TO THE
ARCHIVISTS OF SOUTH ASIA

CONTENTS

PAKISTAN

PREFACE

The archives of the governments of Ceylon, India and Pakistan contain a wealth of historical material relating to the modern history of South Asia. This guide seeks to provide some systematic information about it, albeit in a preliminary way.

The information presented here was initially compiled from those invaluable periodical publications *Indian Archives* and the *Proceedings of the Indian Historical Records Commission*. This was then supplemented by reference to such published guides as were available, many of which have been vital for our entries. Drafts were then sent for comment to the archivists responsible; and it should be recorded that without exception they responded unstintingly to our unheralded, importunate, and all-too-frequent requests—not once, but in most cases twice, and often three or four times as well. Our debt of gratitude to them for the care, trouble and kindness they have displayed is heartfelt and profound. With their assistance the compilers have drawn up the final entries. We alone are responsible for the form they take and the errors which no doubt they still retain.

The lists are arranged by alphabetical order of country with the entries within them—except occasionally for convenience under the National Archives of India—in alphabetical order as well. For a variety of reasons the format of the entries sometimes varies. But at the outset there is usually information about the name and address of the archives office described; the title of its officer directly in charge; and the name and address of the authority in the relevant government that holds responsibility for its administration. There is usually then a note about the latest available information on rules of access; a short historical account of the territory whose archives are described; a short account of the history of its archival administration; a note about the nature and extent of the holdings the archives possess; and a brief guide to any published aids to reference. There follow the holdings lists, which naturally vary from place to place; and there is often a short, select, list of additional publications at the end. We have used the following abbreviations: v for volume(s), f for files, bdl(s) for bundle(s).

The following points need to be emphasized:

a This Guide is only concerned with national and state archives. It does not list (i) district records (ii) High Court records or (iii) private archival collections, except where these are to be found in national or state archives and that is not often. There are substantial manuscript collections in other quarters. They have not been listed here and we very much hope that that task may be performed by other hands.

b Twentieth-century material has only been listed when information about it has been readily available. In most places new, more modern material is being transferred to the archives fairly regularly, and enquiries about this should be made to the officers in charge.

c All dates are A.D. except where they are otherwise specified.

d Rules of access are subject to change. Researchers from outside the country are strongly recommended to seek up-to-date information, and secure authoritative support for their bona fides, both academic and diplomatic, in good time. Archivists are very ready to help, but they have their official responsibilities to fulfil.

We would draw attention to the archival information collected by national and state offices of the History of the Freedom Movement, and by the Regional Records Survey Committees which are to be found in the majority of Indian states. This has not been listed here. Information about it may be found in the books and reports which these bodies publish from time to time.

We regret that we have not been able to incorporate information about archival material in Nepal, Afghanistan and Burma. We hope that information, particularly about Afghan material, may be forthcoming in due course. Burma's modern governmental records suffered grievously from the ravages of war. A great deal has been done by the Burma Historical Commission to secure microfilms of records in London and elsewhere relating to the history of Burma, and typescript catalogues have been produced. But since we have been concerned here to list original manuscripts, we have not felt able to include a digest of these. (It may be noted that there are substantial collections of microfilms on various subjects in other repositories such as the National Archives of India. For the most part these likewise have not been listed.)

There is little information about archives in the smaller Indian Union territories, but we have included notes on Delhi, Manipur and Pondicherry, on which some positive information has become available.

Our most ambitious entry relates to the National Archives of India. Apart from some preliminary work by the first two compilers, most of this was prepared by the third of us, Miss M. D. Wainwright, in the course of a special visit to Delhi in 1964. We are grateful to the London School of Oriental and African Studies for giving her leave to do this; and to the Australian National University for making her visit financially possible. Our especial thanks are due to the officials of all ranks in the National Archives of India who in their invariable way have, on this and other innumerable occasions, put themselves to immense trouble on our behalf. Our friends and helpers there will, we hope, know how grateful we are to them for their assistance and their kindness.

Elsewhere we have others to thank too. If we cannot mention them all by name we hope those whom we do not manage to name will understand. We would, however, thank, for the help they and their associates have given us, Dr P. M. Joshi, Dr K. K. Datta, A. E. M. Shamsul Haque; and Shri V. S. Suri, M. Zaheer, T. K. Mukherji, G. N. Khare, J. K. Jain, M. S. Saletore, Ishwar Dass, K. Dasappa, V. T. Gune, S. C. De, N. S. Natarajan, P. C. Sharma, V. K. Bawa, and the Government Archivist in Ceylon.

Our thanks are also due to Dr Gerald Barrier (particularly for the West Pakistan entry), Dr Tom Metcalf, Dr Peter Reeves, Dr John Broomfield, Dr Hugh Owen, Dr Piet van den Dungen, Mr Ranajit Guha, Dr John Rosselli, Professor C. R. Boxer, Miss Joan Lancaster, Miss Dorothy Woodman, and Dr W. M. Hale. None of these, we must emphasize, holds responsibility for anything which appears in the pages that follow.

This volume could never have been compiled without the support of the Department of History in the Research School of Social Sciences of the Institute of Advanced Studies at the Australian National University, Canberra. We are especially grateful to its former head, Professor Sir Keith Hancock, and the Director of the Research School of Social Sciences, Professor P. H. Partridge, for their warm support. We are also very grateful to Mrs Nan Philips and Mrs May Richardson for all their labours there on our behalf. In England the final typescript has been largely produced by Miss Yvonne Wood in the School of African and Asian Studies at the University of Sussex and we are deeply grateful to her for her patience and assiduity.

D. A. LOW

J. O. ILTIS

M. D. WAINWRIGHT

CEYLON

INTRODUCTION

THE DOMINION OF CEYLON

According to the Mahawamsa chronicle, an Indian prince from the valley
of the Ganges named Vijaya became the first king of the Sinhalese in the
sixth century B.C. This monarchical form of government continued until
1815 when the British subjugated the Kandyan kingdom in the central
highlands. Meanwhile the Portuguese had formed settlements on the west
and south in 1505, which passed to the Dutch when they took over the
administration of the island in 1656. The British Government annexed
these foreign settlements to the presidency of Madras in 1796 and later
separated the maritime provinces from India to form a crown colony in
1802. A unified system of administration was introduced in 1833 under
which the whole island was divided into five provinces, the North, South,
East, West and Ūva provinces, ruled through agencies and subordinate
assistant agencies. As every aspect of administration came under the
purview of the agent these large provinces impeded efficient government,
so further provinces were created. Ceylon reached fully responsible status
within the British Commonwealth when the Ceylon Independence Act,
1947, came into force on 4 February 1948.

HISTORY OF ARCHIVES ADMINISTRATION

From the inception of the Dutch administration in 1656 the Archives
Department in its nuclear form came under the control of the governor.
The main collecting centre was Colombo, with collections also at the provincial centres of Jaffna, Galle, Tuticorin and Hulftsdorp, and local
centres such as Negombo, Kalutara, Mātara and Trincomalee. During the
British period archives were administered as a sub-department of the
Chief Secretary's Office, and suffered many vicissitudes during the
nineteenth century. However, at the turn of the century scattered collections
were brought together and organized, and a start was made on listing and
translations. With the coming of Independence in 1947 the sub-department
was elevated to a separate department. A history of the archives is found in
the introduction to Mrs M. W. Jurriaanse's *Catalogue of the archives of the
Dutch Central Government* (1943).

Department of Government Archives,
Gangodawila, Nugegoda, Ceylon.
Officer in charge: Government Archivist

RULES OF ACCESS

All records more than fifty years old are open for research and sometimes exceptions are made to allow consultation of more recent records. Applications for admittance to the Government Archives search room should be addressed in writing to the Government Archivist at least three days before admission is required, and should state the applicant's profession or business, his place of abode and the particular purpose for which he seeks admission. It is the normal procedure for overseas students attached to a university or other learned institution to include a letter of recommendation from the professor under whom they are working. Other overseas persons engaged in bona fide research are advised to send their applications through the local Ceylon diplomatic representatives and include full particulars of themselves and the research they intend doing. The search room is closed during the first fortnight in September, on Saturdays after 12.30 p.m. and on Sundays. The photography branch is equipped with apparatus for photocopying and for microfilming 16 mm and 35 mm films.

THE GOVERNMENT ARCHIVES DEPARTMENT

The department has a technical branch which preserves, restores and repairs documents, offers technical assistance to other departments and trains other departmental employees in repairing documents and bookbinding. The Historical Manuscripts Commission, a body of twelve members, was constituted in February 1931 to collect, examine and edit private archival and manuscript collections. Unless such collections are donated to the department, photocopies are taken for depositing in the archives and the material repaired and returned to its owners. The Government Archivist is now secretary of the Commission and the Commission is attached to the Archives Department.

The office of the registrar of books and newspapers, established in 1839, was also brought under the control of the Archives Department in October 1947 and has recently been entrusted with the preparation of a national bibliography. A departmental library is attached. (The removal of the archives to a more central, easily accessible and spacious repository has been proposed.)

The Government Record Office, Secretariat, Colombo, originally the record room of the Chief Secretary's Office, came under the jurisdiction of the government archivist in 1947 with a government record keeper in charge. It now holds the secretariat records which are less than fifty years old, and it is hoped that it may become a temporary deposit for non-current records of all government departments until they reach the state of archives (i.e. are more than fifty years old). Research students have sometimes experienced difficulties since some of the earlier files are at Nuwara Eliya while the more recent files are at Colombo. It is against archival principles to transfer volumes by post because of the great risks in sending material bulky in size, weak in condition and unique in number, but this problem should be overcome when the proposal for a more central repository is realized.

ACCESSIONS TO THE DEPARTMENT

As the Ceylon Archives Law is still in draft, accessions to the department are governed by the Manual of Procedure which provides for the transference of departmental records which are over fifty years old. A report on those records considered worthy of preservation and those scheduled for destruction is submitted to the Historical Manuscripts Commission before the transference of custody. Unfortunately the lack of storage space has temporarily put a stop to the acquisition of new accessions although there are many collections lying scattered in the repositories attached to government departments and law courts which are awaiting transfer. These include the records of the Land Settlement Department and Registrar-General's Department and the Kandy District Courts.

In his function as registrar of books and newspapers, the Government Archivist has in his custody all newspapers since 1839 and other publications registered since 1885. Maps from the seventeenth to twentieth centuries are also held.

NATURE AND EXTENT OF HOLDINGS

The archives contain no original Portuguese documents, as the Portuguese *tombos* were allowed to be destroyed when the archives were under Dutch administration. Manuscript copies of a few *tombos* and *forals* pertaining to Ceylon have been obtained from Lisbon, however, and it is hoped to obtain photocopies or microfilms of further material when funds permit. Dutch central government archives are particularly rich and comprehensive despite a fire in 1793 and the physical deterioration of the records during the nineteenth century owing to bad storage, bad handling, and constant removals. Of the two large provincial archives at Jaffna and Galle, the latter are the more complete. Only a few *tombos*, however, have survived of the Jaffna records. The local archives such as those of Negombo and Kalutara have disappeared almost completely except for some files in the Mātara repository. The south coast of India was formerly administered from Colombo, through a *commandeur* or *hoofd* at Tuticorin and sub-ordinates at Cape Comorin, Manapar, Allelande and Kilkare, but none of their archives have been preserved at either Colombo or Madras. The British archives are fairly comprehensive and can be supplemented by material in London. The Kandy records contain much information on the Kandyan kingdom before its surrender to the British.

Microfilms have been made of certain documents held in the Colonial Office, John Rylands Library, Bibliothèque Nationale, Paris, the Historical Archives of Goa, the Bibliotheca Apostolica Vaticana, the India Office Library, the British Museum and the oriental department of the Royal Library, Copenhagen. A list of these records and of photostats obtained from foreign archives is contained in *Government Archives Department and its contents in brief* (1962), 14-15 and 29-30.

AIDS TO REFERENCE

Besides the published catalogues listed on p. 26, reference media include a preliminary list of accessions for lots 2 to 47; summaries of despatches from the secretary of state, 1812-89, and to the secretary of state, 1828-85; a calendar of the Dr N. B. P. Goonatilaka collection; an index to the historical maps in both geographical and chronological order; and a chronological guide to the *plakaats* issued by the Dutch Government. Indexes in greater or less detail have been prepared for those series indi-cated in the list of holdings. In addition, the Historical Manuscripts Com-mission has prepared a National Archives Register of documents at foreign archives, the Government Archives, Kachcheries, etc., St Aloysius College, Galle, the Western, Southern, Ūva, Sabaragamuwa, Central, Northern and North-Western provinces, and D. M. S. S. Kaviraj (owners A-Y, books A-Z). The Department has also typed a 'Calendar of periodicals printed in Ceylon 1885-1900' and 'An index of periodicals 1950-1960'. Portuguese overseas archives in Lisbon, including those pertaining to Ceylon, are being catalogued in a series of volumes entitled *Documentaçao Ultramarina Portuguesa*.

Published and unpublished translations are listed on pp. 24-7.

HOLDINGS

Government Archives Department, Ceylon. Main series

LOT 1. DUTCH ARCHIVES: SUMMARY AND HOLDINGS

CENTRAL GOVERNMENT

COUNCIL MINUTES 1640–1796   *Detailed index*

CORRESPONDENCE ORDINARY

Patria and the Cape of Good Hope 1712–95
Batavia 1712–95
Jaffna and Mannar 1757–95
Galle 1744–95
Tuticorin 1760–95
Trincomalee and Batticaloa 1759–94
Mullaitivu 1785–95
Colombo outposts 1759–94
Kalpitiya and Puttalam 1759–95
Colombo outposts and the outstations 1764–94
Malabar coast 1718–23 and 1746–95
Coromandel coast 1749–97
The Company's agencies in Surat, Bengal, Malacca, Persia, Padang, Siam
    and Canton 1749–92
Maldive Islands 1713–1834
Foreign powers and princes in India 1697–1795
Inland Department 1790–4

MILITARY DEPARTMENT

Patria and Batavia 1790
Galle and Mātara 1791–4
Jaffna, Mannar and Mullaitivu 1790–4
Colombo outposts and Tuticorin 1791–4
Trincomalee and Batticaloa 1790–4
Outstations and the Colombo outposts 1792–3

CORRESPONDENCE SECRET

Patria 1702–95
Batavia 1661–1795
The outstations and the settlements on the Coromandel and Malabar
    coasts 1706–95

INTERNAL AFFAIRS

Statutes of Batavia   1642 and 1768
Orders   1641–1774
Plakaats   1641–1795
Instructions   1660–1796
Agreements with Vanni chiefs 1661–1770
Registers of land grants 1679–1767
Registers of privileges 1743–59
Registers of certificates, passports and licences 1785–96
Acts of appointments 1750–96   *Detailed index*
Secretarial protocols 1690–1795
Memoirs left by governors, commanders, chief officers 1650–1794
Diaries and reports of governors 1662–1760
Annual compendia 1749–90
Reports and other documents relating to the government of the country
    1680–1795
Reports and other documents relating to agriculture and land settlement
    and to irrigation 1678–1794
Rolls, lists and connected documents relating to the status, the possession
    and the taxation of the islanders 1714–91
Documents relating to complaints against the Company's officers in
    function 1664–1794
Documents relating to discontent among the inhabitants 1702–94
Complaints against local chiefs 1678–1795
Farm conditions 1745–96
Pearl fisheries 1674–1794
Documents dealing with trade, audit reports 1772–81
Documents connected with verification 1738–96
Documents relating to salaries 1757 and 1789
Documents relating to the '*Liberale* Gift' 1753–92
Auction sales 1706
Colombo diary 1737–94
Daily paper 1783–94
Translation of *Olas* 1704–96
Sentences on criminal cases by the Court of Justice at Galle sent to the
    Colombo Council 1766–93
Documents dealing with defence and the military in general 1669–1794
Ecclesiastical matters 1679–1785
Documents relating to government dealing with private matters 1767–95
Secretarial indexes 1785 and 1796

Indiscriminately bound papers 1736–95
Miscellaneous documents 1668–1791
Copies and extracts 1640–1794

EXTERNAL AFFAIRS

Relations with other V.O.C. agents 1675–1783
Relations with Kandy 1638–1795
Reports on the relations with South Indian princedoms 1683–1784
Treaties with South Indian princes 1643–1769
Documents relating to the expedition of Ryckloff van Goens (snr) against the French 1672–4
Documents relating to the expedition under Reinicus Siersma against the sea-robbers 1739
Documents relating to the expedition under Christian Wohlfarth to Negapatnam 1773
Documents connected with the war between the Dutch Republic and England 1780–4
Collected documents 1656–1796

'HOOFD-ADMINISTRATEUR'

Documents received from the central government 1749–94
Miscellaneous 1758–91
Documents received from Galle 1759–95
Documents received by the *Sabandar* from the central government 1744–96
Bills of lading 1775–96
Bills of exchange 1742–9
Accounts 1765–96

'DISĀVA'

Correspondence with the central government 1759–96
Correspondence with the outposts in the Colombo Dessawany 1767–96
Miscellaneous documents relating to *Landraad* matters 1751–94
Registers, lists, garden descriptions etc. 1769–93
Tombos 1760, 1766–71   *Detailed index*
Miscellaneous loose documents from *tombos*
Lascoryn rolls 1745, 1768–70
As military commander 1769–93

'SCHOLARCHALE VERGADERING'

Minutes 1765–79
School *tombos* of the Colombo Dessawany

'WEESKAMER' OR ORPHANAGE

Minutes 1747–51
Documents received 1778–9
Accounts 1738–59

'DIACONAL' OR THE BOARD OF DEACONS

Minutes 1739–99
Annexes to minutes 1724–97
Miscellaneous 1780–81
Accounts 1736–79

JUDICIAL

Registers or bonds affecting land 1728–95
Protocols of deeds of emancipation of slaves 1738–95
Protocols of affidavits at the request of the *Hoofd-Administrateur* 1785–8
Civil *presentatie-boeken* 1769–85
Civil rolls 1735–93
Civil *request-boeken* 1761–89
Protocols of affidavits in civil cases 1727–93
Civil *interrogatoria-boeken* 1704–85
Documents in civil cases 1732–95
Documents in civil cases indiscriminately bound together 1678–1791
Criminal rolls 1669–1792
Protocols of affidavits in criminal cases 1704–92
Criminal *proces-boeken* 1712–59
Documents in criminal cases 1739–95
Documents in criminal cases indiscriminately bound together 1739–93
Certificates of execution of sentences in criminal cases 1773–82
Documents received from the central government 1743–92
Collected documents 1675–1796

COLOMBO 'LANDRAAD'

Register of acts in land matters before the Court 1779–91
Rolls of the *Landraad,* and of the sessions of the commissioners only
    1746–93
Protocols of affidavits 1776–91
Proces-boeken 1750–79
Interrogatoria-boeken 1770–84

COLOMBO 'CIVIELE RAAD' OR CIVIL COURT ROLLS 1768
Annexes to rolls 1758–95
Process of the *Civiele Raad* 1791–5
Documents received 1758–81
Miscellaneous documents belonging to court cases indiscriminately bound
 1734–95

SECRET COMMITTEE
Minutes 1762–6
Correspondence
 Patria and Batavia 1762–6
 Colombo outposts, the outstations and the settlements on the Coro-
  mandel and Malabar coasts 1760–6
Miscellaneous documents 1761–5

SPECIAL MISSIONS FROM PATRIA
The *Hooge Commisaris* or High Commissioner 1684–90
The *Commissarissen General* 1792–4
The *Militaire Commissie* 1789–90

GALLE 'COMMANDEMENT'
Council minutes 1664–1796
Correspondence ordinary
 Patria, Batavia and other agents 1727–45
 Colombo 1720–96
Correspondence secret
 Colombo 1713–96
Inland Department
 Colombo 1790–4
Military Department
 Colombo 1790–4
Mātara ordinary 1721–96
Mātara secret 1729–96
Mātara Inland Department 1790–4
Mātara Military Department 1790–4
Outposts ordinary 1757–96
Secret 1729–62
Miscellaneous 1740–78

INTERNAL AFFAIRS

Précis of orders contained in letters from Colombo
   chronological 1729–94
   alphabetical 1736–9
Instructions and order book 1666–1790
Registers of orders issued by the *Commandeur* to heads of departments in
   Galle 1777–92
Registers of extracts of Galle council
   Resolutions sent to Colombo for approval 1766–87
Plakaats and notices 1777–90
Last wills 1651–1796
Secretarial protocols 1699–1774
Various deeds executed at the secretariat, Galle 1773–97
Aparte protocols 1728–96
Attentations by commissioners re the receipt of goods from Company's
   ships, Galle 1750–96
Certificate-boek 1692–1706
Licence books 1774–91
Gifte-boek 1764–95
Acts of Appointments 1645–1791   *Detailed index*
Annexes of Acts of Appointments 1779–92
Native Acts of Appointments 1701–96
Diaries or log-books of ship's commanders 1783–96
Memoirs of *commandeurs* and other officers on departure or temporary
   absence 1701–94
Special reports and diaries 1691–1795
Draft compendia, Galle 1740–94
Annexes to compendia, Galle 1745–92
Daily reports of special commissioners 1761–2
Translations of reports on commissions and mandates issued by the
   Company 1739–95
Translations of *Olas*, etc. 1706–94
Daily papers of the secretariat 1769–93
Petitions 1763–83
Inventories and lists on change of office 1760–95
Papers relating to the farming out of lands in the Galle District 1755–93
Auction sales, registers 1722–94
Auction sales, *Maan Rollen* 1778–80
Uliyam rolls, Moors and Chetties, Galle 1759–93
Uliyam rolls, Moors and Chetties, Mātara 1707–1890

Day registers, Galle 1667–1786
Agriculture lists, Galle 1698–1795
Registers of Tombo commissioners, Galle 1755–85
Papers dealing with the Mātara rebellion 1890–3

JUDICIAL

Protocols of deeds acknowledged before magistrates 1655–1794
Civiele protocols 1700–78
Civil rolls of the Court of Justice 1700–1, 1749–96
Draft of Civil Court proceedings 1782–93
Requests and annexes to the civil rolls 1739–4
Civil process book of the Court of Justice, Galle 1700–92
Affidavits in criminal cases before the Court of Justice, Galle 1776–96
Criminal rolls of the Court of Justice, Galle 1703–84
Criminal process of the Court of Justice, Galle 1756–80
Agenda of civil and criminal cases before the Court of Justice, Galle 1776–9
Interrogatories in judicial proceedings before the Court of Justice, Galle 1721–78
Translation book, Court of Justice, Galle 1790–8
Judicial commissioner's reports 1790–4
Sententie Boeken 1776–95
Letters received by the Court of Justice, Galle 1744–70
Outward letters of the Court of Justice, Galle 1721–51
Miscellaneous 1669–1794
Landraad rolls, Galle 1759–95
Drafts of *Landraad* rolls, Galle 1775–86
Annexes to *Landraad* rolls, Galle 1780–95
Deeds affecting land, sworn before two members of the *Landraad*, Galle 1760–91
Protocols of *Landraad* deeds 1760–97
Outwards letters of the *Landraad*, Galle 1760–93
Miscellaneous 1784–95

LOCAL BOARD

Original proceedings of the Court of Marriage Causes 1750–83
Roll of the Town Court, Galle 1779–81
School Board proceedings, Galle 1747–79
School *Tombos*, Galle District and Mātara Disāvany eighteenth and early nineteenth centuries
Reports on school visits in Galle and Mātara 1718–71

Directors of Poor Widows Fund, Galle 1787–94
Orphans Chamber, Galle 1737–56
Native Poor Board, Galle 1788–95

OFFICERS OF GALLE FISCAL

Extracts from council members and letters sent to the fiscal at Galle 1742–95
    Outward letters 1783–5
Negotie
    Extracts of the Political Council, Galle, sent to the *Negotie* 1757–90
    Extract-boeken (general), *Negotie Kantoor*, Galle 1734–92
    Miscellaneous 1770–84
Ontranger
    Accounts etc. sent to the *Ontranger*, Galle 1772–6
Gecommitteerde Branders
    Extracts of letters, orders etc. 1765–85

MĀTARA 'COMMANDEMENT'

    Council minutes 1784–90
    Correspondence 1790–6

MĀTARA SECRETARIAT

    Protocols civil 1736–69
    Protocols criminal 1771–80

MĀTARA 'LANDRAAD'

    Protocols civil 1791–4
    Protocols criminal 1791–5
    Commissioners' protocols 1790–5
    Deeds of the Mātara *Landraad* passed before two commissioners 1758–88
    Proceedings 1775–95
    Minutes of proceedings 1771–92
    Process papers 1750–92
    Miscellaneous 1790–5
    Ola translations 1751–96
    Mātara rebellion 1790–1
    Mātara rolls 1773–93
    Paddy farming out 1784–94
    Extract-boeken 1765–85
    Miscellaneous 1792–6
    Negotie Boekhonder 1782–5
    Consumptie Boekhonder 1786–90

LOTS 2–11. CHIEF SECRETARY'S OFFICE ARCHIVES:
SUMMARY AND HOLDINGS

2 Executive Council minutes *Indexed*
3 Legislative Council minutes *Indexed*
4 Despatches from the secretary of state *Indexed*
5 Despatches to the secretary of state
6 Inward correspondence up to 1870 and inward and outward correspondence thereafter *Indexed*
7 Outward correspondence up to 1870 *Indexed*
8 Inward correspondence, weeded series
9 Correspondence registers and indexes *Indexed*
10 Miscellaneous collections and cases on special subjects up to 1860
11 Miscellaneous collections and cases on special subjects after 1860

EXECUTIVE AND LEGISLATIVE COUNCILS

2 Executive Council
    Minutes 1802–1931
    Circulated minutes 1834–49
    Papers tabled 1814
3 Legislative Council
    Minutes 1833–1924

GOVERNOR'S DIARIES AND LETTER BOOKS

7 Commercial diaries 1798–1801
  Military diaries 1798–1805
  Public diaries 1798–1805
  Political diaries 1798–1801
  Revenue diaries 1798–1805
  Secret diaries 1798–1805
  Public letter books 1795–1805

CORRESPONDENCE

Correspondence with the secretary of state
4 Inward despatches *Detailed index* 1798–1850
    Ordinary series 1801–1885–1948
    Duplicate series 1811–70
    Circular series 1805–11
    Under secretary of state's series 1824–34
    Miscellaneous special collections 1823–81
    Summaries and schedules 1820–89

    Open despatches (ODs) 1886–1948
    Index to ODs 1890–1913
    Registers to ODs 1886–1948
    Telegrams
        Open 1899–1926, 1940–8
        Open saving 1940–8
        Registers 1939–48
5 Outward despatches
    Ordinary series 1798–1885–1948
    Duplicate series 1805–37
    Annexes 1812–85
    Miscellaneous drafts and copies 1820–53
    Summaries and schedules 1812–85
    Open despatches 1886–1948
    Registers of ODs 1941–6 (8)
    Telegrams
        Open saving 1940–8
        Registers 1917–48

GENERAL DEPARTMENTAL PUBLIC CORRESPONDENCE

7 and 8 REVENUE DEPARTMENTS

    Board of Revenue and Commerce 1802–8
    Commissioners of revenue and commerce 1808–34
    Commissioners of districts and agents of revenue 1822–33
        Colombo 1805–33
        Kalutara 1806–22
        Galle 1805–33
        Mātara 1807–21
        Hambantota 1808–1816/18
        Magam Pattuwa, Hambantota and Tangalla 1817–33
        Batticaloa 1805–33
        Trincomalee 1805–33
        Chilaw 1805–33
        Jaffna 1805–33
        Mannar 1805–33
        Wanny 1806–18
    Collectors of districts 1805–33
    Salt agent, Hambantota 1805–12
    Superintendent of Delft 1811–33
    Superintendent of Cinnamon Plantations 1805–34

FINANCE DEPARTMENTS

Paymaster-general civil and military 1805–33
Deputy paymaster-general king's troops 1811–15
Vice treasurer and accountant-general 1805–33; Treasurer 1833+
Auditor and accountant-general 1805+

JUDICIAL DEPARTMENTS

Judges of the Supreme Court 1812–97
Registrar of the Supreme Court 1815+
Judges or commissioners of minor Courts of Appeal 1833
⎧ Advocate fiscal 1811+
⎨ Queen's advocate
⎩ King's advocate
Provincial judges 1805–33
Sitting magistrates 1805–33
Presidents of *landraad* courts 1811–12
Commissioners and sitting magistrates of Trincomalee 1813
District judges 1833–55
Fiscals 1811+
Commissioners of requests and police magistrates 1844+
Coroners 1844–54
Justices of the peace 1844–53
Stipendiary justices of the peace 1854–6

DEPARTMENTS OF PUBLIC WORKS AND COMMUNICATIONS

⎧ Civil engineer and surveyor general 1805–45
⎩ Surveyor general 1845+
Civil engineer 1845–50
Commissioner of roads 1841–50
⎧ Civil engineer and commissioner of roads 1851–67
⎩ Director of public works 1868+
Government agents in the office of surveyor general
Government agents in the office of civil engineer
Government agents in the office of civil enginee
    of roads 1862–7
Government agents in the office of Pu
    1862+
Town surveyor 1847–9
Masters attendant, Colombo, Galle

Superintendent of cinnamon sorting establishment,
   Colombo 1833–41
   Galle 1834–41
Inspector of the cinnamon oil distillery 1819–23
Government tobacco agent 1812–13
Government chalk agent 1814–15
Commercial agent, Colombo 1805–8

GOVERNMENT AGENTS

Western Province 1833–97
Central Province 1833–97
Southern Province 1833–97
Northern Province 1833–97
Eastern Province 1833–97
North-Western Province 1846–97
North-Central Province 1873–97
Ūva Province 1886–97
Sabaragamuwa Province 1889+

PEARL FISHERY

Superintendent 1803–70
Supervisor of pearl banks 1834–1840/63

COMMISSIONER OF STAMPS 1805+

CUSTOMS DEPARTMENT

Exports and imports warehouse keeper and collector of cus
  Colombo 1805–33
Comptroller general of customs 1809–22
Customs masters 1813–21
Controller of customs 1834–43
   Western Province 1834–43
   Southern Province 1834–70
   Northern Province 1834–70
   Eastern Province 1834–70
   Northern and Eastern Provinces 1840–3
Exports and imports warehouse keepers
  Colombo 1837–47
  Galle 1837–9

Agent for s.s. *Serendib*—see masters attendant above
Superintendent of the steam engine 1813–17
Resident engineer breakwater works 1874+
Colombo waterworks engineer 1883–94
Postmaster-general 1805–97
Deputy superintendent of electric telegraphs 1858–80

RAILWAY DEPARTMENT

Director 1857–61
Ceylon railway agent 1858–60
Ceylon railway–General 1863+
Chief resident engineer railway extensions 1880+

EDUCATIONAL AND ECCLESIASTICAL DEPARTMENTS

Consistory of the Dutch Reformed Church of Ceylon 1805–15
Archdeacon of Colombo 1818–45
Archdeacon of Colombo as king's visitor 1834–43
Bishop of Colombo and other officials of the diocese 1845+
⎧ Colombo chaplain and principal of schools 1805–31
⎨ Secretary of the School Commission 1836–67
⎩ Director of public instruction 1868–97
Secretary of the Society for Promoting Christian Knowledge 1816–23
Director of Colombo museum 1881–97

NAVAL AND MILITARY DEPARTMENTS

⎧ Military secretary 1805–32
⎨ Assistant military secretary 1833–74
⎩ Brigade major 1874+
Officers of the Military Department 1805–40
H.M.'s naval officers 1805–63

MISCELLANEOUS BOARDS, COMMITTEES, COMMISSIONS ETC.

BOARDS OF NATIVE COMMISSIONERS

President of the board and registrar of lands 1805
Commissioners of enquiry 1829–31
Commissioners of the Loan Board 1834+
Committee on Tenders 1851–61
Temple lands commissioners 1857+
Immigrant labour commissioners 1859–62
Stationery Committee 1866–8

Service tenures commissioners 1870–3
Special commissioners for the registration of title to lands 1887–91
Committee, civil service fund 1805–14
Boards and committees—miscellaneous 1809+

DEPARTMENTS OF LOCAL GOVERNMENT

Provincial boards of health 1853–68
Provincial road committees 1854+
Municipalities, Colombo, Kandy and Galle 1866+
Local boards 1880–97

FOREIGN GOVERNMENTS AND AGENCIES OUTSIDE CEYLON

Indian and other empire and foreign governments 1805+
{ Agents for the Ceylon Government in London 1801–79
{ Crown agents in London 1879+
Agents for the Ceylon Government in India 1805–68
Agents for the Ceylon Government, miscellaneous 1807–14

MISCELLANEOUS DEPARTMENTS AND
PUBLIC CORRESPONDENCE

CHIEF TRANSLATOR TO GOVERNMENT 1805–16

MEDICAL DEPARTMENT

Superintendent-general of vaccination 1805–46
Principal civil medical officer 1847+

FOREST DEPARTMENT

Superintendent of government forests 1810–11
Conservator of forests 1887+

SUPERINTENDENT OF THE MINT 1811–16

COMMISSARIAT DEPARTMENT

{ Deputy commissary general 1812–67
{ Colonial storekeeper 1867–97
Storekeeper of building materials 1837–42

SUPERINTENDENT OF BOTANIC GARDENS 1813+

KEEPER OF THE RECORDS 1829–30

POLICE DEPARTMENT

Superintendent of police, Colombo 1833–67
Superintendent of police, Kandy 1843–59
Inspector-general of police 1867+

PRISONS DEPARTMENT

Inspector-general of prisons 1868+
Superintendent convict establishment 1870–8
Superintendent of wrecks 1861–9
Registrar general 1863+
Superintendent of the poor's fund 1806–34
Treasurer of the widows' fund 1833
Directors of the widows' and orphans' pension fund 1884+
Superintendent of census 1890–2
Subordinate government officials 1805–54
Private individuals, associations etc. 1805+

CORRESPONDENCE OF THE SECRETARY FOR THE
KANDYAN PROVINCES

Heads of reference and answers 1815–16
> From the resident at Kandy to the secretary for the Kandyan Provinces
> From the secretary for the Kandyan Provinces to the resident at Kandy
> ⎧ Board of Kandyan commissioners 1816–33
> ⎨ Resident and first commissioner 1815–24
> ⎪ Judicial commissioner 1816–33
> ⎩ Revenue commissioner 1815–33

Agents of revenue in the interior
> Ūva 1817–32
> Saffragam 1817–32
> Three and four Kōrales 1817–32
> Other agents called 'interior' agents 1819–33

Departments in the Maritime Provinces
> Collectors of district 1817–23
> Other departments 1817–32

Private and demi-official correspondence 1817–22
Letters of authority for unfixed contingent charges 1815–33

CORRESPONDENCE OF THE DEPUTY SECRETARY FOR THE
HOME AND JUDICIAL DEPARTMENTS
    Ordinary correspondence 1814–32
    Private and demi-official correspondence 1818–33
    Letters of authority for unfixed contingent charges 1815–33
10 and 11 Miscellaneous collections and cases on special subjects
Unnumbered Pending files, being a special collection of cases on miscellaneous subjects since 1895

GENERAL
6 and 7 Telegrams 1877–83
    Circulars 1805–76
    Reports on inquests 1820–33
    Reports on the state of the country 1824–33
    Returns of cases decided in Provincial Courts and Minor Courts of
        Appeal 1820–32
    Returns of estimates of departmental requirements 1833–35

REGISTERS, INDEXES AND PROTOCOLS ETC.
9   Registers of correspondence 1840–69
    Registers of correspondence 1869–85
    Indexes of correspondence 1805 +
7   Proclamations and advertisements 1795 +
    Governor's minutes and orders 1805–67
    Warrants to fiscals 1866–7
    Warrants of pardon and of remission of prisoners' sentences 1866 +
    Acts of Appointment, commissions and letters patent
        General, public offices 1834 +
        Letters patent 1861 +
        Notarial warrants 1867 +
        Registers of marriage licences
        Gunpowder licences 1879 +
        Passports 1858 +
        Crown grants 1809 +
        Applications for title deeds 1880–99
        Registers of applications for title deeds 1891–8
        General Orders issued by the adjutant-general 1866–7
        Blue Book and annual statistical returns 1827 +
    Expenditure warrants
        Chief secretary 1812–21

Miscellaneous departments 1864–76
Advance warrants 1849–1901
Special expenditure and deposit warrants 1833–1901
Estimates of expenditure
Supply and supplementary 1848–62
Sanctioned estimates 1872–93
Duplicate estimates 1887+
Sanctioned requisitions 1879–84
Indents for stamps 1872–85
Stamp minutes 1858–65
Financial returns and statements from the Treasury and the Pay Office 1823–36
Registers of specifications of payments authorized 1822–37

LOTS 12–48. DEPARTMENTAL ARCHIVES

12 Board of Revenue and Commerce 1801–6 *Indexed*
13 Commissioner of revenue and commerce 1808–33 *Indexed*
14 Civil auditor-general and auditor-general 1802–27 *Indexed*
15 Commissioner of stamps 1805–92 *Indexed*
16 Treasurer 1833–92 *Indexed*
17 Widows' and orphans' pension fund 1884–1910, nos. 1–7690
18 Kandy Kachcheri 1821–58 *Indexed*
19 Commissioners of Enquiry: Colebrooke and Cameron 1831–2 *Incomplete*
20 Jaffna Kachcheri
  ⎰ Diaries 1795–1811 *Indexed*
  ⎱ Grain tax registers 1873–7 *Indexed*
21 Board of Kandyan commissioners 1815–33 *Indexed*
22 Registrar-general
  Index of old deeds of the Anuradhapura District registered in 1873
23 District Courts, Kandy 1815–33 *Indexed*
24 Loan donations
  Consistory of Dutch Reformed Church in Ceylon: Dutch–Sinhalese dictionary compiled by Amos Comenius and an introduction to the study of the language, early eighteenth century
25 Accessions from private sources
  1. Christie section of the Johnstone papers *Indexed*
  2. The Catholic Writers Movement
  3. L. E. Blaze

    4. A. C. Buultjens
    5. Stuart Mackenzie papers *Indexed*
    6. E. B. R. Seuter: collection of papers relating to the civil service of
       Ceylon 1795–1844
    7. Woolf papers, presented by S. C. Fernando, C.C.S.

26 Mātara Kachcheri nineteenth century
27 Hambantota Kachcheri nineteenth and early twentieth century
28 District Courts, Tangalla 1810–35
29 War Emergency Department
    Director of food supply—posters, leaflets, pamphlets etc. 1940–6
    Civil defence commissioner 1941–5
    Commissioner of war risks insurance 1942–6
30 Kegalle Kachcheri nineteenth and early twentieth century (majority are
    Wattōru lists)
31 Mannar Kachcheri nineteenth century
32 District Courts, Kalutara nineteenth and early twentieth century
33 Colombo Kachcheri nineteenth and early twentieth century
34 Matale Kachcheri nineteenth century
35 Kalutara Kachcheri nineteenth and early twentieth century
36 Vavuniya Kachcheri nineteenth and early twentieth century
37 Public trustee late nineteenth century–1930
38 Kurunegala Kachcheri—old colonial secretary's circulars 1849–1910
39 District Courts, Chilaw nineteenth century
40 District Courts, Galle 1809–40
41 Anuradhapura Kachcheri nineteenth and early twentieth centuries.
    Described in *Administration report* 1960 *Indexed*
42 Puttalam Kachcheri nineteenth and early twentieth centuries *Indexed*
43 Galle Kachcheri nineteenth and early twentieth centuries
44 Loan Board Office nineteenth and early twentieth centuries
45 Ratnapura Kachcheri nineteenth and early twentieth centuries
46 Batticaloa Kachcheri nineteenth and early twentieth centuries *Indexed*
47 Nuwara Eliya Kachcheri late nineteenth and early twentieth centuries
48 Department of Wild Life
    Maps seventeenth–twentieth centuries *Indexed*

UNPUBLISHED TRANSLATIONS

Memoir by the *opperhoofd* of Trincomalee, P. van Ommen, for his successor
    Nicholaas van Heuvel 1695.
Memoir by the pro-interim Governor, Daniel Overbeek, for his successor
    Julius Valentijn Stein van Gollenesse 1743.

Memoir by the *Dessave* of Mātara, Gerardus Kersse, for his successor Gerrard Joan Vreelandt 1746.

Memoir by the *Commandeur* of Jaffna, Liebert Hooreman, for his successor Jacob de Jong 1748.

Memoir by Gerrard Joan Vreelandt, *Commandeur* of Galle (Governor-elect of Ceylon), for his successor Frederik Cunes 1751.

Memoir by the *opperhoofd* of Batticaloa, Jacob Burnand, for his successor Johannes Philippus Wambeck 1794.

Diary of the tour of Governor Julius Valentijn Stein van Gollenesse through the *Commandement* of Galle and the Disāvany of Mātara 1745.

Diary of the tour of Governor van Gollenesse from Colombo to Jaffna and the river Musali 1746.

Journal kept during a tour in the District of Kottiyar, Tambalagam and Katukolampattu by the Junior Merchant Jacques Fabrice van Sanden, Governor of Trincomalee in the year 1786.

Report on the state of the Jaffna *Commandement* by the *Commandeur* Floris Blom to Governor Pijl 1690.

Report of Cornelis Zaay van Wezel Disāva of Mātara to the *Commandeur* of Galle 1713.

Report of Abraham Samlant *hoofd administrateur* on the disturbances in the Mātara District 1757–8.

Instructions of the Directors of the V.O.C. to Hendrik van Reede, Lord of Mydrecht, High Commissioner to Bengal, Coromandel, Ceylon etc. 1684.

Instructions for the *hoofd administrateur* Adriaan Maten and other members of the Council, issued by Governor Stephanus Versluys during his absence on visits to Jaffna, Tuticorin and Galle 1730–2.

Instructions by Governor Stein van Gollenesse 1744–5.

Suggestions by Governor van Imhoff to *Commandeur* Danief Agreen and the Council at Jaffna regarding the management of the Jaffna *Commandement* with the marginal replies to the *Commandeur* in Council 1738.

Orders, proclamations, sentences etc. of Julius Vallentijn Stein van Gollenesse 1743–7.

Secret committee minutes 1762–4, 1764, 1765.

PUBLICATIONS

CATALOGUES AND OTHER AIDS TO REFERENCE

R. G. Anthonisz: *Catalogue of the records of the Province of Galle, under the rule of the Netherlands East India Co. 1640–1796* (1906)

M. W. Jurriaanse: *Catalogue of the archives of the Dutch Central Government of Coastal Ceylon 1640–1796* (1943)

Catalogue of books from 1885

Catalogue of newspapers from 1961,

Newspaper indexes, English, Sinhalese, Tamil, Malayalam (cyclostyled)

The Government Archives Department and its contents in brief (1962) (cyclostyled)

The records of the Executive Council of Ceylon 1802–1931 (1962) (cyclostyled)

An index to the articles pertaining to Ceylon in the Colombo Journal, vols I and II, 1832–3 (1963) (cyclostyled)

Papers of the Colebrook-Cameron Commission 1829–31 (1963) (cyclostyled)

TRANSLATIONS

Instructions from the Governor General and Council of India to the Governor of Ceylon 1656–65

Memoirs by Gouverneur Joan Maetsuycker for his successor Jacob van Kittensteijn

Memoir by Governor Rycloff van Goens (snr) for the Governor van Goens (jnr) and the Council 1675 (1932)

Memoir by Commandeur of Jaffna Anthonie Pavilioen for his successor Jorephass Vosch 1665

Memoir by Governor Rycloff van Goens (jnr) for his successor Laurens Pijl 1679

Memoir left by Governor Thomas van Rhee for his successor Gerrit de Heere 1697 (1915)

Memoir left by the Commandeur of Jaffna, Hendrik Zwaardecroon during his absence on leave in Malabar for the Council and for the Jaffna dessave Rycloff de Bitter, with copies of marginal notes by Governor Gerrit de Heere 1697

Memoir left by Governor Cornelis Joan Simons for his successor Hendrik Becker 1707 (1914)

Memoir left by Governor Hendrik Becker for his successor Issac Augustin Rumpf 1716 (1914)

Memoir by Governor Rycloff van Goens (snr) for his successor Jacob Hustaerd 1663

Memoir left by Governor Jacob Christian Pielat for his successor Diederik van Domburg 1734 (1905)

Memoir left by Governor Gustaff Willem Baron van Imhoff for his successor Willem Maurits Bruynink 1740

Memoir by the Chief Officer of Tuticorin Noel Anthony Lebeck for his successor Albertus Domburg 1745 (1910)

Memoir by the Commandeur of Galle Jacob de Jong for his successor Gerrard Joan Vreelandt 1748

Memoir left by the Governor Joan Gideon Loten for his successor Jan Schreuder 1757 (1935)

Memoir by the Commandeur of Jaffna Anthony Mooyart for his successor Noel Anthony Lebeck 1766

Memoir by the Governor Jan Schreuder for his successor Lubbert Jan Baron Van Eck 1762 (1946)

Diary of Governor Gerrit de Heere during his voyage from Colombo to Jaffna 1697 (1914)

MISCELLANEOUS

Constantine de Saa's maps and plans of Ceylon, 1624–8 (1929)

ADMINISTRATIVE REPORTS 1947+

Historical Manuscripts Commission: *Reports*, 1–4
Historical Manuscripts Commission: *Bulletins*

1 *Extracts from the proceedings of the Committee of Investigation 1797–98; the Turnour manuscript* (1937)

2 *Letters of John D'Oyly* (1937; repr. 1962)

3 *Tamil documents in the government archives* (1937)

4 *The Tombo of the Two Kōrales* (1938)

5 *Granville report on the Mātara district 1813*

INDIA

INTRODUCTION

India obtained independence on 14 August 1947. It comprised the former provinces and presidencies of British India less those regions that became Pakistan (q.v.). In the years which immediately followed, those of the former Indian princely states which stood in its area acceded to it. India became a republic in 1950. Under the provisions of the States Reorganization Act, 1956, its internal boundaries were somewhat redrawn so as to form the present linguistic states. Bombay, which was originally a single state, was divided in 1960 to form the two states of Maharashtra and Gujarat, and in 1966 Punjab was divided to form the two states of Punjab and Hariana.

ARCHIVES ADMINISTRATION IN INDIA

The National Archives of India contains the records of the supreme Government of India, under the British East India Company, under the British Crown and, increasingly, since Independence. Most Indian states have set up their own state archives. Apart from containing their own records, these hold either the records of the presidencies or provinces that extended over their present areas in the past, or such records pertaining to their area as they have managed to collect, particularly those belonging to local erstwhile princely states. A coordinating body concerned with archives in India is the Indian Historical Records Commission which publishes its *Proceedings*.

NATIONAL ARCHIVES OF INDIA

National Archives of India, Janpath, New Delhi
Officer in Charge: Director of Archives
Authority: Ministry of Education

RULES OF ACCESS

In general, records relating to all Ministries except the Ministry of External Affairs are open for consultation by bona fide research students up to 1945. Home Affairs records relating to Kashmir are not however open for the period after 31 December 1913 unless quite special permission has been secured. Records of the Ministry of External Affairs which are over 30 years old are open to inspection except those of a later date than

31 December 1913 which may relate to India's relations with areas which now comprise Pakistan, Kashmir, Nepal, Tibet, China, Sikkim, Bhutan and North East Frontier Agency. However, prior permission from the Ministry of External Affairs can sometimes be obtained to consult some of this later material. Excerpts of material of the open period are released without scrutiny. Students wishing to use the archives must produce a recommendation from an appropriate authority.

ADMINISTRATION OF CENTRAL GOVERNMENT ARCHIVES

The National Archives of India (formerly known as the Imperial Record Department) came into existence in 1891, as a result of the efforts of the Government of India to find an adequate and permanent solution to the problem of storage and preservation of the ever-increasing bulk of their records, which were till then kept in the custody of each creating department. In 1889 Professor (afterwards Sir) G. W. Forrest was placed by the Government of India on special duty to examine the records of the Foreign Department. In his report dated 17 August 1889 Forrest recommended that all the records relating to the administration of the East India Company should be placed in one central records office. The proposal was duly approved by the secretary of state for India, and Mr Forrest was appointed as the first officer-in-charge of the records of the Government of India. Thus the Imperial Record Department came into existence in Calcutta on 11 March 1891.

The Imperial Record Department was under the administrative control of the Home Department till 1910, when it was transferred to the care of the newly created Department of Education. The designation of the officer-in-charge of records was subsequently changed to Keeper of Records of the Government of India. With the transfer of the capital of India from Calcutta to Delhi in 1911, it was felt necessary to transfer the official records also to the new headquarters. The present archives building was completed in 1926, but the transfer of the entire bulk of records to Delhi could not be accomplished till March 1937. With the advent of independence in India in 1947, the name of the Imperial Record Department was changed to National Archives of India, and the post of Keeper of Records was redesignated as the Director of Archives. A departmental library is attached.

NATURE AND EXTENT OF HOLDINGS

Holdings occupy about 75,000 running feet of shelves. The main archival series date from 1748 although copies of earlier collections have been obtained from various sources, notably the India Office Records, a section of the Commonwealth Relations Office, London, and from France, the Netherlands and Denmark. The Bombay and Madras factory records are available in the Bombay Secretariat Record Office (q.v.) and the Madras Record Office (q.v.). The early Bengal records are unfortunately not available in either the National Archives of India or in West Bengal, apparently having been destroyed partly by the cyclone and flood of 1737 and partly during the sack of Calcutta in 1756, but they are available in the India Office Records, London. The later records of the Government of Bengal, including those of the period when it was the supreme government, and of the several boards and offices subordinate to it, are partly in the custody of the National Archives of India and partly of the West Bengal Secretariat Record Office (q.v.). With the abolition of the office of the crown representative, and the residencies and the political agencies after 1947, those of their records which were not already dispersed were centralized in the National Archives. About one million files of the Ministry of States previously held at Simla were transferred to the National Archives during 1949–50. One result of this has been to break the integrity of some of the series held in the states, as local government records of the Indian States were separated and removed to the Residencies in 1937 with the inauguration of provincial autonomy. The National Archives has a substantial collection of microfilms of material in other repositories, particularly in Britain. Since this is regularly enlarged it has not been listed here.

CENTRAL GOVERNMENT RECORDS OUTSIDE NEW DELHI

The National Archives has confined its attention mainly to records produced at the capital, but many important offices of the central government are outside Delhi, as for instance the geological and zoological surveys of India, Calcutta; the survey of India, Dehra Dun; the office of the government epigraphist for India, Ootacamund; the iron and steel controller, Calcutta; and the textile commissioner, Bombay. The director of archives inspects these records. A regional office of the National Archives was opened at the Moti Mahal, Bhopal, in 1954 as a result of an offer from the late government of Bhopal to hand over all its historical records as a gift. Central government records are also held in the Assam Secretariat Office, Shillong (q.v.) and at repositories now under the administration of Madhya Pradesh, Andhra Pradesh, Uttar Pradesh, Kerala, Madras, Rajasthan, Mysore and Gujarat (q.v.).

AIDS TO REFERENCE

The compilation of reference media forms one of the main items in the records administration programme of the National Archives. Printed indexes of records after 1859 already exist. Press lists were issued in tabular form until 1917 when the run-on style was adopted. They were abandoned in 1939 in favour of indexing but have subsequently been resumed. The survey and listing of various groups of records in connection with the projected revision of the *Handbook to the records in the National Archives of India* was begun in 1940, but with the unprecedented flow of new accessions after 1947 much of this work was made obsolete and had to be restarted. However, part I of the new *Guide to records* was published in 1959. Handlists of the Persian letters have been prepared and an *Index* to the handlists published. Printed press lists, calendars, handbooks and reference aids are listed here under 'Additional Publications' in the pages which follow those giving the lists of holdings in the National Archives.

PUBLICATIONS

On the recommendation of the Royal Asiatic Society of England the Government of India in June 1900 decided to publish through the Society two series, the 'Indian text series' and the 'Indian records series'. In 1905 the secretary of state entrusted the publication of the 'Indian records series' to John Murray under the supervision of the India Office, and the work proceeded until coming to a sudden close in 1913. In January 1942 the recently reconstituted Indian Historical Records Commission urged upon the government the necessity of resuming their long-interrupted publishing activities, presenting to the government a publication programme divided into three parts. Under scheme I the *Fort William–India House correspondence 1748–1800* is being printed *in extenso* in 21 volumes edited by scholars under the general editorship of the director of archives and under scheme II 'Selections from the English records' are directly edited by the director of archives. These represent the resuscitated 'Indian record series' in a new form. Under scheme III(a) 'Records in Oriental languages' and (b) 'Selections from English records', in the custody of the National Archives, are published in collaboration with private institutions. Other official publications include a number in which records from the National Archives have been printed *in extenso* or in extracts. Details of other publications in which the archives have been used extensively appear in the bibliographies appended to the volumes of the *Fort William–India House correspondence*, volume v of the *Cambridge History of India* and other standard works on modern Indian history. A select list of administrative publications and publications of the Indian Historical Records Commission appear under 'Additional Publications' in the pages which follow the ensuing lists of holdings in the National Archives.

I

NATIONAL ARCHIVES OF INDIA, PRE-MUTINY SERIES

A guide to these records, *Handbook to the records of the Government of India in the Imperial Record Department 1748–1859* (Calcutta, 1925) is still of considerable use and contains much more detail than is included here. For this period the main departmental categories are Finance, Foreign, Home, Legislative, Military and Public Works. These records are those of the supreme Government of the British East India Company in India.

The Company was incorporated under a charter granted by Queen Elizabeth I on 31 December 1600 which conferred the exclusive privilege of trade in the East Indies. The first trading factory established in India proper was at Surat in 1612. A factory at Fort St George, which eventually became the seat of the Madras presidency, was established in 1639, and a factory at Hooghly in Bengal proper in 1651. These and other agencies and factories were by 1700 administered as three presidencies, Bombay, Madras and Bengal, by presidents or governors with headquarters at Bombay, Fort St George and Calcutta. Business, which related almost exclusively to trade, was carried on in direct correspondence with the Court of Directors in London. This period of the Company's transactions, until the passing of the Regulating Act in 1773, is known as the Factory period.

As the Company became increasingly involved in political administration and territorial expansion in conflict with other European and Indian powers, the period from the 1750s saw the growth of special committees and secretariats to deal with different aspects of administration. With the passing of the Regulating Act in 1773 the Government of Bengal became the supreme Government of British India. The early nineteenth century saw a further increase in political and social responsibilities and a consequent increase in the numbers of boards and departments, until it became necessary by the Charter Act of 1833 to introduce important changes in the Indian administration. The overgrown presidency of Bengal was divided into the presidencies of Fort William in Bengal and of Agra. Although the governor-general of India remained in addition the governor of Bengal, certain functions of the secretariat and their records were divided and the activities of the Company as a commercial body also ceased. In 1843 the secretariat of the Government of India was separated completely from that of Bengal. By the passing of the Government of India Act in 1858 the control of the Government of India was transferred from the Company to the British Crown.

At the time when the business of the Company related only to trade and cognate subjects disposed of by the governor in council, records of council business were entered into a 'diary and consultation book', later a 'consultation book', which with two other volumes, 'letters to' and 'letters from' the Court of Directors in London, contained the complete records of a factory. With the growth of business these latter were abolished and all documents were entered in full in the 'consultation books' which came to be known as 'proceedings volumes' and summary minutes or 'body sheets' were bound separately. The original documents from which copies were made were called 'original consultations' and were kept in chronological bundles. As the Company extended its interests and sub-heads such as Public, Revenue, Secret, Political, Military, Commercial and Judicial were created, separate proceedings for each were started. 'Indexes', containing abstracts of the documents arranged alphabetically under broad heads, were prepared and bound separately. The 'order books' contained copies of routine correspondence not formally brought before the Council. Thus the most important records to which all the others were subsidiary were the 'proceedings volumes', 'original consultations' and 'letters to and from the Court of Directors'.

HOLDINGS: PRE-MUTINY SERIES

SUMMARY LIST OF HOLDINGS

Finance Department	1810–59
Foreign Department	1756–1859
Home Department	1704–1859
Legislative Department	1777–1859
Military Department	1771–1859
Persian Department	1801–81
Public Works Department	1850–9
Thagi and Dakaiti Department	1830–1904

FINANCE DEPARTMENT 1810–59

This department originated as a branch of the Public Department in January 1810. A distinct secretariat was formed in August 1812 when the Colonial Department, concerned with Mauritius, Java and the Malaccas, was attached, but on the abolition of the Colonial Department in November 1815 the Finance Department was made a part of the Revenue Secretariat, then styled the Territorial Department. Transferred to the Public Department in 1830, it was transformed into an independent secretariat in January 1843. The records consist of two series, the one starting in 1810 and relating to the supreme Government, the other relating to the Government of Bengal 1834–54. The first series includes financial papers from other departments, also records relating to commerce, a function of the Financial Secretariat from 1879 when it became the Finance and Commerce Department. Mint matters were recorded separately from March 1832. The Bengal series remained with the Finance Department when the two governments were separated in May 1854. There are no Bengal financial proceedings before 1834, and those for May 1854–6 are incorporated with the revenue records in West Bengal. The Colonial Department records are lost, but duplicate copies exist in London.

GOVERNMENT OF INDIA RECORDS

FINANCIAL PAPERS

Proceedings	11 Jan. 1811–18 Dec. 1857	250 v
Abstract of proceedings	1816; 1825; Apr. 1842–1855	17 v
Index to proceedings	1811–57	39 v
Body sheets	1810–56	41 v
Order book	1810–55	55 v
Original consultations	14 Jan. 1790–22 Dec. 1854	177 bdls
General letters from Court	18 Mar. 1812–1857	47 v
Abstract general letters from Court with index	Sept. 1785–Apr. 1838	1 v
Index to general letters from Court	1834–Nov. 1853	1 v
General letters to Court	1809–57	56 v
Abstract of general letters to Court	1835–52	1 v
Index to general letters to Court	1834–51	1 v

MINT PAPERS

Proceedings	27 Mar. 1832–18 Dec. 1857	27 v
Index to proceedings	1832–57	27 v
Body sheets	1832–55	7 v
Order book	Mar. 1832–1856	9 v
Original consultations	3 May 1833–18 Dec. 1857	16 bdls

MISCELLANEOUS   1750–1857   28 v

Includes Bengal revenue statements 1843–4 and 1855–6; Bombay supplies; Accounts Committee proceedings; Madras contingent expenses 1827–8; and resolutions and orders by the department 1834–48.

GOVERNMENT OF BENGAL RECORDS

FINANCIAL PAPERS

Proceedings	21 Nov. 1834–30 Dec. 1853	25 v
Abstract of proceedings	1837–May 1853	6 v
Index to proceedings	1834–54	20 v
Body sheets	1836–Apr. 1854	12 v
Order book	July 1835–Apr. 1854	16 v
Original consultations	21 Nov. 1834–28 Apr. 1854	31 bdls
General letters from Court	1834–54	21 v
General letters to Court	1835–54	14 v

MINT PAPERS

Proceedings	15 Apr. 1835–28 Apr. 1854	19 v
Index to proceedings	1836–54	16 v
Body sheets	1 Dec. 1834–50	5 v
Order book	1835–Feb. 1854	8 v
Original consultations	15 Apr. 1835–17 Feb. 1854	7 bdls

SEPARATE REVENUE BRANCH

'Separate' revenue denotes government income accruing from sources other than land revenue, namely salt and opium from 1790; customs from 1790 except May 1810–May 1821; stamps from 1828; *akbari* from 1829; and assessed taxes from 1843. Previously the assessed taxes were administered by the Public Branch and then by the Financial Branch, while earlier records under the other heads appear in the proceedings of the governor-general in Council in the Revenue or Territorial Department, in the possession of West Bengal, as also do the customs records for 1810–21. Between 1843 and 1863 Separate Revenue Branch became part of the Home Department.

Proceedings	20 Aug. 1790–1856	130 v
Index to proceedings	1794–1857	57 v
Order books	5 Dec. 1815–1834	14 v
Original consultations	Aug. 1790–1857	208 bdls
Body sheets	1817–20	4 v

Body sheets	1821–56	18 bdls
Letters from Court	1795–1856	17 v
Letters from Court	1838; 1843–57	1 bdl
Letters to Court	1795–1857	31 v
List of packets to Court	1844–50	1 v
Governor-general's proceedings (or abstracts)	1839–52	2 bdls
Proceedings (ceded and conquered provinces)	Oct. 1804–Apr. 1805	5 v
Original consultations (ceded and conquered provinces)	March 1803–July 1805	5 bdls
Body sheets (ceded and conquered provinces)	1803	1 bdl

INTERMEDIATE AUTHORITIES

Board of Customs, salt and opium (Fort William)

Customs proceedings	1819–21	6 v
Index to Customs proceedings	1819–20	2 v

Board of Commissioners, ceded and conquered provinces (known as the Board of Revenue, Western Provinces from 23 April 1822)

Customs proceedings	Sept. 1807–1825	72 v
Index to Customs proceedings	1811–24	12 v

Board of Commissioners, Bihar and Benares (known as the Board of Revenue, Central Provinces from 9 April 1822)

Customs proceedings	Feb. 1816–1826	17 v
Index to Customs proceedings	1817–26	9 v

Board of Revenue (Fort William), salt

Proceedings	May 1788–1892	15 v

FOREIGN DEPARTMENT 1756–1859

SECRET (SELECT) COMMITTEE

Created after the capture of Calcutta by Siraj-ud-daula in June 1756, the Secret Committee functioned from August until December 1756 when it was replaced by a Select Committee constituted on similar lines for similar purposes. After the end of 1762 the governor and Council resumed charge of the special duties allotted to it until May 1765 when it was reconstituted with absolute jurisdiction over all military and political concerns. Subordinated to the Council in August 1768 the Select Committee was dissolved in October 1774. Its records constitute one series. Wanting portions may be found in the Orme MSS in the India Office Records and in the possession of West Bengal (q.v.).

Proceedings	1756–74	27 v
Copies of letters received	10 Dec. 1771–24 Nov. 1772	1 v
Copies of letters issued	7 May–27 Dec. 1765; 1768	3 v
Original consultations and body sheets (stray)	1762–74	1 bdl
Letters from Court	1756–61; 1766–71	2 v

A number of letters from and to the Court were misplaced amongst the records of the Public Department. Those under notice furnish an excellent narrative of the contemporary military and political situation in India and contain material relating to all the rival European powers, the Moguls, the Nawab Wazir of Oudh, the Rohillas, the Pathans, the Maratha dynasties, the Sikhs and Jats, the Nizam of Hyderabad, the Nawab of the Carnatic, the Nawab Nazim of Bengal, Haidar Ali and Ahmad Shah Abdali.

SECRET BRANCH

The Secret Department functioned under this name from December 1763 until May 1765 and from August 1768 until May 1786 when it became known as the Secret and Political Department and, after May 1789, the Political Department. Upon the creation of the Foreign Department in May 1843 the Secret Department became one of its branches and as such continued until October 1859. Proceedings of the governor-general in Council at Ootacamund, in 1834 and 1855, are included in the following papers and total 4 volumes and 2 bundles.

Index to proceedings	1772–1859	67 v
Decennial indexes	1830–80	47 v
Secret proceedings	1763–1859	812 v
Draft secret proceedings	1778–9	1 v
Secret order book	1763–4	1 v
Body sheets	1765–75	4 v
	1776–1848	36 bdls
Original consultations	1763–1859	[no bulk given]
Index to letters from Court	1824–6	1 v
Letters from Court and secretary of state	1778–1857	20 v
	1787–1859	12 bdls

Index to letters to Court	1806	1 v
Letters to Court and secretary of state	1764–1860	99 v
Letters to Court and secretary of state	1803–59	24 bdls
Draft letters to Secret Committee of Court of Directors	1806–20	6 v
Letters to secretary, India House	1844–59	1 v
Duplicate copies of Secret Department letters	1825–6	2 bdls
Original letters from Secret Committee	1841–3	2 sheets only
Index to Ootacamund proceedings (proceedings of governor-general in Council at Ootacamund)	1834	1 v
Ootacamund proceedings	June–Oct. 1834	1 v
Ootacamund original consultations	June–Oct. 1834	1 bdl
Ootacamund letters to Court	1834–7, 1855	2 v
Copies of governor-general's letters to Secret Committee of Court, from Ootacamund	Mar.–Aug. 1855	1 bdl

FOREIGN BRANCH

The Foreign Branch (or Department) conducted transactions with foreign European nations. It emanated from the Secret Department in December 1783 and merged into the Political Department in August 1842, although from May 1818 it was associated with the General Department under the charge of the same secretary.

Proceedings	1784–1842	69 v
Index to proceedings	1784–1840	27 v
Diary of letters issued	Nov. 1784–5; 1811–59	57 v
Diary of letters received	1819–59	55 v
Original consultations	10 Dec. 1783–1842	99 bdls
Letters from Court	Apr. 1792–Apr. 1827	3 v
Letters to Court	Feb. 1784–1825	14 v

POLITICAL BRANCH

This department came into existence in June 1789, its proceedings being included in those of the Secret Branch until 1790 when they form a distinct series. In August 1841 the Foreign Branch merged with the Political Branch, the combined establishment becoming part of the newly constituted Foreign Department in May 1843 under the name Foreign Branch. Ootacamund papers for 1834 and 1855, totalling 13 volumes and 14 bundles, are included in the following papers. The diaries of letters issued, 1811–59, and of letters received, 1819–59, are listed under the Foreign Branch.

Index to political proceedings	1775–1859	110 v
Political proceedings	1790–1860	1860 v
Body sheets	1790–1828	10 bdls
Original consultations	1790–1860	1329 bdls +9 big bdls
Index and abstracts of letters from Court	1824–39	2 v
Register of letters from Court and secretary of state	1786–1859	78 v
Register of letters from Court and secretary of state	1800–59	13 bdls
Index to letters to Court	1829–33	3 v
Abstract and content of letters to secretary of state	1859	1 bdl
Political letters to Court and secretary of state	1789–1859	159 v
Governor-general's political despatches to Court and secretary of state	1810–59	3 bdls
Letters to Court and secretary of state	1796–1859	34 bdls
Index to Ootacamund proceedings	June–Oct. 1834	1 v + duplicate
Ootacamund political proceedings	June–Oct. 1834	8 v
Letters to Court (Ootacamund)	1834, 1855	4 v
Ootacamund original consultations	1834	7 bdls

SECRET AND SEPARATE BRANCH

The functions of this branch were confined to the consideration of certain special questions as they arose and its proceedings were unconnected with any other branch. From 1796 it acted as a kind of political intelligence bureau. Subjects dealt with include the conduct of Ram Charan Roy in corresponding with Kamgar Khan 1761–2; alleged maladministration of revenues by Raja Shitab Rai of Bihar 1773; trial of Muhammad Riza Khan of Bengal for grain monopoly 1773–4; capture of the Dutch settlements in Bengal 1781–3; designs of Tipu Sultan 1787; revision of the civil establishment and reduction of political charges at native courts 1788–90; Persia and Turkey 1796; expedition to Manilla 1797; Wazir Ali' insurrection at Benares 1799; diplomatic negotiations with Arabia, Persia, Turkey, Kabul, Sind, Ranjit Singh and others, and expeditions against hostile European nations in India and the East 1808–11.

Proceedings	Apr. 1761–Mar. 1811	42 v
Index to proceedings	1787–8; 1797; 1799; 1808–11	9 v
Original consultations	1770–Mar. 1811	35 bdls
Body sheets	1773–Mar. 1811	4 bdls
Letters to Court or their Secret Committee	Jan–Nov. 1789; Oct. 1810	3 v
Ootacamund and presidency letters to the Secret Committee	1834–8	1 v

SECRET DEPARTMENT OF INSPECTION

This branch came into existence in 1766 under the name 'Committee of Inspection'. An adjunct to the Public Department, it was associated with the Secret Department in 1784 and merged with the Secret and Separate Department in 1787. Known variously as the Board of Inspection, Secret Department of Inspection or Department of Reform, its functions were to examine and arrange the working of government administration.

Proceedings	1782; Oct.–Dec. 1785; Apr.–Dec. 1786	2 v
Copies of letters issued	1782–6	1 v
Original consultations	1770; 1778; 1784–7	4 bdls
Body sheets	1770; 1784–7	1 v

DEPARTMENT OF CEDED AND CONQUERED PROVINCES

The Revenue Department of the ceded provinces was created in February 1803 to deal with matters of justice and revenue relating to those territories, other matters being administered through the ordinary departments of government. In November 1804 the conquered provinces were brought within the jurisdiction of the department and the name changed to the Department of the Ceded and Conquered Provinces. The proceedings were recorded under three heads, Revenue and Judicial, the few remaining papers of which are entered under the Foreign Department miscellaneous records, and Public (Separate Revenue, i.e. customs, salt, opium) held under the Finance Department Separate Revenue Branch.

TENASSERIM PAPERS

These are the original consultations of the Government of Bengal, transferred to the Government of India when it took over the administration of Tenasserim.

The papers are incomplete.

Original consultations (judicial)	Jan. 1830–9 Nov. 1854	26 bdls
Original consultations (revenue)	16 Dec. 1833–15 June 1854	6 bdls
Original consultations (general)	1 Dec. 1834–28 Sept. 1854	3 bdls
Original consultations (separate-customs)	1835; 1842; 1844–8	1 bdl
Original consultations (marine)	9 May 1838–29 Apr. 1854	6 bdls
Original consultations (marine-steam)	4 Jan. 1838–12 Jan. 1854	1 bdl
Original consultations (ecclesiastical)	6 Jan.–24 Mar. 1853	1 bdl
Index		1 v

BENGAL ORIGINAL POLITICAL PAPERS

1834–43   5 bdls

These papers appear to have been transferred to the Government of India in October 1843 when the branches of business with which they deal were allotted to that government.

Original political consultations.

A selection relating to the North-East Frontier, Sambalpur (South-West Frontier), Tenasserim Provinces and Khasia Hills and the affairs of the Nawabs of Murshidabad and Dacca and of the princes of Tipu Sultan's family.

Original General (Foreign) consultations with body sheets.

These contain transactions in respect of foreign powers and external politics generally and represent entire proceedings of each date.

BHUTAN, SIKKIM AND TIBET PAPERS

1845–59   1 bdl

A selection of original consultations recorded in the General, Judicial and Political Branches which relate to British diplomatic relations with these countries and which were later transferred to the Government of India.

SAMBALPUR PAPERS

From the time of its annexation by the British in 1849 until its incorporation into the Central Provinces in 1862, Sambalpur was administered by Bengal. After 1912 it formed part of Bihar and Orissa. The papers, apparently incomplete, were transferred to the Government of India as a result of the transfer of administrative control.

Original consultations (general)	May 1849–3 July 1850; 10 Aug. 1857	1 bdl
Original consultations (judicial)	1857–9	3 bdls

NORTH-WESTERN PROVINCES ORIGINAL CONSULTATIONS

1840–58   4 bdls

The majority of these are political consultations for the period 1840–3, the others judicial and revenue consultations 1842–58. They relate to certain principalities and native states including Bundelkhand, Saugor and Nerbudda and represent only those portions of the series to which they belong which were transferred to the Government of India.

CHINA PAPERS

1840–50; 1855   12 bdls

Original correspondence and accounts relating to the Second China Expedition 1840–4 (Opium War), and copy of Siam treaty, 1855.

KABUL PAPERS

1839–59   6 v and 2 bdls

Four sets of a collection of letters received in or issued from the Foreign Department Political and Secret Branches relating to British relations with Afghanistan and printed in 1884–5 when the Russian and British commission to fix the northern boundary was appointed.

JAGIR STATEMENTS

1847–57   225 statements

215 statements of conditional land grants (hereditary or life) in the Punjab, also 5 pension statements of the royal family of Oudh. These are original consultations of the Foreign (Political) and Secret Branches.

PERSIA DESPATCHES
1834–59   40 v, 1 bdl

Copies of letters from the British envoy in Persia to the Secret Committee of the Court, later the secretary of state for India.

CORRESPONDENCE
1838–58   4 bdls

Including letters between the secretaries to government at the presidency and the secretary in camp, e.g. with the governor-general on tour.

MALACCA PROCEEDINGS
1851–60   5 v

TENASSERIM AND MARTABAN PROCEEDINGS
1855–9   5 v

Abstracts of the weekly proceedings of the commissioner.

CENTRAL INDIA AGENCY RECORDS
1806–59   1 bdl

Printed copies of selected files belonging to the office of the principal political officer (later agent to the governor-general in Central India), with a printed index.

MISCELLANEOUS RECORDS
1796–1859   398 v and
11 bdls

Relating to particular subjects kept separate from the regular series of proceedings, also private correspondence and other documents, these records are listed in *A Handbook to the records of the Government of India… 1748–1859*. They include correspondence with the residents or agents at Ava, Delhi, Ajmer, Alwar, Rajputana, Hyderabad, Indore, Peshawar, Saugor and other places; list of packets; report of the Malabar Commission; copies of correspondence relating to the secret expeditions against Mauritius, Batavia etc.; proceedings of the Board of Commissioners for Mysore 1832; newsletters relating to Kabul and Western India 1839–42; accounts of political events in Persia and neighbouring countries; administration reports and other accounts of the Punjab, including C. M. Wade's report; Tanjore Raj case papers.

HOME DEPARTMENT 1704–1859

PUBLIC BRANCH

This group contains the Council's consultations from 1704, before the creation of separate departments, continued by the records of the Public Department created in 1763 and charged with the business relating to shipping, revenues, fortifications, accounts, appointments, etc. The name was changed to General Department in June 1818, until May 1843 when it became the General Branch, later the Home, then (1847) the Public Branch of the Home Department. It was generally responsible for all matters not covered by other branches, and more particularly for political matters. Records were at different times transferred to relevant younger departments and are now included in those series. The main series begins in 1748, but earlier series are held in London.

Proceedings	1748–1859	644 v

The volumes for 1859 contain, besides public, the ecclesiastical, education, electric telegraph, judicial, marine, post office, revenue and separate revenue proceedings.

Proceedings (monthly)	1857–9	8 bdls
Abstracts of proceedings	1799–1832	18 v
Index to proceedings	1748–1859	99 v
Contents of proceedings	1859	1 v
Diaries, including all branches of the Home Department	1843–57	13 v
Registers of letters issued	1845–57	24 v
Original consultations and collections	1761–1859	842 bdls
Body sheets	1763–1856	96 bdls
Governor-general's proceedings	Jan.–Nov. 1855 and Feb. 1858–Jan. 1859	6 v

The volumes for February 1858–January 1859 contain the proceedings of the ecclesiastical, education, electric telegraph, judicial, marine, post office, public, revenue, and separate revenue branches.

Governor-general's original consultations	1837–59	20 bdls
Foreign Department secret consultations	1858–9	1 bdl

These relate to the concerns of the Public Branch and the police in the affairs of the Punjab and Oudh.

Letters from Court	1755–1859	133 v

Include copies of letters obtained from the India Office, London. Some of the volumes contain miscellaneous letters and papers as well; others public as well as ecclesiastical, military and secret general letters.

Letters from Court	1818–59	6 bdls
Abstract	1778–1818	3 v
Register	1844–59	2 v
Letters to Court	1748–1859	150 v
Letters to Court	1845–59	2 bdls
Drafts	1859	1 v
Abstract	1807–18	1 v
Register	1858–9	1 v
Letters from secretary, India House	1843–58	3 v, 1 bdl
Letters to secretary, India House	1800–57	9 v
Letters to under secretary of state	1858–9	1 v, 1 bdl

The last three items contain the public as well as various other heads.

ECCLESIASTICAL BRANCH

Until 1815, when an Ecclesiastical Branch of the Public Department was established, the work pertaining to the clerical establishment was conducted   .
both in the Public and Military Departments. Correspondence with the Home authorities on matters affecting chaplains not on the Company's regular establishment remained with the Military Department.

Proceedings	Nov. 1815–1859	45 v
Index to proceedings	1815–59	23 v
Contents of proceedings	1859	1 v
Body sheets	1842–56	10 v
Original consultations and collections	1815–59	65 bdls
Governor-general's original consultations	1848–51 and 1858	3 bdls
Letters from Court	1824–59	5 v, 2 bdls
Register of letters from Court	1858–9	2 v
Letters to Court	1820–59	21 v, 2 bdls
Register of letters to Court	1858–9	1 v

JUDICIAL BRANCH

The judicial records of the governor-general in Council prior to the establishment of the Judicial Department in 1834 are held in West Bengal. The Department became a branch of the Home Department in 1843.

Proceedings	Dec. 1834–1859	87 v
Abstract of proceedings	1839	1 v
Index of proceedings	Dec. 1834–1859	29 v

The Revenue index is also held in vol. I (December 1834–June 1835) and the indexes for the Legislative and Revenue Branches in vol. III (July–December 1835).

Contents of proceedings	1859	1 v
Diaries	1836–47	6 v
Body sheets (also revenue body sheets up to 1837)	1835–56	22 v
Original consultations and collections	Oct. 1834–1859	111 bdls
Governor-general's original consultations	1831–59	20 bdls
Letters from Court	1835–59	19 v
Letters from Court	1836–56	3 bdls
Index	1835–49	1 v
Register	1835–59	2 v
Letters to Court	1835–59	40 v, 2 bdls
Register	1858–9	1 v
Letters to the secretary, India House, judicial, marine, ecclesiastical, electric telegraph	1837–59	4 v, 1 bdl

REVENUE BRANCH

The earliest information on revenue matters is found in the records of the Public and Secret Departments and Select Committee. The proceedings relating to revenue which were recorded separately from 1771 to 1834 are held in West Bengal. A Revenue Branch was established in 1834 and was incorporated with the Home Department in 1843.

Proceedings	June 1834–1859	82 v
Index to proceedings	1857–67	1 v
Diary of letters received	1834–47	5 v
Original consultations	1830–59	62 bdls

The papers prior to 1834 originally belonged to the Territorial (Revenue) Department series of the Government of Bengal and are not continuous. Later they were transferred to the central government. Many relate to the tea industry.

Letters from Court relating to cotton and silk cultivation, irrigation	1835–59	16 v

Letters from Court	1837–58	2 bdls
Index	1859	1 v
List	1836–58	1 v
Letters to Court	1834–59	20 v
Letters to Court	1838–59	1 bdl
List of packets to Court	1847–56	3 v
Draft letters to the secretary, India House	1838–51	1 v
Home Department consultations		
Foreign, public and legislative (emigration)	1830–57	1 bdl

The emigration papers after 1858 are with the Crown records of the Commerce Department.

Public (fibres and silk)	1836; 1855–6 1858–9 etc.	1 bdl
Public (revenue)	1843; 1851–3; 1855	1 bdl
Public (agriculture)	1851–2; 1855–7	1 bdl
Public (meteorology)	1857–8	1 bdl
Public (surveys)	1855–7	1 bdl
Public Works Department, forests		
A. Proceedings	1859	1 bdl

This is the start of the Forest series, which continues successively under the headings General, Agriculture and Revenue in the Public Works Department.

EDUCATION BRANCH

Matters relating to education were recorded with the proceedings of the Public or General Department until 1784 and from September 1830 to 1856, the Revenue or Territorial (Revenue Branch) from 1785 to 17 July 1823, and the Political Department from 18 July 1823 to August 1830, in this case the correspondence being conducted through the Persian secretary. Certain records are held in West Bengal (q.v.).

Proceedings	1859	1 v
Index to proceedings	1857–9	4 v
Contents of proceedings	1859	1 v
Original consultations and collections	1857–9	4 bdls
Governor-general's original consultations and collections	1858	1 bdl
Spare copies (letters, etc.)	1854–9	1 bdl
Letters from Court	1859	1 bdl
Register	1858–9	2 v

Letters to Court (also some printed duplicates)	1856–9	8 v
Letters to Court	1859	1 bdl
Register	1858–9	1 v

MEDICAL BOARD

The records of the Hospital and Medical Boards up to 1857 are with the Home Department.

Proceedings	May 1786–June 1854	292 v
Index to proceedings	1787–1857	74 v
Original letters received	1853	12 v
Diary of letters received	Sept. 1845–June 1846	1 v
Original consultations	Apr. 1845–57	66 bdls
Miscellaneous	1817–57	37 v
Service certificates of military and medical officers	1817–26	1 v
Graduation list of the Medical department and of officers (up to the rank of adjutant) attached to the various corps and regiments of the Bengal army	1824	1 v
Quarterly returns on medical sub-ordinates and native doctors	1824–57	11 v
Monthly returns of medical officers	1851–7	7 v
Monthly returns of medical sub-ordinates	1851–7	7 v
Medical certificates granted to military officers and others	1853–7	10 v

MISCELLANEOUS RECORDS

	1680–1859	574 v and 12 bdls

These records, listed in *A handbook to the records of the Government of India…1748–1859*, pp. 35–48, include the narrative of proceedings of Agra and North-Western Provinces in the Judicial and other departments 1835–62; Bengal civil lists for 1805, 1822, 1824, 1825, 1828, 1835, 1837, 1846, 1859; papers laid before the Board in various departments 1811–34; extracts from proceedings of the Board of Revenue, Madras, 1830–51; narrative of the affairs and war in the Carnatic 1751–8; proceedings of the

governor in Council at Fort Marlbro' with index 1787–99; proceedings of
the commissioner (afterwards resident) at Fort Marlbro' September 1800–
March 1818; Board of Trade proceedings regarding Fort Marlbro' 1809–
April 1826; proceedings of the College of Fort William *c.* 1801–54; copies
of letters from the Court of Directors 1680–1 and 1703–48, the originals in
London; Java records; Judicial Department original consultations 1834;
proceedings of the Indian law commissioners 1844–7; lists of packets;
index to Legislative, Revenue and Judicial proceedings 1836–7; orders and
advertisements issued from the Public Department 1787–May 1843; copies
of Public Department records obtained from London 1749–September
1799; and Straits Settlements proceedings.

LEGISLATIVE DEPARTMENT 1777–1859

Originally the legal concerns of the East India Company were dealt with in
the Public Department (see under the Public Branch of the Home Depart-
ment, above). Later these responsibilities were shared in part with the
Revenue Department (see under the Revenue Branch of the Home
Department, above), the records of civil and criminal justice administration
being included in the Revenue consultations until the creation of the
Judicial Branch in August 1790. The records of the Judicial Branch before
1834 are held in West Bengal; for those after 1834 see pages 48–9 above.
The first proceedings dealing exclusively with law were recorded in the
Revenue Department 1777–85, and another series headed 'law' was
started in the Public Department in 1794. In January 1835 the law proceedings were incorporated with the Judicial proceedings, passing to the
newly created Legislative Department, an adjunct to the Judicial Department, the following May. The Legislative Department became a branch of
the Home Department in 1843 and was abolished in May 1854 when its
duties were taken over by the Legislative Council. With a few unrelated
exceptions the Council records have disappeared although papers relevant
to a particular matter are found in the proceedings of the departments
concerned, assents to bills are recorded in the Public Branch, and printed
journals of proceedings of the Council are available. The Legislative
Branch of the Home Department was revived in 1861 and converted into a
distinct secretariat in 1869, the Legislative Council, transformed into an
implementing rather than a policy body, becoming a branch. At different
times the functions of the different law bodies have been extended to
include matters relating to movements and residence of Europeans, passports, Anglo-Indians, emigration of Indians to various British colonies,
municipalities and other matters.

Law proceedings	1781; 1796–1830	25 v

The subject matter in the 1781 volume is confined to Bengal proper.

Abstract of law proceedings	1800	1 v
Index to law proceedings	1796–1834	6 v

The index to the separate public proceedings relating to law for 1794 is included in the Public Department index for 1794.

Original law consultations	Dec. 1777; 1780; 1794–Jan. 1835	47 bdls
Law letters from Court	1795–1803; 1806; 1819–32	3 v

Mostly concerned with the emigration of Indians to other colonies.

Law letters to Court	1796–1806; 1824–31	3 v
Legislative proceedings	July 1835–May 1854	111 v
Index to legislative proceedings	1835–54	21 v
Legislative body sheets	1835–May 1854	
Diary of legislative letters received	1835–47	4 v
Original legislative consultations	July 1835–Sept. 1854	117 bdls
Legislative letters from Court	1835–58	33 v
Legislative letters from Court	1837–59	1 bdl
Index to legislative letters from Court	1837–44	1 v
Legislative letters to Court	1835–54	30 v
Legislative letters to Court	1839–51	1 bdl
Index to legislative letters to Court	1835–7	2 v
List of packets to Court	1847–May 1854	2 v
Legislative letters to secretary, India House	1835–54	3 v
Governor-general's legislative proceedings	1838–Jan. 1840	5 bdls
Governor-general's up-country legislative proceedings	Apr. 1842–56	19 bdls

INDIAN LAW COMMISSION

Appointed in 1833 and subordinate to the Legislative Department, the duties of the Commission were to enquire into the jurisdiction, powers and rules of the existing courts of justice and police establishments, all forms of judicial procedure and the operation of all laws, civil or criminal, written or customary, prevailing in any part of India to which the subjects of the Company were then amenable. The Commission began work in 1835, drafted the Indian Penal Code, laid the basis for the Codes of Civil and Criminal Procedure and several other codes, but after 1849 became practically defunct.

Proceedings	1837–8	I v
Index to proceedings	1835–45	I v

MILITARY DEPARTMENT 1771–1859

Until the formation of a general Indian army under the control of the supreme Government in 1895, separate armies were maintained for the three Presidencies. The Bengal army was under the Government of India, those of Bombay and Madras under their respective local governments. Until mid-1756, and also in 1763, the Public Department was in charge of military administration while one or other branch of the Foreign Department governed policy according to its jurisdiction in particular cases. A separate office, the Controlling Military Committee, was created in March 1771 to take over the administrative functions of the Public Department. Abolished in January 1774, it was revived as the Military Board in 1777, the Public Department being re-entrusted with its previous responsibilities during the intervening years. Indeed, that department never entirely ceased its concern with military affairs, particularly in local matters and internal defence, until 1786 when the military secretariat was replaced by two new departments, the Secret and Military Department, called the Military Department after May 1789, and the Military Department of Inspection, abolished in 1793 when its duties were divided between the Military Department, Adjutant General and Town Major. The records of the Military Department of Inspection are unknown in both New Delhi and London, but the other records date from 1786 and include those Bombay and Madras papers which contribute to the history of the growth of the Indian army.

GOVERNMENT OF INDIA RECORDS

Proceedings	Jan.–June 1779; 31 May 1786–1859	1,725 v
Index to proceedings	1786–1859	296 v
Diaries of letters received	1819–51	82 v
Order book	1792–Feb. 1813	67 v
Letters written by the secretaries under the orders of the Board.		
Rough drafts of the above order book	1813–50	822 v
Body sheets	Apr.–June 1805; Jan.–Mar. 1806; 1825–59	137 v
Body sheets (incomplete)	1786–1810	4 bdls
Original consultations	1786–1859	1,437 bdls

Ootacamund proceedings	June–Oct. 1834	3 v
Abstract of Ootacamund proceedings	Mar.–16 Sept. 1855	1 v
Index to Ootacamund proceedings	1834	2 v
Ootacamund original consultations	June–Oct. 1834; Mar.–Nov. 1855	11 bdls
Up-country index	1837–Jan. 1859	16 v
Up-country diary	1837–58	16 v
Up-country rough drafts	Nov. 1837–59	78 v
Up-country original consultations	Dec. 1837–Jan. 1852; Mar.–Nov. 1855–Feb. 1858–Dec. 1859	126 bdls
General letters from Court	1780–1859	134 v
Duplicate copies	1835–58	43 bdls
General letters to Court	1790–1859	96 v
Drafts	1818–59	98 v
General letters from Court to Bengal	1835–54	87 bdls
Duplicate copies of general letters relating exclusively to the Bengal army	1835–54	17 bdls
General orders (minutes of Council	Apr. 1776–1826; 1828–59	105 v
Drafts	1822–41 (gaps)	26 v
General orders by commander-in-chief	1816–59	102 v
General orders by commander-in-chief		
Home Department	1796–1801; 1816–59	2 v
Finance Department	1831; 1833–57	37 v
Public Works Department	1831–59	25 v
Surgeon-general's office	1816–58	55 v
General orders (King's Troops)	1817–18; 1821; 1823–37	15 v
General orders (Queen's Troops)	1838–68	15 v
Bengal annual military statements and other returns	1760–1858 (gaps)	52 v
Medal and prize rolls	1794–1855	36 v
Passenger list book	1797–1850 (gaps)	21 v
Furlough book	1805–25	1 v
Furlough papers	1832–59 (gaps)	51 v

Service certificate book	1829–56 (gaps)	15 v
Death reports and promotion rolls	1837–58 (gaps)	18 v
Proceedings of Medical Boards on sick and wounded officers	1858–9	4 v
Bengal Military Widows' Fund proceedings	1806–8–11; 1813–18; 1822–4	16 v
Bengal Military Widows' Fund correspondence	1818; 1824	2 v
Bengal Military Fund proceedings	Jan.–May 1826	1 v
Bengal Military Fund correspondence	1825–39	29 v
Clothing Board proceedings	May 1816–June 1850	82 v
Clothing Board letter book	Jan.–Aug. 1817; 1821–54	69 v
Estates proceedings	1843–59	125 bdls
Papers relating to the estates of deceased		
European officers in Bengal: estate proceedings	1842–59	102 bdls
Index	1824–59	11 v
Index to letters of administration obtained in respect of estates	1844–59	1 v
Estates deposit number book	1851–4	2 v
Estates correspondence	June–Aug. 1846; Sept.–Dec. 1853; Sept.–Dec. 1856; Mar.–Apr. 1859	10 v
Estate diaries of letters received	1855–9	6 v
Number book: registers of letters issued	1851; 1855; 1858	3 v
Registers of estates	1824–59	10 v
Java or Batavia proceedings	1813–14	10 v
Correspondence	1812–17	3 v
Military letter book	Nov. 1812–Jan. 1815	1 v
Statements of letters received and orders passed thereon in the quarter-master-general's office	1835–59	24 v

GOVERNMENT OF MADRAS RECORDS

Abstract of proceedings	July–Sept. 1840; Jan.–Mar. 1845; 1850–5	15 bdls
General letters from Court	1787–1859	66 v
General letters from Court (duplicates)	1810–59	41 bdls

Index	1846–59	11 v
General letters to Court	1796–8; 1800–59	83 v
Index	1846–58	12 v
General orders	1820–59	40 v
Annual military statements	1796–1857	52 v
Records of the old Madras army	1757–9	7 papers

The bulk of these records are held in the Madras Record Office.

GOVERNMENT OF BOMBAY RECORDS

Abstract of proceedings	15 Oct. 1835–1859	26 bdls
General letters from Court	1797–1801–3; 1805–6; 1808–59	57 v
General letters from Court (duplicates)	1810–59	40 bdls
General letters to Court	1808–26; 1830–59	50 v
General orders	Aug. 1820–1859	48 v
Annual military statements	1807–59	48 v
Records of the old Bombay army	1819–93	

The bulk of these records are held in the Bombay Secretariat Record Office. The following were retained in the N.A.I.

Adjutant general's correspondence and miscellaneous papers	1819–93	196 v
Quarter-master-general's correspondence	1839–90	46 v
Correspondence relating to the Royal Artillery	1864–8	8 v

GOVERNMENT OF THE PUNJAB RECORDS

	1854–9	15 v

MARINE BRANCH

A Marine Department was created in May 1838, attached to the Home Department until 1867 when it was transferred to the Military Department. Previously its duties had been performed by the Public Department, a Marine Board being formed in May 1795.

Proceedings	May 1838–1859	31 v
Index to proceedings	May 1838–1867	20 v
Contents of proceedings	1859–May 1860	1 v
Body sheets	1842–55	9 v
Original consultations	May 1838–1859	44 bdls
Collection proceedings	1857–8	3 bdls

Governor-general's original consultations	1842–51; 1858	2 bdls
Letters from Court	1838–59	13 v
Letters from Court	1842–60	4 bdls
Letters to Court	1838–59	20 v
Letters to Court	1843–60	2 bdls
Index to letters to Court	1845	I v
Register of letters to Court	1858–61	I v
List of packets to Court	1842–4	I v
Letters from the secretary, India House, to the secretary to the Government of India; also naval appointments and lists of volunteers in the Bengal pilot service	1855; 1857–8; 1848; 1852; 1855; 1857; 1861	I bdl
Letters to the secretary, India House	1857–8	I v
Letters to the under secretary of state	1859–61; 1864	I bdl
Letters from the secretary, Marine Board	1824–6	I v
Draft of letters to the secretary, Marine Board	9 Jan. 1839–17 Aug. 1841	I bdl
Miscellaneous records	1837–58	3 v
Bengal Marine Superintendent's proceedings	2–27 Feb. 1854	
Bombay annual marine statements	1837/8–1854/5 (gaps)	
Bombay Marine Department general, standing and squadron orders	1838–9; 1840–1; 1848; 1851; 1858	

QUARTER-MASTER GENERAL

This office for the Bengal presidency was created in 1773. The post was abolished September 1785–May 1786 and was combined with the post of commissary-general from 1809 until 1812. The staff was considerably strengthened in 1837. The duties included the provision of supplies, transport, and housing, the supervision of military roads and the checking of the advance of a foreign or internal enemy.

Copies of letters received	1817–59	135 v
Copies of letters issued	1809–40	109 v
Original correspondence (receipts and issues), including charts, maps and plans	1841–59	214 bdls
Progress reports and letters from officers commanding regiments	1851–9	48 bdls

BOARD OF ORDNANCE

Created in April 1775 to regulate military expenses, this board was succeeded by the Military Board in May 1786, the records of both forming one series.

Proceedings with index	Nov. 1775–July 1785	25 v
Letter books, issues, with index	1777–May 1786	6 v

MILITARY BOARD

Replacing the Board of Ordnance in May 1786, this Board was reorganized in December 1830 when, in addition to the duties of inspection and the regulation of expenses, it controlled ordnance, public works, canal embankment, commissariat and stud. The office of commissary-general was incorporated in 1843. From 1850 its functions began to be curtailed, the civil division of public works passing to the Home Department and then in February 1855 to the newly created Public Works Department, the Commissariat Branch being separated in 1853, a superintendent of studs created in June 1854 and an inspector general of ordnance and magazine in May 1855. In May 1855 the Board was abolished, its remaining functions passing to the Public Works Department.

Proceedings with index	25 May 1786–Sept. 1858	1,442 v
Letter books, issues, with index	May 1786–1858	651 v
Bill books with index: divided into 15 series relating to the different departments.	1829–55	534 v

MISCELLANEOUS RECORDS

59 v and
4 o.c.

These include correspondence regarding disembarkation and disposition of troops in Bengal 1858–9; Jones' and Neufville's report on Assam; annual reports of the Military Board, Bengal, 1843–53; passenger and pilot's certificate report book 1829–31 and 1851–4; and J. N. Jackson's intelligence report on Rangoon and Ava 1824–7.

PERSIAN DEPARTMENT 1801–81
(these records have not been divided at 1860)

The Persian Department conducted the East India Company's political and diplomatic transactions with Indian notables, and also the correspondence with foreign oriental potentates. Until 1801 the officer in charge was designated Persian translator, and thereafter Persian secretary. In 1830 the department became a branch of the Political Department, and from 1843 of the Foreign Department, in the charge of an attaché.

Persian indexes	1801–84	29 v
Persian Department proceedings (in English)	1826–9	15 v
Original consultations (English)	1826–9	6 bdls
Persian original receipts	1764–1881 (gaps)	336 bdls, 1 v
Copies of letters received Bahi-i-Khutut-i-Anadari [copies of original receipts], some vols. in Urdu, Bengali and Nagri scripts. One or two in Arabic.	1769–1861	168 v
English translation of Persian receipts	1763–1832 (gaps)	97 v
English translation of Persian receipts (copies of the above)	1765–1859	37 bdls
Nizamat letters received in the Persian Department	1821	1 v
English abstract of letters received	1759–1853	38 v
Persian Department letters issued	1771–1825	25 v
Copies of letters written by the Perisan secretary to residents and others.		
Copies of letters issued [mostly in name of governor-general] (Bahi-i-Huzuri)	1766–1874 (gap 1768)	125 v (many duplicates)
Drafts of letters issued	1805, 1810–71	61 bdls
English translations of letters issued	1761–1839 (gaps)	82 v
English translation of letters issued (copies of the above)	1778–1859 (gaps)	12 bdls
English abstracts of letters issued	1759–1819 (gaps)	5 v
Abstracts of letters written to the residents and others from the Persian Department	1802–24	14 v
Copies of letters issued by the Persian secretary	1804–46 (gaps)	32 v
Diary of letters written	1827	1 v
Index to the diary	1828	1 v
Minto Papers (containing translations of some correspondence in Persian between the chiefs, nobles and mag-	1808–13	9 v

nates of India and the government of the first Lord Minto, governor-general of Fort William in Bengal)		
Abstracts and extracts of receipts and issues of the political correspondence of Lord Minto	1807–13	1 v
Darbar proceedings (Persian: accounts of darbars, etc., held by governors-general during their tours)	1790–1868 (gaps) 1791–1877	11 v 3 bdls
Treaties, sanads, engagements, *farmans*	1760–1885 (gaps)	3 bdls, 13 v
Correspondence with the resident at Nagpur	1788–1832 (gaps)	2 v
Urdu and Persian newspapers	1824–99 (gaps)	38 v
Petitions		
Register	1847–78	37 v
Index	1847–61	1 v
English abstract	1879	1 v
Original petitions	1827–61	2 bdls
Mutiny papers (collection of Persian and Urdu papers, cuttings from newspapers, etc. originally collected for the trial of Bahadur Shah II)	1857	210 collections
Miscellaneous records [items listed in the *Handbook* have been rearranged. Those records which could not be amalgamated with other regular series are included here].	1769–1888	23 v

PUBLIC WORKS DEPARTMENT 1850–9

The superintendence of public works was the concern successively of the Public Branch of the Home Department, the Board of Ordnance from 1775 and the Military Board from 1786. From about 1850 civil works, as distinct from military works, reverted to the Public Branch of the Home Department or to the Foreign Department according to the territory. The Public Works Department, created in February 1855, took over these functions, the administration of the railways, the remaining duties of the Military Board when it was abolished in May 1855, and the post office and electric telegraph, formerly administered by the Home Department. The following list includes the relevant papers transferred from the Home and Foreign

Departments, apart from those relating to military works which were transferred to the Army Department.

Proceedings	9 Feb. 1855–1859	133 v
Indexes	1850–8	13 v
Diary of letters received	Feb. 1855–1859	9 v
Original consultations and collections	Feb. 1850–1859	153 bdls
General letters from Court	1855–9	6 v
Index	1855–9	2 v
General letters to Court	1855–9	16 v
Foreign Department, Hindusthan and Tibet		
Road papers	1850–55	3 bdls
Index and list		1 v
Railway proceedings	Nov.–Dec. 1858	2 v
Index	19 July 1850–1859	9 v
Railway original consultations and collections	July 1850–1859	65 bdls
General letters from Court, railway	1852–9	8 v
Index	1852–9	2 v
Register of railway financial letters	1856	1 v
Diary of railway general letters from Court	1851–8	1 v
Railway general letters to Court	1850–9	11 v
Contract between the East India Company and the East India Railway Company, Delhi line	15 Feb. 1854	1 copy
Governor-general's proceedings	Apr. 1858–1859	18 v
Governor-general's diaries of letters received	1858–9	2 v
Governor-general's original consultations	Apr. 1858–1859	11 bdls
Governor-general's Ootacamund original consultations	1855	2 bdls
Index to general orders and notifications	1858	1 v
Public Works Department number book	1855–9	1 v
Straits Settlements Public Works Department proceedings, quarterly narratives	1855–9	2 v
Post Office proceedings	1859	2 v
Index	1857–9	3 v
Contents	1859	1 v
Post Office original consultations	1857	3 bdls
Post Office general letters to Court	1856–7	4 v

List of Post Office and electric telegraph general letters to Court	1856–8	1 v
Electric telegraph proceedings	1859	2 v
Indexes	1857–9	6 v
Contents	1859	1 v
Electric telegraph original consultations and collections	1857–9	28 bdls
Electric telegraph general letters from Court	1850–9	4 v, 3 bdls
Register	1858–9	2 v
Electric telegraph general letters to Court	1856–9	9 v
Register	1858–9	1 v

THAGI AND DAKAITI DEPARTMENT 1830–1904
(*These records have not been divided at* 1860)

Systematic measures for the suppression of *thagi* were begun in 1830, under Sir William Sleeman. In 1839 the department organized for the suppression of *thagi* was entrusted with the additional duty of suppressing dacoits. After the reorganization of the police in 1860–3 this special department was no longer needed for British territory and it became mainly concerned with the suppression of organized *dakaiti* in Central India and Hyderabad, and the capture of dacoits who had fled from British to princely territory. At the head of the department was the general superintendent, immediately subordinate to the Government of India in the Foreign Department. The department was abolished in 1904.

DEPARTMENT RULES AND PROCEDURE

Rules for the guidance of arresting parties, instructions to inspectors etc.	1836–88	13 files or papers

CRITICISMS OF DEPARTMENTAL WORKING

Judicial comment	1833–92	18 files and papers

Copies of judgements and judicial comments including judgements in dacoity cases etc.

Correspondence

Letters containing criticisms of work done, suggestions, accounts of trials of dacoits etc.	1832–97	45 items

Printed correspondence, containing the condemnation by a magistrate of the department, with the general superintendent's satisfactory defence	1859	I V

GENERAL ORGANIZATION ETC.

Papers relating to costs, reorganizations etc	1864–1902	10 items

CONDITIONS IN NATIVE STATES

Reports from officers in Udaipur, Marwar, Jaipur, Bikaner border, Alwar, Gwalior, Baroda, Nizam's territory, Punjab, Bhopal, Rajputana, Mewar, Hyderabad	1835–92	21 items

INTERESTING CASES OF SPECIAL CRIMINALS

Papers relating to particular thugs and dacoits	1831–93	23 items
Confessions of particular thugs and dacoits	1834–1900	36 items
Confession of Ameerali, a noted thug, recorded by W. H. Sleeman	1832	I V
Confessions of thugs recorded by Sleeman	1833	I V
Copies of confessions of thugs	1834–7	I V
Copies of confessions of noted dacoits	1840	I V

OTHER PAPERS

Papers of general interest throwing light on contemporary conditions of life or of historical interest	1837–67	13 items

FIGURES OF CRIME AT DIFFERENT INTERVALS, ANNUAL REPORTS ETC.

Annual reports from various officials for the years 1846, 1850, 1852, 1860, 1861(2), 1862(2) and 1865	1847–66	9 items
Report in book form of the proceedings during 1862 of Major Chamberlain, Assistant General Superintendent for Oudh and the North-West Provinces, in connection with professional poisoning	1863	I V

CORRESPONDENCE

Copies of letters issued by General Superintendent W. H. Sleeman, Officiating Superintendent Reynold, General Superintendent J. Sleeman, and General Superintendent C. Hervey, to their assistants and others, and to the various governments	1832–73	53 v
Copies of letters received by General Superintendents W. H. Sleeman and J. Sleeman from the different governments	1833–4, 1841–5, 1849–56, 1856–9	4 v
Copies of letters to the General Superintendent and others from the Assistant General Superintendent at Sholapur, the Superintendent in the Deccan, the Assistant General Superintendent in Malwa, the Superintendent at Jubbulpur, the Assistant General Superintendents at Belgaum, Saugor and Lucknow	1836–63	13 v
Letters from the agent to the governor-general in Rajputana to W. H. Sleeman; from the General Superintendent to the Assistant General Superintendent at Sholapur, and to the Assistant General Superintendent at Belgaum	1833–48	4 v

II

NATIONAL ARCHIVES OF INDIA POST-MUTINY SERIES

In 1860 the supreme Government of India consisted of the following five departments: Home, Foreign, Financial, Military, and Public Works. By 1947 these had developed into eighteen ministries, namely: Home Affairs, External Affairs and Commonwealth Relations, Defence, Commerce, Communications, Finance, Transport, Railways, Education, Health, Agriculture, Food, Industries and Supplies, States, Law, Works and Mines and Power, Labour, and Information and Broadcasting. Since 1947 there

LGA

has been further reorganization, but few records of the post-Independence period have yet been transferred to the National Archives and therefore it is not necessary to trace those changes here. (It should be noted that post-Mutiny records of the Persian, and the Thagi and Dakaiti Departments are all listed under the pre-Mutiny records.)

A new system of record keeping was introduced into the secretariats of the Government of India in April 1860. The system of recording by weekly consultations was abolished, and from 1860 to 1921 papers were divided into 'A' and 'B' proceedings, the most important being placed in category 'A' and printed, the less important being placed in category 'B' and remaining generally in manuscript, although some of the more important of these were also printed. A third class of proceedings, known as 'Deposit' proceedings, consisted of ordinary petitions, forwarding letters from other presidencies, and similar papers. Papers were sometimes placed in a fourth category known as 'C' proceedings: these were routine papers of little importance. The papers continued to be indexed, and the indexes were printed. The records within each department, therefore, from 1860 to 1921, consist essentially of (1) proceedings, bound chronologically into volumes (including the contents only of 'B' proceedings), (2) 'A', 'B', perhaps 'C', and 'Deposit' proceedings, kept in bundles or carton boxes, (3) despatches to and from the secretary of state, (4) indexes, diaries, registers etc. and perhaps (5) miscellaneous papers.

The system of record keeping was again changed in 1921, first in the Home Department, and then at later dates in all departments. The new simplified system, known as the 'File System', was to keep all papers on one subject together in a file, a method which has been essentially retained to the present day. These files are kept in bundles or carton boxes. It should be noted, however, that in some departments (e.g. Commerce Department and Railway Department) the files continued to be classified into 'A', 'B', 'C', and 'Deposit' proceedings even after the file system had been introduced, and in the Military Department the proceedings system continued to a later date than elsewhere.

In the pages which follow the records are listed under the heads of the various departments arranged alphabetically and an explanation of the business is attached wherever possible. The development of the five departments of 1860 into the eighteen ministries of 1947 is shown in the attached chart.

To use the records the searcher should consult first the indexes belonging to the department in which he is interested, and there he will find the information necessary for the production of the documents required—branch, date, type of document or file number, and so on. Some types of business, however, were dealt with in different departments at different times, and therefore an attempt has been made in the pages that follow to show to which department various subjects were transferred at later dates. Ecclesiastical affairs might be taken as an example: ecclesiastical matters were dealt with in the Home Department between 1860 and 1910, in the Department of Education and its successors between 1910 and 1924, in the Commerce Department between 1925 and 1937, and after 1937 in the Defence Department.

It should be noted that in the following lists numbers of volumes, bundles, boxes etc. though correct at the time of compilation are approximate only, as documents in bundles are gradually being transferred to carton boxes (and one bundle might fill several boxes); and as volumes are rebound bulky ones are sometimes split and thin ones bound together. The dates given are covering dates: gaps are not usually noted.

HOLDINGS: POST-MUTINY SERIES

SUMMARY LIST OF HOLDINGS

Department of Commerce and Industry	1905–20
Department of Commerce	1920–47
Ministry of Commerce	1947 onwards
Department of Education, Health and Lands (including records of predecessor bodies)	1923–45
(i) Department of Revenue, Agriculture and Commerce	1871–9
(ii) Home, Revenue and Agriculture Department	1879–81
(iii) Department of Revenue and Agriculture	1881–1923
(iv) Department of Education	1910–21
(v) Department of Education and Health	1921–3
(vi) Department of Education, Health and Lands	1923–45
Department/Ministry of Education	1945 onwards
Department/Ministry of Health	1945 onwards
Department/Ministry of Agriculture	1945 onwards
Directorate General of Health Services	1896–1947
Imperial Council of Agricultural Research	1929–47
Financial Department	1860–79
Finance and Commerce Department	1879–1905
Finance Department	1905–47
Central Board of Revenue (including Office of the Salt Commissioner)	1924–47

Ministry of Finance	1947 onwards
Foreign Department (including records of successor bodies)	
(i) Foreign Department	1860–1914
(ii) Foreign and Political Department	1914–37
(iii) Department of External Affairs	1937–47
(iv) Political Department	1937–47
(v) Ministry of States	1947–54
Home Department	1860–1947
Ministry of Home Affairs	1947 onwards
Indian Munitions Board	1917–20
Board of Industries and Munitions	1920–1
Department of Industries	1921–3
Department of Industries and Labour	1923–37
Legislative Department	1861–1947
Military Department (including records of successor bodies)	
(i) Military Department	1860–1906
(ii) Military Finance Department	1860–4
(iii) Army Department	1906–36
(iv) Military Supply Department	1906–9
(iv) Defence Department	1936–42
(v) War Department	1942–6
Public Works Department	1860–1923
Railway Board/Railway Department	1905–47
Reforms Office	1919–21, 1930–40
Survey of India	1777–1902

DEPARTMENT OF COMMERCE AND INDUSTRY 1905–20

From 1860 to 1871 commercial matters were dealt with mainly in the Public Branch of the Home Department. In 1871 they were transferred to the newly formed Revenue, Agriculture and Commerce Department, and in 1879 to the new Finance and Commerce Department. In 1905 a new Department of Commerce and Industry was created, and work was transferred to it from Home, Revenue and Agriculture, and Public Works Departments, in addition to the Commerce branches of the former Finance and Commerce Department. The new department dealt with trade and commerce (including statistics), supply of stores, customs, post office and telegraph, merchant shipping, and railways (until 1908). The department was divided into two in 1920—Commerce and Industries (later (1923), Industries and Labour).

Index	1905–20	217 v

ACETONE BRANCH

Index	1917, yearly	1 v
Monthly proceedings	Jan.–Mar. 1917	6 v
Yearly proceedings volumes	1917	4 v
'A' and filed proceedings	Jan.–Mar. 1917	1 bdl

CARBIDE BRANCH

Index, yearly	1905–15	19 v
Index and contents	1905–12	11 v
Monthly proceedings	1906–15	31 v
Yearly proceedings volumes	1905–15	15 v
Files	1905–7	2 v
'A', 'B', 'C' and filed proceedings	July 1905–Oct. 1914	1 bdl

CASH BRANCH

Diary	1905–12	13 v
Deposit proceedings	1905–20	2 bdls

CIVIL AVIATION BRANCH

For the years after 1920, see Department of Commerce 1920–1, Public Works Department 1922–3 and Department of Industries and Labour 1923–33.

Index, yearly	1919	1 v
Monthly proceedings	Oct. 1919–Feb. 1920	6 v
Yearly proceedings	1919	4 v
'A', 'B', filed and MS proceedings	1919–20	2 bdls

COAL BRANCH

Yearly index	1917–19	3 v
Monthly proceedings	Jan.–Dec. 1917	12 v
Yearly proceedings	1917–19	12 v
'A', 'B', filed and MS proceedings	1917–20	6 bdls

COAL AND IRON BRANCH

'A' proceedings	June 1905	1 bdl

COAL AND STEEL BRANCH

Deposit proceedings	1919–20	1 bdl

COMMERCE BRANCH

Diary	1905–16	30 v
Deposit proceedings	Feb. 1912–18	1 bdl

COMMERCE (WAR) BRANCH

Yearly index	1914–19	10 v
Monthly proceedings	Jan. 1918–Feb. 1920	26 v
Yearly proceedings	1918–19	8 v
Diary	1914–16	6 v
Filed, deposit and MS proceedings	1907–20	7 bdls

COMMERCE AND TRADE BRANCH

Yearly index	1905–16	22 v
Index and contents	1905–12	19 v
Monthly proceedings	1906–16	141 v
Yearly proceedings	1905–16	43 v
Files	1905–7	7 v
File registers	1905–15	20 v
Miscellaneous registers		23 v
'A', 'B', 'C' and filed proceedings	1905–16	37 bdls

COMMERCIAL EXHIBITION BRANCH

From 1895 to 1904 this branch was part of the Department of Revenue and Agriculture and in 1917 its work was transferred to the Internal Trade Branch of the Commerce and Industry Department (from 1920 Commerce Department). In 1923 the work was transferred to the Commerce Branch.

Yearly index	1905–16	22 v
Index and contents	1905–12	22 v
Monthly proceedings	1906–16	97 v
Yearly proceedings	1905–16	43 v
Files	1905–7	4 v
File registers	1906–14 (1911–13, gap)	5 v
'A', 'B' and filed proceedings	1905–16	4 bdls

COMMERCIAL INTELLIGENCE BRANCH

Yearly index	1917–19	3 v
Monthly proceedings	1917–20	36 v
Yearly proceedings	1917–19	12 v
'A', 'B', filed and MS proceedings	1917–19	4 bdls

COMPANIES BRANCH

Yearly index	1913–15	4 v
Monthly proceedings	1913–16	43 v
Yearly proceedings	1913–16	11 v
Registers	1913–16	4 v
'A', 'B', filed and MS proceedings	1913–16	8 bdls

COMPANY LAW BRANCH

Monthly proceedings	1917–20	25 v
Yearly proceedings	1917–19	9 v
'A', filed, deposit and MS proceedings	1916–20	5 bdls

COTTON DUTIES BRANCH

Yearly index	1905–16	22 v
Index and contents	1905–12	18 v
Monthly proceedings	1906–16	66 v
Yearly proceedings	1905–16	46 v
Files	1905–7	4 v
'A', 'B', 'C' and filed proceedings	1905–16	2 bdls

CUSTOMS BRANCH

See also the Departments of Revenue and Agriculture 1871–9, Finance and Commerce 1879–1905, and Central Board of Revenue from 1924.

Yearly index	1906–16	25 v
Index and contents	1906–12	18 v
Monthly proceedings	1906–16	140 v
Yearly proceedings	1905–16	45 v
Files	1905–7	8 v
'A', 'B', 'C' and filed proceedings	1905–16	44 bdls

CUSTOMS DUTIES BRANCH (INCLUDING COTTON EXCISE)

Yearly index	1917–19	4 v
Monthly proceedings	1917–20	50 v

Yearly proceedings	1917–19	11 v
'A', 'B', filed and MS proceedings	1917–20	9 bdls

CUSTOMS ESTABLISHMENT

Yearly index	1906–19	25 v
Index and contents	1906–12	11 v
Monthly proceedings	1906–20	170 v
Yearly proceedings	1906–19	49 v
Files	1906–7	3 v
Registers	1907–16	1 bdl
'A', 'B', 'C', filed and MS proceedings	1906–20	23 bdls

ECONOMIC PRODUCTS BRANCH

The Economic Products Branch was attached to this department only for the years 1906–10. The work was mainly the concern of the Department of Revenue and Agriculture and its successors (Economic Products Branch 1895–1905, and Agriculture Branch 1910–44).

Yearly index	1906–10	14 v
Index and contents	1905–10	16 v
Monthly proceedings	1906–10	109 v
Yearly proceedings	1907 and 1910	2 v
Files	1905–7	4 v
File register	1908–9	2 v
'A', 'B', 'C' and filed proceedings	1905–9	1 bdl

ELECTRICITY BRANCH

Yearly index	1906–11	12 v
Index and contents	1906–11	9 v
Monthly proceedings	1906–11	60 v
Yearly proceedings	1906–10	11 v
Files	1906	1 v
'A', 'B', 'C' and filed proceedings	1906–11	1 bdl
File registers	1906–7	5 v

EMIGRATION BRANCH

Emigration was the concern of the Commerce Departments only from 1906 to 1921. The main records are to be found in the Department of Education, Health and Lands, Emigration Branch.

Yearly index	1906–19	25 v
Index and contents	1906–15	18 v

Monthly proceedings	1906–20	175 v
Yearly proceedings	1905–19	59 v
Files	1905–7	10 v
File registers	1906–15	12 v
'A', 'B', 'C', filed, deposit and MS proceedings	1905–20	69 bdls

EXCISE BRANCH

Yearly index	1910–16	17 v
Index and contents	1910–12	3 v
Monthly proceedings	1910–17	85 v
Yearly proceedings	1910–17	26 v
File registers	1910–15	24 v
'A', 'B', filed, deposit and MS proceedings	1910–16	34 bdls

EXCISE GENERAL BRANCH

Yearly index	1917–19	3 v
Monthly proceedings	1918–20	26 v
Yearly proceedings	1918–19	7 v
'A', 'B', filed and MS proceedings	1917–20	9 bdls

EXPLOSIVES BRANCH

Yearly index	1905–20	26 v
Index and contents	1905–12	11 v
Monthly proceedings	1906–20	147 v
Yearly proceedings	1905–19	30 v
Files	1906–7	2 v
'A', 'B', 'C' and filed proceedings	1905–20	10 bdls

FACTORIES BRANCH

Yearly index	1906–20	25 v
Index and contents	1905–12	11 v
Monthly proceedings	1906–20	145 v
Yearly proceedings	1905–19	30 v
Files	1906–7	2 v
'A', 'B', 'C', filed and MS proceedings	1905–20	13 bdls

FISHERIES BRANCH

This branch was part of the Department of Revenue, Agriculture and Commerce and its successors from 1871 to 1904, and the Department of Commerce from 1920 to 1923. The work of the branch was then transferred to the Shipping Branch (1923–9) and Mercantile Marine II branch (1929–44) of the Commerce Department. In 1945–6 there was again a separate Fisheries Branch in the Department of Agriculture.

Yearly index	1905–19	24 v
Index and contents	1905–15	25 v
Monthly proceedings	1906–20	183 v
Yearly proceedings	1905–20	62 v
Files	1905–7	4 v
File registers	1905–10	9 v
'A', 'B', 'C', deposit and filed proceedings	1905–20	6 bdls

FOREIGN TRADE BRANCH (INCLUDING DYES)

Yearly index	1917–19	3 v
Monthly proceedings	1917–20	37 v
Yearly proceedings	1917–19	11 v
'A', 'B', filed and MS proceedings	1917–20	7 bdls

GENERAL BRANCH

Yearly index	1905–19	25 v
Index and contents	1905–12	19 v
Monthly proceedings	1906–19	167 v
Yearly proceedings	1905–19	47 v
Files	1905–7	5 v
Diary	1906–15	14 v
File registers	1905–12	19 v
'A', 'B', 'C', filed and deposit proceedings	1905–20	27 bdls

GENERAL CASH BRANCH

'B', 'C' and filed proceedings	1905–16	4 bdls

GENERAL LIBRARY BRANCH

'A', 'B', 'C' and filed proceedings	1905–14	3 bdls

GEOLOGY AND MINERALS BRANCH

This branch was part of the Department of Revenue, Agriculture and Commerce, and its successors, from 1871 to 1904, the Department of Industries from 1921 to 1923, and the Department of Industries and Labour from 1923 to 1937.

Yearly index	1905–16	21 v
Index and contents	1906–12	10 v
Monthly proceedings	1906–16	136 v
Yearly proceedings	1905–16	24 v
Files	1906–7	6 v
File registers	1906	2 v
'A', 'B', 'C', filed, deposit and MS proceedings	1905–19	45 bdls

GEOLOGY AND MINERALS ESTABLISHMENT BRANCH

Yearly index	1917–20	4 v
Monthly proceedings	1917–20	41 v
Yearly proceedings	1917–19	6 v
'A', 'B', filed and MS proceedings	1917–20	4 bdls

IMPORT AND EXPORT REGULATIONS

Yearly index	1917–19	3 v
Monthly proceedings	1917–20	38 v
Yearly proceedings	1917–19	13 v
'A', 'B', filed and MS proceedings	1917–19	44 bdls

INDUSTRIES BRANCH

Yearly index	1905–20	37 v
Index and contents	1906–11	15 v
Monthly proceedings	1906–20	292 v
Yearly proceedings	1906–19	38 v
Files	1906–7	3 v
File registers	1908–15	7 v
'A', 'B', 'C', filed and deposit proceedings	1905–20	27 bdls

INLAND NAVIGATION BRANCH

Yearly index	1917–19	3 v
Monthly proceedings	1917–20	36 v

| Yearly proceedings | 1917–19 | 12 v |
| 'A', 'B' and filed proceedings | 1917–20 | 3 bdls |

INSURANCE BRANCH (INSURANCE COMPANIES BRANCH 1917–19)

Yearly index	1913–18	8 v
Index and contents	1913	1 v
Monthly proceedings	1913–20	77 v
Yearly proceedings	1913–19	26 v
File registers	1913 and 1916	3 v
'A', 'B' and filed proceedings	1913–20	10 bdls

INTERNAL LAND TRADE AND INLAND TRADE BRANCH

Yearly index	1906–7	4 v
Index and contents	1906–7	6 v
Monthly proceedings	1905–7	6 v
Yearly proceedings	1905–7	4 v
Files	1906	1 v
File registers	1906–7	2 v
'B' and 'C' proceedings	1905–6	1 bdl

INTERNAL TRADE BRANCH (INCLUDING COMMERCIAL EXHIBITIONS)

Yearly index	1917–19	3 v
Monthly proceedings	1917–20	39 v
Yearly proceedings	1917–19	12 v
'A', 'B', filed and MS proceedings	1917–20	8 bdls

INTOXICATING DRUGS BRANCH

Yearly index	1918–19	2 v
Monthly proceedings	1918–20	26 v
Yearly proceedings	1918–19	6 v
'A', 'B', filed and MS proceedings	1918–20	4 bdls

INVENTIONS AND DESIGN BRANCH

See also the Patents and Design branches of the Departments of Revenue and Agriculture (1888–1905), Commerce and Industry (1913–20), Indian Munitions Board (1920), Industries (1921–3), and Industries and Labour (1923–37).

| Yearly index | 1905–11 | 10 v |
| Monthly proceedings | 1908–11 | 46 v |

Yearly proceedings	1905–11	22 v
Files	1905–9	11 v
'A' proceedings	1905–11	6 bdls

JUTES, HIDES AND WOOL BRANCH

Yearly index	1917	1 v
Monthly proceedings	1917	12 v
Yearly proceedings	1917	5 v
'A', 'B', filed and MS proceedings	1917	11 bdls

LASCAR SEAMEN BRANCH

Yearly index	1918–19	2 v
Monthly proceedings	1918–20	25 v
Yearly proceedings	1918–19	8 v
'A', 'B', filed and MS proceedings	1918–20	7 bdls

LIBRARY BRANCH

Deposit proceedings	1905–20	7 bdls

LIGHTING OF COASTS BRANCH

Yearly index	1905–6	23 v
Index and contents	1905–10	15 v
Monthly proceedings	1906–16	94 v
Yearly proceedings	1905–16	48 v
Files	1905–7	4 v
File registers	1914–15	10 v
'A', 'B', 'C' and filed proceedings	1905–16	3 bdls

LIQUOR EXCISE BRANCH

Yearly index	1918–19	2 v
Monthly proceedings	1918–20	21 v
Yearly proceedings	1918–19	4 v
'A', 'B', filed and MS proceedings	1918	2 bdls

MERCHANDISE MARKS BRANCH

Yearly index	1905–19	25 v
Index and contents	1906–12	16 v
Monthly proceedings	1906–20	131 v
Yearly proceedings	1906–19	39 v
File volumes	1906–7	3 v
'A', 'B', 'C', filed and MS proceedings	1906–20	6 bdls

MERCHANT SHIPPING BRANCH

Yearly index	1905–19	24 v
Index and contents	1906–12	19 v
Monthly proceedings	1906–20	181 v
Yearly proceedings	1905–19	57 v
Files	1905–7	5 v
File registers	1906–14	11 v
'A', 'B', 'C', filed and MS proceedings	1905–20	43 bdls

MINERAL RESERVES BRANCH

Yearly index	1917–20	4 v
Monthly proceedings	1917–20	36 v
Yearly proceedings	1917–19	6 v
'A', 'B', filed and MS proceedings	1917–20	6 bdls

MINES REGULATIONS BRANCH

Yearly index	1917–20	4 v
Monthly proceedings	1917–20	39 v
Yearly proceedings	1917–19	6 v
'A', 'B', filed and MS proceedings	1917–19	4 bdls

PATENTS AND DESIGNS BRANCH

Yearly index	1913–20	21 v
Monthly proceedings	1913–20	181 v
Yearly proceedings	1913–19	26 v
File registers	1913–14	2 v
'A', 'B' and filed proceedings	1913–20	3 bdls

PETROLEUM BRANCH

Yearly index	1905–20	24 v
Index and contents	1905–12	11 v
Monthly proceedings	1906–20	156 v
Yearly proceedings	1905–19	30 v
Files	1906–7	2 v
'A', 'B', 'C', filed and deposit proceedings	1905–20	9 bdls

PORTS AND LIGHTING BRANCH

Yearly index	1917–19	3 v
Monthly proceedings	1917–20	33 v

Yearly proceedings	1917–19	9 v
'A', 'B', filed and MS proceedings	1917–20	8 bdls

PORTS, PORT DUES AND PILOTAGE BRANCH

Yearly index	1905–16	24 v
Index and contents	1905–12	17 v
Monthly proceedings	1906–16	146 v
Yearly proceedings	1905–16	35 v
Files	1905–7	6 v
File registers	1907–15	10 v
'A', 'B', 'C' and filed proceedings	1905–16	21 bdls

POST AND TELEGRAPH ESTABLISHMENT BRANCH

Yearly index	1914–19	8 v
Monthly proceedings	1914–20	72 v
Yearly proceedings	1914–19	13 v
File registers	1906–7	2 v
'A', 'B', filed, deposit and MS proceedings	1906–20	32 bdls

POST OFFICE BRANCH

This branch came under the Home Department from 1860 to 1867, the Commerce Department from 1920 to 1921, the PWD from 1921 to 1923, and the Industries and Labour Department from 1923 to 1937. From 1867 to 1905 business relating to Post Offices was dealt with in the Separate Revenue Branch of the Financial (Finance and Commerce) Department.

Yearly index	1905–19	26 v
Index and contents	1906–12	11 v
Monthly proceedings	1906–20	184 v
Yearly proceedings	1905–19	30 v
Files	1906–7	4 v
Diary	1908–9	2 v
'A', 'B', 'C', filed and MS proceedings	1905–20	37 bdls

POST OFFICE ESTABLISHMENT BRANCH

Yearly index	1911–13	6 v
Index and contents	1911–12	2 v
Monthly proceedings	1911–13	35 v
Yearly proceedings	1911–13	6 v
'A', 'B' and filed proceedings	1911–14	8 bdls

PRACTICAL ARTS AND MUSEUM BRANCH

For the years 1871–1905 and 1911–23, see Department of Revenue and Agriculture.

Yearly index	1910	1 v
Index and contents	1905–10	17 v
Monthly proceedings	1905–10	90 v
Yearly proceedings	1905–10	9 v
Files	1905–7	6 v
'A', 'B', 'C', filed and MS proceedings	1905–10	7 bdls

PURCHASE SCHEMES BRANCH

Yearly index	1918–19	2 v
Monthly proceedings	1918–20	23 v
Yearly proceedings	1918–19	8 v
Filed proceedings	1918–20	11 bdls

RAILWAYS BRANCH

Until 1905 railway matters were dealt with in the Public Works Department (Railway Branch) but in 1905 a Railway Board was established under this department. The Board became a separate department in 1908.

Yearly index	1910–11	4 v
Index and contents	1906–11	8 v
Monthly proceedings	1908–11	14 v
Yearly proceedings	1910–11	3 v
File registers	1906–10	4 v
Diary	1906–7	2 v
'A', 'B', 'C', filed, MS and deposit proceedings	1905–11	5 bdls

RAILWAY QUESTIONS BRANCH

Yearly index	1906 and 1908	2 v
Index and contents	1905	1 v
Yearly proceedings	1905–7	2 bdls
'A' proceedings	1906–7	1 bdl

SALT BRANCH

Yearly index	1911–16	17 v
Index and contents	1910–12	3 v

Monthly proceedings	1910–16	76 v
Yearly proceedings	1910–16	26 v
File registers	1910–15	5 v
Diary	1910	1 v
'A', 'B', filed, deposit and MS proceedings	1910–17	11 bdls

SALT AND SALTPETRE BRANCH

Yearly index	1907–18, 1919–20	3 v
Monthly proceedings	1917–20	41 v
Yearly proceedings	1917–19	9 v
'A', 'B' and filed proceedings	1917–20	9 bdls

SALT ESTABLISHMENT BRANCH

Yearly index	1918 and 1920	2 v
Monthly proceedings	1918–20	30 v
Yearly proceedings	1918–19	5 v
'A', 'B', filed and MS proceedings	1918–20	4 bdls

SHIPPING CONTROL BRANCH

Yearly index	1918–19	2 v
Monthly proceedings	1918–20	26 v
Yearly proceedings	1918–19	8 v
'A', 'B', filed, deposit and MS proceedings	1918–20	15 bdls

STATIONERY AND PRINTING BRANCH

Yearly index	1905–20	25 v
Index and contents	1905–12	12 v
Monthly proceedings	1906–20	180 v
Yearly proceedings	1905–19	29 v
Files	1906–7	2 v
File registers	1915	10 v
'A', 'B', 'C', filed and MS proceedings	1905–20	22 bdls

STATISTICS BRANCH

Yearly index	1906–19	25 v
Index and contents	1905–12	17 v
Monthly proceedings	1906–20	153 v
Yearly proceedings	1906–19	53 v

Files	1906–7	4 v
'A', 'B', 'C', filed and MS proceedings	1906–20	11 bdls

STEAM BOILERS BRANCH

Yearly index	1905–20	25 v
Index and contents	1905–12	12 v
Monthly proceedings	1906–20	111 v
Yearly proceedings	1905–19	25 v
Files	1905–7	2 v
'A', 'B', 'C' and filed proceedings	1905–15	2 bdls

STORES BRANCH

Yearly index	1905–16	22 v
Index and contents	1905–12	19 v
Monthly proceedings	1906–16	264 v
Yearly proceedings	1905–16	44 v
Files	1906–7	4 v
File registers	1907–15	9 v
'A', 'B', 'C', filed, MS and deposit proceedings	1905–16	41 bdls

STORES AND PLANT BRANCH

Yearly index	1917	1 v
Monthly proceedings	1917 (Jan.–Sept.)	23 v
Yearly proceedings	1917	2 v
'A', 'B', filed and deposit proceedings	1917	5 bdls

SUSPECTED FIRMS BRANCH

Yearly index	1919	1 v
Monthly proceedings	1919	10 v
Yearly proceedings	1919	4 v

TELEGRAPHS BRANCH

Telegraphs came under the Public Works Department from 1870 to 1905 and again from 1921 to 1923. From 1923 they were the concern of the Department of Industries and Labour.

Yearly index	1905–19	24 v
Index and telegraph	1905–12	11 v

Monthly proceedings	1906–20	189 v
Yearly proceedings	1905–19	30 v
Files	1906–7	4 v
Registers	1907	1 v
Diary	1908–11	4 v
'A', 'B', 'C', filed and MS proceedings	1905–20	54 bdls

TELEGRAPH ESTABLISHMENT BRANCH

Yearly index	1906–18	14 v
Index and contents	1905–12	9 v
Monthly proceedings	1906–13	99 v
Yearly proceedings	1905–13	18 v
Files	1906–7	5 v
'A', 'B', 'C' and filed proceedings	1905–14	22 bdls
Despatches	1908	1 bdl

TRADE AFTER THE WAR BRANCHES

COTTON

Yearly index	1919	1 v
Monthly proceedings	May–Dec. 1919	5 v
Yearly proceedings	1919	4 v
'A' and filed proceedings	1919	1 bdl

DYES

Yearly index	1919	1 v
Monthly proceedings	1919–20	9 v
Yearly proceedings	1919	4 v
'A' and filed proceedings	1919–20	1 bdl

GENERAL

Yearly index	1919	1 v
Monthly proceedings	1919–20	10 v
Yearly proceedings	1919	4 v
'A', 'B' and filed proceedings	1919–20	2 bdls

HIDES, SKINS AND LEATHER

Yearly index	1919	1 v
Monthly proceedings	1919–20	12 v
Yearly proceedings	1919	4 v
'A', 'B' and filed proceedings	1919–20	2 bdls

IMPERIAL PREFERENCE

Yearly index	1919	I v
Monthly proceedings	1919–20	II v
Yearly proceedings	1919	4 v
'A', 'B' and filed proceedings	1919–20	I bdl

JAPANESE ACTIVITIES

Yearly index	1919	I v
Monthly proceedings	1919–20	II v
Yearly proceedings	1919	4 v
'A', 'B' and filed proceedings	1919–20	I bdl

JUTE

Yearly index	1919	I v
Monthly proceedings	1919–20	9 v
Yearly proceedings	1919	4 v
'A' and filed proceedings	1919–20	I bdl

OLEAGINOUS PRODUCTS

Yearly index	1919	I v
Monthly proceedings	1919–20	6 v
Yearly proceedings	1919–20	5 v
'A' and filed proceedings	1919–20	I bdl

RUBBER

Yearly index	1919	I v
Monthly proceedings	July 1919	I v
Yearly proceedings	1919	4 v
'A' proceedings	July 1919	I bdl

WOOL

Yearly index	1919	I v
Monthly proceedings	1919–20	7 v
Yearly proceedings	1919–20	5 v
'A', 'B' and filed proceedings	1919–20	I bdl

TRADING BY FOREIGNERS BRANCH

Yearly proceedings	1917	I v
'A', 'B' and filed proceedings	1917–19	18 bdls

WEIGHTS AND MEASURES BRANCH

Before 1890 Weights and Measures were dealt with in the Public Branch of the Home Department, and from 1890 to 1905 in the General Branch of the Department of Revenue and Agriculture. From 1920 the work was the concern of the Commerce Department (Weights and Measures Branch, 1920-1, Internal Trade Branch 1921-3 and Commerce Branch 1923-47).

Yearly index	1905-19	24 v
Index and contents	1906-12	12 v
Monthly proceedings	1906-20	83 v
Yearly proceedings	1905-19	46 v
Files	1905-7	4 v
File registers	1905-15	7 v
'A', 'B' and filed proceedings	1906-20	3 bdls

WHEAT BRANCH

Yearly index	1917-20	4 v
Monthly proceedings	1917-20	20 v
Yearly proceedings	1917-20	16 v
'A', 'B' and filed proceedings	1917-20	2 bdls

DEPARTMENT OF COMMERCE 1920-47

The Department came into existence in 1920 on the division of the Department of Commerce and Industry into two parts. The business handled included matters relating to shipping, trade and commerce, import and export regulations, and insurance. In 1947 the Department became the Ministry of Commerce in the independent Government of India.

Although the file system of record keeping was adopted in this Department in 1924, the files continued to be classified into 'A', 'B', 'C' and 'Deposit' proceedings, and they are arranged in this way.

General index	1920-52 (gaps)	61 v

ACTUARIAL BRANCH

Yearly index	1922	I v
Monthly proceedings	1922-3	51 v
Yearly proceedings	1922	2 v

ASSAM LABOUR AND EMIGRATION ACT

Yearly index	1921	I V
Monthly proceedings	Aug.–Nov. 1921	II V

CASH BRANCH

Deposit proceedings	1920–4	I bdl

CIVIL AVIATION BRANCH

Yearly index	1920–1	
Monthly proceedings	1920–1	30 V
Yearly proceedings	1920	I V
'A', 'B', filed and MS proceedings	1920–1	4 bdls

COAL BRANCH

Yearly index	1920–1	2 V
Monthly indexes	1920–1	7 V
Yearly proceedings	1920	4 V
Filed proceedings	Mar.–Aug. 1920	I bdl

COMMERCE BRANCH

'A', 'B', 'C', deposit and MS proceedings	1920–42	69 bdls
Registers	1925–39	4 bdls

COMMERCE (WAR) BRANCH

Yearly index	1920–1	2 V
Monthly proceedings	1920–1	18 V
Yearly proceedings	1920–1	6 V
'A', 'B' and filed proceedings	1920–1	2 bdls

COMMERCIAL EDUCATION BRANCH

Yearly index	1920	I V
Monthly proceedings	April 1920	I V
Yearly proceedings	April 1920	3 V
Filed proceedings	April 1920	I bdl

COMMERCIAL INTELLIGENCE BRANCH

Yearly index		
Monthly proceedings		
Yearly proceedings		8 V
'A', 'B', filed and MS proceedings	1920–3	9 bdls

COMPANY LAW BRANCH

Yearly index	1921–2	2 v
Monthly proceedings	1921–3	101 v
Yearly proceedings	1920–2	8 v
'A', 'B', filed, deposit and MS proceedings	1920–3	6 bdls

CUSTOMS DUTIES BRANCH (INCLUDING COTTON EXCISE)

Yearly index	1920–2	3 v
Monthly proceedings	1920–3	91 v
Yearly proceedings	1920	2 v
'A', 'B', filed and MS proceedings	1920–3	13 bdls

CUSTOMS ESTABLISHMENT BRANCH

Yearly index	1920–2	3 v
Monthly proceedings	1920–3	95 v
Yearly proceedings	1920	3 v
'A', 'B', filed and MS proceedings	1920–3	13 bdls

EMIGRATION BRANCH

Yearly index	1920–1	2 v
Monthly proceedings	1920–1	31 v
Yearly proceedings	1920	2 v
'A', 'B', filed, deposit and MS proceedings	1920–1	9 bdls

ESTABLISHMENT BRANCH

'B', 'C' and deposit proceedings	1924–35	7 bdls

EXCISE GENERAL BRANCH

Yearly index	1920–2	2 v
Monthly proceedings	1920–3	97 v
Yearly proceedings	1920	3 v
'A', 'B', and filed proceedings	1920–3	3 bdls

EXHIBITION BRANCH

Yearly index	July–Aug. 1923	1 v
'B' and filed proceedings	1923	1 bdl

EXPORT CESSES-LAC (TEA AND JUTE) BRANCH

Yearly index	August 1923	1 bdl

FISHERIES BRANCH

The work of this branch was transferred to the Shipping Branch in 1923, and the Mercantile Marine II Branch in 1929.

Yearly index	1920–2	3 v
Monthly proceedings	1920–3	77 v
Yearly proceedings	1921–2	4 v
'A', 'B' and filed proceedings	1920–3	3 bdls

FOREIGN TRADE BRANCH

Yearly index	1920–2	3 v
Monthly proceedings	1920–2	103 v
Yearly proceedings	1920–2	7 v
'A', 'B' and filed proceedings	1920–3	12 bdls

GENERAL BRANCH

Yearly index	1920–2	7 v
Monthly indexes	1921–3	1 bdl
Monthly proceedings	1920–3	103 v
Yearly proceedings	1920–2	7 v
Registers	1936–8	3 registers
'A' proceedings and files	1920–35	1 bdl
'B' proceedings and files	1920–38	16 bdls
'C' proceedings and files	1923–39	7 bdls
Filed proceedings	1923 (Mar.–Nov.)	12 bdls
Deposit proceedings	1920–3	1 bdl

GENERAL (LIBRARY) BRANCH

Filed proceedings	1923	1 bdl

IMPORT AND EXPORT REGULATIONS BRANCH

Yearly index	1920–2	3 v
Monthly proceedings	1920–2	64 v
Yearly proceedings	1920–2	7 v
'A', 'B' and filed proceedings	1920–1	4 bdls

INLAND NAVIGATION BRANCH

Yearly index	1920–2	2 v
Monthly proceedings	1920–3	84 v

Yearly proceedings	1920–2	8 v
'A', 'B' and filed proceedings	1920–3	3 bdls

INSURANCE BRANCH

Yearly index	1920–2	3 v
Monthly proceedings	1920–3	104 v
Yearly proceedings	1920–2	8 v
Registers	1938	11 v
'A', 'B', 'C' and filed proceedings and files	1920–43	42 bdls

INTERNAL TRADE BRANCH

The work of this branch was transferred to the Commerce Branch in 1923.

Yearly index	1920–2	3 v
Monthly proceedings	1920–3	104 v
Yearly proceedings	1920–2	8 v
'A', 'B', filed and MS proceedings	1920–3	8 bdls

INTOXICATING DRUGS BRANCH

Yearly index	1920–2	3 v
Monthly proceedings	1920–3	90 v
Yearly proceedings	1920	3 v
'A', 'B', filed and MS proceedings	1920–3	5 bdls

LASCAR SEAMEN BRANCH

Yearly index	1920–2	3 v
Monthly proceedings	1920–3	103 v
Yearly proceedings	1920–2	8 v
'A', 'B' and MS proceedings	1920–3	8 bdls

LIBRARY BRANCH

Registers	1925–38	3 bdls, 4 v
'B', 'C' and deposit proceedings	1920–36	8 bdls

LIQUOR EXCISE BRANCH

Yearly index	1920–2	3 v
Monthly proceedings	1920–2	78 v
Yearly proceedings	1920	4 v
'A', 'B', filed and MS proceedings	1920–2	3 bdls

MERCHANDISE MARKS BRANCH

Yearly index	1920–2	3 v
Monthly proceedings	1920–3	86 v
Yearly proceedings	1920–1	6 v
'A', 'B', filed and MS proceedings	1920–3	4 bdls

MERCANTILE MARINE I BRANCH

Registers	1929–38	2 bdls
'A', 'B' and 'C' proceedings	1929–41	54 bdls

MERCANTILE MARINE II BRANCH

Registers	1925–37	4 bdls
'A', 'B' and 'C' proceedings	1929–46	36 bdls

MERCANTILE MARINE III BRANCH

'B' and 'C' proceedings	1944–7	2 bdls

MERCHANT SHIPPING BRANCH

Yearly index	1920–2	3 v
Monthly proceedings	1920–3	103 v
Yearly proceedings	1920–2	8 v
'A', 'B', filed and MS proceedings	1920–3	17 bdls

OFFICE ESTABLISHMENT AND CASH BRANCH

Yearly index	1923	I v
Monthly proceedings	May–Aug. 1923	12 v
Filed proceedings	May–Nov. 1923	1 bdl

PORTS AND LIGHTING BRANCH

Yearly index	1920–2	3 v
Monthly proceedings	1920–3	98 v
Yearly proceedings	1920–2	5 v
'A', 'B', filed and MS proceedings	1920–3	11 bdls

PORTS AND LIGHTHOUSES BRANCH

Registers	1930–7	2 bdls
'A', 'B' and 'C' proceedings	1930–7	50 bdls

POST AND TELEGRAPH ESTABLISHMENT BRANCH

Yearly index	1920–1	2 v
Monthly proceedings	1920–1	31 v

Yearly proceedings	1920	2 v
'A', 'B', 'C', filed and deposit proceedings	1920–1	17 bdls

POST OFFICE BRANCH

Yearly index	1920–1	2 v
Monthly proceedings	1920–1	30 v
Yearly proceedings	1920	2 v
'A', 'B' and filed proceedings	1920–1	5 bdls

PURCHASE SCHEME BRANCH

Yearly index	1920–1	2 v
Monthly proceedings	1920–1	24 v
Yearly proceedings	1920–1	6 v
'B' and filed proceedings	1920–1	2 bdls

SHIPPING BRANCH

Registers	1923–8	1 bdl
'A', 'B', 'C' and deposit proceedings	1922–9	55 bdls

SHIPPING CONTROL BRANCH

Yearly index	1920–2	3 v
Monthly proceedings	1920–3	77 v
Yearly proceedings	1920–2	8 v
'A', 'B', filed and MS proceedings	1920–2	4 bdls

STAMPS BRANCH

Yearly index	1921–2	2 v
Monthly proceedings	1921–3	54 v
'A' proceedings	1921–3	1 bdl

STATISTICS BRANCH

Yearly index	1920–2	3 v
Monthly proceedings	1920–3	107 v
Yearly proceedings	1920–2	8 v
'B', filed and MS proceedings	1920–2	5 bdls

STORES BRANCH

'A' proceedings	Sept. 1938	1 bdl

SUSPECTED FIRMS BRANCH

Yearly index	1920	1 v
Monthly proceedings	August 1920	1 v
Yearly proceedings	1920	2 v

TARIFFS BRANCH

Yearly index	1923	1 v
Monthly proceedings	1923	6 v
Registers	1923–38	7 bdls
'A', 'B', 'C', filed and deposit proceedings	1923–36	41 bdls

TARIFF VALUATIONS BRANCH

'A' and filed proceedings	1923	1 bdl

TELEGRAPHS BRANCH

Yearly index	1920–1	2 v
Monthly proceedings	1920–1	30 v
Yearly proceedings	1920	2 v
'A', 'B', filed and MS proceedings	1920–1	8 bdls

TRADE AFTER THE WAR BRANCHES

COTTON

Yearly index	1920–1	2 v
Monthly proceedings	1920–1	12 v
Yearly proceedings	1920–1	6 v
'A' and filed proceedings	1920–1	1 bdl

DYES

Yearly index	1920–1	2 v
Monthly proceedings	1920–1	40 v
Yearly proceedings	1920–1	6 v
'A', 'B' and filed proceedings	1920–1	2 bdls

GENERAL

Yearly index	1920–1	2 v
Monthly proceedings	1920–1	40 v
Yearly proceedings	1920–1	6 v
'A', 'B', filed and MS proceedings	1920–1	3 bdls

HIDES, SKINS AND LEATHER

Yearly index	1920–1	2 v
Monthly proceedings	1920–1	41 v
Yearly proceedings	1920–1	6 v
'A', 'B' and filed proceedings	1920–1	3 bdls

IMPERIAL PREFERENCE

Yearly index	1920–1	2 v
Monthly proceedings	1920–1	34 v
Yearly proceedings	1920–1	6 v
'A', 'B' and filed proceedings	1920–1	2 bdls

JAPANESE ACTIVITIES

Yearly index	1920–1	2 v
Monthly proceedings	1920–1	25 v
Yearly proceedings	1920–1	5 v
'A', 'B' and filed proceedings	1920–1	1 bdl

JUTE

Yearly index	1920–1	2 v
Monthly proceedings	1920–1	13 v
Yearly proceedings	1920–1	6 v
'A', 'B', and filed proceedings	1920–1	1 bdl

OLEAGINOUS PRODUCTS

Yearly index	1920	1 v
Monthly proceedings	Nov.–Dec. 1920	2 v
Yearly proceedings	1920	3 v
Filed proceedings	Nov. 1920	1 bdl

WOOL

Yearly index	1920	1 v
Monthly proceedings	1920–1	26 v
Yearly proceedings	1920–1	5 v
'A' and filed proceedings	1920–1	1 bdl

TRADING BY FOREIGNERS BRANCH

Filed proceedings	1920–1	8 bdls

TREATIES

Registers	1929–38	6 bdls
'A', 'B' and 'C' proceedings	1934–41	16 bdls

TREATIES AND ECCLESIASTICAL BRANCH
(including A and G branch)

The Ecclesiastical Branch was part of the Home Department from 1860 to 1910 and of the Department of Education and its successors from 1910 to 1924. After 1937 ecclesiastical affairs were transferred to the Defence Department.

Registers	1929–38	6 bdls
'A', 'B', 'C' and deposit proceedings	1925–39	47 bdls

WEIGHTS AND MEASURES BRANCH

Yearly index	1920–1	2 v
Monthly proceedings	1920–3	28 v
Yearly proceedings	1920–1	6 v
Filed proceedings	1920–1	1 bdl

WIRELESS TELEGRAPHY (SHIPPING) BRANCH

Yearly index	1923	2 v
Monthly proceedings	1923	13 v
'A', 'B' and filed proceedings	1923	1 bdl

MINISTRY OF COMMERCE: M. III SECTION

'B' and 'C' proceedings	1947–8	2 bdls

DEPARTMENT OF EDUCATION, HEALTH AND LANDS 1923–45

(including records of predecessor bodies, DEPARTMENT OF REVENUE, AGRICULTURE AND COMMERCE 1871–9; HOME, REVENUE AND AGRICULTURE DEPARTMENT 1879–81; DEPARTMENT OF REVENUE AND AGRICULTURE 1881–1923; DEPARTMENT OF EDUCATION 1910–21; DEPARTMENT OF EDUCATION AND HEALTH 1921–3)

The Department of Education, Health and Lands was created in 1923 with the amalgamation of the two departments, Education and Health and Revenue and Agriculture. It continued under this name until 1945 when the department was divided into its three component parts, Education, Health, and Lands. All the records which were transferred to the new department on its creation in 1923 are kept with the records of this department, not with those of the originating departments. They are, however, divided into two wings corresponding to the two amalgamating departments in 1923.

I. REVENUE AND AGRICULTURE

This wing consists of the records of the Department of Revenue and Agriculture and its predecessors, and of those branches of the Department of Education, Health and Lands which continued to deal with the relevant subjects after the amalgamation. The Department of Revenue, Agriculture and Commerce was created in June 1871 and work was transferred to it from the Home Department (Public and Revenue Branches), the Foreign Department (relevant matters relating to the territories under its jurisdiction), the Military Department (Government studs, horse and cattle breeding and, in 1874, marine administration relating to commerce), the Financial Department, and the Public Works Department (forests and fisheries). In 1879 the work of the department was redistributed between the two Departments of Finance and Commerce, and Home, Revenue and Agriculture. However, in 1881 a new Department of Revenue and Agriculture was established to deal with land revenue, surveys, agriculture and horticulture, fisheries, cattle-breeding and diseases, minerals, meteorology, and famine. Various other subjects were transferred to the department from time to time, including practical arts, economic museums and exhibitions (1882), forests (1886), archaeology and fine arts (1887), patents (1888), horse-breeding (1889), and weights and measures (1890). Certain items of business were transferred to the new Department of Education in 1910, and in 1923 the two Departments (with Health) were amalgamated.

The file system was used in the Department of Revenue and Agriculture from 1895 until 1923 and was reintroduced into the Department of Education, Health and Lands in 1932.

General index	1875–1922	652 v
General proceedings volumes	1871–9	242 v
General files volumes	1907–18	177 v
Despatches of secretary of state	1871–3, 1881–1911	43 v

AGRICULTURE BRANCH

This branch was part of the Departments of Revenue, Agriculture and Commerce and its successor bodies from 1871. For the years 1860–71 see Home Department, Public Branch.

Index and contents	1873–1915	120 v
Proceedings volumes	1871–1921	204 v

Files volumes	1895–1919	216 v
Monthly proceedings	1906–17	17 bdls
'A' proceedings	1871–1932	158 bdls
'B' proceedings	1871–1932	127 bdls
'C' proceedings	1892–1906	9 bdls
Deposit proceedings	1923–32	3 bdls
Filed proceedings	1899–1925	9 bdls
Files	1932–44	61 bdls
MSS	1923–42	19 bdls
Despatches from the secretary of state	1869–1910	2 v
Despatches to the secretary of state	1880	2 v

CIVIL VETERINARY ADMINISTRATION (HORSE-BREEDING AND AGRICULTURAL STOCK) BRANCH

This branch was administered by the Department of Revenue, Agriculture, Commerce and its successors from 1871 to 1923. For the years before 1871 see the Military Department, and for those after 1923 see the Department of Education, Health and Lands, Agriculture Branch.

Index and contents	1873–1920	110 v
Proceedings volumes	1871–1921	163 v
Files volumes	1895–1918	123 v
Monthly proceedings	1906–17	12 bdls
'A' proceedings	1871–1923	78 bdls
'B' proceedings	1871–1923	47 bdls
'C' proceedings	1893–1905	4 bdls
Deposit proceedings	1923	1 bdl
Filed proceedings	1896–1923	4 bdls

COMMERCE AND TRADE BRANCH

This branch was part of the Department of Revenue, Agriculture and Commerce from 1871 to 1879. For the years before 1871 see the Home Department, Public Branch, and for those after 1879 see the Departments of Finance and Commerce and Commerce and Industry.

Index and contents	1871–9	1 v
Proceedings volumes	1871–9	8 v
'A' proceedings	1871–9	6 bdls
'B' proceedings	1871–9	2 bdls

COMMERCIAL EXHIBITIONS BRANCH

This branch came under the Department of Revenue and Agriculture from 1895 to 1904. For the years 1905–16 see the Department of Commerce and Industry, Commercial Exhibitions Branch; 1917–20, Commerce and Industry, Internal Trade Branch; 1920–2, Commerce Department, Internal Trade Branch; 1923, Commerce Department, Exhibitions Branch; and from 1924, Commerce Department, Commerce Branch.

Index and contents	1895–1904	25 v
Proceedings volumes	1897–1904	23 v
'A' proceedings	1897–1905	4 bdls
'B' proceedings	1895–1904	2 bdls
'C' proceedings	1892–1903	1 bdl
Filed proceedings	1900–4	1 bdl

CUSTOMS BRANCH

This branch was part of the Department of Revenue, Agriculture and Commerce from 1871 to 1879. For the years before 1863 see the Home Department, for those from 1863 to 1871 see the Financial Department, and after 1879 see the Department of Finance and Commerce and from 1924 the Central Board of Revenue. For the years 1905–20 see also the Department of Commerce and Industry.

Index and contents	1873–9	1 v
Proceedings volumes	1871–8	3 v
Questions volumes	1875–81	4 v
'A' proceedings	1862–79	4 bdls
'B' proceedings	1871–9	1 bdl
Stamps account registers	1914, 1917–18	6 v

ECONOMIC PRODUCTS BRANCH

Economic products were dealt with in the Agriculture Branch of the Department of Revenue, Agriculture and Commerce and its successors until 1895, and again from 1910. In 1895 the Economic Products Branch was established, and was attached to the Department of Commerce and Industry from 1906 to 1910.

Index and contents	1895–1904	23 v
Proceedings volumes	1895–1904	30 v
Files volumes	1895–1904	20 v
'A' proceedings	1895–1905	8 bdls
'B' proceedings	1895–1905	9 bdls

7

'C' proceedings	1895–1905	2 bdls
Filed proceedings	1899–1904	1 bdl
Despatches from secretary of state	1867–1906	1 v

FAMINE BRANCH

This branch was part of the Department of Revenue, Agriculture and Commerce from 1871 to 1877 and of the Department of Home, Revenue and Agriculture from 1879 to 1881. Before 1871 famine was dealt with in the Public Branch of the Home Department, from 1877 to 1879 in the Public Works Department, and from 1881 in the Department of Revenue and Agriculture. After the amalgamation in 1923 the work of the Famine Branch was transferred to the Agriculture Branch of the Department of Education, Health and Lands.

Index and contents	1874–1919	97 v
Proceedings volumes	1873–1921	278 v
Files volumes	1895–1918	175 v
Monthly proceedings	1878, 1906–17	13 bdls
'A' proceedings	1873–1923	123 bdls
'B' proceedings	1874–1923	37 bdls
'C' proceedings	1897–1906	3 bdls
Filed proceedings	1899–1923	6 bdls
Deposit proceedings	1923	1 bdl
Despatches from secretary of state	1869–1904	1 v
Famine Commissioners' Reports	1877–1904	110 v

FAMINE (BENGAL, N.W. AND BIHAR ETC. SCARCITY)

Index	1873–5	14 v
Proceedings volumes	1873–5	40 v

FIBRES AND SILK BRANCH

This branch was part of the Department of Revenue, Agriculture and Commerce and its successors from 1871 until 1894 when its work was transferred to the Agriculture Branch of the Department of Revenue and Agriculture and its successors. Previously matters relating to cotton, silk etc. had been dealt with in the Public Branch of the Home Department.

Index and contents	1874–9, 1881–94	38 v
Proceedings volumes	1871–9, 1881–94	79 v
'A' proceedings	1871–9, 1881–93	7 bdls
'B' proceedings	1871–9, 1881–94	18 bdls
'C' proceedings	1892–4	1 bdl
Despatches from secretary of state	1870–95	1 v

FISHERIES BRANCH

Previously the concern of the Home Department, Public Branch, and the Public Works Department, this branch was part of the Department of Revenue, Agriculture and Commerce and its successors 1871–1904, the Department of Commerce and Industry 1905–20, and the Department of Commerce 1920–3. For the years 1923–9 see the Commerce Department, Shipping Branch, for 1929–44 see the Commerce Department, Mercantile Marine II Branch, and for 1945–6 the Department of Agriculture, Fisheries Branch.

Index and contents	1871–9, 1881–1904	58 v
Proceedings volumes	1871–9, 1881–1904	98 v
Files volumes	1895–1904	5 v
'A' proceedings	1871–9, 1882–1904	3 bdls
'B' proceedings	1871–9, 1881–1904	1 bdl

FOODSTUFFS BRANCH

'A' proceedings	1919–22	5 bdls
'B' proceedings	1919–22	20 bdls
Filed proceedings	1919–22	1 bdl

CENTRAL TRANSPORT AND FOODSTUFFS BOARD

General 'B' proceedings	1918	1 bdl
General filed proceedings	1918	1 bdl
Foodstuffs 'B' proceedings	1918–19	2 bdls

DEPUTY FOODSTUFFS COMMISSIONER'S OFFICE

Foodstuffs 'B' proceedings	1919–21	6 bdls

FOREST BRANCH (FOREST AND LANDS BRANCH 1940–4)

Matters relating to forests were dealt with in the Home Department, Public Branch, from 1860 to 1865, and in the Forest Branch which was successively part of the Public Works Department 1865–71, and the Department of Revenue, Agriculture and Commerce and its successors from 1871 onwards, except for 1881–6 when the Branch was part of the Home Department. The Forest Branch became the Forest and Lands Branch between 1940 and 1944.

Index and contents 1871–1925	1871–1925	136 v
Proceedings volumes	1871–1924	324 v
Monthly proceedings	1906–17	

Files volumes	1895–1918	249 v
'A' proceedings	1871–1932	225 bdls
'B' proceedings	1872–1932	150 bdls
'C' proceedings	1893	11 bdls
Deposit proceedings	1923–32	3 bdls
Filed proceedings	1898–1922	8 bdls
Files	1932–44	22 bdls
MS proceedings	1922–40	12 bdls
Despatches from secretary of state	1868–1910	6 v
Despatches to secretary of state	1910	1 v

INSPECTOR GENERAL OF FORESTS BRANCH

This was a subordinate office under the Forest Branch, having separate indexes. Its proceedings are not entered in the general indexes.

MS indexes	1874, 1881–92	4 v
Printed indexes	1889, 1895–1911	12 v
Proceedings volumes	1871–2, 1884–1909	51 v
Monthly proceedings	1905–9	
Abstract of proceedings	1880–4	1 v
'A' proceedings	1871–1909	10 bdls
'B' proceedings	1864–1923	66 bdls
'C' proceedings	1884–1905	15 bdls
Deposit proceedings	1923	1 bdl
Filed proceedings	1905–23	22 bdls
Working plan	1905–22	15 bdls
'B' proceedings relating to Burma, C.P., N.W.P., Oudh etc.	1864–70	1 bdl

GENERAL BRANCH

Index and contents	1871–1923	119 v
Proceedings volumes	1871–1921	170 v
Monthly proceedings	1906–17	10 bdls
Files volumes	1895–1918	142 v
'A' proceedings	1871–1922	64 bdls
'B' proceedings	1871–1923	78 bdls
'C' proceedings	1895–1907	9 bdls
Filed proceedings	1899–1922	14 bdls
Despatches from secretary of state	1871–1910	1 v

GEOLOGY AND MINERALS BRANCH

This branch was part of the Department of Revenue, Agriculture and Commerce and its successors from 1871 to 1904, the Department of Commerce and Industry from 1905, the Board of Industries and Munitions 1920-1, the Department of Industries 1921-3, and the Department of Industries and Labour 1923-37. For the years 1860-71 see Home Department, Public Branch.

Index and contents	1871–1904	33 v
Proceedings volumes	1871–1904	73 v
'A' proceedings	1871–83	3 bdls
'B' proceedings	1871–83	2 bdls
Originals	1884–1904	26 bdls

LAND REVENUE BRANCH
(LANDS BRANCH FROM 1923)

This branch came under the Home Department until 1871 when it was transferred to the new Department of Revenue, Agriculture and Commerce and its successors. After the amalgamation in 1923, the Survey Branch and the Land Revenue Branch were also amalgamated to become the Lands Branch in the new Department of Education, Health and Lands. In 1932 its work was transferred to the Emigration Branch which was re-designated Lands and Overseas Branch, and in 1940 the Lands part of the work of this branch was transferred to the Forest Branch, which then became the Forest and Lands Branch. The Home Department records are kept with those of this department.

Decimal index	1857–67	1 v
Index and contents	1862–1925	130 v
Proceedings volumes	1860–1925	523 v
Monthly proceedings	1906–17	13 bdls
Files volumes	1895–1921	395 v
'A' proceedings	1860–1932	376 bdls
'B' proceedings	1860–1932	207 bdls
'C' proceedings	1862–1908	7 bdls
Deposit proceedings	1913–32	2 bdls
Filed proceedings	1896–1923	9 bdls
Despatches from secretary of state	1858–1907, 1918–21	4 bdls, 9 v
Despatches to secretary of state	1858–82	1 bdl, 5 v

| Despatches, Bombay revenue | 1858–71 | 2 bdls, 11 v |
| Despatches, Madras | 1860–71 | 1 bdl, 11 v |

PATENTS BRANCH (PATENTS ON INVENTIONS AND DESIGNS BRANCH 1895–7)

This branch was part of the Home Department from 1875–88, when it was transferred to the Department of Revenue and Agriculture. From 1860 to 1875 patents had been dealt with in the Public Branch of the Home Department. For the years 1905–11 see the Department of Commerce and Industry, Inventions and Designs Branch, and for the years 1913–37 see the Patents and Designs Branches of, successively, the Department of Commerce and Industry, the Indian Munitions Board, the Department of Industries, and the Department of Industries and Labour.

Index and contents	1875–1901	15 v
Proceedings volumes	1874–1904	75 v
Files volumes	1895–1904	17 v
'A' proceedings	1875–1905	17 bdls

KHEDDAH BRANCH

The Kheddah Branch was part of the Military Department, but when the work of the branch was transferred to the Forest Branch of the Department of Revenue and Agriculture in 1904, the records were also transferred. From 1902 to 1904 the work of the branch came under the Burma Government.

| Index | 1866–1904 | 14 v |
| 'A', 'B' and 'C' proceedings | 1866–1904 | 4 bdls |

METEOROLOGY BRANCH

This branch was part of the Department of Revenue, Agriculture and Commerce and its successors from 1871 to 1923. For the years 1860–71 see the Home Department, Public Branch, and for those after 1923 see the Department of Industries and Labour, Meteorology Branch.

Index and contents	1907–15	9 v
Proceedings volumes	1871–1914	81 v
Monthly proceedings	1906–17	
'A' proceedings	1871–82	1 bdl
'B' proceedings	1871–82	6 bdls
Original proceedings	1883–1923	48 bdls
Despatches from secretary of state	1873–1910	1 v

STATISTICS BRANCH

Index and contents	1873–95	15 v
Proceedings volumes	1871–98	53 v
Files volumes	1897–8	2 v
'A' proceedings	1873–98	3 bdls
'B' proceedings	1871, 1884–98	2 bdls

SURVEY BRANCH

The Survey Branch was part of the Department of Revenue, Agriculture and Commerce and its successors from 1871 to 1923. For the years 1864–71 see the Home Department, Public Branch. For 1923–32 see the Lands Branch, for 1932–9 the Lands and Overseas Branch (formerly Emigration) and for 1940–4 the Forests Branch of the Department of Education, Health and Lands.

Index and contents	1869–1923	131 v
Proceedings volumes	1869–1923	98 v
Monthly proceedings	1906–17	
Files volumes	1895–1923	105 v
'A' proceedings	1869–1923	87 bdls
'B' proceedings	1869–1923	55 bdls
'C' proceedings	1905	1 bdl
Filed proceedings	1900–23	1 bdl
Despatches from secretary of state	1869–1910	8 v
Despatches to secretary of state	1869–1901	5 v

TAKAVI BRANCH

The work of the Takavi Branch was transferred to the Land Revenue Branch in 1879.

Index and contents	1874, 1876, 1879	4 v
Proceedings volumes	1871–7	2 v
'A' proceedings	1871–9	2 bdls
'B' proceedings	1871–9	1 bdl

II. EDUCATION AND HEALTH

This wing consists of the records of the Department of Education, 1910–21, the Department of Education and Health, 1921–3, and of those branches of the Department of Education, Health and Lands which continued to deal with the relevant subjects after the amalgamation with the Department of Revenue and Agriculture. Until 1910 education affairs came under the control of the Home Department, where an Education Branch had been established in 1857, but in 1910 a separate Department of Education was established to deal with all matters relating to education, examinations, archaeology, census, gazetteers, record offices, the Imperial Library, books and publications, copyright etc. Various other subjects were transferred to the department from time to time, including oriental languages, ethnography, and zoological gardens (1911), and in 1921 the work relating to public health and medical matters was also transferred to the Education Department from the Home Department. The department was then redesignated the Department of Education and Health, and in 1923 the Department of Education, Health and Lands.

All the records which were transferred to the Education Department and its successors from the Home Department and elsewhere are now kept with the records of the Department of Education, Health and Lands, not with those of the originating departments.

General indexes	1911–35	58 v

ARCHAEOLOGY BRANCH (ARCHAEOLOGY AND CONSERVATION OF ANCIENT MONUMENTS BRANCH, 1881–7; ARCHAEOLOGY AND EPIGRAPHY BRANCH FROM 1895)

Matters relating to archaeology were dealt with in the Public Branch of the Home Department from 1860 to 1879, the Survey Branch of the Department of Home, Revenue and Agriculture from 1879 to 1881, and the Archaeology Branch of, successively, the Home Department from July 1881, the Revenue and Agriculture Department from April 1887, the Home Department from May 1905 and the new Department of Education from December 1910. In 1923 archaeology ceased to be an independent branch and archaeological matters were dealt with in the Education Branch and from 1932 the Forests Branch, and from 1945 the General Branch, of the Department of Education, Health and Lands. In 1946 an independent Archaeology Branch was again established. All the records of the Archaeology Branch from 1881 to 1923 are kept together.

Manuscript indexes	1882–6	5 v
Index and contents	1881–1917	59 v
Proceedings volumes	1881–1922	136 v
'A' proceedings	1881–1922	37 bdls
'B' proceedings	1881–1923	25 bdls
'C' proceedings	1894–1905	1 bdl
Deposit proceedings	1905–23	4 bdls

Filed proceedings	1900–3	1 bdl
Manuscript proceedings	1909–19	9 bdls
Despatches from secretary of state	1881–9	3 v
Despatches to secretary of state	1881–2	2 v
Despatch sheets	1881–9	2 v
Miscellaneous volumes (Diaries of file registers etc.)	1881–1903	5 v

BOOKS PUBLICATION BRANCH
(BOOKS GENERAL BRANCH, 1912–22)

The work of this branch was dealt with in the Public Branch and, from 1882, a separate branch, of the Home Department. In 1910 the branch was transferred to the new Department of Education. After the creation of the Department of Education, Health and Lands in 1923 the work of the Books Publication Branch was taken over by the Education Branch (1924–44).

Index and contents	1881–1917	53 v
Proceedings volumes	1882–1922	100 v
Monthly proceedings volumes	1882–95	1 bdl
'A' proceedings	1880–1922	22 bdls
'B' proceedings	1880–1923	30 bdls
Deposit proceedings	1890–1923	2 bdls
Manuscript proceedings	1911–18	4 bdls
Despatches from secretary of state	1896–1906	1 bdl

ECCLESIASTICAL BRANCH

This Branch was part of the Home Department (Home Revenue and Agriculture Department 1879–81) from 1860 to 1910, when it was transferred to the new Department of Education. From 1925 to 1937 ecclesiastical matters were dealt with in the Treaties and Ecclesiastical Branch of the Commerce Department, and in 1937 they were transferred to the Defence Department.

MS indexes	1860–80	19 v
Indexes	1857–95	11 v
Index and contents	1859–97	10 v
Monthly proceedings volumes	1908 (Jan.–Sept.)	10 v
'A' proceedings	1860–1924	49 bdls
'B' proceedings	1860–1924	28 bdls
Deposit proceedings	1892–1923	2 bdls
Manuscript proceedings	1909–18	14 bdls
Despatches from secretary of state	1860–77, 1860–1906	15 v, 3 bdls

Register of despatches	1858–91	2 v
Despatches to secretary of state	1860–95, 1860–92	32 v, 2 bdls
Register of despatches	1866–96	2 v
Despatches to under secretary of of state	1860–79, 1860–92	14 v, 3 bdls
Registers of despatches	1878–1903	2 v

EDUCATION BRANCH

Education was a branch of the Home Department (Home, Revenue and Agriculture Department, 1879–81) from 1860 to 1910. A new Department of Education was created in December 1910, succeeded in 1921 by the Department of Education and Health, and in 1923 by the Department of Education, Health and Lands. All the education papers are kept with the records of this department.

MS indexes	1860–1904	30 v
Decimal index	1857–67	1 v
Indexes	1936–44	16 v
Index and contents	1860–1920	50 v
Proceedings volumes	1860–1932	379 v
'A' proceedings	1860–1932	188 bdls
'B' proceedings	1860–1932	95 bdls
Deposit proceedings	1896–1932	16 bdls
Files	1932–44	74 carton boxes
Manuscript proceedings	1909–41	72 bdls
Despatches from secretary of state	1860–90	12 v
Despatches to secretary of state	1860–95	29 v
	1860–93	4 carton boxes
Despatch book	1872	1 v
Despatches to under secretary of of state	1865–75	6 v
	1862–92	1 box
Despatch sheets	1897–1906	4 v
Issue and receipt registers etc.	1924–32	19 v

EMIGRATION BRANCH (OVERSEAS BRANCH 1923–32 AND FROM 1938; LANDS AND OVERSEAS BRANCH 1933–8)

Emigration was dealt with in the Public Branch of the Home Department from 1860 to 1871. From 1871 to 1905 the Emigration Branch was part of the Department of Revenue, Agriculture and Commerce, and its successors. In 1905 emigration business was transferred to the new Department of Commerce and Industry, but returned to the Department of Revenue and Agriculture in 1921, and from 1923 was dealt with in the Department of Education, Health and Lands, Overseas Branch, except for emigration to Egypt, Palestine, and Mesopotamia and foreign countries other than Surinam—this work was dealt with by the Foreign and Political Department, General Branch. For the emigration records for the years 1905–21 see Commerce and Industry Department, Emigration Branch, 1905–20, and Commerce Department, Emigration Branch, 1920–1. And for the years 1923–37 see also Foreign and Political Department, General Branch.

In 1941 a separate Department of Indians Overseas was created, which in 1944 was redesignated the Department of Commonwealth Relations, and this department in turn was amalgamated in 1947 with the External Affairs Department to become the Department of External Affairs and Commonwealth Relations.

Index and contents	1871–1905, 1922–40	78 v
Proceedings volumes	1871–1905, 1923–5	220 v
Bengal emigration proceedings volumes	1868–1903	38 v
Emigrants registers	1863–1938	255 v
'A' proceedings	1871–1905, 1922–32	118 bdls
'B' proceedings	1871–1905, 1922–32	57 bdls
Deposit proceedings	1921–32	3 bdls
Filed papers	1901–5, 1922–3	5 bdls
Files	1932–41	69 bdls
Manuscript proceedings	1921–38	14 bdls
Despatches from secretary of state	1871–1903, 1881–2	1 carton box, 1 v
Despatch register	1858–71	2 v
Despatches to secretary of state	1880	2 v
Deposit register	1923–6	1 v

EXAMINATIONS BRANCH

The Examinations Branch was part of the Home Department (Home, Revenue and Agriculture Department, 1879–81) from 1874 to 1910 when it was transferred to the new Department of Education. In 1923 the work was transferred to the Education Branch of the Department of Education, Health and Lands. For the years before 1874 see the Home Department, Public Branch.

Manuscript indexes	1874–1906	12 v
Index and contents	1874–1917	59 v
Proceedings volumes	1874–1922	105 v
Monthly proceedings volumes	1874–95	2 bdls
'A' proceedings	1874–1922	29 bdls
'B' proceedings	1874–1923	10 bdls
Deposit proceedings	1899–1921	2 bdls
Manuscript proceedings	1912–17	4 bdls
Examination lists	1875–87	9 v

GENERAL BRANCH

Indexes	1923, 1934–42	26 v
Index and contents	1912–17	12 v
Proceedings volumes	1910–22	39 v
'A' proceedings	1910–32	10 bdls
'B' proceedings	1910–32	46 bdls
Deposit proceedings	1911–32	12 bdls
Files	1932–44	55 bdls
Manuscript proceedings	1910–40	14 bdls

GENERAL A BRANCH

| 'B' proceedings | 1923 | 1 bdl |

LOCAL BOARDS BRANCH

Local Boards were institutions of local government in the rural areas, the rural counterparts to municipal government. The Local Boards Branch was part of the Home Department from 1889 to 1910 when it was transferred to the new Department of Education. In 1923 the Local Boards Branch was amalgamated with the Municipalities Branch to become the Local Self-Government Branch of the Department of Education, Health and Lands. For the years to 1871 see the Home Department, Public Branch, and for those from 1871 to 1889 see the Municipalities Branch.

MS indexes	1889–95	8 v
Index and contents	1889–1919	30 v
Proceedings volumes	1889–1923	74 v
'A' proceedings	1889–1921	9 bdls
'B' proceedings	1889–1923	17 bdls
Deposit proceedings	1900–21	1 bdl
Manuscript proceedings	1908–20	4 bdls
Local Boards Administration Reports	1918–21	1 bdl
Issue register and despatch sheets	1905–17	3 v
Diaries	1889–1905	16 v

MEDICAL BRANCH

Medical matters were dealt with in the Public Branch, and from 1873 the Medical Branch, of the Home Department. In 1921 the branch was transferred to the Education Department which was then redesignated the Department of Education and Health, and from 1923 the Department of Education, Health and Lands. In 1923 the Medical and Sanitary Branches were amalgamated to become the Health Branch.

MS indexes	1874–1907	22 v
Index and contents	1874–1906	23 v
Proceedings volumes	1873–1923	267 v
Monthly proceedings volumes	1873–1912	11 bdls
'A' proceedings	1873–1923	177 bdls
'B' proceedings	1873–1923	47 bdls
Deposit proceedings	1886–1923	5 bdls
Proceedings relating to lunatic asylums	1873–1921	2 bdls

MUNICIPALITIES BRANCH (FROM AUGUST 1923 LOCAL SELF-GOVERNMENT BRANCH)

Until 1871 municipalities were dealt with in the Public Branch of the Home Department. The Municipalities Branch was created in 1871 and came under the new Department of Revenue, Agriculture and Commerce until 1876, the Home Department 1876–9, the Home, Revenue and Agriculture Department 1879–81, and again the Home Department 1881–1910, and the new Department of Education from 1910. In 1923 it was amalgamated with the Local Boards Branch and redesignated the Local Self-Government Branch. In 1932 the work of the branch was transferred to the Health Branch (formerly Sanitary Branch).

MS indexes	1876–92	5 v
Index and contents	1871–1919	66 v
Proceedings volumes	1871–1930	179 v
Monthly proceedings volumes	1876–95	7 bdls
'A' proceedings	1871–1932	86 bdls
'B' proceedings	1871–1932	68 bdls
Deposit proceedings	1892–1932	5 bdls
MS proceedings	1898–1932	14 bdls
Despatches to secretary of state	1874–82, 1892–1910	5 v, 1 bdl
Diaries, registers, lists etc.	1876–87	12 v

MUSEUMS BRANCH (VARIOUS TITLES)

Business relating to museums was dealt with in the Public Branch of the Home Department until 1871 when a separate Museums Branch was created. Part of the new Department of Revenue, Agriculture and Commerce, and its successors from 1871 to 1905, the Commerce and Industry Department from 1905 to 1910, and the new Education Department from 1911, the branch was absorbed by the Education Branch in 1923. For the records of the years 1905–10 see the Commerce and Industry Department, Practical Arts and Museums Branch.

Index and contents	1871–1904, 1911–21	75 v
Proceedings volumes	1871–1904, 1911–22	140 v
Monthly proceedings volumes	1881–1905	6 bdls
'A' proceedings	1871–1904, 1911–22	20 bdls
'B' proceedings	1871–1904, 1911–23	18 bdls
Deposit proceedings	1915–21	1 bdl
Filed proceedings	1901–4	1 bdl
Manuscript proceedings	1912–17	2 bdls
File registers etc.	1895–1904	10 v

SANITARY BRANCH (FROM AUGUST 1923 HEALTH BRANCH)

Sanitary matters were dealt with in the Public Branch, then from 1867 a separate Sanitary Branch, of the Home Department. This Branch came under the Department of Revenue, Agriculture and Commerce from 1871 to 1873, the Home Department again from 1873 to 1879, the Home, Revenue and Agriculture Department from 1879 to 1881, and the Home Department again from 1881 to 1910. The branch was then transferred to the new Department of Education, and in 1923 amalgamated with the Medical Branch and redesignated the Health Branch.

MS indexes	1870–1908	12 v
Index and contents	1869–1942	112 v
Proceedings volumes	1868–1930	450 v
Sanitary Commissioners proceedings volumes	1868–73	17 v
'A' proceedings	1868–1932	187 bdls
'B' proceedings	1868–1932	106 bdls
Deposit proceedings volumes	1897–1902	10 v
Deposit bundles	1890–1932	16 bdls
Files	1932–44	92 bdls
Manuscript proceedings	1899–1940	55 bdls

Despatches from secretary of state	1867–74	8 v
	1867–92	6 boxes
Despatches to secretary of state	1868–95	25 v
	1868–92	6 boxes
Despatches to under secretary of	1868	1 v
state	1868–87	2 boxes
Sanitary lists	1869–82	9 v
Issue and receipt registers	1868–1944	13 v

ZOOLOGICAL SURVEY BRANCH 1915–23

The work of the Zoological Survey Branch was transferred to the Lands Branch in 1923.

Index and contents	1916–17	4 v
Proceedings volumes	1916–22	14 v
'A' proceedings	1916–23	2 bdls
'B' proceedings	1916–23	1 bdl
Deposit proceedings	1915–23	1 bdl
Manuscript proceedings	1916–23	1 bdl

III. SUBORDINATE OFFICES

BOOKS DISTRIBUTION BRANCH

This was a subordinate office with separate indexes, its proceedings not entered in the general index. The work was done in the Imperial Record Office.

Monthly index and contents	1917–40	1 bdl
Proceedings volumes	1912–21	13 v
'A' proceedings	1912–20	1 bdl
'B' proceedings	1912–31	5 bdls
Deposit proceedings	1912–40	2 bdls
Files	1932–41	6 bdls
Diary, issue and receipt registers	1932–40	4 v

BUREAU OF EDUCATION

The Bureau of Education was constituted in 1915, under the supervision and control of the Educational Commissioner. The head of the Bureau was the Curator, and its duties included the collection and collation of information on educational matters in India and abroad, and the publication of reports and pamphlets on educational subjects. The Bureau was abolished in May 1923 as an economy measure.

Files	1916–22	1 bdl

CENTRAL ADVISORY BOARD OF EDUCATION

This Board was constituted in 1920 to give advice to the Government of India on matters concerning university legislation, university examinations, management of government educational institutions, preparation of educational reports, monographs, surveys etc. The Board was abolished in 1923 as an economy measure, but revived in 1935.

Indexes	1935–9	13 v
Files	1921–3, 1935–44	16 bdls
Manuscripts	1935–8	1 bdl

DIRECTOR-GENERAL OF EDUCATION

The post was created in 1901 on the recommendation of the educational conference convened by Lord Curzon, to establish an understanding between the central and local Governments in the educational sphere. The post was abolished on the creation of the Department of Education in December 1910.

Files	1903–10	1 bdl

EDUCATIONAL COMMISSIONER

The office was created in 1915, being a revival of the post of Director-General of Education (abolished in 1910) under a new name. The Educational Commissioner supervised and controlled the Bureau of Education and from 1920 acted as chairman of the Central Advisory Board of Education.

Files	1915–22	10 bdls

LINGUISTIC SURVEY OF INDIA

In 1896 Dr G. A. Grierson was appointed to undertake a systematic survey of the vernacular languages of India. Until 1910 the survey came under the Public Branch of the Home Department, and from 1910 under the Education Branch of the Department of Education.

Bombay	Nos. 1–36	2 bdls
Bengal	Nos. 1–53	2 bdls
N.W.P. and Oudh	Nos. 1–47	2 bdls
Central Provinces	Nos. 1–32	2 bdls
Punjab	Nos. 1–32	1 bdl
Assam	Nos. 1–14	1 bdl
Princely states	Nos. 1–30	2 bdls
Miscellaneous	Nos. 1–13	1 bdl

DEPARTMENTS/MINISTRIES OF EDUCATION, HEALTH AND AGRICULTURE 1945 ONWARDS

In 1945 the Department of Education, Health and Lands was divided into three departments, and in 1947 these departments became ministries in the independent Government of India.

MINISTRY OF EDUCATION (DEPARTMENT OF EDUCATION 1945–7) 1947 ONWARDS

A2 SECTION (ADMINISTRATION)

Files	1946–51	34 bdls

D III(U) SECTION

Files	1948	4 carton boxes

E I SECTION (EDUCATION)

Indexes	1945–7	3 v
Files	1945–7	32 carton boxes

E I AND D III SECTION (SECONDARY EDUCATION)

Files	1948	7 bdls

E III–IV SECTIONS

Indexes	1948	2 v
Files	1945	2 carton boxes

GENERAL SECTION

Files	1945–9	14 bdls

RESETTLEMENT SECTION

Files	1945–8	1 carton box

MINISTRY OF HEALTH (DEPARTMENT OF HEALTH 1945–7) 1947 ONWARDS

HEALTH SECTION

Files	1945	7 bdls

PUBLIC HEALTH SECTION

Index	1945	1 v
Files	1945–6	8 bdls

PUBLIC HEALTH I SECTION

Files	1946	3 bdls

PUBLIC HEALTH II SECTION

Files	1946–7	10 bdls

PLANNING AND RESETTLEMENT SECTION

Files	1946–7	15 bdls

TRAINING SECTION

Files	1947	5 bdls

MINISTRY OF AGRICULTURE (DEPARTMENT OF AGRICULTURE 1945–7) 1947 ONWARDS

Indexes	1946, 1954–6	9 v

ADVISERS' SECTION

Files	1948	1 bdl

AGRICULTURE SECTION

Files	1945	3 bdls

CROPS SECTION

Files	1946–7	3 bdls

ECONOMICS AND STATISTICS SECTION

Files	1946	1 bdl

ESTABLISHMENT SECTION

Files	1946	1 bdl

FISHERIES SECTION
Files   1945–6   3 bdls

FOOD PRODUCTS SECTION
Files   1945   1 bdl

FOREST AND LANDS SECTION
Files   1945–6   1 bdl

GENERAL SECTION
Files   1946   1 bdl

INSTITUTES SECTION
Indexes   1948   4 v
Files   1948   13 carton boxes

LIVESTOCK SECTION
Files   1946–8   6 bdls

PLANNING SECTION
Files   1945   5 bdls

POLICY SECTION
Files   1946–7   11 bdls + 23 carton boxes

PROGRESS SECTION
Files   1946   1 bdl

REVENUE SECTION
Files   1945   2 bdls

SEEDS AND VEGETABLES SECTION
Files   1946–7   2 bdls

DIRECTORATE GENERAL OF HEALTH SERVICES
1896–1947

In April 1896 the Bengal, Madras and Bombay medical services were amalgamated into the Indian Medical Service, with the Surgeon-General (Government of India), his designation changed to Director General, at its head. In July 1914 the office of Sanitary Commissioner (Government of India) was amalgamated with the Indian Medical Service to become the Public Health Section of the Directorate. The Directorate came under the administrative control of the Home Department from its inception until 1918, of the Education Department from 1918 to 1921, of the Department of Education and Health from 1921 to 1923, of the Department of Education, Health and Lands from April 1923 until August 1945, and then of the Department of Health. In August 1947 the Department of Health and Director-General, Indian Medical Service became the Ministry of Health and Directorate-General, Health Services, and the post of Public Health Commission (Government of India) was abolished. Work relating to Air Raid Precautions (Medical) became the responsibility of the Directorate during World War II. Work relating to Planning and Purchase and Medical Stores was transferred to the Directorate-General, Industries and Supplies in July 1943. Work relating to the recruitment of nurses and medical officers for the army was transferred to the Medical Directorate, G.H.Q. India, in 1947.

D.G.I.M.S. (Miscellaneous) Medical Department, Bengal Folded and stray documents	1855–98 (many gaps)	14 bdls
Air Raid Precautions	1941–5	16 bdls
Cash	1943–6	15 bdls
	1947	2 files
Central Medical Employment Bureau	1946–7	4 bdls
Civil Medical Practitioners in army (General)	'	9 bdls, arranged alphabetically by names
Civil Medical Practitioners in Army (Licentiate)		5 bdls, arranged alphabetically by names
Drugs	1945–7	7 bdls
Rules	1901	4 bdls
General	1912–46	140 bdls
Indian Army Medical Corps	1943–5	10 bdls

Indian Medical Directorate (personal files)		126 bdls, arranged alphabetically by names
		99 bdls, arranged alphabetically by names and numbers
Indian Medical Directorate	1912–47	164 bdls
Indian Medical Service (personal files)		137 bdls, arranged alphabetically by names and numbers
Indian Medical Service (Personal I, II and III)		
Personal I and II combined	1912–47	295 bdls
Personal II	1946–7	8 bdls
Personal III	1947	3 bdls
Medical	1937–48	76 bdls
Nursing	1941–2	7 bdls
Planning and Development	1943	9 bdls
Public Health	1901–47	276 bdls
Recruitment (recruitment of medical officers and nurses for the army)	1941–7	107 bdls
Resettlement	1940–8	33 bdls, 32 boxes
Record	1942–7	16 bdls
Research	1914–46	182 bdls
Stores	1891–1941	267 bdls
Stores (general)	1942–5	34 bdls
Stores (import and export)	1942–6	11 bdls
Stores (indent I)	1940–7	39 bdls
Stores (indent II)	1942–6	28 bdls
Stores (planning)	1941–2	1 bdl
Civil provisioning	1942–3	1 bdl
Social insurance	1945–8	4 bdls
Indents (stores) F.R.	1946	2 bdls
Statistical	1942	7 bdls
Inspection Reports	1852–66	18 v

THE IMPERIAL COUNCIL OF AGRICULTURAL RESEARCH 1929–47

The Imperial Council of Agricultural Research came into existence as a separate department in May 1929. From January 1939 the Council was attached to the Department of Education, Health and Lands, and from 1945 to the Department (1947 Ministry) of Agriculture. The name of the Council was changed to the Indian Council of Agricultural Research in June 1947.

Agriculture Branch		
'B' proceedings	1930–45	162 bdls
'Deposit' proceedings	1930–3	2 bdls
Agriculture II Branch: 'B' proceedings	1938–42	11 bdls
Coffee Cess Branch: 'B' proceedings	1937–8	2 bdls
Crop Costing Branch: 'B' proceedings	1934–7	3 bdls
Finance Branch: 'B' proceedings	1944–5	2 bdls
General Branch		
'B' proceedings	1929–45	109 bdls
'Deposit' proceedings	1929–33	3 bdls
Imperial Bureau: 'B' proceedings	1933–4	1 bdl
Lac Cess Branch		
'B' proceedings	1934–41	16 bdls
'Deposit' proceedings	1932–3	1 bdl
Library Branch: 'B' proceedings	1933–45	18 bdls
Locust Branch		
'B' proceedings	1930–40	15 bdls
'Deposit' proceedings	1930–2	3 bdls
Marketing Branch: 'B' proceedings	1934	1 bdl
Oil Seeds Branch: 'B' proceedings	1933–4	3 bdls
Planning Branch: 'B' proceedings	1945	1 bdl
Publication Branch: 'B' proceedings	1930–45	25 bdls
Research Branch		
'B' proceedings	1929–30	2 bdls
'Deposit' proceedings	1929–30	1 bdl
Statistical Branch: 'B' proceedings	1933–45	17 bdls
Sugar (Institute-Development) Branch: 'B' proceedings	1936–45	32 bdls
Veterinary (Animal Husbandry) Branch		
'A' proceedings	1930–2	1 bdl
'B' proceedings	1930–45	96 bdls
'Deposit' proceedings	1930–3	1 bdl
Registers		
Diary registers (all branches)	1933–49	114 v
Proceedings register (Agricultural Branch B)	1929–33	2 v
Issue registers	1930–9	13 v

File registers	1930–45	70 v
Deposit registers	1929–37	3 v
Record register (General Branch 'A' and 'B')	1929–33	1 v
Receipt diary register (Accounts Branch)	1945	3 v

FINANCIAL DEPARTMENT 1860–79

A distinct Financial Department was first created in 1843. From 1879 to January 1905 it was part of the amalgamated Finance and Commerce Department, becoming a separate department again in January 1905, and a ministry in the independent Government of India in 1947.

Index	1860–79	36 v
Contents	1868–79	17 v
Proceedings volumes	1860–77	327 v

ACCOUNTS BRANCH

This branch included such subjects as money orders, banks, alienation of imperial revenue, estimates, loans, escheats, administration of the estates of intestates etc.

Proceedings volumes	1867–79	8 bdls, 17 v
'A' proceedings	1860–79	54 bdls
'B' proceedings	1861–79	1 bdl

ESTABLISHMENT BRANCH

Proceedings volumes	1860–3	36 v
'A' proceedings	1860–3	6 bdls
'B' proceedings	1861–2	1 bdl

EXPENDITURE BRANCH

Proceedings volumes	1863–79	9 bdls, 38 v
'A' proceedings	1863–79	29 v
'B' proceedings	1863–79	3 bdls

INCOME TAX BRANCH (TRANSFERRED FROM HOME DEPARTMENT 1861)

'A' and 'B' proceedings	1862–4	1 bdl

LEAVE BRANCH

Proceedings volumes	1867–79	3 bdls, 12 v
'A' proceedings	1860–79	21 bdls
'B' proceedings	1864–77	1 bdl

LICENCE TAX BRANCH (TRANSFERRED FROM HOME DEPARTMENT 1861)

	1862	1 file only

MINT AND CURRENCY BRANCH

Proceedings volumes	1867–79	2 bdls, 10 v
'A' proceedings	1860–79	8 bdls

MISCELLANEOUS BRANCH

Proceedings volumes	May–June 1876	2 v
'A' proceedings	1860–4	3 bdls
'B' proceedings	1862–4	1 bdl

PAY AND ALLOWANCES BRANCH

Proceedings volumes	1876–9	1 bdl, 10 v
'A' proceedings	1876–9	8 bdls
'B' proceedings	1876–9	1 bdl

PENSIONS AND GRATUITIES BRANCH

Proceedings volumes	1867–79	4 bdls, 10 v
'A' proceedings	1860–79	21 bdls
'B' proceedings	1862–78	1 bdl

SEPARATE REVENUE BRANCH

This branch was transferred from the Home Department in 1864, and dealt with assessed taxes, excise, opium, stamps and (from 1867) Post Offices. The work of the Post Office Branch of the Home Department was transferred to this branch in 1867.

Proceedings volumes	1867–79	8 bdls, 13 v
'A' proceedings	1864–79	24 bdls
'B' proceedings	1864–79	9 bdls
'C' proceedings	1876–9	1 bdl

FINANCE AND COMMERCE DEPARTMENT 1879–1905

Between 1879 and 1905 the Finance and Commerce Departments were amalgamated.

Index	1879–1905	173 v
Contents	1879–1904	45 v
Proceedings volumes	1880–6	18 v

ACCOUNTS AND FINANCE BRANCH

Index	1891–1902	6 v
Proceedings volumes	1879–1905	6 bdls, 199 v
'A' proceedings	1879–1905	128 bdls
'B' proceedings	1879–1905	17 bdls
'C' proceedings	1880–1905	5 bdls

COMMERCE AND TRADE BRANCH

Proceedings volumes	July–Dec. 1879	7 v
'A' proceedings	July–Dec. 1879	1 bdl
'B' proceedings	July–Dec. 1879	1 bdl

EXPENDITURE BRANCH

Proceedings volumes	July–Dec. 1879	6 v
'A' proceedings	July–Dec. 1879	1 bdl
'B' proceedings	July–Dec. 1879	1 bdl

LEAVE AND LEAVE ALLOWANCES BRANCH
(1880–1 LEAVE, ALLOWANCES, PENSIONS AND GRATUITIES BRANCH)

Index	1891–5	2 v
Proceedings volumes	1897–1905	3 bdls, 64 v
'A' proceedings	July 1879–Jan. 1905	23 bdls
'B' proceedings	1880–Jan. 1905	3 bdls
'C' proceedings	1903–4	1 v

MINT AND CURRENCY BRANCH

'A' Proceedings	July–Dec. 1879	1 bdl

PAY AND ALLOWANCES BRANCH [FOR 1880–1
SEE LEAVE, ALLOWANCES ETC. BRANCH ABOVE]

Index	1891–5	3 v
Proceedings volumes	July–Dec. 1879 and 1882–1905	60 v and 1 bdl
'A' proceedings	July–Dec. 1879 and 1882–1904	30 bdls
'B' proceedings	1882–1905	3 bdls
'C' proceedings	1894–1904	1 bdl

PENSIONS AND GRATUITIES BRANCH
[FOR 1880–1 SEE LEAVE, ALLOWANCES ETC. BRANCH ABOVE]

Index	1891–1900	2 v
Proceedings volumes	July 1879–Jan. 1905	66 v, 1 bdl
'A' proceedings	July 1879–Jan. 1905	40 bdls
'B' proceedings	July 1879–Jan. 1905	4 bdls
'C' proceedings	1889–Jan. 1905	1 bdl

SALARIES, ESTABLISHMENT AND OTHER EXPENDITURE BRANCH

Index	1891–5	6 v
Proceedings volumes	1884–1905	1 bdl, 81 v
'A' proceedings	1884–1904	43 bdls
'B' proceedings	1884–Jan. 1905	13 bdls
'C' proceedings	1885–1904	2 bdls

SEPARATE REVENUE BRANCH

Index	1890–1902	14 v
Index and contents	1882–3	1 v
Proceedings volumes	1879–1905	7 bdls and 171 v
'A' proceedings	July 1879–Jan. 1905	91 bdls
'B' proceedings	July 1879–Jan. 1905	41 bdls
'C' proceedings	1880–Jan. 1905	3 bdls

STATISTICS BRANCH

Proceedings volumes	July–Dec. 1879	7 v
'A' proceedings	Oct. 1879	1 file only

STATISTICS AND COMMERCE BRANCH

Index	1891–1903	22 v
Contents	May 1900–Feb. 1905	1 v
Proceedings volumes	March 1885–Feb. 1905	97 bdls
'A' proceedings	Mar. 1885–Jan. 1905	50 bdls
'B' proceedings	Mar. 1885–Feb. 1905	24 bdls
'C' proceedings	Mar. 1885–Feb. 1905	4 bdls

FINANCE DEPARTMENT 1905–47

In 1905 the Finance Department was separated once again from the Commerce Department.

Index	1905–23	59 v and 2 slips
Contents	1910–12	4 v
File volumes	1924–9	11 v

ACCOUNTS AND FINANCE BRANCH (FROM APRIL 1925 ACCOUNTS BRANCH)

Index	1915–28	12 v
Proceedings volumes	1905–24	90 v
'A' proceedings	Feb. 1905–Jan. 1925	71 bdls
'B' proceedings	Feb. 1905–Mar. 1925	50 bdls
'C' proceedings	Feb. 1905–Mar. 1925	48 bdls

ACCOUNTS BRANCH

Index	1925–8	4 v
File volumes	1927	1 v
Files	1925–9	12 bdls

BUDGET BRANCH

Index	1930–45	10 v
Files	1930–46	23 bdls
Ordinary files	1930–46	1 bdl

CASH BRANCH

Index	1925–37	3 v
Files	1925–42	1 bdl

CIVIL SERVICE REGULATION BRANCH

Index	1924–6	2 v
Files	1924–7	14 bdls

COMMUNICATION BRANCH

Files	1941–2	6 bdls

ESTABLISHMENT III AND ESTABLISHMENT SPECIAL BRANCH

Indexes	1944–6

[kept with Ministry of Finance Establishment III and Establishment Special Branch indexes]

EXPENDITURE I BRANCH

Index	1926–43	10 v
Files	1925–42	103 bdls
Deposit files	1932	1 bdl

EXPENDITURE II BRANCH

Index	1927 and 1937	2 v
Files	1927–42	75 bdls

FINANCE BRANCH

Index	1924–36	7 v
File volumes	1927	1 v
Files	1925–44	160 bdls
Ordinary files	1924–46	24 bdls

FINANCE I BRANCH

Files	1945–6	12 bdls

FINANCE II BRANCH

Files	1945–6	17 bdls

FINANCIAL ESTABLISHMENT BRANCH

Index	1924–6	3 v
Files	1924–7	15 bdls

GENERAL BRANCH

Files	1925–39	8 bdls

LEAVE AND LEAVE ALLOWANCES BRANCH

Index	1915–24	9 v
Proceedings volumes	1905–22	34 v
'A' proceedings	Feb. 1905–23	6 bdls
'B' proceedings	Feb. 1905–May 1924	5 bdls
'C' proceedings	Feb. 1905–May 1924	5 bdls

MILITARY FINANCE BRANCH AND FINANCIAL
ADVISER MILITARY FINANCE

Files	1906–43	19 bdls, 165 v

PAY AND ALLOWANCES BRANCH

Index	1915–24	8 v
Proceedings volumes	1905–23	37 v
'A' proceedings	Feb. 1805–June 1924	20 bdls
'B' proceedings	Feb. 1905–May 1924	32 bdls
'C' proceedings	Feb. 1905–May 1924	15 bdls

PENSIONS AND GRATUITIES BRANCH

Index	1915–24	7 v
Proceedings volumes	1904–23	35 v
'A' proceedings	Feb. 1905–May 1924	13 bdls
'B' proceedings	Feb. 1905–May 1924	15 bdls
'C' proceedings	Feb. 1905–May 1924	9 bdls

PLANNING BRANCH

Files	1944–6	15 bdls

REFORM BRANCH

Index	1937	I v
Files	1928–37	9 bdls

REGULATION I BRANCH

Index	1927–31	2 v
Files	1928–42	38 bdls

REGULATION II BRANCH

Index	1927–38	II v
Files	1926–42	61 bdls

SALARIES, ESTABLISHMENT AND OTHER EXPENDITURE BRANCH

Index	1915–24	8 v
Proceedings volumes	1905–22	39 v
'A' proceedings	Feb. 1905–Jan. 1925	20 bdls
'B' proceedings	Feb. 1905–Mar. 1925	46 bdls
'C' proceedings	Feb. 1905–May 1925	16 bdls

SCHEDULE BRANCH

Files	1930–2	1 bdl

SEPARATE REVENUE BRANCH [INCLUDES CUSTOMS ETC.]

Index	1915–24	7 v
Proceedings volumes	1905–22	67 v
'A' proceedings	Feb. 1905–Oct. 1923	39 bdls
'B' proceedings	Feb. 1905–Mar. 1924	26 bdls
'C' proceedings	Feb. 1905–Mar. 1924	13 bdls
Filed proceedings	1921–2	1 bdl

WAR BRANCH

Files	1941–3	18 bdls

DESPATCHES

Accounts despatches from secretary of state	1917–28	4 bdls, 2 v
Finance despatches from secretary of state	1860–1928	16 bdls, 74 v
Financial Funds despatches from secretary of state	1879–1914	2 v
Financial stores despatches from secretary of state	1879–1914	4 v
Despatches to secretary of state from Government of India	1860–1917	147 v
Judicial despatches from secretary of state	1886–1907	2 v
Military despatches from secretary of state	1881–1914	1 v
Political despatches from secretary of state	1889–1911	2 v
Public despatches from secretary of state	1879–1920	9 v
Revenue despatches from secretary of state	1884–1921	11 v
Finance despatches from secretary of state to Government of Bombay	1879–98	1 v
Finance despatches from Government of Bombay to secretary of state	1879–98	1 v
Financial stores despatches from secretary of state to Government of Bombay	1879–89	1 v
Financial stores despatches from secretary of state to Government of Madras	1879–89	1 v

MISCELLANEOUS GROUPS

Consolidated abstracts of receipts and disbursements, Hyderabad	1884–1900	9 v
Consolidated abstracts of receipts and disbursements, Indian and provincial governments	1870–1900	37 v

Expenditure shown under separate budget heads	1870–1	I v
Finance and revenue accounts	1911–23	II v
Receipts and disbursements of Home and Indian accounts	April 1912–Mar. 1920	I v
Financial statements and budget estimates	1909–23	15 v
Net military disbursements	1880–4	I v
Register for the office of the Controller-General	1884–93	I v
Register of sanctions, expenditure branch	1903–4	I v
Register of confidential 'B' and 'C' cases removed for destruction	1910–11	I v
Register of cases received in the Record Office (Finance Department) for former papers	1893–1914	I v
Miscellaneous file volumes	1870–8	8 v
Minutes and notes	1856–1915	3 bdls, 39 v
Report of the Indian Retrenchment Committee	1922–3	I v
Report of Lord Welby's Commission on Indian Expenditure, vol. II, appendix	1896	I v
Esher's Report, parts III–IX (Committee on Indian Home effective charges)	1920	I v
Report of the Public Accounts Committee on the accounts of 1921–2	1921–2	2 v
Audit report of the Army, Marine and Military works of the Government of India	1922–3	2 v
Appendices Indian Army Budget estimates	1909–24	II v
List of 'B' and 'C' proceedings of the Finance Department destroyed	1882–1913	I v
Graduation list of officers of the Financial Department	1871–3	3 v

Financial Department consultations	1860	1 bdl
Finance and Commerce Department confidential reports on the officers of the Postal Department	1894-1904	1 bdl

CENTRAL BOARD OF REVENUE 1924-47

The Central Board of Revenue was constituted on 1 April 1924 to control and manage the various heads of revenue. Although not a separate and independent department the Board was permitted to address communications directly to other departments. All matters concerning customs were entrusted to the Board, with the control and management of the income tax, and work relating to salt, opium, excise, and stamps.

Administration I: files		1 bdl
Administration (War): files	1945	1 bdl
Central Excise: files	1935-46	17 bdls
Central Excise (Tobacco): files	1943-6	6 bdls
Central Excise (Miscellaneous)		
(1) Central Excise, Madras	1920-49	1 bdl
(2) Records of the Assistant Controller of Excise, Baroda	1917-42	10 carton boxes
Customs		
'C' proceedings	1924	3 bdls
Files	1925-46	117 bdls
Customs II: files	1928-44	49 bdls
Customs (War): files	1939-46	9 bdls
Customs (Establishment)		
'C' proceedings	1924-5	2 bdls
Files	1925-46	82 bdls
Customs (Miscellaneous)		
(1) Records of the Collector of Customs, Bombay	1849-1923	2 bdls
(2) Records of the Collector of Customs, Calcutta	1860-1933	1 bdl
(3) Records of the Collector of Customs, Madras	1907-33	1 bdl
Excise—Opium: files	1925-46	101 bdls
General: files	1925-46	28 bdls
Income Tax		
'B' proceedings	1924	1 bdl

'C' proceedings	1924	5 bdls
Files	1925–46	155 bdls
Income Tax Administration: files	1937–46	31 bdls
Intoxicating Drugs		
'C' proceedings	1924–5	1 bdl
Filed proceedings	1924–5	1 bdl
Opium Administration: files	1938–46	5 bdls
Opium (Miscellaneous)		
(1) Allahabad, opium	1911–26	3 bdls
(2) Bengal, opium	1891–1912	2 bdls
Salt: files	1925–46	85 bdls
Salt II: files	1928–30	8 bdls
Salt: Establishment		
'A', 'B' and 'C' proceedings	1924	1 bdl
Salt (miscellaneous)		
(1) Bengal, salt. 'A' and 'B' proceedings	1874–1905	3 bdls
(2) Bombay, salt	1899–1925	8 bdls
(3) Madras, salt	1890–1925	34 bdls
Stamps		
'C' proceedings	1924–5	1 bdl
Files	1925–46	14 bdls

OFFICE OF THE SALT COMMISSIONER

This was a small separate office, part of the Financial Department and its successors, and from 1924 coming under the control of the Central Board of Revenue.

Accounts Branch	1927–46	20 bdls
Budget Branch	1876–1924	7 bdls
Establishment Branch	1878–1947	36 bdls
General Branch	1870–1946	68 bdls
Revenue Department (Salt Customs and Akbari)	1862–1909	72 v
Revenue (Customs)	1911–15	11 v

MINISTRY OF FINANCE 1947 ONWARDS

With the advent of independence in 1947 a Ministry of Finance was created.

BUDGET SECTION

Files	1947–8	6 bdls
Ordinary files	1947–8	1 bdl

ESTABLISHMENT SECTION

Establishment III index	1947–54	21 v
Establishment special index	1947–50	5 v
(includes also indexes for 1944–6 of Finance Department)		

EXTERNAL FINANCE SECTION

Files	1947	1 bdl

FINANCE SECTION

Finance I files	1947–8	10 bdls
Finance II files	1947–8	19 bdls

PLANNING SECTION

Planning I files	1947–8	7 bdls
Planning II files	1947	1 bdl

DEPARTMENT OF ECONOMIC AFFAIRS, STATE BANKS SECTION

1956	4 bdls

FOREIGN DEPARTMENT 1860–1914

(including records of successor bodies, FOREIGN AND POLITICAL DEPARTMENT 1914–37; DEPARTMENT OF EXTERNAL AFFAIRS 1937–1947; POLITICAL DEPARTMENT 1937–47; MINISTRY OF STATES 1947–54)

The Foreign Department of the Government of India was created in the reorganization of 1843, from the former Political, Foreign and Secret branches. The details of the business conducted within the various branches varied from time to time, but essentially the work of the Foreign Department was to deal with politics generally, to control relations with foreign states, the princely states in India and frontier and hill tribes, and to control the frontier districts and administration of various territories which came under its jurisdiction. Ajmer-Merwara, Assam, Baluchistan, British Burma, Central Provinces, Coorg, Hyderabad, Mysore and Rewa, North-West Frontier Provinces, Oudh and the Punjab were all controlled by the Foreign Department at some time. The department also dealt with the business relating to political prisoners, political pensions, honours and ceremonial, extradition and extra-territorial jurisdiction, grant of passports, and subjects later transferred to other departments such as electric telegraph (1867–70), the preparation of gazetteers (transferred to the Home Department in 1868) and various matters in the territories under its jurisdiction such as education (transferred to the Home Department in 1861), police and jails (transferred to the Home Department in 1862), revenue (transferred to the Revenue and Agriculture Department at various dates between 1871 and 1884), ecclesiastical, medical and other business. In 1920 business relating to emigration to Egypt, Palestine and Mesopotamia and to foreign countries other than Surinam was transferred to the Foreign Department from the Commerce Department.

From April 1860 to September 1861 the records of the department were divided simply into 'A' and 'B' proceedings, but from October 1861 to September 1882 the papers were dealt with in six different branches, namely Judicial, which dealt with all papers relating to civil courts, criminal courts, police (to 1862), *thagi* and *dakaiti* (see under pre-Mutiny records), and similar matters in those territories which came under the jurisdiction of the Foreign Department; Revenue, which dealt with all papers relating to the land-tax, special cesses, transit duties and customs in those territories; Revenue, Irrigation (from 1868); Finance, which dealt with all questions relating to funds for the support of contingents, pensions and Nizamat fund, and also prepared reports on the financial condition of native states and British provinces; Military, which dealt with all correspondence concerning the organization and discipline of the forces which came under the Foreign Department and questions of leave to England or out of India; Political, which dealt with all matters relating to the native states except those items specifically dealt with in other branches; and General, which dealt with all correspondence not included in the work of the branches, such as leave other than military, the clergy, medical department etc.

In September 1882 the office was divided into four branches, Internal, External, Frontier and General, but the former subject headings were not abolished until 1884, and for these two years the papers were recorded thus—'A' Judicial I(nternal), 'B' Military E(xternal), 'A' Revenue G(eneral) etc. The Frontier Branch recorded its papers with the External Branch to the end of August 1884 and the General Branch secret papers were recorded with those of the Internal Branch. The Internal Branch was concerned with relations with the native states and Bhutan and Sikkim. The External Branch dealt with relations with Baluchistan, Persia, Aden, Turkish Arabia, the Red Sea and Egypt, Nepal, Assam, Manipur, Burma, Siam, China, and foreign settlements in India. The Frontier Branch dealt with Afghanistan, Central Asia, the North-West Frontier, Kashmir, Chitral and Yarkand. The General Branch was concerned with personal and miscellaneous matters, such as appointments, leave and pay, political pensions etc. With the abolition of the subject headings in 1884 the papers were recorded as 'A' or 'B' proceedings within each branch. Secret papers were recorded in a separate series throughout the period.

As the work of the Foreign Department increased new branches were created and old branches divided. In 1906 the branches were as follows: Frontier Branch A, dealing with Afghanistan, Afghan refugees, Central Asia, Kashmir frontier, miscellaneous, newsletters and diaries, North-West Frontier, and petitions; Frontier Branch B, dealing with Baluchistan, confidential, Khorasan and Seistan, newsletters and diaries, and Persia; External Branch A, dealing with Aden, confidential, miscellaneous, Persian Gulf, pilgrim traffic, Red Sea and Somali Coast, Turkish Arabia, Zanzibar and East Africa; External Branch B, dealing with Assam, Bhutan, Burma, China, confidential, miscellaneous, Nepal, Siam, Sikkim and Tibet; Internal Branch A, dealing with Ajmer, arms and armament returns, Baroda, Bombay, census, confidential, famine, foreign settlements, Madras, miscellaneous, Mysore, petitions, plague, Punjab, Rajputana, *thagi* and *dakaiti*; and titles and salutes; Internal Branch B, dealing with Bengal, Central India, Central Provinces, confidential, exhibitions, Hyderabad, Imperial Cadet Corps, Imperial Service troops, Kashmir (internal), local corps, miscellaneous, petitions, railways, state prisoners, and United Provinces; General Branch, dealing with appointments, books, foreign service, leave and furlough, miscellaneous office matters, pay and allowances, personal confidential files, political pensions, returns and reports, service pensions, and *toshakhana*; Cypher Branch (cr. 1904), dealing with cypher codes, foreign consuls and decorations; Registrar's Branch (cr. 1903–5), dealing with the general registry of papers coming to the office etc.; Issue Branch (cr. 1903), concerned with the fair copying and despatch of papers; Persian Branch (cr. 1903–5), which prepared translations; and Toshakhana (i.e. storehouse) Branch which had custody of presents made to viceroy and officers of the government, purchased gifts for native chiefs and others, arranged for the entertainment of government guests, had the custody of insignia and darbar paraphernalia, and made arrangements for the darbar reception of chiefs.

An attempt was made in 1907 to relieve the pressure on the department by transferring all non-political business emanating from British Baluchistan, the agency territories, and British areas administered by the governor-general in Council in the native states, including cantonments, to other departments. Various items of business were transferred to the Army Department (army except business connected with the Imperial Service troops, cantonments, Cantonment Magistrates' Department and volunteers), the Finance Department (general finance, separate revenue, currency and banking, Civil Account Department, Army Finance and Military Accounts Department), and the Revenue and Agriculture Department (forests, land revenue except that of jaghirs in the North-West Frontier Provinces and British Baluchistan, land surveys, agriculture, the civil veterinary administration, meteorology and famine). None, however, was transferred to the Home Department, which was itself suffering under a great increase of business.

The problem of relieving the pressure of work on the department was solved more satisfactorily in 1914 by redesignating it Foreign and Political Department, with two secretaries, foreign secretary and political secretary. The Foreign section dealt with all matters relating to the frontiers of India and to territories outside India through its General (foreign cases) Establishment 'A' and 'B' (foreign cases), External 'A' and 'B' and Frontier branches. The Political section dealt with all matters concerning the native states and areas administered by the Foreign and Political Department through its General (political cases), Internal 'C' (honours etc.), Establishment 'A' (political cases) and 'B' (political cases), Internal 'A' and 'B', Cypher, Registrars, and Library branches.

In 1923 there was another reorganization of the branches, and their designation was changed as follows: Internal 'A' became Political; Internal 'B', Internal; Establishment 'A', Establishment; Establishment 'B', Accounts; General 'A', General; General 'B', Honours; Frontier remained the same; External 'A', External; and External 'B', Mid Asia. The distribution of work among the reorganized branches was thus:

Political, political matters, not specially classified, relating to Indian states; Internal, matters in Indian states and administered areas relating to jurisdiction, railways, customs, excise, opium, salt, petitions for mercy, cantonments, military employment, police, extradition, rights of British subjects in Indian states; Establishment, all matters concerning Political and Medical Departments, and miscellaneous establishments, appointments, and pensions; Accounts; Honours; Frontier, matters relating to the North-West Frontier, Baluchistan, Afghanistan, and revision of the map of India; External, relations with foreign countries, Gilgit, Bolshevik intrigue, and League of Nations; Mid Asia/Near East, matters relating to Egypt, the Somali Coast, the Red Sea, Turkey, Palestine, Aden and hinterland, Arabia, Iraq, Persian Gulf and Persia, and pilgrims in the Hedjaz; General, political pensions, commercial treaties and conventions, official publications and maps, returns and reports, arms licences, jails, convicts, sanitation, plague and cholera, foreign settlements, foreign consuls, passports and permits, emigration, exhibitions, conferences and congresses, petitions, map cases and miscellaneous.

A Reforms Branch was created in April 1928, which took over work from both the Political and Internal Branches including the acquisition by ruling princes and chiefs and notables of property in British India, visits of British officials and Europeans and others to Indian states, chiefs' colleges, employment in Indian states (excluding military), matters relating to the reforms and the chamber of princes and standing committee (except such as fell under the technical headings of E and A branches), land revenue settlements, irrigation, forests, aviation, posts, telegraphs, telephones, geology, mines, mining concessions and industrial concerns, education (excluding education of ruling princes and chiefs), census, archaeology, epigraphy, zoology, returns of births and deaths, execution of commissions and service of summons issued by Indian state courts and by courts in British dominions and colonies.

A Special Branch was created in 1930 to deal with the work arising from the Butler Committee's Report and cognate subjects, and to consider the question of the future economic and financial relations between British India and the Indian states in connection with the discussions to take place at the Round Table Conference.

Two temporary branches were created in 1935, the Earthquake, to deal with the Quetta earthquake, and the Federation, to deal with all work relating to the proposed federal system (1935 Act).

In 1937 the Foreign and Political Department was split into two, the External Affairs Department and the Political Department. The External Affairs Department included the following branches: Accounts; External, which dealt with all matters relating to Tibet, Nepal, Sinkiang, Gilgit, Bhutan, Sikkim, China, Japan, Russian refugees expeditions, French and Portuguese settlements, estates of Indians dying abroad, expenditure in connection with the Lhasa Mission and Sikkim Agency, the Burma Boundary Commission, Assam Rifles, and extradition; Frontier, which was concerned with all business relating to the North-West Frontier, Baluchistan, and Afghanistan; General, which was concerned with foreign consuls in India, honours, ceremonials, passports, visas, and other matters not coming within the scope of other branches; Near East, which dealt with relations with the Persian Gulf, Aden, Iraq, Turkey, Egypt, Palestine, Afghan refugees, Somali coast, Abyssinia, the Red Sea, and Arabia; Establishments; Central Cypher Bureau; Issue; Registry Section; Library; and Toshakhana.

In 1947 the Department of External Affairs became the Ministry of External Affairs and Commonwealth Relations in the independent

Government of India, and the Political Department was redesignated the Ministry of States (abolished 1954).

The records of the External Affairs Department and the Political Department (from 1937) are at present kept with those of the Foreign (and Political) Department, but probably they will eventually be kept separately and the papers of the Political Department at present described with those of the Political Branch, Foreign Department will be extracted. The papers of the Ministry of States will be kept as a continuation of those of the Political Department.

FOREIGN DEPARTMENT
INDEXES

Consolidated (from 1937 split into External Affairs and Political)	1860–1951	426 v, including spare copies
Diaries of letters issued	1859–72	36 v
Diaries of letters received (including camp diaries)	1859–80	

NON-SECRET RECORDS, APRIL 1860–SEPTEMBER 1861

Part 'A' consultations	1860–1	28 bdls
'A' proceedings volumes	1860–1	39 v
Part 'B' consultations	1860–1	5 bdls
'B' proceedings volumes	1860–1	23 v

NON-SECRET RECORDS, OCTOBER 1861–AUGUST 1884: ELECTRIC TELEGRAPH BRANCH

Index	1867–70	5 v
'A' proceedings	1868–70	5 boxes
'B' proceedings	1867–70	1 bdl
Despatches to secretary of state	1867–9	1 box

NON-SECRET RECORDS, OCTOBER 1861–AUGUST 1884: FINANCE BRANCH

Indexes	1862–8	12 v
Despatches to secretary of state	1865–7	4 v
Despatches from secretary of state (see below Mixed Des-	1862–79	3 bdls

patches, which contains
despatches for all branches)

'A' proceedings	1861–82 (with gaps)	36 bdls
'B' proceedings	1861–82 (with a few gaps)	30 bdls
'A' Finance E	1883–4 (with gaps)	1 bdl
'B' Finance E	1882–4 (with gaps)	1 bdl
'A' Finance G	1882–4 (with gaps)	3 bdls
'B' Finance G	1882–4	4 bdls
'A' Finance I	1883–4	2 bdls
'B' Finance I	1882–4 (with gaps)	

NON-SECRET RECORDS, OCTOBER 1861–AUGUST 1884: GENERAL BRANCH

Indexes	1862–7	12 v
Despatches to secretary of state	1865–7, 1862–78	4 v, 7 bdls
Despatches from secretary of state (see Mixed Despatches, below)		
'A' proceedings	1861–82	134 bdls, 12 v
'B' proceedings	1861–82	65 bdls
'A' General E	1882–4	6 bdls
'B' General E	1882–4 (gaps)	1 bdl
'A' General G	1882–4 (gap)	7 bdls
'B' General G	1882–4	5 bdls
'A' General I	1882–4 (gaps)	13 bdls
'B' General I	1882–4	4 bdls

NON-SECRET RECORDS, OCTOBER 1861–AUGUST 1884: JUDICIAL BRANCH

Indexes	1862–7	12 v
Despatches from secretary of state	1859–63, 1860–7	1 v, 1 bdl
Despatches to secretary of state	1865–7	4 v
	1862–79	2 bdls
'A' proceedings	1861–82 (gaps)	57 bdls
'B' proceedings	1861–82 (gaps)	6 bdls
'A' Judicial E	1882–4 (gaps)	1 bdl
'B' Judicial E	Jan. 1884	1 proceeding only

'A' Judicial G	Jan.–Feb. 1883	1 bdl
'B' Judicial G		nil
'A' Judicial I	1882–4	5 bdls
'B' Judicial I	1882–4 (gaps)	1 bdl

NON-SECRET RECORDS, OCTOBER 1861–AUGUST 1884:
MILITARY BRANCH

Indexes	1862–7	11 v
Despatches to secretary of state	1865–7 (gaps), 1862–74 (gaps)	2 v, 1 bdl
Despatches from secretary of state (see Mixed Despatches, below)		
'A' proceedings	1861–84 (gaps)	12 bdls
'B' proceedings	1861–82 (gaps)	4 bdls
'A' Military E	1883, May–Dec. (gaps)	1 bdl
'B' Military E		nil
'A' Military G	1882–4 (gaps)	1 bdl
'B' Military G	1882–4 (gaps)	1 bdl
'A' Military I	1882–4 (gaps)	1 bdl
'B' Military I	1883–4 (gaps)	in bundle with 'B' Military G

NON-SECRET RECORDS, OCTOBER 1861–AUGUST 1884:
POLITICAL BRANCH

Despatches from secretary of state	1860–80 (gaps)	10 bdls, 33 v
Despatches to secretary of state	1860–83 (gaps)	77 bdls, 53 v
'A' proceedings volumes	1861–80 (gaps)	273 v
'B' proceedings volumes	1861–4 (gaps)	55 v
'A' proceedings	1861–82	568 bdls, 1 v
'B' proceedings	1861–82 (gap)	64 bdls
'A' Political E	1882–4	43 bdls
'B' Political E	1882–4 (gaps)	2 bdls
'A' Political G	1882–4	5 bdls
'B' Political G	1882–4 (gaps)	1 bdl
'A' Political I	1882–4	35 bdls
'B' Political I	1882–4 (gaps)	2 bdls

NON-SECRET RECORDS, OCTOBER 1861–AUGUST 1884:
REVENUE BRANCH

Indexes	1862–7	12 v
Despatches to secretary of state	1865–7, 1862–79 (gaps)	6 v, 5 bdls
Despatches from secretary of state (including despatches of Revenue Irrigation Branch)	1865–7 1860–7 (gaps)	6 v 1 bdl
'A' proceedings	1861–82 (gaps)	87 bdls
'B' proceedings	1861–82	10 bdls
'A' Revenue E	1883–4 (gaps)	1 bdl
'B' Revenue E		nil
'A' Revenue G		nil
'B' Revenue G	July 1883	1 proceeding only
'A' Revenue I	1882–4 (gaps)	3 bdls
'B' Revenue I	1882–4 (gaps)	1 bdl

NON-SECRET RECORDS, OCTOBER 1861–AUGUST 1884:
REVENUE IRRIGATION BRANCH

Despatches to and from secretary of state (see Revenue Despatches, above)		
'A' proceedings	1868–82 (gaps)	3 bdls
'B' proceedings	1869–78 (gaps)	1 bdl
'A' and 'B' Revenue Irrigation E		nil
'A' and 'B' Revenue Irrigation G		nil
'A' Revenue Irrigation I	1883–4	1 bdl
'B' Revenue Irrigation I		nil

NON-SECRET RECORDS, OCTOBER 1861–AUGUST 1884:
MIXED DESPATCHES

Mixed despatches to secretary of state (comprising despatches of almost all branches)	1862–73 (gaps)	4 v
Mixed despatches from secretary of state	1860–79 (gaps)	5 v, 1 bdl

NON-SECRET RECORDS, POST SEPTEMBER 1884:
ACCOUNTS BRANCH

Files	1922–40	229 bdls
Originals	1922–40	10 bdls
File registers	1930–3 ⎫	1 bdl
File movement registers	1922–3 ⎭	
Records	1940–7	[no bulk]

NON-SECRET RECORDS, POST SEPTEMBER 1884:
AITCHISON TREATIES BRANCH

Files	1933	5 bdls

NON-SECRET RECORDS, POST SEPTEMBER 1884:
CASH BRANCH

Files	1938–40	7 bdls

NON-SECRET RECORDS, POST SEPTEMBER 1884:
CROWN OFFICE BRANCH

Files	1937	1 box (belonging to Political Dept.)
	1942	

NON-SECRET RECORDS, POST SEPTEMBER 1884:
EARTHQUAKE BRANCH

Files	1935–7	10 bdls
Originals	1935–6	1 bdl

NON-SECRET RECORDS, POST SEPTEMBER 1884:
ESTABLISHMENT BRANCH

'A' proceedings	1908–22 (gaps)	47 bdls
'B' proceedings	1908–23 (gaps)	313 bdls
Deposit proceedings/tables	1908–23 (gaps)	10 bdls
Originals (Deposit)	1913–21 (gaps)	1 bdl
Files (secret and non-secret)	1922–41	191 bdls (with 1 bdl of Political Dept. 1937–40)
Originals (secret and non-secret)	1922–39 (gaps)	18 bdls

Movement registers	1922–33	2 bdls
File registers	1931–3 (gaps)	1 bdl
Records	1941–7	[no bulk]

NON-SECRET RECORDS, POST SEPTEMBER 1884: EXTERNAL BRANCH

'A' proceedings	1884–1921	258 bdls
'B' proceedings	1884–1923 (gap Feb. 1922)	275 bdls
Deposit proceedings (tables/ proceedings)	1882–1923 (gaps)	16 bdls
Files (secret and non-secret)	1922–41	163 bdls
Originals (secret and non-secret)	1923–40	41 bdls
Issue registers	1937–45	2 bdls
File movement registers	1922–3	1 bdl
Records	1941–5	[no bulk]

NON-SECRET RECORDS, POST SEPTEMBER 1884: FEDERATION BRANCH
(created in 1935 to apply new Constitution Bill)

Files	1935–41	19 bdls
Originals	1935–9	30 bdls

NON-SECRET RECORDS, POST SEPTEMBER 1884: FOREIGN OFFICE BRANCH

Files	1925–40	49 bdls
Originals	1926–37 (gaps)	1 bdl

NON-SECRET RECORDS, POST SEPTEMBER 1884: FRONTIER BRANCH

'A' proceedings	1884–1922 (gaps)	142 bdls
'B' proceedings	1884–1923 (gaps)	254 bdls
Deposit proceedings and tables	1884–1923 (gaps)	9 bdls
Files (secret and non-secret)	1922–41	219 bdls
Originals (secret and non-secret)	1922–41	114 bdls
File movement registers	1922–3	1 bdl

NON-SECRET RECORDS, POST SEPTEMBER 1884:
GENERAL BRANCH

'A' proceedings	1884–1922 (gaps)	101 bdls
'B' proceedings	1884–1923 (gaps)	383 bdls
Deposit tables/proceedings	1881–1922 (gaps)	16 bdls
Files (secret and non-secret)	1922–41	175 bdls (including some Political Dept. files)
Originals (secret and non-secret)	1922–41	12 bdls
File movement registers	1922–3	1 bdl
Records	1941–6	[no bulk]

NON-SECRET RECORDS, POST SEPTEMBER 1884:
HONOURS BRANCH

Files	1923–37	33 bdls
	1946	1 file
Originals	1923–37	17 bdls
Records	1937–46	[no bulk]

NON-SECRET RECORDS, POST SEPTEMBER 1884:
INTERNAL BRANCH

'A' proceedings	1884–1921 (gaps)	625 bdls
Originals	1907–22	123 bdls
'B' proceedings	1884–1923 (gaps)	612 bdls
Originals	1900–22	91 bdls
Deposit proceedings/tables	1883–1922 (gaps)	37 bdls
Originals	1910–21 (gaps)	2 bdls
Files (secret and non-secret, during 1934–41 divided into 'A' and 'B')	1922–42	214 bdls
Originals (secret and non-secret)	1922–41	70 bdls
'A' proceedings (Coronation Darbar)	Nov. 1912	1 bdl
'B' proceedings (Coronation Darbar)	1912–14 (gaps)	19 bdls
Deposit proceedings/tables (Coronation Darbar)	1912–14 (gaps)	4 bdls
Originals (Coronation Darbar)	Apr.–Dec. 1912 (gaps)	4 bdls

Press cuttings and the military arrangement report (1 vol.) re Coronation Darbar of 1911–12	1911–12	1 bdl
Records	1942–7	[no bulk]

NON-SECRET RECORDS, POST SEPTEMBER 1884:
MID ASIA (FROM MAY 1925, NEAR EAST) BRANCH

Files (secret and non-secret)	1921–40	180 bdls
Originals (secret and non-secret)	1922–35	53 bdls
Records	1940–1	[no bulk]

NON-SECRET RECORDS, POST SEPTEMBER 1884:
MIDDLE EAST BRANCH

Files	1944–5	1 bdl of 4 files only

NON-SECRET RECORDS, POST SEPTEMBER 1884:
PASSPORT BRANCH

Indexes	1862–4	3 v
Despatch books	1848–72	3 v
Files	1946	1 bdl of 1 file only

NON-SECRET RECORDS, POST SEPTEMBER 1884:
POLITICAL BRANCH

Files	1922–43 (gaps)	84 bdls
Originals	1922–43 (gaps)	30 bdls
Records	1943–7	[no bulk]

NON-SECRET RECORDS, POST SEPTEMBER 1884:
REFORMS BRANCH

'A' proceedings	1920–2 (gaps)	3 bdls
Originals	1920–2	4 bdls
'B' proceedings	1920–2 (gaps)	6 bdls
Originals	1920–1	4 bdls
Deposit proceedings	1922	1 bdl
Files (secret and non-secret)	1928–34	43 bdls
Originals (secret and non-secret)	1928–34	7 bdls

NON-SECRET RECORDS, POST SEPTEMBER 1884:
SPECIAL BRANCH

Files	1930–1	12 bdls
Originals	1930–1	2 bdls

NON-SECRET RECORDS, POST SEPTEMBER 1884:
TOSHAKHANA BRANCH

Files	1925–40 (gaps)	4 bdls
Salary bills	1871–8	2 v

NON-SECRET RECORDS, POST SEPTEMBER 1884:
WAR BRANCH

Files	1939–40	6 bdls
Files	1940–5	[no bulk]
Diaries and despatch registers	1942–6	2 bdls

SECRET RECORDS

Where possible secret files after 1922–3 are amalgamated with non-secret records.

Secret despatches from secretary of state	1860–1901 (gaps)	7 v
Secret despatches to secretary of state	1860–99 (gaps)	43 v
	1860–83 (gaps)	32 bdls

SECRET RECORDS: CYPHER BUREAU

Deposit G proceedings	1898–1910	2 bdls
Deposit proceedings	1910–32	15 bdls
Deposit E proceedings	1903–8 (gaps)	1 bdl
Confidential proceedings	1908–39	17 bdls

SECRET RECORDS: SECRET ESTABLISHMENT BRANCH

Proceedings volumes (unbound)	1908–21	3 bdls
Proceedings	1908–21	10 bdls
Originals	1908–21	11 bdls
Confidential 'A' proceedings	1910–17 (gap 1912)	1 bdl
Confidential 'B' proceedings	1911–22	4 bdls
Deposit proceedings	1913–21 (gaps)	1 bdl
Records	1921–37	[no bulk]

SECRET RECORDS: SECRET HOME BRANCH

roceedings volumes	1868–71	1 bdl
Proceedings	1868–71	7 bdls

SECRET RECORDS: SECRET INDIA BRANCH

Proceedings volumes	1869–71	2 bdls
Proceedings	1869–71	11 bdls

SECRET RECORDS: SECRET INTERNAL BRANCH

Proceedings volumes	1883–1922	41 bdls
Proceedings	1882–1922	96 bdls
Originals	1905–22	74 bdls
Confidential 'A'		
Section 'A' proceedings (printed and originals)	1891–1915 (gaps)	6 bdls
Section 'B' proceedings (printed and originals)	1891–1907 (gaps)	1 bdl
Confidential 'B'		
Section 'A' proceedings	1891–1918 (gaps)	2 bdls
Section 'B' and 'C' proceedings (printed and originals)	1891–1920 (gaps)	1 bdl
Deposit proceedings	1910–23	6 bdls
Issue registers	1890–1908	1 bdl

SECRET RECORDS: SECRET MISCELLANEOUS BRANCH

Proceedings volumes	1870	1 bdl
Proceedings	1870–1	2 bdls

SECRET RECORDS: SECRET REFORMS BRANCH

Proceedings volumes	1920–2	1 bdl
Proceedings	1920–2	2 bdls
Originals	1920–2	5 bdls

SECRET RECORDS: SECRET BRANCH

Index	1876–80	1 v
Proceedings volumes	1871–80	27 bdls, 11 v
Proceedings	1871–82	192 bdls
Originals	Aug. 1882	2 bdls

SECRET RECORDS: SECRET EXTERNAL

Proceedings volumes (un-bound)	1883–1923	
Proceedings	1882–1923	5
Deposit proceedings	1908–22	1 b
Originals	1882–1923 (gaps)	258 b
Confidential External 'A', 'B' and 'C' sections	1891–1922	15 bdls
Originals	1891–1921	8 bdls
Issue registers	1885–1905	2 bdls

SECRET RECORDS: SECRET FRONTIER BRANCH

Proceedings volumes (un-bound)	1884–1923	83 bdls
Proceedings	1884–1923	314 bdls
Originals	1905–23	105 bdls
Confidential proceedings volumes 'A' and 'B' (un-bound)	1891–1908	1 bdl
Confidential 'A' proceedings	1891–1921 (gaps)	4 bdls
Originals	1891–1921 (gaps)	9 bdls
Confidential 'B' proceedings	1891–1922 (gaps)	7 bdls
Frontier Watch and Ward Committee proceedings	1936	1 bdl
North-West Frontier Enquiry Committee Report	1922	3 v in 1 bdl
Originals	1922	2 bdls
Issue registers	1891–1905	1 bdl
Diary registers	1909–18	1 bdl

SECRET RECORDS: SECRET GENERAL BRANCH

Proceedings volumes	1905–22	9 bdls
Proceedings	1883, 1905–22	20 bdls
Originals	1905–22	19 bdls
Confidential 'A' proceedings	1907–18	2 bdls
Originals	1906–18	1 bdl
Confidential 'B'	1891–1921 (gaps)	3 bdls
Originals	1904–16	1 bdl
Deposit proceedings	1913–22 (gaps)	1 bdl
Originals	1913–18	1 bdl

SECRET RECORDS: SPECIAL BUREAU OF INFORMATION (SECRET)
Set up in January 1920 to check the presence of Bolshevik agents in India.

| Weekly reports | Feb.–Dec. 1920 | 1 bdl |
| Originals | 1920 | 2 bdls |

SECRET RECORDS: SECRET SUPPLEMENTARY BRANCH

| Proceedings volumes | 1878–81 | 10 bdls |
| Proceedings | 1878–81 | 65 bdls |

SECRET RECORDS: SECRET WAR BRANCH

Proceedings volumes	1914–20	5 bdls
Proceedings	1914–41 (gaps)	44 bdls
Originals	1914–41 (gaps)	44 bdls
'A' proceedings	1914–19 (gap 1918)	1 bdl
Originals	1914–19	1 bdl
'B' proceedings	1914–20	12 bdls
Originals	1914–20	9 bdls
Deposit proceedings	1915–18	1 bdl

MINOR GROUPS OF RECORDS

Darbar ceremonial proceedings: secret as well as non-secret proceedings pertaining to various darbars.

| | 1826–1914 | 5 bdls, 19 v |

Papers relating to the Orders of the Indian Empire

| | 1876–90 | 7 bdls |

Mussoorie and Rawalpindi Conference: cash-books, contingent bills etc. of the Indo-Afghan Trade Conference.

| | 1919–20 | 1 carton box |

Notes: duplicates of some of the more important notes, available also in the Foreign Department proceedings, arranged by serial numbers, not chronologically. Subject list available.

	1860–1905	60 bdls
Papers belonging to the Seistan Agency	1870	1 bdl
Papers relating to the Order of the Star of India	1861–90	19 bdls

Tours in India. Papers relating to the tours of:

| Prince of Wales | 1920–2 | 4 bdls |

Duke of Connaught	1920–1	3 bdls
Prince Arthur of Connaught	1924–5	3 bdls
Prince of Sweden	1926–7	2 bdls
King and Queen of Belgium	1925	2 bdls
Papers of the Thagi and Dakaiti Department	1889–97	1 box
Kabul Mission papers	1920–3	3 bdls
British Trade Delegation, Kabul	1922–3	1 bdl
Frontier Watch and Ward Committee	1936	1 bdl

MISCELLANEOUS RECORDS

'Looshai File', v. 2 [v. 1 missing]   1 folio v

Official correspondence and papers relating to the Lushai raids in Hill Tipperah, Cachar and Manipur, and to the Lushai Expeditionary Force 1871–2.

Frederick Henvey (with assistance of H. M. Durand), *Note of correspondence in the Foreign Office of the Government of India relating to the subsidiary and contingent forces of Hyderabad* (Calcutta, Foreign Dept. Press, 1874)

Translation of Nazim Ibrahim's narrative of his tour from Kabul to Bokhara, Khiva etc., under instructions from D. C. Macnabb, Commissioner and Superintendent at Peshawar, 1873 (Calcutta, Foreign Dept. Press, 1875)

Papers relating to the negotiation of a Treaty of Commerce and Extradition with the Government of Portuguese India 1877.

Papers relating to Portuguese trade and privileges

Part 1	1821, 1870–6	1 v
Part 2	1876–7	1 v
Part 3	1877	1 v

Note on the ports of Carwar and Marmagao, with appendices, by T. C. Hope: And, Memorandum by Captain Bythesea, consulting naval officer with the Government of India, on the same subject. To accompany the report of the delegates to negociate a treaty of commerce with Portugal, dated 11 August 1877 (Simla, Government Central Branch Press, 1877)

Despatch (no. 38, 21 August 1877) from the Government of Bombay to the secretary of state, enclosing *An appeal...by Zalla Verabhai Narsungjee... of Kittywar...against an order...relating to the division of land in 3 villages between co-sharers*, with appendices containing documents relating to the appeals.

Précis of correspondence regarding railways in Native States, part II, Down to the end of the year 1883, by J. S. Crawford (Calcutta, Foreign Dept. Press, 1884)

Despatch from Governor of Natal to the Viceroy of India, 9 January 1897, with enclosures (including a copy of his despatch to the Colonial Secretary of the same date about the recruitment of emigrants in India), and newspaper cuttings 31 December 1896–16 January 1897. The cuttings contain protests against the migration of Indians to Natal, and many relate to M. K. Gandhi.

POLITICAL DEPARTMENT

The records of the Political Department for 1937–54 are at present kept with those of the Political Branch of the Foreign (Foreign and Political) Department, but they will probably be extracted at a later date and kept separately. The papers of the Ministry of States will then be kept as a continuation of those of the Political Department.

MINISTRY OF STATES 1947–54

After independence the Political Department was redesignated Ministry of States. Once the integration of the former princely states into the Republic of India had been completed in 1954 the Ministry was abolished and the remaining work was transferred to the Ministry of Home Affairs. The records of the Ministry of States are not yet sorted and it is impossible to give the bulk.

Index	1947–54
Accounts Branch. Files	1947–9
Communication Branch. Files	1949–51
Defence and Security Branch. Files	1949
Establishment Branch. Files	1947–9
Federal Financial Integration Branch. Files	1949–51
Internal Branch. Files	1947–8
Hyderabad Branch. Files	1948–50
Judicial and General Branch. Files	1949–50
Kashmir Branch. Files	1948
Labour and Agriculture Branch. Files	1949–50
Political Branch. Files	1947–54
Services Branch. Files	1949–50

HOME DEPARTMENT 1860–1947

The Home Department of the Government of India, which had been created in the reorganization of 1843, continued as a separate department until 1947 except for one short period, 1879–81, when the department was part of the Home, Revenue and Agriculture Department. In the independent Government of India it was transformed into the Ministry of Home Affairs. The Home Department dealt with law and justice, jails and police, civil service questions, internal politics, judicial and administrative establishments, census, and a number of other subjects which were later transferred to younger departments. In addition, provinces administered through chief commissionerships, and known as 'minor administrations' were administered under the direct control of the Central Government acting mainly through the Home Department, except for Ajmer-Merwara, British Baluchistan, and the North-West Frontier Province, which were controlled through the Foreign and Political Department.

The original branches of the Home Department in 1843 were Revenue, Separate Revenue, General, Marine, Judicial, Legislative, and Ecclesiastical, but as the work of the department increased new branches were formed, which in turn sometimes developed into separate departments or were transferred to other (younger) departments during reorganizations of the secretariat. In 1860 the branches of the Home Department were Ecclesiastical (1843–1910), Education (1857–1910), Electric Telegraph (1856–67), Judicial (1843–1947), Marine (1843–67), Post Office (1856–67), Public (1847–1947), Revenue (1843–71), and Separate Revenue (1843–64). The Legislative Branch, which had been abolished in 1854, was revived in 1861 (1861–9). The records of a number of these branches, however, are now to be found with those of the departments to which they were later transferred, namely: Ecclesiastical and Education Branches with the records of the Department of Education, Health and Lands; Marine Branch with the records of the Military Department; Legislative Branch with the records of the Legislative Department; and Revenue Branch with the records of the Department of Education, Health and Lands (Revenue and Agriculture wing). The records of a number of branches of the Home Department created at later dates are also now kept with those of the Department of Education, Health and Lands, where they were transferred on the creation of the Department of Education in December 1910, or the Department of Education and Health in 1921, namely: Archaeology (1881–7, 1905–10), Books and Publications (1880–1910), Examinations (1874–1910), Local Boards (1889–1910), Medical (1873–1921), Municipalities (1871–1910), and Sanitary (1868–1910). The records of the Home

Department Patents Branch (1875–88) are also kept with those of the Department of Education, Health and Lands (Revenue and Agriculture wing).

Indexes	1868–1947	Yearly, 1879 and 1881 are half-yearly, Jan.–June, July–Dec.
Index and Contents	1885–97	Half-yearly, Jan.–June 1891 wanting
Contents	1880–9	Monthly, 1881–6 consolidated in one volume; 1888 wanting; 1890–8 wanting
Contents	1899–1910	Half-yearly
Index and Contents	1911–12	1 bdl
Index	1886–7	1 bdl
Consolidated indexes	1858–64; 1865–70; 1871–5; 1876–80; 1881–5; 1886–90; 1891–5; 1896–1900; 1900–6; 1917–18; 1919–20; 1921–2; 1927–9; and 1901–5, incomplete	

ACCOUNTS AND GENERAL BRANCH

Files	1947	5 bdls

ACCOUNTS AND GENERAL: PRISONER OF WAR BRANCH

Files	1939–42	2 bdls

APPOINTMENTS BRANCH

Files	1946–7	5 bdls

SPECIAL APPOINTMENTS BRANCH

Files	1947	1 bdl

CENSUS BRANCH

Until 1871 census matters were dealt with in the Public Branch of the Home Department; from 1871 to 1879 in the Statistics Branch of the Revenue, Agriculture and Commerce Department; and from 1879 to 1881 in the Home, Revenue and Agriculture Department. From 1911 to 1923 the Census Branch came under the Department of Education and the Department of Education and Health, but the records are kept here with those of the Home Department. After 1923 the business was transferred to the Public Branch of the Home Department.

Index and Contents	1880–1917 (with gaps)	
Proceedings volumes	1880–1921	68 v
'A' proceedings	1880–1922	11 bdls
'B' proceedings	1880–1923	4 bdls
Deposit proceedings	1899–1923	1 bdl
Manuscript proceedings	1910–14	1 bdl
List of 'A' and 'B' files	1880–1903	1 bdl
Diary register	1881–1903	4 v
Despatches to secretary	1880–3	3 v
of state	1881–3	1 bdl
Register of despatches to secretary	1880–81, 1891	2 v
of state		
Register of despatches from secre-	1880–91	1 v
tary of state		

CENTRAL PUBLICITY BOARD

This branch was formed in 1918 as a result of the war conference held in Delhi in 1918 for the purpose of carrying on internal war propaganda. It was dissolved in 1919.

'A' proceedings	1918–19	1 bdl
'B' proceedings	1918–19	2 bdls
Deposit proceedings	1918–19	1 bdl

DELHI BRANCH

This branch dealt with the transfer of the capital from Calcutta to Delhi. After 1913 business relating to Delhi was dealt with mainly in the Public Branch of the Home Department.

Proceedings volumes	1911–13	1 v
'A' proceedings	1911–13	4 bdls
'B' proceedings	1911–13	1 bdl
Deposit proceedings	1912–13	1 bdl

ELECTRIC TELEGRAPH BRANCH

This branch came under the Home Department until 1867 when it was transferred to the Foreign Department. From 1870 to 1905 and again from 1921 to 1923 the Telegraph Branch was part of the Public Works Department; from 1905 to 1920 part of the Commerce and Industry Department; from 1920 to 1921 part of the Commerce Department; and from 1923 to 1937 part of the Department of Industries and Labour.

Index	1857–67	3 v
Index and contents	1859–67	3 v
Proceedings volumes	1860–7	13 v
'A' proceedings	1860–7	5 bdls
Despatches from secretary of state	1860	1 v
Despatches to secretary of state	1859–67	12 v

ESTABLISHMENT BRANCH

This branch was established in 1874; until then the work was carried out in the Public and other relevant (Ecclesiastical, Education, Judicial, Jails etc.) branches.

Indexes	1874–5	Half-yearly
	1876–95	Yearly
Index and contents	1874–1907 (with gaps)	Yearly
Proceedings volumes	1874–1921	240 v
Unbound monthly proceedings	1874–80	2 bdls
'A' proceedings	1874–1921	199 bdls
'B' proceedings	1874–1921	55 bdls
Deposit proceedings	1886–1921	9 bdls
Files	1921–47	173 bdls
Deposit registers	1911–21	3 bdls
Diary files	1921–32	4 bdls

ESTABLISHMENT (SPECIAL) BRANCH

Files	1930–47	78 bdls

ESTABLISHMENT (RECRUITMENT) BRANCH

Files	1945–7	16 bdls

INDIAN CIVIL SERVICE BRANCH

Files	1940–3	3 bdls

INTERNEES INFORMATION BUREAU

Files	1943–7	1 bdl

JAILS BRANCH

All business relating to jails was entrusted to the Home Department in 1862, but a separate branch was not established until 1888. Before that date matters relating to jails will be found in the Judicial Branch of the Home Department.

Indexes	1888–95	Yearly
Index and contents	1888–1912	Yearly, 1895, 1898–1905 wanting
Proceedings volumes	1888–1921	101 v
'A' proceedings	1888–1921	58 bdls
'B' proceedings	1888–1921	19 bdls
Deposit proceedings	1888–1921	2 bdls
Files	1921–47	114 bdls
File registers	1926–42	13 v
Diary registers	1926–38	13 v

JUDICIAL BRANCH

The Judicial Department became a branch of the Home Department in 1843.

Indexes	1857–67	Consolidated
	1860	Yearly
	1861	Half-yearly
	1868–89	Half-yearly
	1890–5	Yearly
Index and contents	1892–7	Yearly
Contents	1862–77	Yearly
	1867–70; 1871–4; 1874–7	Consolidated
Proceedings volumes	1860–1921	Approx. 719 v
Unbound monthly proceedings	1871–80	5 bdls
'A' proceedings	1860–1921	469 bdls
'B' proceedings	1860–1921	150 bdls
Deposit proceedings	1884–1921	10 bdls
Files	1921–41	158 bdls
Deposit registers	1904–7; 1913–18	2 v
File registers	1921–2; 1928–41	16 v
Diary registers	1921–37; 1940–1	15 v
Diary of the Commissioner of the Hyderabad Districts	1866–7	1 v
'A', 'B', 'C' proceedings of Finance, Account and miscel-	1863–78	1 bdl

laneous proceedings of escheated
and inland estates

Despatches from secretary of state	1860–92	32 v
	1860–1905	3 bdls
Register of despatches from secretary of state	1866–91	3 v
Despatches to secretary of state	1858–95	71 v
	1860–92	7 bdls
Register of despatches to secretary of state	1858–63; 1869–96	3 v
Despatches to under secretary of of state	1861; 1863–77	9 v
Register of despatches to under secretary	1878–96	1 v

LUNATIC ASYLUM BRANCH

This branch only existed between February and July 1921, but 'Lunatic Asylums' was a separate section within the Medical Branch from 1899 to 1921 and the proceedings are kept together. From 1860 to 1873 lunatic asylums were dealt with in the Public Branch, from 1873 to January 1921 in the Medical Branch, and from July 1921 onwards in the Jails Branch.

'A' proceedings	1899–1921	1 bdl
'B' proceedings	1899–1921	3 bdls

MANPOWER BRANCH

Files	1939–45	4 bdls

MISCELLANEOUS BRANCH

Proceedings volumes	1921	2 v
'A' proceedings	1921	1 bdl
'B' proceedings	1921	1 bdl
Despatches from secretary of state	1918–28	1 bdl

POLICE BRANCH

The Home Department was entrusted with all business relating to police in 1862—previously some relating to the territories under its jurisdiction had been dealt with in the Foreign Department, the rest in the Judicial Branch of the Home Department.

Indexes	1862–7	Consolidated
	1868–80, 1888–95	Yearly

Index and contents	1862–8; 1871–4 1865; 1869–70; 1874–9; 1892–7; 1906–9; 1913	Consolidated Yearly
Index and despatches	1881–7	Yearly
Proceedings volumes	1862–1921	459 v
Unbound monthly proceedings	1872–93	4 bdls
'A' proceedings	1862–1921	178 bdls
'B' proceedings	1862–1921	82 bdls
Deposit proceedings	1886–1921	9 bdls
Files	1921–47	158 bdls
Secret files	1944–7	4 bdls
Special files	1946–7	5 bdls
Receipt register	1907–8	1 v
Issue registers and diaries	1919–40	17 v
Movement Registers	1921–44	25 v
Diaries	1921–40	2 bdls

POLITICAL BRANCH

The Political Branch was created in July 1907 owing to the heavy and increasing volume of work relating to unrest in India and cognate subjects. The new branch dealt with all business relating to internal politics and political agitation, much of which had previously been dealt with in the Public Branch. These records, many concerned with political disturbances, are essential for all students of the Indian national movement. Among the subjects dealt with by this branch are agitation, arrests, books and publications, censorship, civil disobedience movement, Congress, conspiracy cases, foreigners, information, Indian revolutionaries, Legislative Assembly, newspapers (including reports on native newspapers), passports, political prisoners, public security, publicity and propaganda, questions in Parliament, sedition, terrorists etc.

Indexes	1907–47	Yearly
Proceedings volumes	1907–20	100 v
'A' proceedings	1907–21	66 bdls
'B' proceedings	1907–21	37 bdls
Deposit proceedings	1907–21	16 bdls
Files	1921–33	227 carton boxes
Closed files	1934–47	105 carton boxes and 147 bdls

PORT BLAIR BRANCH

The Home Department administered the penal settlements on the Andaman and Nicobar Islands from the foundation of the penal settlement at Port Blair in 1858. The Port Blair branch was established in 1871 (for the years before 1871 see the Public and Judicial branches). The branch was abolished in 1921 and the work transferred to the Jails branch, but in 1945 a separate Andaman and Nicobar Branch was again established.

Indexes	1873–80; 1890–5	Yearly
Index and contents	1871–3; 1876–9	Consolidated
	1874–5; 1888–1909	Yearly
Diary and index	1871	Yearly
	1872	Half-yearly
Despatch and index	1881–7	Yearly
Proceedings volumes	1873–1921	338 v
'A' proceedings	1871–1921	48 bdls
'B' proceedings	1871–1921	23 bdls
Deposit proceedings	1894–1921	2 bdls
Deposit register	1908–21	3 v
Andaman papers	1860–3	5 v
Administration reports of Port Blair and Nicobar	1864–7	4 v

ANDAMAN AND NICOBAR BRANCH

Files	1945–7	19 bdls

POST OFFICE BRANCH

Business relating to post offices was dealt with in the Public Branch of the Home Department until 1856, when a separate branch was created. From 1867 to 1879 post offices came under the Financial Department (Separate Revenue Branch), from 1879 to 1905 under the Finance and Commerce Department (Separate Revenue Branch), from 1905 to 1920 under the Commerce and Industry Department (Post Office Branch), from 1920 to 1921 under the Commerce Department (Post Office Branch), from 1921 to 1923 under the Public Works Department (Post Office Branch), and from 1923 to 1937 under the Department of Industries and Labour (Post Office Branch).

Index and Contents	1860–7	1 v
Proceedings volumes	1860–7	12 v

| 'A' proceedings | 1860–7 | 3 bdls |
| 'B' proceedings | 1860–7 | 1 bdl |

PRIORITY PASSAGE BRANCH

| Files | 1943–7 | 14 bdls |

PUBLIC BRANCH

The Public Branch dealt with all business which did not come within the scope of the other branches of the Home Department, including much that was later dealt with in separate branches of the Home Department, or in other, younger, departments. Work was also sometimes transferred to the Public Branch from separate branches which were being closed. The records of this branch cover such a wide field that students of almost any subject would be wise to consult the Home Indexes for information about possible relevant documents among the records of the Public Branch.

This branch dealt with matters of internal politics, conducted the correspondence with other departments of the Government of India, and between the Government of India and the Provincial Governments, administered the minor administrations (i.e. Chief Commissionerships other than Assam, Central Provinces, Ajmer-Merwara, British Baluchistan, and North-West Frontier Province) which were administered under the direct control of the Central Government through Chief Commissioners, dealt with Civil Service questions, newspapers, and much of the business relating to political disturbances which from 1907 was dealt with by the Political Branch.

Among other subjects which came within the scope of this branch from time to time are the following: agriculture (to 1871), archaeology (to 1879), books (to 1880), census (to 1871 and from 1923), commerce and trade (to 1871), copyright (to 1910), Delhi (to 1910), emigration (to 1871), establishments (to 1873), examinations (to 1874), exhibitions (to 1882), famine (to 1871), fibres and silk (to 1871), fisheries (to 1871), food and foodstuffs (to 1871), foreign missionaries (1932–6), forests (to 1865), gazetteers, geology and minerals (to 1871), health (to 1868), hospitals and medical matters (to 1873), industry (to 1871), inventions (to 1875), internal political disturbances (to 1907), Linguistic Survey (1896–1910), meteorology (to 1881), minerals and geological survey (to 1871), municipalities (to 1871), museums (to 1871), Patent Law (to 1875), Port Blair (to 1871), the Registration Act, sanitation (to 1867), science and art (to 1876), statistics (to 1871), various reports (including reports on native newspapers), telegraphs (to 1867), and weights and measures (to 1890).

Indexes	1857–63, 1864–8	Consolidated
	1860–1, 1873, 1876, 1879, 1880	Yearly
	1868–89	Half-yearly
Contents	1859–61, 1862–3, 1864–6	Consolidated
	1860–80	Yearly
	1860, 1864	Half-yearly
Index and contents	1889–97	Yearly
Proceedings volumes	1860–1921	675 v
Unbound monthly proceedings	1869–81	5 bdls
'A' proceedings	1860–1921	314 bdls [these are being 're-bundled', i.e. very large bundles are being split]
'B' proceedings	1860–1921	142 bdls
Deposit proceedings	1880–1921	30 bdls
	1899–1903	1 v
Files	1921–46	192 bdls
Manuscript proceedings	1927–40	1 bdl
Diary files	1921–9	1 bdl
Diary registers	1929–38	9 v
Deposit registers	1902–9	2 v
Movement registers	1923–35	14 v
Despatches from secretary of state	1860–88	47 v
	1860–1904	10 bdls
Register of despatches from secretary of state	1879–89	1 v
Despatches to secretary of state	1860–1910	77 v
	1860–99	21 bdls
Register of despatches to secretary of state	1869–96	1 v
Despatches to under secretary of state	1861–1908	27 v
	1860–89	4 bdls
Register of despatches to under secretary	1877–96	1 v

PUBLIC BRANCH A

Files	1947	8 bdls

PUBLIC BRANCH B

Files	1947	3 bdls

PUBLIC BRANCH C

Files	1943–5	9 bdls

PUBLIC SERVICE COMMISSION

Files	1924	2 bdls

RE-EMPLOYMENT AND RECONSTRUCTION BRANCH

Files	1947	2 bdls

SEPARATE REVENUE BRANCH

The Separate Revenue Branch was transferred to the Financial Department in 1864, and continued thereafter to be administered by that Department and its successors.

Proceedings volumes	1860–3	11 v
'A' proceedings	1860–3	4 bdls
'B' proceedings	1860–3	1 bdl
Despatches to secretary of of state	1858–62	1 v

SPECIAL BRANCH

Index	1927–9	3 v
Files	1927–30	13 carton boxes

UPPER BURMA BRANCH

Indexes	1886–8	32 v
Proceedings volumes	1886–8	18 v
Unbound monthly proceedings	1887–8	1 bdl
Ecclesiastical 'A' and 'B' proceedings	1886–7	1 bdl
Establishment 'A' proceedings	1886–8	2 bdls
Establishment 'B' proceedings	1886–8	1 bdl
Judicial 'A' proceedings	1886–8	4 bdls
Judicial 'B' proceedings	1886–8	1 bdl
Medical 'A' proceedings	1886–8	2 bdls

Medical 'B' proceedings	1886–8	2 bdls
Police 'A' proceedings	1886–8	3 bdls
Police 'B' proceedings	1886–8	1 bdl
Public 'A' proceedings	1886–8	3 bdls
Public 'B' proceedings	1886–8	1 bdl
Public Municipal 'A' proceedings	1888	1 bdl

WAR BRANCH

Indexes	1919	4 v
Proceedings volumes	1919–20	4 v
'A' proceedings	1918–20	4 bdls
'B' proceedings	1918–20	14 bdls
Deposit proceedings	1918–20	1 bdl
Deposit register	1918–19	1 v

GENERAL ORDERS

1870–1913	49 v

MISCELLANEOUS VOLUMES, GENERAL

Petition Diary	1857–9	1 v
List of public despatches addressed to secretary of state	1860	1 v
Electric telegraph and education letters to secretary of state	1862	1 v
Demi-official letters from secretary of state	Oct. 1869–June 1870	1 v
Despatches to the secretary of state from ecclesiastical, education, judicial, municipal, public, and sanitary branches	1896, 1898–1901	5 v
Office of the Record Committee: letters sent	May 1861–Aug. 1863	1 v
Minutes of proceedings of the Prison Conference	1877	1 v
List of Officers serving in the Assam Commission	July 1879–June 1883	1 v

MISCELLANEOUS VOLUMES, BENGAL

Bengal: Separate Revenue Department to secretary of state	1860–3	3 v
Bengal: Education letters to secretary of state	1868–70	1 v

MISCELLANEOUS VOLUMES, BRITISH BURMA

Circular letters from the Judicial Commissioner, British Burma	1872–8	1 v
Circular orders from the Judicial Commissioner, British Burma	1872–8	1 v
Graduation list of Officers in the British Burma Commission	July 1879–Dec. 1881	1 v

MISCELLANEOUS VOLUMES, NORTH-WEST PROVINCES

Abstract of proceedings of the North-Western Provinces in the Separate Revenue Department	Jan.–Aug. 1860	1 v

MISCELLANEOUS VOLUMES, OUDH

Oudh Police Circulars	1864–70, 1865–70	2 v

MISCELLANEOUS VOLUMES, BOMBAY

DESPATCHES FROM THE SECRETARY OF STATE TO THE BOMBAY GOVERNMENT

Ecclesiastical	1859–67, 1870–7	8 v
Education	1860–77	10 v
Judicial	1860–74	13 v
Legislative	1861–8	2 v
Marine	1860–1	2 v
Public	1860–77	3 v
Public Works Department	1860–2, 1864–6, 1869–71	9 v
Public Works Department: telegraph letters	1858–69	4 v
Sanitary	1867–8	1 v
Statistics and commerce	1874–5	1 v

REGISTER OF DESPATCHES FROM THE SECRETARY OF STATE TO THE BOMBAY GOVERNMENT

Education	1859–67	1 v
Judicial	1859–91	2 v
Legislative	1861–8	2 v
Public	1858–91	3 v

DESPATCHES TO THE SECRETARY OF STATE FROM THE BOMBAY
GOVERNMENT

Ecclesiastical	1867–74	3 v
Education	1861, 1865, 1867–75	6 v
Ecclesiastical and Education	1866	1 v
Judicial	1860–75	14 v
Legislative	1862–9	7 v
Marine	1860–1	2 v
Public	1860–7, 1869–75, 1877	15 v
Public Works Department	1860–6, 1869–71	10 v
Public Works Department: telegraph letters	1864–5	1 v

REGISTERS OF DESPATCHES TO THE SECRETARY OF STATE FROM
THE BOMBAY GOVERNMENT

Education	1858–67	1 v
Judicial	1856–85	2 v
Legislative	1862–8	2 v
Public	1856–81	3 v

DESPATCHES TO AND FROM THE SECRETARY OF STATE

Public Works Department	1867	1 v
Public Works Department: telegraph letters	1867–8, 1870	2 v
Municipalities register from secretary of state	1881–5	1 v
Municipalities register to secretary of state	1881–6	1 v
Indo-European telegraph: correspondence	1866–9	1 v

MISCELLANEOUS VOLUMES, MADRAS

DESPATCHES FROM THE SECRETARY OF STATE TO THE MADRAS
GOVERNMENT

Education	1864–70, 1876–7	4 v
Revenue	1860–9	5 v
Sanitary	1867–8	1 v

REGISTER OF DESPATCHES FROM THE SECRETARY OF STATE TO
THE MADRAS GOVERNMENT

Education and telegraph	1859–67	1 v
Judicial	1858–91	2 v
Legislative	1868	1 v
Public	1858–91	3 v
Revenue	1858–67	1 v
Sanitary	1868, 1874–91	2 v

DESPATCHES TO THE SECRETARY OF STATE FROM THE MADRAS
GOVERNMENT

Ecclesiastical	1861–9, 1875–7	5 v
Education	1861, 1864–5, 1873, 1875	4 v
Marine	1861	1 v

REGISTER OF DESPATCHES TO THE SECRETARY OF STATE FROM
MADRAS GOVERNMENT

Education and telegraph	1961–7	1 v
Judicial	1856–85	2 v
Legislative	1864–8	2 v
Public	1856–84	2 v
Sanitary	1873–8	1 v
Madras Separate Revenue Proceedings	1891	1 v

MISCELLANEOUS VOLUMES, BOMBAY AND MADRAS

Despatches from the secretary of state to the Bombay and Madras Governments: education, ecclesiastical, financial, judicial, marine, and revenue	1858–63	1 v
Register of despatches from the secretary of state to the Bombay and Madras Governments: education, ecclesiastical	1868–91	1 v
Register of despatches to the secretary of state from the Bombay and Madras Governments: education, ecclesiastical	1868–86	1 v

MISCELLANEOUS VOLUMES, SINGAPORE

Singapore general abstracts	1859–66	12 v
Singapore judicial abstracts	1861–6	6 v
Singapore marine abstracts	1860–6	7 v
Singapore revenue abstracts	1861–6	6 v

MINISTRY OF HOME AFFAIRS 1947 ONWARDS

With the advent of Independence a Ministry of Home Affairs was created.

Indexes	1948–58	Yearly. From 1955, volumes within a year are alphabetical not chronological, e.g. 1955 A–M, N–Z, not 1955 Jan.–June, July–Dec.

Files

Administrative Section	1948–50	80 boxes
Andaman and Nicobar Section	1948–50	35 carton boxes
Appointment Section	1948–9	12 bdls
Appointment Section (Special)	1948–9	17 bdls
Central Services Section	1949–51	6 bdls
Establishment Section	1948–50	15 bdls
Foreigners Section	1948–53	48 bdls
Gazetted Services Section (later All India Services Section)	1948–50	17 bdls
Non-Gazetted Services Section	1948–50	11 bdls
Priority Passage	1948–51	4 bdls
Police Section: Police (i)	1948–9	12 bdls
Police Section: Police Special (ii)	1948–55	29 bdls
Public Section	1948–50	25 bdls
Recruitment, Promotion and Seniority Section	1949–50	1 bdl
Special Recruitment Board	1948–51	4 bdls
Reorganization Section	1948–50	7 bdls
Reorganization Section (Civil Service)	1949	1 bdl

INDIAN MUNITIONS BOARD 1917–20

The Indian Munitions Board was created as a temporary organization during the First World War. In 1920 it was reorganized as the 'Board of Industries and Munitions' which formed the nucleus of the separate Department of Industries, created in 1921 with the separation into two parts of the Department of Commerce and Industry.

CHEMICALS AND MINERALS BRANCH

Index (loose), proceedings and files	1917–20	3 bdls

ESTABLISHMENT BRANCH

Index (loose) and files	1917–20	6 bdls

EXPORTS AND IMPORTS BRANCH

'A' and 'B' proceedings	1917–20	1 bdl

GENERAL BRANCH

Index (loose), files and miscellaneous	1920	3 bdls

HOME INDENTS BRANCH

'A' and 'B' proceedings	1918–20	1 bdl

INTELLIGENCE BRANCH

Index (loose)	1917–18	1 bdl

INDUSTRIAL INTELLIGENCE BRANCH

Index (loose), proceedings and files	1917–20	16 bdls

HIDES AND WOOL BRANCH

Files	1917–20	1 bdl

PATENTS AND DESIGNS BRANCH

Files	1920	1 bdl

PRIORITY BRANCH

Proceedings volumes and 'A' and 'B' proceedings	1917–20	2 bdls

POST-WAR BRANCH

Files	1919	1 bdl

STORES BRANCH
Index (loose), 'A' and 'B' proceedings and files   1917–20   3 bdls

TEXTILE BRANCH
'A' proceedings and files   1918–20   2 bdls

WOOL BRANCH
Files   1918   1 bdl
Diary registers   1917–20   2 bdls

BOARD OF INDUSTRIES AND MUNITIONS 1920–1
CHEMICALS AND MINERALS BRANCH
Index, proceedings volumes and files   1920–1   6 bdls

ESTABLISHMENTS BRANCH
Loose index and files   1920–1   6 bdls

ELECTRICITY BRANCH
Files   1920–1   1 bdl

EXPLOSIVES BRANCH
Files and Deposit   1920–1   2 bdls

FACTORIES BRANCH
'A' and 'B' proceedings, and files   1920–1   2 bdls

GENERAL BRANCH
Loose index and miscellaneous files   1920–1   4 bdls

GEOLOGY AND MINERALS ESTABLISHMENT BRANCH
'A' and 'B' and filed proceedings   1920–1   1 bdl

GENERAL TECHNICAL INDUSTRIAL EDUCATION BRANCH
Files   1920   1 bdl

INDUSTRIES BRANCH
Proceedings volumes and files   1920–1   3 bdls

INDUSTRIAL INTELLIGENCE BRANCH
Index, proceedings volumes and files   1920-1   6 bdls

LABOUR BRANCH
Files   1920-1   2 bdls

MINES REGULATIONS BRANCH
Files   1920-1   1 bdl

MINERAL RESOURCES BRANCH
'A' and filed proceedings, and files   1920-1   2 bdls

STORES BRANCH
Proceedings volumes, files and miscellaneous 'C'   1920-1   5 bdls
proceedings

INDUSTRIAL EXHIBITION BRANCH
Files   1920   1 bdl

PATENTS AND DESIGNS BRANCH
Index and files   1920-1   2 bdls

PETROLEUM BRANCH
'A', 'B' and filed proceedings   1920-1   1 bdl

STEAM BOILER BRANCH
Files   1920   1 bdl

STATIONERY AND PRINTING BRANCH
Files   1920-1   1 bdl

TECHNICAL EDUCATION BRANCH
Files   1920-1   1 bdl

LEATHER BRANCH
Files   1920   1 bdl

TEA CESS BRANCH
Files   1920   1 bdl

DEPARTMENT OF INDUSTRIES 1921-3

This department was created following the division of the former Department of Commerce and Industry into two in 1921. It lasted until 1923.

CHEMICALS BRANCH

Loose index, proceedings volumes and files	1921-3	3 bdls

ESTABLISHMENTS BRANCH

Files	1921-3	4 bdls

ELECTRICITY BRANCH

Files	1921-3	2 bdls

EXPLOSIVES BRANCH

Files	1921-3	1 bdl

FACTORIES BRANCH

Files	1921-3	2 bdls

GEOLOGY AND MINERALS ESTABLISHMENT BRANCH

'A', 'B', filed and deposit proceedings	1921-3	6 bdls

GENERAL BRANCH

Files	1921-3	4 bdls

INDUSTRIES BRANCH

Index, proceedings volumes and files	1921-3	4 v, 3 bdls

INDUSTRIAL INTELLIGENCE BRANCH

Index, proceedings volumes and files	1921-3	3 bdls

INDUSTRIAL EXHIBITION BRANCH

Files	1921-3	1 bdl

INTER-PROVINCIAL MIGRATION BRANCH

Files	1921-3	1 bdl

LEATHER BRANCH

Files	1921-2	1 bdl

LABOUR BRANCH

Files   1921–3   11 bdls

MINES AND GEOLOGICAL EDUCATION BRANCH

Files   1921–3   1 bdl

MINES REGULATIONS BRANCH

'A', 'B', deposit and filed proceedings and files   1921–3   3 bdls

MINERAL RESOURCES BRANCH

Files   1921–3   3 bdls

PATENTS AND DESIGNS BRANCH

Index, proceedings volumes and files   1921–3   4 bdls

PETROLEUM BRANCH

'A', 'B', and filed proceedings   1921–3   1 bdl

STORES BRANCH

Index, proceedings volumes, files, and miscel-   1921–3   12 bdls
laneous 'C' files

STATIONERY AND PRINTING BRANCH

Files   1921–3   10 bdls

TEA CESS BRANCH

Files   1921   1 bdl

STEAM BOILERS BRANCH

Files   1921–3   1 bdl

TECHNICAL EDUCATION BRANCH

Files   1921–3   2 bdls

DEPARTMENT OF INDUSTRIES AND LABOUR
1923–37

The Department of Industries and Labour was created in 1923 by the
amalgamation of the Public Works Department with the Department of
Industries. In 1937 the Department was divided into two departments of

Labour and of Communications, but the records of these departments have not yet been transferred to the National Archives.

Indexes   1923–37   34 v

ACCOUNTS CIVIL WORKS BRANCH

Files   1923–35   15 bdls

ACCOUNTS GENERAL BRANCH

Files   1923–35   14 bdls

ACCOUNTS IRRIGATION BRANCH

Files   1924–35   4 bdls

CHEMICALS BRANCH

Files 1923–7   1923–7   1 bdl

CIVIL AVIATION BRANCH

Files   1923–33   2 bdls

COPYRIGHT BRANCH

Files 1924–37   1924–37   1 bdl

For post-1937 see Department of Education, Health and Lands.

CIVIL WORKS BUILDING BRANCH

'B' proceedings and files   1923–34   9 bdls

CIVIL WORKS COMMUNICATION BRANCH

Files   1923–34   2 bdls

CIVIL WORKS MISCELLANEOUS BRANCH

'B' proceedings and files   1923   7 bdls

CIVIL WORKS IRRIGATION BRANCH

Files   1923–35   18 bdls

CONSULTING ENGINEERS BRANCH

Files   1923–30   2 bdls

DECORATION BRANCH

Files   1927–35   3 bdls

ESTABLISHMENT BRANCH

Files	1923–35	17 bdls

ELECTRICITY BRANCH

Files	1923–35	4 bdls

EXPLOSIVES BRANCH

Files	1923–35	5 bdls

FACTORIES BRANCH

Files	1923–35	9 bdls

GENERAL BRANCH

Files	1923–35	20 bdls

GEOLOGY AND MINERALS BRANCH

Files	1923–35	32 bdls

GEOLOGY AND MINERALS ESTABLISHMENT BRANCH

Files	1923	1 bdl

INTER-PROVINCIAL MIGRATION BRANCH

Files	1923–35	6 bdls

INDUSTRY BRANCH

Files	1923–36	13 bdls

INDUSTRIAL INTELLIGENCE BRANCH

Files	1923–7	1 bdl

LABOUR BRANCH

Index	1938–40	4 v
Files	1923–35	52 bdls

LEATHER BRANCH

Files	1927	1 bdl

MINES AND GEOLOGICAL EDUCATION BRANCH

Files	1923	1 bdl

MINERAL RESOURCES BRANCH

Files   1923   1 bdl

METEOROLOGY BRANCH

Files   1923–34   14 bdls

PATENTS AND DESIGNS BRANCH

Index and files   1923–37   9 bdls

PETROLEUM BRANCH

Files   1928–35   3 bdls

POST AND TELEGRAPH ESTABLISHMENT BRANCH

Files   1923–31   28 bdls

POST AND TELEGRAPH GENERAL BRANCH

Files   1926–32   7 bdls

POST OFFICE BRANCH

Files   1923–30   7 bdls

PUBLIC WORKS ESTABLISHMENT BRANCH

'A' and 'B' proceedings and files   1923–35   26 bdls

PUBLIC WORKS GENERAL BRANCH

Files   1923–35   16 bdls

STATIONERY AND PRINTING BRANCH

Files   1923–36   44 bdls

STORES BRANCH

Files   1923–36   30 bdls

STEAM BOILERS BRANCH

Files   1923–35   4 bdls

TELEGRAPH BRANCH

Files   1923–7   10 bdls

TECHNICAL EDUCATION BRANCH

Files   1923–35   4 bdls

MISCELLANEOUS

Inventory of plant and machinery engineers in the   1925   86 v
telegraph workshop etc.

MINISTRY OF LABOUR

LABOUR INVESTIGATION COMMITTEE

Records created by the Committee appointed by   1944–6   3 bdls
the Government of India

DIRECTOR-GENERAL OF CIVIL AVIATION

Records created by the Committee appointed by   1947–53   1 bdl
the Government of India

LEGISLATIVE DEPARTMENT 1861–1947

The Legislative Branch was abolished in 1854 and until it was again
revived in 1861, subordinate to the Home Department, legislative functions
were vested in the Council of India. In 1864 a separate Legislative Department was created, not to initiate, but to prepare measures decided upon
elsewhere, and to advise other departments on questions involving the
interpretation of law. In 1947 the Legislative Department became the
Law Ministry. There were no separate branches in the Legislative Department until 1920.

Indexes	1861–1935	632 v
Papers relating to Acts (total number	1860–1923	1,419 v
of Acts—1,277)	1880–1923 (with gaps)	23 bdls
Minute book	1862, 1867–9, 1873	4 v
Proceedings volumes	1861–1924	761 v
Legislative Council proceedings volumes	1860–7, 1869–72, 1876–80	10 v
'A' proceedings	1861–1924	412 bdls
'B' proceedings	1861–1924	154 bdls

Deposit proceedings	1915–24	24 bdls
Assembly and Council files	1924–7	44 bdls
Assembly files	1928	2 bdls
Council and General Files	1927–46	88 bdls

DESPATCHES

Despatches from secretary of state	1860–1910 (gaps —1886–96)	16 v
Despatches to secretary of state	1861–9, 1877–87	23 v
Secret despatches to secretary of state	1874–7	1 v
Despatches to under secretary of state	1861–5, 1867–8	7 v
Registers of despatches to secretary of of state	1860–78, 1910–35	7 v
Registers of despatches to under secretary	1869–87, 1898–1927	4 v

ISSUES AND RECEIPTS REGISTERS, DIARIES ETC.

Issue registers	1908–34	62 v
Miscellaneous registers	1910–37	18 v
Receipt registers	1909–36	82 v
Diaries	1908–29	14 v
Pay bills, etc.	1874–1944	39 v
Stamps accounts	1913–34	13 v
Miscellaneous volumes	1879–1921	4 v

UNOFFICIAL

Proceedings	1872–1931	257 bdls (not indexed)
Registers and receipts registers	1873–1904	25 v
Index to unofficial register	1873–1904	5 v
Diary registers	1905–32	55 v
Issue registers	1910–15	4 v

ESTABLISHMENT BRANCH

'B' proceedings	1921–4	6 bdls
Deposit proceedings	1921–4	5 bdls
Files	1924–40	29 bdls

GENERAL BRANCH

'A' proceedings	1921–4	31 bdls
'B' proceedings	1921–4	21 bdls
Deposit proceedings	1921–4	6 bdls
Files	1924–7	52 bdls
Receipts register	1920–3	16 v
Movement register	1924–35	14 v

PUBLICATIONS BRANCH

'A' and 'B' proceedings	1921–3	1 bdl: 'A', 1922–3; 'B', 1921–2
'B' proceedings	1922–4	2 bdls
Deposit proceedings	1921–4	2 bdls
Files	1924–40	92 bdls

LIBRARY BRANCH

Files (relating to the purchase of books)	1923–35	8 bdls, not indexed

PAY BILLS

Files	1920–33	1 bdl

PEACE TREATY

'A' proceedings	1920–4	1 bdl
'B' proceedings	1920–2	13 bdls
Files	1922–37	7 bdls
Enemy debts files	1920–37	5 bdls

SOLICITOR BRANCH (SEE ALSO RECORDS OF THE SOLICITOR-GENERAL)

'B' proceedings	1920–30	3 bdls
Deposit proceedings	1921–30	2 bdls
Diaries	1920–31	3 v

SOLICITOR BRANCH (UNOFFICIAL)

Files (dealing with matters sent for opinion and advice by other departments)	1920–30	21 bdls, not indexed

ADVOCATE-GENERAL'S OPINIONS

Opinions	1885–1911	11 bdls
'B' proceedings	1912–19, 1921–37	2 bdls
Opinions, Bengal	1888–95, 1897– 1911	12 v
	1885–9	1 bdl

LEGAL OPINIONS

Index	1885–1910	4 v
'B' proceedings	1870–86	7 bdls

PRIZE COURT

'B' proceedings	1914–17	1 bdl

MISCELLANEOUS

Minutes and Notes by Lord Hobhouse and others	1874–6	1 bdl
Notes on procedure and ruling of the Royal Commission on compensation for suffering and damage by enemy action. Prepared by A. L. Saunders		1 bdl
Travelling Allowance Bills of the Members of Council	1921–38	11 bdls

SOLICITOR-GENERAL'S RECORDS

It would seem that there have been two transfers of Solicitor-General's records. (1) Title-deeds, conveyances, contracts, licences, leases, agreements, bonds, assignments, trust deeds etc. 1761–1920. These documents are numbered 1–925 (with gaps), and there is available an unofficial manuscript list. (2) Correspondence and papers (including briefs) relating to various cases dealt with by the Solicitor-General's office, 1919–42 (88 bundles). These records are at present unsorted and unarranged, being still in their original bundles, which are kept in NAI bundles.

MILITARY DEPARTMENT 1860–1906

(including records of successor bodies, MILITARY FINANCE DEPARTMENT, 1860–4; ARMY DEPARTMENT, 1906–36; MILITARY SUPPLY DEPARTMENT, 1906–9; DEFENCE DEPARTMENT, 1936–42; WAR DEPARTMENT, 1942–6)

Until 1895 three separate armies were maintained for the presidencies of Bengal, Bombay and Madras. The Bengal army was under the Government of India; the other two under the local governments. In 1895 they were united to form the Indian army controlled by the supreme Government. The Military Department had been transferred to the Government of India in 1833, and continued thereafter as a separate department until 1906, dealing with all matters relating to the administration of the army in all the presidencies. In 1867 the Marine Branch was transferred to the Military Department from the Home Department. Some of the work of the Marine Branch, namely that relating to commerce (lighting, buoys, beacons, ports, pilots and pilotage) was later transferred (1874) to the Department of Revenue, Agriculture and Commerce, but in 1879 the work was re-transferred to the Marine Branch, finally being taken over by the Department of Commerce and Industry in 1905. The Military Department also dealt with matters relating to government studs and the improvement of the breed of horses and cattle, but this business was transferred to the Department of Revenue, Agriculture and Commerce in 1871; horse-breeding was transferred to the Department of Revenue and Agriculture in 1889. In 1906 as a result of the Kitchener/Curzon controversy the Military Department was abolished and replaced by the Army Department (to conduct all business relating to the army, except that specifically given to the Military Supply Department), and the Military Supply Department (to take charge of all army contracts, purchase of army stores and ordnance, to have custody of army stores, ordnance, etc., the management of military works, clothing and manufacturing sections, the Indian Medical Service, the Royal Indian Marine, the marine surveys, and damage to navigation). However, in 1909 the Military Supply Department was abolished and its business taken over by the Army Department. In 1923 the Air Force came under the charge of the Army Department, which in 1936 became the Defence Department. Ecclesiastical matters were transferred to it in the following year (1937). In 1942 a new Defence Department was set up and the old Defence Department renamed War Department, but at the end of World War II the two departments were amalgamated as the Defence Department; becoming the Ministry of Defence in the independent Government of India (1947). In the Military Department (and its successors) proceedings were numbered consecutively, not separately within the various branches; therefore the records of the branches are not kept separately as in other departments. Records up to 1938 have been transferred to the National Archives, and the proceedings system continued in the department to that date.

MILITARY DEPARTMENT, ARMY DEPARTMENT, DEFENCE
DEPARTMENT, 1860–1938

Unbound proceedings	1860–1938	Approx. 2,800 bdls (average 94 files in each)
Bound proceedings	1860–1930	Approx. 2,100 v (19 shelves)
Confidential 'B' proceedings	1882–1930	114 bdls (100 in each)
Confidential 'A' proceedings	1891–1912	14 bdls (100 in each)
Body sheets	1860–77	17 v
Index	1860–1936, 1940	140 v
Monthly index	1860–78	64 v
Index and contents	1860–83	58 v
Tabular statements	1879–1923	80 v
Notes	1888–1923	51 bdls
Confidential notes	1889–1922	3 bdls (100 in each)
War proceedings	1914–17	14 bdls
Despatches to secretary of state	1860–1904	129 v
	1886–1929	150 bdls (150 in each)
Rough drafts	1860–74	29 v
Despatches to under secretary of state	1878–84, 1890–1905	15 v
	1894–1919	9 bdls (150 in each)
Miscellaneous despatches to secretary of state	1907–10	4 bdls (150 in each)
Despatches from secretary of state	1860–1905	157 v
	1890–1929	20 bdls (150 in each)
Financial despatches from secretary of state	1862–87	16 v
Military stores despatches from secretary of state	1888–97	10 v
Up-country index	1860–9	17 v
Up-country body sheets	1867–70	11 v
Up-country consultations	1860–71	7 bdls (100 in each)
Up-country rough drafts of letters	1860–70	58 v

MILITARY SUPPLY DEPARTMENT, 1906–9

'B' proceedings	1906–9	190 bdls (100 in each)

MILITARY DEPARTMENT, ARMY DEPARTMENT

MILITARY P.W.D. (MILITARY WORKS) 1863–1912

Index	1865–79	6 v
Unbound 'B' proceedings	1871–1906	118 bdls (100 in each)
Unbound 'A' proceedings	1863–1906	190 bdls (100 in each)
Bound proceedings	1882–1909	53 v
Confidential 'B' proceedings and notes	1885–1912	16 bdls (100 in each)

MILITARY DEPARTMENT

GENERAL ORDERS ETC. 1860–1901

General orders (minutes of Council)	1860–87	33 v
General orders (C.-in-C.)	1860–1901	54 v
Standing orders	1861–92	41 v
Various miscellaneous items	1862–81	10 v
Rough drafts of telegraphic messages	1863–70	10 v

EXPEDITIONS

Indexes to Field Operations: Duffla, 1874–5, 1 v; Straits Settlement, 1875–6, 1 v; Waziri, 1881, 1 v; China, 1900–3, 2 v; Tirah, 1897–8, 1 v; Tochi, 1897–8, 1 v; Suakin, 1896–7, 1 v; Hazara, 1888–9, 1891–2, 2 v; Malta, 1878–9, 1 v; Manipur, 1891–2, 1 v; Miranzai, 1890–2, 1 v; Hunza Nagar, 1892, 1 v; Malakand, 1897–8, 1 v; Chitral, 1895–6, 1 v; Waziristan, 1895–6, 1 v; Chin Lushai, 1889–91, 1 v; Lushai, 1889, 1 v; North-West Frontier, 1877–8, 1 v.

Unbound proceedings, Field Operations, Confidential: Chitral Relief Force, 1895, 10 f; Hazara proceedings, 1888–91, 3 f; Sikkim proceedings 1888–9, 2 f; Manipur proceedings, 1891, 7 f; Hunza proceedings, 1892, 6 f; Isazai proceedings, 1892–3, 3 f; Waziristan proceedings, 1895, 10 f; Suakin proceedings, 1896, 3 f; Tirah proceedings, 1897–8, 40 f; Tochi proceedings 1897–8, 10 f; Miranzai proceedings, 1891, 44 f; Malakand proceedings, 1897–8, 10 f; China proceedings, 1901–3, 20 f; Notes of Chitral Relief Force and China, 1895–1902, f 4.

Bound proceedings, Field Operations: Duffla, 1874–5, 1 v; Straits Settlement, 1875, 1 v; Waziri, 1881, 1 v; China, 1900–3, 2 v; Tochi, 1897–8, 1 v; Tirah, 1897–8, 1 v; Suakin, 1885, 1896–7, 2 v; Hazara, 1888–9, 1891–2, 2 v; Manipur, 1891–2, 1 v; Miranzai, 1890–2, 1 v; Hunza Nagar 1892, 1 v; Malakand, 1897–8, 1 v; Chitral, 1895–6, 1 v; Waziristan, 1895–6, 1 v;

Chin Lushai, 1889–91, 1 v; Malta, 1878–9, 2 v; Naga, 1875, 1880–1, 2 v; Egypt, 1882–3, 2 v; extract from Egypt expedition, 1882, 1 v; North-West Frontier, 1877–8, 2 v; Lushai, 1889, 1 v; Burma, 1875, 1885–6, 2 v; Isazai, 1892–3, 1 v; Sikkim, 1888–90, 1 v; Quetta, 1885, 1 v; Kabul, 1878–81, 1 v.

SUPPLY AND TRANSPORT PROCEEDINGS

	1879–82	13 v

MUTINY MEDALS

	1863–9	3 v

MARINE BRANCH

The Marine Branch was transferred to the Military Department from the Home Department in 1867.

Unbound 'A' and 'B' proceedings	1873–83	60 bdls (100 in each)
Unbound 'B' proceedings	1884–1923	160 bdls (100 in each)
Bound proceedings	1860–1922	67 v
Confidential 'A' and 'B' proceedings and notes	1887–1937	63 bdls (100 in each)
War confidential and 'B' proceedings	1914–17	8 bdls (100 in each)
Originals of printed notes and collections and printed notes	1907–13	11 bdls
Despatches from secretary of state	1860, 1863–6, 1860–7, 1881–91, 1860–7	24 v, 2 bdls
Despatches to secretary of state	1866, 1887, 1888–91, 1892–5	9 v
Confidential despatches to secretary of state	1892–1923	6 bdls (200 in each)
Index to despatches to secretary of state	1867–1903, 1905	3 v
Confidential despatches to under secretary of state	1860–84	4 f

MILITARY MISCELLANEOUS RECORDS (POST-MUTINY)

Adjutant-General's circular letters	1861–5	5 v
Proceedings of the Bengal Sanitary Commission on the health of the army	1866	
State of the Nepal Residency escort	1867–78	
Distribution of troops in the three Presidencies, with copies of correspondence on the military occupation of Darjeeling etc.	1865–70	
Distribution return of the army in Bengal	1869	
List of changes in war material and of patterns of military stores of H.M.'s army in India	1920–3, 1925	

Digest of service of 63rd Light Infantry, 1758–1922; 4th Bombay Grenadiers (3rd Battalion, vol. I, 1768–1893; vol. II, 1894–1926; vol. III, 1927–30; 4th Battalion, vol. I, 1768–1887; vol. II, 1887–1916; vol. III, 1917–30; 10th Battalion, vol. I, 1800–1921; vol. II, 1922–30); 14th Regiment of Madras Native Infantry, 1775–1913; the 74th Punjabi Regiment, afterwards the 4/2 Punjab Regiment, 1776–1937; 79th Carnatic Infantry, 1777–1923; Historical records of the 18th (Alipore) Infantry, vol. I, 1795–1915; vol. II, 1916–22; Digest of service of the 3rd Brahman Indian Infantry, 1798–1861; 1/3rd (Brahman) Regiment of Native Infantry (vol. I, 1861–1914; vol. II, 1914–22); 83rd Walajahbad Light Infantry, 1799–1923; History of the Burma Sappers and Miners, 1887–1921; Digest of service of the Burma Sappers and Miners, 1922–9; 1/3rd Madras Regiment, 1907–28; 2/3rd Madras Regiment, 1914–26.

WAR DEPARTMENT

Files	1942–6	9 bdls

PUBLIC WORKS DEPARTMENT 1860–1923

The P.W.D. was first established in 1855 to supervise and control all matters relating to buildings, roads and irrigation. It also dealt with railways, electric telegraph (taken over from the Foreign Department in 1870), and forests and fisheries (handed over to the Department of Revenue, Agriculture and Commerce in 1871). In 1905 telegraph business was transferred to the new Department of Commerce and Industry, and in the same year the railway system was entrusted to the newly created Railway Board which came under that department as well. In 1908 a separate Railway Department was created. In 1921 business relating to posts and telegraphs was transferred to the P.W.D. from the Commerce Department. In 1923 the P.W.D. was amalgamated with the Department of Industries, in the new Department of Industries and Labour. It should be noted that the records of this department are not yet completely arranged.

GENERAL

General indexes	1860–1923	180 v
Index and contents	1872	6 v
General proceedings volumes	1860–1922	2,600 v

ACCOUNTS BRANCH

'A' and 'B' proceedings	1864–81	5 bdls

ACCOUNTS (CIVIL AND MILITARY WORKS) BRANCH

'A' and 'B' proceedings	1874–81	1 bdl

ACCOUNTS (CIVIL WORKS) BRANCH

'A' and 'B' proceedings	1882–1923	15 bdls

ACCOUNTS (ESTABLISHMENT) BRANCH

'A' and 'B' proceedings	1880–1910	25 bdls

ACCOUNTS (GENERAL) BRANCH

'A' and 'B' proceedings and files	1870–1922	26 bdls

ACCOUNTS (IRRIGATION) BRANCH

'A' and 'B' proceedings and files	1864–1923	18 bdls
Despatches to secretary of state	1868–89	1 bdl

CIVIL AVIATION BRANCH

For 1919–20 see also Department of Commerce and Industry; for 1920–1 see Department of Commerce; and for 1923–33 see Department of Industries and Labour

'A' and 'B' proceedings	1922–3	2 bdls

CIVIL WORKS (AGRICULTURAL, BUILDING, COMMUNICATION, INDUSTRIES, MISCELLANEOUS) BRANCH

'A' and 'B' proceedings and files	1862–1905	30 bdls

CIVIL WORKS (BUILDING) BRANCH

'A', 'B', deposit proceedings and files	1887–1923	86 bdls
Copies of circular letters addressed to Provincial Government	1908–11	3 bdls
Despatches to secretary of state	1864–1911	2 bdls

CIVIL WORKS (COAL AND IRON) BRANCH

Proceedings volumes	1901–5	16 v
'A' and 'B' proceedings	1882–1905	17 bdls
Despatches to secretary of state	1883–1903	1 bdl

CIVIL WORKS (COMMUNICATION) BRANCH

'A' and 'B' proceedings	1882–1921	9 bdls
Despatches to secretary of state	1861–97	1 bdl

CIVIL WORKS (ELECTRICITY) BRANCH

'A' and 'B' proceedings and files	1899–1920	14-bdls
Despatches to secretary of state	1906–9	1 bdl
Notifications	1905–10	3 bdls

CIVIL WORKS (IRRIGATION) BRANCH

'A' and 'B' proceedings and files	1867–1923	146 bdls
Notification and resolutions, and copies of circular letters		3 bdls
Despatches to secretary of state	1867–1911	8 bdls
Despatches from secretary of state	1898–1904	1 bdl
Portfolio of plans 'A' and 'B'	1920	2 v
Irrigation maps	1883	1 v

CIVIL WORKS (IRRIGATION) BRANCH: CANAL SERIES

Proceedings	1855–92	54 v
	1870–97	67 bdls

ESTABLISHMENT BRANCH

Service books of officers		130 v
Proceedings volumes	1905–10	12 v
'A' and 'B' proceedings	1862–1923	81 bdls
Despatches to secretary of state	1880–1912	6 bdls

ESTABLISHMENT (ACCOUNTS) BRANCH

'A' and 'B' proceedings	1869–1908	4 bdls
Despatches to secretary of state	1877–82	1 bdl

ESTABLISHMENT (BUILDING, ROADS, CIVIL WORKS, MILITARY) BRANCH

'A' and 'B' proceedings	1872–81	3 bdls

ESTABLISHMENT (GENERAL) BRANCH

'A' and 'B' proceedings	1870–9	6 bdls
Despatches to secretary of state	1861–87	2 bdls

ESTABLISHMENT (IRRIGATION) BRANCH

'A' and 'B' proceedings	1867–79	3 bdls

FORESTS BRANCH

For post 1871 see Department of Revenue, Agriculture and Commerce.

Index	1865–71	2 v
Proceedings volumes	1861–71	32 v
'A' and 'B' proceedings	1861–73	33 bdls
Book docket covers	1861–71	1 bdl
Despatches from secretary of state	1861–70	5 v
Despatches to secretary of state	1861–70	1 v
Revenue, Agricultural and Commerce despatches to under secretary	1873	1 v

GENERAL BRANCH

Indexes	1863–9	10 v
Proceedings volumes	1859–1904	59 v
General Order volume	1900–5	1 v
'A' and 'B' proceedings and files	1860–1923	83 bdls
Despatches from secretary of state	1860–71	2 bdls
Despatches to secretary of state	1886–1904	9 bdls

GOVERNOR-GENERAL'S PROCEEDINGS

'A' and 'B'	1860–3	14 bdls
Diaries	1860–3	2 v

MISCELLANEOUS BRANCH

'A' and 'B' proceedings and files	1862–1922	34 bdls
Resolutions	1902–11	6 bdls
Despatches to secretary of state	1864–1906	2 bdls

POST OFFICE BRANCH

For pre-1921 see Department of Commerce; and for post-1923 see Department of Industries and Labour.

'A', 'B' and MS proceedings and files	1921–3	8 bdls

RAILWAYS BRANCH

Index	1882–1901	4 v
Accounts Guaranteed Railway		
'A' and 'B' proceedings	1871–9	8 bdls
Accounts Railway		
'A' and 'B' proceedings	1864–1905	9 bdls
Railway Construction		
'A' and 'B' proceedings	1879–1905	55 bdls
Guaranteed Railway		
'A' proceedings	1863–72	1 bdl
Railway Establishment		
'A' and 'B' proceedings and files	1869–1905	17 bdls
Railways Accounts		
'A' proceedings	1872–94	1 bdl
Railway Project		
'A' and 'B' proceedings	1898–1905	6 bdls
Railway		
'A' and 'B' proceedings	1860–79	30 bdls
Railway Traffic		
'A' and 'B' proceedings	1879–1905	36 bdls
Despatches to secretary of state	1861–71	1 bdl
State Railway		
'A' and 'B' proceedings	1872–4	3 bdls
Railway statistics		
'A' and 'B' proceedings	1891–1905	27 bdls
Railway stores		
'A' and 'B' proceedings	1879–1905	5 bdls
Despatches		
Public Works and railway despatches from secretary of state	1860–74	76 v

Despatches to secretary of state	1861–84	71 v
Papers and documents of various railways	1848–1904	81 v
Miscellaneous		
Inspection reports	1858–62, 1865–7	2 v
Indian Railways Capital and Revenue Accounts	1897–1904	15 v
Register State Railways Capital	1894–1905	22 v

CIVIL WORKS TELEGRAPH BRANCH

For pre-1867 see Home Department; for 1867–70 see Foreign Department; for 1905–20 see Department of Commerce and Industry; and for 1920–1 see Commerce Department.

'A' and 'B' proceedings	1870–1923 [except 1905–21]	42 bdls
Despatches to secretary of state	1870–1904	3 bdls

TELEGRAPH BRANCH

Files	1922–3	5 bdls

TELEGRAPH ESTABLISHMENT BRANCH

'A' and 'B' proceedings	1871–1905	12 bdls
Despatches to secretary of state	1889–1900	1 bdl

POST AND TELEGRAPH BRANCH

'A' and 'B' and filed proceedings	1921–3	13 bdls
Circulars	1861–91	43 v
Notification	1865–1911	22 v

PUBLIC WORKS: DESPATCHES

Despatches from secretary of state	1884–1909	1 bdl
Despatches to secretary of state from Ecclesiastical, Agricultural, Educational, Industrial, Accounts, Establishment	1862–88	1 bdl
Accounts despatches to secretary of state	1864–89	3 bdls
Public Works Building and Roads despatches to secretary of state	1862–1911	14 bdls

CIVIL WORKS BUILDING SERIES

New Imperial Secretariat building at Calcutta	1889–92	1 bdl

CIVIL WORKS FRONTIER ROADS

Dera Ghazi Khan Pishon Road, vol. II   1887–93   1 bdl

RENT CHARGEABLE FOR GOVERNMENT BUILDINGS
OCCUPIED AS RESIDENCIES
1887–96   1 bdl

SUPPLY OF STORES FOR THE PUBLIC SERVICE
1872–96   1 bdl

CIVIL WORKS BUILDING AND ROADS ETC.
1872–95   5 bdls

PUBLIC WORKS FAMINE COMMITTEE GENERAL

Note   1888   1 v
Famine relief works, Rajputana, Burma   1891–2   2 bdls

MISCELLANEOUS VOLUMES

Acquittance rolls	1861–1904	77 v
Simla allowance bills	1889–1907	18 v
Other miscellaneous volumes	1877–1910	31 v
Registers	1901–6	12 v
Files	1905–23	2 bdls
Resolutions	1900–11	10 bdls
Circulars	1884–1911	7 bdls
Cash book	1865	1 v
Stamp accounts	1911	1 v
Issue and receipt registers		21 v
Transferred list		6 v
Office order books		4 v

RAILWAY BOARD 1905–8; RAILWAY DEPARTMENT
1908–47

Until 1905 railway matters were dealt with in the Railway Branch of the
Public Works Department. In 1905 control of the railway system was
entrusted to a newly established Railway Board (under the Department of
Commerce and Industry). In 1908 the Railway Department became a
separate department, and in 1947 a ministry in the independent Government of India. Although the file system of record keeping was adopted in

this department in 1924 the files continued to be classified into A, B, C and Deposit 'proceedings', and they are both arranged and indexed in this way.

Indexes	1902–56	55 v

ACCOUNTS BRANCH
'A' and 'B' proceedings	1905–25	21 bdls

ACCOUNTS, ESTABLISHMENT BRANCH
'A' and 'B' proceedings	1905–18	2 bdls

ACCOUNTS I BRANCH
'B' proceedings	1941–4	10 bdls

ACCOUNTS II BRANCH
'B' proceedings	1941–3	10 bdls

AIR RAID PRECAUTIONS BRANCH
'B' proceedings	1943–4	4 bdls

BUDGET BRANCH
'A', 'B', 'C' proceedings	1924–38	30 bdls

CASH BRANCH
'B' proceedings	1931–43	18 bdls

CODE BRANCH
'A' and 'B' proceedings	1937–41	4 bdls

CONSTRUCTION BRANCH
'A' proceedings	1905–15	77 bdls
'B' proceedings	1905–15	40 bdls
Files	1907	1 bdl

ESTABLISHMENT BRANCH
'A' proceedings	1905–41	47 bdls
'B' proceedings	1905–44	344 bdls
Files	1905–19	1 bdl

FINANCE BRANCH
'A' proceedings	1916–42	19 bdls
'B' and 'C' proceedings	1916–43	138 bdls
Files	1921–9	1 bdl

GENERAL BRANCH

'A' proceedings	1910–15	9 bdls
'B' and 'C' proceedings	1910–43	52 bdls
Files	1911–16	1 bdl

LABOUR BRANCH

'A' proceedings	1929–35	5 bdls
'B' proceedings	1929–35	10 bdls

LIBRARY BRANCH

'B' proceedings	1932–43	1 bdl

PRIORITY BRANCH

'A' and 'B' proceedings	1918–19	1 bdl

PROJECT BRANCH

'A' proceedings	1905–25	38 bdls
'B' proceedings	1905–25	36 bdls
Files	1915–23	1 bdl

PROGRAMME BRANCH

'A' proceedings	1925–9	13 bdls
'B' proceedings	1925–9	28 bdls

REGISTRAR BRANCH

'B' proceedings	1916–23	3 bdls
Files	1909–23	1 bdl

STATISTICS BRANCH

'A' proceedings	1905–31	5 bdls
'B' and 'C' proceedings	1905–43	165 bdls
Files	1912–22	1 bdl

STORES BRANCH

'A' proceedings	1905–39	25 bdls
'B' proceedings	1905–44	265 bdls
Files	1915–21	1 bdl

TECHNICAL BRANCH

'A' and 'B' proceedings	1925–9	24 bdls

TRAFFIC BRANCH

'A' proceedings	1905–36	59 bdls
'B' proceedings	1905–43	214 bdls

WAY AND WORKS BRANCH

'A' proceedings	1916–25	10 bdls
'B' proceedings	1916–25	52 bdls
Files	1916–21	1 bdl

WORKS BRANCH

'A' proceedings	1930–7	12 bdls
'B' proceedings	1930–43	99 bdls

RECORDS OF THE ACCOUNTANT-GENERAL, RAILWAYS

Accounts (various)	1911–29	33 bdls
Records relating to various railways	1886–1923	35 v

RECORDS OF THE CONTROLLER OF RAILWAY ACCOUNTS

Accounts	1929–41	56 bdls
Administration	1929–41	60 bdls
Capital Accounts and Code	1929–40	21 bdls
Establishment	1930–41	65 bdls
General	1929–41	11 bdls
Revenue Accounts	1929–39	20 bdls
Statistics 'B' and 'C' proceedings	1931–5	9 bdls

MISCELLANEOUS

Budget supplement	1935–41	11 v
Indian railways capital and revenue accounts	1905–40	36 v
Finance accounts	1907–40	31 v
Finance and revenue accounts of the Government of India	1917–35	18 v
Combined finance and revenue accounts of central and provincial Governments in India	1938–9	1 v
Journal, ledger and technical reports	1913–29	16 v
Monthly home accounts file	1904–21	4 v
Final home accounts of the secretary of state and the High Commissioner for India	1928–30	3 v

Home accounts of the secretary of state and the High Commissioner for India	1928-31	4 v
Accounts current of the secretary of state and the High Commissioner for India	1938-40	3 v
Statement of payments made in England by the secretary of state and the High Commissioner for India	1935-8	2 v
Payments register	1924-7	1 v
English payments register	1932-3	1 v
Report by the Agent	1936-7	1 v

STATE RAILWAYS

State railways capital register	1905-33	57 v
Abstract register, capital	1931-3	2 v
Imperial register, State Railways capital	1921-7	1 v
London accounts	1907-22	10 v
London account—account current	1921-30	2 v
London account—Quarterly Abstract Reports	1910-21	1 v
Monthly London account current	1921-2	1 v
London stores accounts	1910-21	1 v
Register—State railways revenue	1909-32	28 v
Abstract revenue accounts	1932-3	1 v
State railways stores branch—journal	1913-17	4 v
State railways stores branch—register of receipts and charges	1908-24	2 v

REFORMS OFFICE 1919-21, 1930-40

The Reforms Office was an independent establishment from 1919 to 1921, and again from 1930 to 1940. For the years between these dates see Home Department, Public Branch and Special Branch (1927-30). From 1940 to 1947 the Reforms Office was attached to the Governor-General's secretariat, and after 1947 it was merged in the Ministry of Law. The office dealt with questions relating to constitutional reforms.

FEDERATION BRANCH

Files	1937-40	17 boxes
Diaries	1937-40	1 box
Miscellaneous	1937-8	1 bdl

FRANCHISE BRANCH

'A' proceedings	1920–1	13 boxes
'B' proceedings	1919–21	3 boxes
'Deposit' proceedings	1920–1	1 box
Files	1935–6	14 boxes
Diaries	1936	1 box

GENERAL BRANCH

'A' proceedings	1919–21	4 boxes
'B' proceedings	1919–21	4 boxes
'Deposit' proceedings	1919–21	3 boxes
Files	1937–40	12 boxes
Files (A)	1935–7	10 boxes
Files (B)	1935–7	10 boxes
Diaries	1937–40	1 box
Diaries (A)	1936–7	1 box
Diaries (B)	1936–7	1 box
Notes	1935–8	1 bdl

REFORMS BRANCH

'A' proceedings	June 1920	
'B' proceedings	1919–20	1 box
'Deposit' proceedings	1919–21	
Files	1930–48	64 boxes
Diaries	1930–48	2 boxes
Notes (secret)	1930–31	1 bdl

SPECIAL BRANCH

Files	1935–8	11 boxes
Diaries	1935–8	1 box
Notes	1927–9	2 bdls
Miscellaneous volumes	1934–5	1 bdl
Code		1 bdl

SUBJECT BRANCH

'A' proceedings	1920–1	2 boxes
'B' proceedings	1920–1	1 box
'Deposit' proceedings	1920–1	1 box

MISCELLANEOUS

Miscellaneous notes	1929–37	2 bdls
Departmental memoranda	1923–32	2 bdls
Opinions of the provincial government on the re-commendations of the Indian Statutory Commission		1 bdl
Orders in Council	1936–7	1 bdl

GOVERNOR-GENERAL'S SECRETARIAT

Indexes	1937–42	6 v
'A' section	1939–47	29 bdls
'B' section	1938–47	42 bdls
'G' section (judicial)	1934–8	2 bdls
Police (confidential)	1937	1 bdl

OFFICE OF THE PRIVATE SECRETARY TO THE VICEROY
(*name changed in 1948 to Prime Minister's secretariat records*):
HONOURS BRANCH

Indexes	1937–42	12 v
Files	1918–54	71 bdls

SURVEY OF INDIA 1777–1902

The three survey branches, Trigonometrical, Topographical and Revenue, were at first virtually separate departments, each with its own superintendent. Topographical surveys began in the eighteenth century and in 1763 Major James Rennell was appointed Surveyor-General of Bengal by Lord Clive. The Great Trigonometrical Survey of India began in 1802 in Madras, and remained under the control of the Madras Government until 1818, when it was transferred to the direct control of the governor-general in Council, all its records and plans being removed to Calcutta. Revenue surveys began in 1822. In 1839 the records of all surveys conducted by various departments were ordered to be deposited in one place, Calcutta; in 1847 the Revenue survey work was placed under a separate superintendent (Colonel Thuiller); in 1862 the surveyor-generalship was separated from the superintendency of the Trigonometrical Survey.

The first regular organization of the Survey Department was in 1866, but the three branches remained virtually separate departments, each with its own cadre and establishment until in January 1878 the three were amalgamated under the designation of the Survey of India, and placed under the orders of a surveyor-general.

Surveys were controlled by the Military Department from 1860 to 1864, the Home Department (Public Branch) from 1865 to 1871, the Department of Revenue, Agriculture and Commerce from 1871 to 1879, and the Department of Home, Revenue and Agriculture from 1879 to 1881. In July 1881 a separate Revenue and Agriculture Department was constituted and the Survey of India remained under the control of this Department until April 1923. From April 1923 until August 1945 the Survey came under the control of the Department of Education, Health and Lands (Land Revenue Branch 1923-32; Lands and Overseas Branch 1933-9; and Forest and Lands Branch 1940-5), and from September 1945 under the control of the Department of Agriculture, which became the Ministry of Agriculture in the independent Government of India, and in February 1951 the Ministry of Food and Agriculture. In June 1952 the Survey of India came under the control of the Ministry of Natural Resources and Scientific Research.

SURVEY OF INDIA RECORDS

Field office records of the Survey of India	1865-99	50 bdls; 183 carton boxes
Index to the correspondence records of the Survey of India	1874-99	25 v
Revenue survey records (belonging to the Director, Land Records, Bengal)	1837-60	92 v
Annual reports	1880-1902	26 v
Correspondence records of the Survey of India (DDn. volumes)	1772-1894	1,028 v
Diaries of trans-Himalayan exploration by Nain Singh, Kishen Singh, Hari Ram, Ganga Ram, and other Indian explorers who mapped out parts of Central Asia and Tibet, till then unexplored	1867-86	13 v, written in colloquial Hindi
Memoirs and field books	1774-1866	342 v
Revenue records (village plans, traverse records etc.)		1,430 v
Originals of cantonment plans (revenue)		90 folios
Survey of India historical maps	1700-1900	206 folios
Survey of India M.R. 10, miscellaneous maps	1725-1861	21 folios

III

NATIONAL ARCHIVES OF INDIA RECORDS
OF RESIDENCIES AND AGENCIES

Control over the Indian princely states during the British period, from about 1813 onwards, was exercised by the governor-general through his agents, the political officers, who generally resided in the states. In the larger states the Government of India was represented by a resident, while some of the other states (as in Rajputana and Central India) were grouped together under a single agent to the governor-general, who was assisted by local residents or political agents. The 'paramount power' acted for the native states in relation to foreign powers and other native states, but respected the internal authority of the princes. The political officers formed the channel of communication between the states and the Government of India (Foreign Department), the officials of British India, and other native states. They also advised and assisted the rulers over any matters on which they were consulted. The agents were under the control of the Foreign (later Foreign and Political) Department, and from 1937 of the Political Department. After Independence, relations with the states were dealt with by a Ministry of States, which was abolished in 1954 on the final integration of the former princely states into the Republic of India. With the lapse of 'paramountcy' the records of the residencies and agencies were dispersed. Some were sent to the United Kingdom (where they are now in the custody of the India Office Library); some were transferred to the successor states; while others were deposited in the National Archives of India. The records described below are those now in the custody of the National Archives. It should be noted that it is not always possible to give the covering dates of a particular series, and that the records of specific agencies or residencies often include those of its predecessor, and sometimes successor, bodies as well. Many of the later records, especially those from about 1924 onwards, are of a routine nature, which may be weeded out when the papers are finally sorted and arranged.

CENTRAL INDIA STATES AGENCY

The Central India Agency (after 1933 the Central India States Agency) was established in 1854 and included at various times the following residencies and agencies:

(1) BHOPAL AGENCY

This was created in 1818 when a political officer was accredited to the Bhopal Darbar with collateral charge over the other states in the vicinity. He ranked as agent to the governor-general until 1842, when the charge was made into a political agency. In 1854 the Bhopal Agency became part of the Central India Agency. The agency included the states of Bhopal, Dewas Junior and Dewas Senior (from 1931), Rajgarh, Narsinghgarh, Khilchipur, Kurwai, Makrai (from 1933), Mohammadgarh and Pathari.

(2) BUNDELKHAND AGENCY

The Bundelkhand Agency was created in 1802 after the treaty of Bassein, and in 1854 was included in the new Central India Agency. Until 1857 the Baghelkhand states formed part of the agency, but from 1857 to 1862 there was a separate agency attached to the Rewa Darbar (Rewa was the first among the Baghelkhand states), and from 1871 to 1931 there was a separate Baghelkhand Agency. In 1931 the two agencies were amalgamated as the Bundelkhand Agency, but two years later the first among the Baghelkhand states (Rewa) came into direct political relations with the agent to the governor-general (later resident) at Indore. The amalgamated agency now included the following states: Ajaigarh, Alipura, Banka Pahari, Baoni, Baraundha (Pathar Kachhar), Beri, Bhaisaunda, Bihat, Bijawar, Bijna, Charkhari, Chhatarpur, Datia, Dhurwal, Garrauli, Gaurihar, Hasht-bhaya jagirs, Jaso, Jigni, Kamta Rajaula, Kothi, Lugasi, Maihar, Naigawan Rebai, Orchha (Tikamgarh), Pahra (Chaubepur), Paldeo (Nayagaon), Panna, Samthar, Sarila, Sohawal, Taraon (Pathraundi), and Tori-Fatehpur.

(3) BAGHELKHAND AGENCY

The Baghelkhand states formed part of the Bundelkhand Agency until 1857 when a separate political agent was appointed, attached to the Rewa Darbar and in direct subordination to the agent to the governor-general in Central India. The agency was abolished in 1862, but revived as the Baghelkhand Agency in 1871, when it comprised the states of Rewa, Nagod, Maihar, Sohawal, and Kothi. In 1896 the states of Baraundha or Pathar Kachhar, Jaso, Paldeo, Bhaisaunda, Pahra, Taraon and Kamta Rajaula were transferred to the Baghelkhand Agency from the Bundelkhand Agency. In 1931 the agency was amalgamated with the Bundelkhand Agency, and in 1933 Rewa State came into direct political relations with the agent to the governor-general (later resident) at Indore.

(4) INDORE AGENCY

A political officer was first attached to the Court of the Maharaja Holkar of Indore in 1818, and in 1854 this appointment was merged in that of the newly created agent to the governor-general in Central India. From 1899 to 1916 there was a separate resident appointed to conduct political relations with the Maharaja Holkar under the supervision of the agent to the governor-general, but in 1916 the old system was revived. The resident supervised and controlled the Bhopal, Bundelkhand and Malwa Political Agencies, and conducted direct relations with Indore State and (from 1933, after the abolition of the Baghelkhand Agency) Rewa State, the first among the Baghelkhand states.

(5) MALWA AGENCY

The Malwa Agency was established in 1818, under the commandant of the local corps stationed at Mehidpur. In 1860 when the Central India Horse was regularly constituted, the charge of the agency (then called Western Malwa Agency) was entrusted to the commandant, with headquarters at Agar. However, in 1895 the Malwa Agency was created under a separate political officer, with headquarters at Nimach. From 1907 to 1931 the two Dewas states were included in the agency: in the latter year they were transferred to the Bhopal Agency. In 1925 the Malwa Agency was amalgamated with the Southern States (formerly Bhopawar) Agency, with the designation Malwa and Southern States Agencies: in 1934 the designation was changed to Malwa Agency.

(6) BHOPAWAR AGENCY
(from 1914 SOUTHERN STATES AGENCY)

This charge was originally divided into two sections known as the Bhil and Deputy Bhil Agencies, with headquarters at Bhopawar and Manpur respectively. After 1857 the officer commanding the Bhil Corps was entrusted with the political control of the agency, with headquarters at Sardarpur. But in 1882 the Bhil and Deputy Bhil Agencies were amalgamated, and a regular agency was constituted at Sardarpur. In 1911 the headquarters of the agency was transferred to Manpur, and in 1914 its designation was changed to Southern States Agency. In 1925 it was amalgamated with the Malwa Agency and designated the Malwa and Southern States Agency, with headquarters at Manpur, and from 1932 at Indore. In 1934 the designation of the amalgamated agency was changed to Malwa Agency.

(7) MALWA AND SOUTHERN STATES AGENCY

This agency was established in 1925 when the Malwa Agency was amalgamated with the Southern States Agency. In 1934 the designation was changed to Malwa Agency. The agency comprised the states of Alirajpur, Barwani, Dhar, Jaora, Jhabua, Jobat, Kathiwara, Mathwar, Piploda, Ratanmal, Ratlam, Sailana and Sitamau.

(8) GWALIOR POLITICAL AGENCY

The Gwalior Residency was established in 1782, and formed part of the political charge of the agent to the governor-general in Central India from 1854 to 1921, when it was placed in direct relations with the Government of India. The state of Khaniadha was attached to the residency from 1888 when it separated from the Bundelkhand Agency, and the states of Rampur and Benares (formerly part of the political charge of the governor of the United Provinces) were added in 1936. From 1860 to 1896 the officer commanding the Central India Horse at Guna was also in political charge of the surrounding minor states, later included in the Gwalior Residency.

AGENCY RECORDS

Receipt registers	1817–80	
Issue registers	1817–80	
Miscellaneous letters	1806–56	2 boxes
Loose letters		
Letters issued	1845–82	58 boxes
Letters received	1818–83	90 boxes
Letters received from different political agents, in bound volumes		140 boxes
Unlocated letters		
Cantonment	1858–1903	12 boxes
General records	1857–1903	188 boxes
Vernacular files	1822–1914	36 boxes
Baghelkhand Agency	1858–1901	17 boxes
Baghelkhand boundary	1891–1901	1 box
Baghelkhand vernacular	1825–1909	4 boxes
Baghelkhand vernacular (Rewa)	1812–1907	7 boxes
Bagli		4 boxes
Bagli vernacular		3 boxes
Bhopal Agency	1857–1903	18 boxes
Bhopal boundary		9 boxes
Bhopal vernacular	1850–1908	8 boxes

Bhopawar Agency	1858–1901	19 boxes
Bhopawar vernacular	1819–1901	9 boxes
Bundelkhand Agency	1858–1901	33 boxes
Bundelkhand boundary	1801–1905	14 boxes
Bundelkhand vernacular	1804–1902	16 boxes
Dewas, Junior and Senior		25 boxes
Dewas vernacular	1868–1903	3 boxes
Dewas Tankedar	1858–98	1 box
Goona	1858–1901	3 boxes
Gwalior Agency	1857–1903	14 boxes
Indore Darbar	1858–1901	19 boxes
Indore vernacular	1824–1904	13 boxes
Malwa Agency	1850–1901	17 boxes
Malwa vernacular	1817–1904	17 boxes
Miscellaneous boxes		15 boxes
Alphabetical index of Central India Agency files	1917–46	30 v
A.R.P.	1942–3	3 boxes
Boundary Settlement Office	1930	4 boxes
Census	1910–44	48 boxes
Confidential	1886–1953	19 boxes
Confidential miscellaneous		105 boxes
Educational Branch	1917–24	4 boxes
Excise Office	1902–41	64 boxes
Federal (A, B and C)	1947–9	16 boxes
Finance	1904–54	380 boxes
Budget	1926–45	12 boxes
Budget: pay bills	1903–44	6 boxes
Budget contingent bills	1917–48	1 box
Receipt and issue registers (Finance)	1906–54	13 v
General D	1904–21	16 boxes
Receipt and issue registers		76 v
General G	1947–50	38 boxes
Information	1947–9	7 boxes
Judicial B	1904–51	237 boxes
File registers, receipt and issue registers	1912–46	125 v
Judicial B, High Court civil appeal	1922–45	7 boxes
Judicial B, High Court criminal appeal	1921–46	5 boxes
Judicial B, High Court revision	1921–46	5 boxes
Judicial B, High Court civil revision	1928–45	10 boxes
Judicial B, High Court miscellaneous	1925–42	2 boxes
Judicial B, small cause suits	1932–44	9 boxes

Judicial B, railway lands (criminal)	1931–45	4 boxes
Judicial B, railway lands (miscellaneous)	1942	1 box
Judicial B, criminal cases	1924–43	4 boxes
Judicial B, criminal cases (miscellaneous)	1936	1 box
Judicial B, civil cases	1936–45	1 box
Judicial B, civil miscellaneous	1946	1 box
Judicial B, civil suits	1931–47	1 box
Judicial B, cases	1929–46	1 box
Judicial B, sessions cases	1921–4	1 box
Judicial B, railway lands (W.C.O.)	1944	1 box
Judicial B, civil courts: Pay Bills	1917–24	4 boxes
Judicial B, small cause execution	1936	1 box
Judicial Officer, Mhow Cantonment	1914–47	28 boxes
Miscellaneous registers		
Malwa Bhil Corps	1918–48	116 boxes
N.W.F.	1942–5	4 boxes
O.T.C.	1940–1	5 boxes
Petrol	1942–50	10 boxes
Plague		7 boxes
Police general		1 box
Police Cr. Branch		93 boxes
Police Cr. Registers	1905–46	27 v
Office of I.G.P. (Jails)	1914–43	7 boxes
Political A	1904–47	170 boxes
Political file registers		
Political Branch	1901–10	1 box
Political Branch, receipt and issue registers		
Political Branch, Coronation Darbar	1911	1 box
Political Branch, Prince of Wales visit	1921	3 boxes
Political Branch, Viceroy's visit to Indore	1922	1 box
Calcutta files	1906–47	65 boxes
Public Works Department		283 boxes
Railway registers		
Red Cross	1940–5	17 boxes
Treasury Office	1890–1951	18 boxes and 54 v (registers)
War	1939–47	96 boxes
War receipt and issue registers		
Extracts from records	1818–57	18 boxes
Central India miscellaneous registers		8 v

SUBORDINATE AGENCY RECORDS

BAGHELKHAND AGENCY

Indexes, receipt and issue registers	1805–1932	1,040 v
Vernacular files	1805–1916	
Rewa vernacular files	1824–99	2 boxes
Baghelkhand Political Agency	1829–1932	548 boxes
	1928–33	2 boxes
Baghelkhand excise	1916–19	4 boxes
Baghelkhand census	1901–30	6 boxes
Baghelkhand boundary	1834–1911	7 boxes
Baghelkhand famine	1895–1908	5 boxes

BHOPAL AGENCY

Bhopal vernacular		110 boxes
Bhopal Political Agency	1830–1936	332 boxes
Bhopal accounts and finance	1931–47	82 boxes
Bhopal excise	1941–7	6 boxes
Bhopal notes relating to weeding		1 box
Bhopal gazettes	1944	1 box
Bhopal judicial branch	1931–47	34 boxes
Bhopal Makrai		10 boxes
Bhopal pensions branch	1914–46	3 boxes
Bhopal political branch	1931–47	35 boxes
Bhopal railway civil cases	1910–36	4 boxes
Bhopal criminal cases	1911–36	40 boxes
Bhopal miscellaneous cases	1912–36	9 boxes
Bhopal Boundary Settlement Office		116 boxes
Bhopal War	1914–45	49 boxes
Bhopal miscellaneous volumes		170 v

BUNDELKHAND AGENCY

Bundelkhand registers		770 v
Bundelkhand vernacular files	1805–1916	228 boxes
Bundelkhand vernacular miscellaneous	1805–72	1 box
Bundelkhand Political Agency English files	1805–1947	482 boxes
War	1940–7	7 boxes
Bundelkhand excise	1915–31	28 boxes
Bundelkhand boundary	1829–1911	21 boxes
Bundelkhand census	1920–41	7 boxes
Bundelkhand famine	1904–19	91 boxes

Bundelkhand Nowgong Sub-Jail	1918–47	11 boxes
Bundelkhand Nowgong Week files	1937–9	3 boxes
Bundelkhand Local Excise Authority	1915–46	10 boxes
Bundelkhand rationing	1921–45	15 boxes
Bundelkhand priority branch	1945–7	5 boxes
Bundelkhand Judicial Officer, Nowgong	1864–1946	132 boxes
Bundelkhand Agency Surgeon	1891–1947	131 boxes
Bundelkhand confidential	1919–47	2 boxes
Bundelkhand Red Cross	1942–5	3 boxes
Bundelkhand duplicate lists		1 box

GWALIOR POLITICAL AGENCY

Gwalior Political Agency files	1907–47	339 boxes
Gwalior receipt and issue registers, including copies of letters sent and received (i.e. correspondence volumes)		400 v
United Provinces Secretariat	1890–1905 ⎫	
Benares	1889–1942 ⎬ 35 boxes	
Rampur	1852–1935 ⎭	

INDORE AGENCY

Indore files	1885–1916	24 boxes
Indore boundary		3 boxes
Indore receipt and issue registers		74 v

BHOPAWAR POLITICAL AGENCY (LATER SOUTHERN STATES AGENCY)

Bhopawar Political Agency files		51 boxes
Bhopawar vernacular		135 boxes
Bhopawar vernacular: various	1891–1932	40 boxes
Bhopawar (Bagode)		1 box
Bhopawar Political Agency English files	1907–24	33 boxes
Southern States (Forest Department)		1 box
Southern States	1893–1934	12 boxes
Southern States: various legal cases	1907–34	72 boxes

MALWA AND SOUTHERN STATES AGENCY

Agency files	1925–31	19 boxes

MALWA POLITICAL AGENCY

Malwa Political Agency files	1860–1925	69 boxes
Malwa finance	1932–47	123 boxes

Malwa judicial	1928–47	78 boxes
Malwa receipt and issue registers		15 v
Malwa political branch	1932–47	71 boxes
Malwa political branch registers		
Malwa war branch	1939–47	33 boxes
Malwa war branch registers		
Malwa boundary (English)		45 boxes
Malwa vernacular		97 boxes
Malwa confidential	1937–46	1 box
Malwa residency functions	1947–8	1 box
Malwa library catalogue of books		1 v

EASTERN STATES AGENCY

The Eastern States Agency was established in 1933 when the states formerly in political relations with the governments of Bengal, Bihar and Orissa, and the Central Provinces (except Makrai State, which was included in the Bhopal Political Agency in Central India) were placed in direct relations with the Government of India through the agent to the governor-general, Eastern States. In 1936 the states of Cooch Behar and Tripura and Mayurbhanj State were also included in the agency. The Eastern States Agency included the following agencies:

(1) BENGAL STATES AGENCY

This agency consisted of the states of Cooch Behar, Tripura, and Mayurbhanj, which were included in the Eastern States Agency from 1936. Cooch Behar was a feudatory state in North Bengal, with a British Government superintendent of the state acting as vice-president of the Council. There had been a political agent in Tripura from 1871 to 1878 and again from 1910: in 1922 the state had been placed in direct political relations with the Government of India, the Governor of Bengal in Council acting as agent to the governor-general. Mayurbhanj was formerly one of the Orissa tributary states.

(2) ORISSA STATES AGENCY

Established in 1937, this was formerly known as the Sambalpur Agency and consisted of most of the former Orissa tributary states, namely: Athgarh, Athmallik, Bamra, Baramba, Baud, Bonai, Daspalla, Dhenkanal, Gangpur, Hindol, Keonjhar, Khandpara, Kharsawan, Narsinghpur, Nayagarh, Nilgiri, Pal-Lahara, Rairakhol, Ranpur, Seraikela, Sonpur, Talcher, and Tigiria.

(3) CHHATTISGARH STATES AGENCY

Established in 1936 this comprised the states of Bastar, Changbhakar, Chhuikhadan, Jashpur, Kalahandi, Kanker, Kawardha, Khairagarh, Korea, Nandgaon, Patna, Raigarh, Sakti, Sarangarh, Surguja and Udaipur. This agency was a revival of the old Raipur Agency, that is the political agency controlling the Chhattisgarh feudatory states, with headquarters at Raipur.

AGENCY RECORDS

Files	1933–47	69 bdls
War branch files	1939–47	17 bdls
Administration files	1949–50	1 bdl
Pay Bills, T.A. Bills and Provident Fund	1933–48	7 bdls
Registers	1924–49	4 bdls
Character and Service Roll, miscellaneous papers etc.		5 bdls

CHHATTISGARH STATES AGENCY RECORDS

Files	1901–47	19 bdls
Pay Bills	1892–1947	8 bdls
Miscellaneous boundary disputes	1902–4	2 bdls

ORISSA STATES AGENCY RECORDS

Files	1918–47	24 bdls
War files	1943–7	10 bdls
Miscellaneous boundary disputes		1 bdl

HYDERABAD RESIDENCY

The Hyderabad Residency was established in 1779/80 when J. Holland of the Madras Civil Service was appointed resident. The succession of residents was unbroken from that date until the lapse of paramountcy in 1947. From 1853 to 1903 the resident also held administrative charge of the province of Berar, and from 1853 to 1860 of certain district in the Raichur Doab and on the western frontier of Hyderabad.

RESIDENCY RECORDS

Indexes	1782–1938	26 v
Correspondence to and from the resident	1785–1884	891 v
Extracts of correspondence	1790–1873	85 v

English proceedings of the Inam Commission	1850–1	5 v
Inward diary registers	1946–8	14 v
File movement registers	1946–52	28 v
Service books and leave accounts	1906–48	50 v
Contingent registers and contingent bills	1924–53	13 v, 7 bdls
Acquittance rolls	1895–1953	26 v
Pay bills	1915–53	33 bdls
Registration of foreigners		19 bdls
Registers showing establishment changes	1915–51	6 v
Registers of births and deaths	1891–1945	9 v
Marriage register books	1898–1947	4 v
Miscellaneous registers	1911–54	27 v
Miscellaneous papers		1 bdl
Files		
Accounts branch	1896–1953	47 bdls
Judicial	1916–47	11 bdls
Political and war	1832–1948	43 bdls
Confidential	1938–48	1 bdl
P.W.D. and State Counsellor's	1902–53	1 bdl
Miscellaneous		1 bdl

KASHMIR RESIDENCY

The Kashmir Residency was established in 1885, although political relations with the Government of India had begun in 1846, being conducted at that time by the Punjab Government through the Maharaja's agent at Lahore. No officer resided in Kashmir until 1852, when an officer on special duty was appointed, but he resided in Kashmir during the summer months only. In 1877 the officer on special duty was placed under the immediate orders of the Government of India, and in 1885 his designation was changed to resident and he was permanently stationed in Kashmir. There was a political agent in Gilgit from 1877 to 1881, and when the Gilgit Agency was re-established in 1889 it came under the control of the Kashmir Residency.

RESIDENCY RECORDS

Accounts registers	1837–1949	21 v
Miscellaneous registers	1938–49	14 v
Files not classified under subjects	1891–1950	17 bdls (521 files)

KOLHAPUR RESIDENCY AND THE DECCAN STATES AGENCY

The Kolhapur Residency and the Deccan States Agency was established in 1933 from the former Kolhapur and Southern Maratha Country States Agency, with the addition of Akalkot, Aundh, Bhor, Janjira, Jath, Phaltan, Savanur and Savantvadi. The Southern Maratha Country States Agency (established 1819) and the Kolhapur Agency (established 1843) had been amalgamated in 1862.

RESIDENCY AND AGENCY RECORDS

Accounts branch files	1935–49	14 boxes
Confidential files	1940–8	3 boxes
Control section files	1946–7	1 box
Various other records	1936–48	4 boxes, 1 v

MADRAS RESIDENCY

Before 1923 the states which at that date became the Madras States Agency were in political relations with the Government of Madras. These states were (1) Travancore and Cochin, where there had been a residency from 1800 to 1923; (2) Pudukottai, which from 1807 to 1841 had been in the charge of the resident of Tanjore and Pudukottai, from 1841 to 1865 in the charge of the collector of Madura, from 1865 to 1874 in the charge of the collector of Tanjore, and from 1874 to 1923 in the charge of the collector of Trichinopoly; (3) Banganapalle, which had been previously in the charge of the collector of Kurnool, and (4) Sandur, which had been in the charge of the collector of Bellary. In 1937 the Madras States Agency became the Madras Residency, and in 1939 Banganapalle and Sandur were transferred to the Mysore Residency.

MADRAS GOVERNMENT RECORDS (*these records will be returned to the Madras Government at a later date*)

Political Department proceedings, confidential and non-confidential	1857–1926	86 bdls
Political Department proceedings, in bound volumes	1801–1931	105 v
Public Department proceedings, including Public Political and Public Works Departments	1859–1937	5 bdls
Judicial Department proceedings	1866–1901	1 bdl

Revenue Department proceedings	1801–1920	8 bdls
Ecclesiastical Department proceedings, Military Department proceedings and Railway Department proceedings	1866–1911	3 bdls
Co-operative societies proceedings, and abstracts of papers of common interest	1672–1935	3 bdls

TRAVANCORE AND COCHIN RESIDENCY RECORDS

Letters to and from the Government of Madras in the Political, Secret and Military Departments	1759–1891	29 v
Letters to the Dewan of Travancore and the Dewan of Cochin	1841–91	39 v
Political files	1913–40	1 bdl
Travancore Residency files	1890–1922	19 bdls

COLLECTORATE RECORDS

Files relating to the office of the Political Agent Sandur	1895–1926	2 bdls
Files relating to the Collector of Bellary office, Revenue Board and Forest Department	1843–1918	2 bdls
Pudukottai Agency files	1825–1926	10 bdls
Pudukottai Political Department letters	1801–89	167 v
Pudukottai Agency correspondence regarding Chinnarakanai Jaghir	1849–52	1 v

MADRAS STATES AGENCY RECORDS

Madras States Agency files, political, special, and those relating to the Church case, Trichur	1913–41	12 bdls
Passports	1934–47	18 bdls
Confidential files relating to federal negotiations with Banganapalle and Sandur	1935–8	1 bdl

MYSORE RESIDENCY

There was a resident in Mysore from 1799 to 1843, when the office of resident was abolished and the duties of the resident were discharged by the commissioner for the affairs of Mysore. From 1867 to 1881 the commissioner was designated chief commissioner; the post was then abolished and the office of resident revived. From 1881 the resident for Mysore was also appointed chief commissioner for Coorg. In 1939 the states of Banganapalle and Sandur were transferred from the Madras States Agency to the Mysore Agency. The Mysore Residency records were dispersed as follows: (1) all important records of historical interest, confidential records relating to the private lives of rulers and the internal affairs of their states, and other records of interest to the British Government were sent to the United Kingdom High Commissioner in Delhi, and subsequently deposited in the India Office Library; (2) records relating to the administration of the Mysore Assigned Tract, and records of administrative value to Mysore, Banganapalle, and Sandur, were transferred to the states concerned; (3) ephemeral records were destroyed; (4) ephemeral records ('E' records) which it was intended to destroy on the lapse of paramountcy, and records of administrative value to the Government of India ('G' records) were transferred to the National Archives of India.

RESIDENCY RECORDS

'E' category files	1881–1947	361 bdls
'G' category files	1885–1947	24 bdls
Files relating to the Establishment cases	1900–50	16 bdls
Press files	1947–9	1 bdl
Retrocession files	1932–46	16 bdls
Political files relating to Banganapalle and Sandur: Madras States Agency files	1895–1947	24 bdls
Federation files	1928–38	2 bdls
Madras States Agency files	1935–8	1 bdl
Confidential branch	1772–1948	11 boxes
War branch files	1939–47	37 bdls
Papers relating to increments to the staff of Mysore Residency		1 bdl
Files relating to the transfer of records to the Government of India	1947–8	1 box
Papers relating to Mysore State Agency (Ration Depot)		1 bdl
Mysore Residency control of expenditure	1947–8	1 box
Abstracts of old records	1672–1931	16 v
Files relating to the lapse of paramountcy	1947	1 bdl
Miscellaneous and other papers		3 bdls
Fort St George: diary, consultation books (57 v) and indexes (12 v)	1690–1841	69 v
Indexes to the proceedings	1880–1947	19 v
File registers	1880–1948	22 v

Registers, various	1863–1949	205 v
Cash books	1929–49	18 v
Bills (salary, office etc.)	1881–1949	11 bdls, 87 v
Files relating to the Judicial Commissioners, Coorg	1883–1947	11 bdls
Indexes belonging to the Chief Commissioners, Coorg	1834–1939	4 v

NEPAL RESIDENCY

A residency was established at Katmandu in 1802 but withdrawn the next year. It was re-established in 1817.

Papers of the British Residency in Nepal	1817–1921	43 bdls, 26 v

THE PUNJAB STATES AGENCY

The Punjab States Agency was established in 1921 when the states which had formerly been in political relations with the Punjab Government were placed in direct relations with the Government of India. These states were Patiala, Bahawalpur, Jind, Nabha, Kapurthala, Mandi, Sirmur, Bilaspur, Malerkotla, Faridkot, Chamba, Suket and Loharu. Khairpur State, which had been in political relations with the Bombay Government since 1843, was added in 1933. In 1936 Pataudi and Dujana, which had been previously in the charge of the Punjab Government, were added to the agency. The Punjab Hill States Agency was constituted as a subordinate agency in 1936, and included states which had been previously in the political charge of the Punjab Government, through the Superintendent Hill States, Simla, together with Sirmur and Bilaspur (transferred from the Punjab States Agency), Tehri Garhwal (formerly within the political charge of the Commissioner of Bareilly), and Kalsia (formerly in political relations with the Government of the United Provinces through the Commissioner of Kumaon). The Punjab Hill States Agency included Baghal, Baghat, Balsan, Bashahr, Bhajji, Bilaspur (Kahlur), Darkoti, Dhami, Jubbal, Kalsia, Keonthal (Junga), Kumharsain, Kunihar, Kuthar, Mahlog, Mangal, Nalagarh (Hindur), Sangri, Sirmur (Nahan), Tehri (Garhwal), and Tharoch.

PUNJAB GOVERNMENT RECORDS (*N.B. these records are to be returned to the Punjab Government*)

Commissioner Amballa Division	1867–1936	71 bdls
Confidential files Native States	1897–1931	1 bdl
Financial Commissioner Punjab Excise Cases		1 bdl

Forest A proceedings	1888–1918	1 bdl
General and Judicial Departments proceedings	1849–60	3 bdls
Native States 'A' proceedings	1871–1935	5 bdls
Native States 'B' proceedings	1881–1936	46 bdls
Native States 'C' proceedings	1919–36	3 bdls
Native States miscellaneous files		2 bdls
Pataudi State special bundle	1881–1900	1 bdl
Political Department proceedings	1849–68	13 bdls
Punjab Government consolidated circulars		2 v
Punjab Government miscellaneous files and Political Department 'B' proceedings	1827–1932	9 bdls
Revenue, and Revenue and Agriculture Department proceedings	1849–60, 1890–1900	2 bdls

PUNJAB STATES AGENCY RECORDS

Alphabetical indexes of the office records of the agent to the governor-general, Punjab States	1927–37	60 v
Accounts	1922–47	58 bdls
Confidential		5 bdls
Control	1943–6	21 bdls
Finance	1943–6	6 bdls
General, including records of predecessor bodies	To 1946	255 bdls
Judicial	1922–47	113 bdls
Military	1929–46	81 bdls
Political	1928–46	158 bdls
Residency files	1946–7	51 bdls

TEHRI GARHWAL RECORDS

U.P. Government records	1884–1936	6 bdls
Accounts and General papers	1936–42	7 bdls and 6 bdls of predecessor body

PUNJAB HILL STATES AGENCY RECORDS

Records of the Punjab Hill States Agency and of predecessor bodies	1887–1947	122 carton boxes
Registers		3 v

REGIONAL COMMISSIONER P.E.P.S.U. RECORDS

1947–54　94 bdls

REGISTERS, VARIOUS

85 bdls

RAJPUTANA AGENCY

There was an agent to the governor-general in Rajputana from 1832, when this appointment was also given to the superintendent of Ajmer, with headquarters at Abu. The agency included at various times the following residencies and agencies:

(1) MEWAR RESIDENCY (from 1931 MEWAR AND SOUTHERN RAJPUTANA STATES AGENCY)

The Mewar Agency was established in 1818 when Captain J. Tod became the first political agent, but was abolished in 1831 when the agency came under the superintendent of Ajmer. However, in 1836 the agency was re-established, and in 1881 it became the Mewar Residency. In 1931 the states of Dungarpur, Banswara and Partabgarh, and the Kushalgarh Chiefship, which had formed the Southern Rajputana States Agency, came into political relations with the Mewar Residency, and the designation was changed to the Mewar and Southern Rajputana States Agency.

(2) WESTERN RAJPUTANA STATES AGENCY

The Western Rajputana States Agency was established in 1879. A political agent had first been appointed to Jodhpur in 1839; in 1869 Jaisalmer was added to the agency, and in 1879 Sirohi state. There had been a political agent in Sirohi from 1823 to 1832, but the state had been for the most part in political relations with an assistant to the governor-general's agent until 1870, when it was placed in the political charge of the commandant of the Erinpura Irregular Force: this officer became political agent to the three states of Jodhpur, Jaisalmer and Sirohi in 1879. A year later the name of the charge became the Western Rajputana States Agency. In 1882 the agency became a residency. In 1909 Bikaner state was added to the agency on the abolition of the Bikaner Political Agency. In 1918 Bikaner, Jaisalmer and Sirohi were placed in political relations with a newly appointed political agent, Western Rajputana States, leaving the state of Jodhpur under the resident, who was styled resident, Marwar. But a year later the new political agency was abolished, Jaisalmer was again put under the resident, Marwar, who was again designated resident, Western Rajputana States.

Bikaner and Sirohi states were now placed in direct political relations with the agent to the governor-general in Rajputana. The Western Rajputana States Residency was abolished in 1932, and the two states of Marwar (Jodhpur) and Jaisalmer were added to the Jaipur Residency. However, in 1934 the Western Rajputana States Residency was revived and included, in addition to Marwar and Jaisalmer, the states of Palanpur and Danta which were formerly under the Government of Bombay (Banaskantha and Mahikantha Agencies). Sirohi State was returned to this residency in 1939.

(3) JAIPUR AGENCY

A political officer was first stationed at Jaipur in 1821, but in 1830 the charge was transferred to the superintendent of Ajmer (who was subsequently, from 1832, also agent to the governor-general for the states of Rajputana). However in 1838 the Jaipur Agency was re-instituted. In 1879 it was amalgamated with the Eastern Rajputana States Agency, which now included Bharatpur, Karauli, Alwar, and Jaipur. In 1882 Alwar became a separate charge, and Bharatpur and Karauli States were placed in political relations with the new political agent stationed at Karauli. In 1887 the Jaipur Residency was instituted and the Eastern Rajputana States Agency reconstituted. Tonk State was part of the Jaipur Residency from 1911 to 1915, during which period the Haraoti and Tonk Agency had been abolished, and again from 1934 when the agency was finally abolished. In the same year Shahpura (which had been part of the Haraoti and Tonk Agency), Alwar (from the Eastern Rajputana States Agency), and the Nimrana Chiefship were also placed in political relations with the Jaipur Residency. For the short period 1932–4, when the Western Rajputana States Residency was abolished, the states of Jodhpur and Jaisalmer were also included in the Jaipur Residency. And from 1933 to 1934 Palanpur State (formerly part of Banaskantha Agency) and Danta State (formerly part of Mahikantha Agency) were also included in the residency. In 1941 the designation was changed to Jaipur Agency.

(4) EASTERN RAJPUTANA STATES AGENCY

The Eastern Rajputana States Agency was established in 1869 and comprised the states of Alwar, Bharatpur, Dholpur, and Karauli. The Alwar Agency had been created in 1858, the Bharatpur Agency in 1853 (Dholpur was added in 1863), and the Karauli Agency in 1850. From 1879 to 1882 the Jaipur Agency was amalgamated with the Eastern Rajputana States Agency, which now included Bharatpur, Karauli, Alwar and Jaipur (Dholpur was a separate agency from 1873 to 1885). However in that year (1882) Alwar became a separate charge, and Bharatpur and Karauli were included in the new Karauli Agency. In 1885 Dholpur was re-transferred to the Eastern Rajputana States Agency, which two years later was re-constituted to comprise Bharatpur, Alwar, Karauli, and Dholpur. In 1922 Kotah state was included in the agency on the abolition of the Kotah and Jhalawar Agency.

(5) HARAOTI AND TONK AGENCY

Until 1876 the political agency of Haraoti included the states of Bundi and Kotah, but in that year a separate agent was appointed at Kotah. The Haraoti and Tonk Agency included the states of Bundi and Tonk and the chiefship of Shahpura. In 1911 the agency was abolished and Tonk state was transferred to the Jaipur Residency, but in 1915 the Haraoti and Tonk Agency was revived, to be finally abolished in 1934. Tonk and Shahpura then became part of the Jaipur Residency, while Bundi was included in the Eastern Rajputana States Agency. Jhalawar state, which had been included in the Haraoti and Tonk Agency in 1922 when the Kotah and Jhalawar Agency was abolished, was also (in 1934) included in the Eastern Rajputana States Agency.

(6) KOTAH AND JHALAWAR AGENCY

Until 1876 the state of Kotah was included in the Haraoti Agency, but in that year a separate agent was appointed at Kotah. The Kotah and Jhalawar Agency was abolished in 1922, and Kotah was transferred to the Eastern Rajputana States Agency, while Jhalawar was included in the Haraoti and Tonk Agency until 1934 when it also was transferred to the Eastern Rajputana States Agency.

(7) BIKANER AGENCY

There was a separate political agency at Bikaner from 1883, but in 1909 the agency was abolished and Bikaner state was included in the Western Rajputana States Agency. In 1920 the state was placed in direct relations with the agent to the governor-general (from 1937, Resident), Rajputana.

(8) ALWAR AGENCY

The Alwar Agency was created in 1858, but in 1869 Alwar state was included in the Eastern Rajputana States Agency, and remained in the charge of that agency (except for the period 1882-7, when it was a separate charge) until 1934, when Alwar state was transferred to the Jaipur Residency.

(9) BHARATPUR AGENCY

The Bharatpur Agency was created in 1853, consisting of Bharatpur state only. In 1863 Dholpur State was added, and in 1869, with Alwar and Karauli, the agency became part of the Eastern Rajputana States Agency.

(10) DHOLPUR AGENCY

Dholpur state was part of the Bharatpur Agency from 1863 to 1869, and of the Eastern Rajputana States Agency from 1869 to 1873. From 1873 to 1885 Dholpur was a separate agency, but in the latter year it was again transferred to the Eastern Rajputana States Agency.

(11) KARAULI AGENCY

The Karauli Agency was created in 1850, but in 1869 the state was included in the Eastern Rajputana States Agency. It was again a separate agency (including the states of Bharatpur and Karauli) from 1882 to 1887, when it was again transferred to the re-instituted Eastern Rajputana States Agency.

AGENCY RECORDS

Indexes and registers		
Indexes		11 v
Issue and receipt registers	1836–80	95 v
Political, general, receipt registers	1881–1936	189 v
Political, general, issue registers	1881–1936	148 v
Camp issue registers	1881–1905	19 v
Camp receipt registers	1884–1936	26 v
Camp diary books	1889–1910	14 v
Camp P.W.D. issue registers	1869–1933	56 v
Vernacular issue and receipt registers	1869–1921	100 v
P.W.D. receipt registers	1867–1941	187 v
P.W.D. issue registers	1867–1941	135 v
Miscellaneous letter books	1805–80	293 v
Palanpur and Mahikantha letter books	1827–81	19 v
Political branch records	pre-1927	119 bdls, 13 v
Vernacular records	1880–1931	215 v, 51 bdls
Records of the administrative medical officer	1929–47	24 bdls, 55 v (registers)
Records of the director of civil supply	1945–9	47 bdls, 8 v
Confidential records	1898–1951	30 bdls, 4 v (registers)
Co-operative Thrift and Savings Society records		5 bdls, 3 boxes

Office files of the co-ordinating officer		1 bdl
Office of the district magistrate		
Files	1928–47	7 bdls
Price control office; commissioner for workmen's compensation		1 bdl
Miscellaneous papers		1 bdl
Miscellaneous registers		43 v
Establishment files	1937–48	5 bdls
Finance files	(i) pre-1926	6 bdls
	(ii) 1927–54	129 bdls
File registers		12 v
Office of the superintendent gazetteers files		4 v
General branch files	(i) pre-1933	9 bdls
	(ii) 1934–48	49 bdls
General branch registers		12 v
Imperial Indian relief fund		1 bdl
Passports branch files	(i) pre-1926	3 bdls
	(ii) 1927–41	17 bdls
Passports		2 boxes
Press and library files		1 bdl
Political branch files	1857–1952	214 bdls
Political branch return files	1928–48	1 bdl
Political branch miscellaneous files		1 bdl
Public Works Department		69 bdls, 9 v
War Branch	1942–7	4 v, 39 bdls
Tehsil Office, Abu		50 bdls, 76 v
List of retained files and weeding notes etc.		22 bdls
Miscellaneous loose papers		39 bdls
Miscellaneous registers (receipt, accounts, issue, file, etc.)		556 v
Loose indexes		234 booklets, 10 bdls, 6 boxes
Bikaner Agency		2 bdls
Eastern Rajputana Agency	1853–1948	30 v, 105 bdls
Jaipur Agency:		
Correspondence, registers, miscellaneous volumes, etc.	1818–1947	350 v
Political officers' diaries	1839–78	22 v
Jaipur Agency files	pre-1926	39 bdls
Jaipur Agency files	1927–47	151 bdls

Boundary English files	1869–1923	4 bdls
Confidential files	to 1947	9 bdls
Civil	1916–39	8 bdls
Criminal	1902–42	3 bdls
Judicial and Session cases	1914–29	2 bdls
Returns	1929–47	3 bdls
Alwar files		5 bdls
Nimrana files (English)		2 bdls
Alwar–Nimrana files	1927–39	2 bdls
Alwar–Nimrana correspondence	1859–77	1 bdl
Haraoti and Tonk files	pre-1925	7 bdls
Kishangarh supervisors' office files	1939–47	16 bdls
Shahpura		
Vernacular files		4 bdls
Boundary files (vernacular)		18 bdls
Indian Soldiers' Board, Rajputana: miscellaneous files; index, lists etc.; printed documents; account registers		6 bdls
Printed miscellaneous files of Shahpura and Sirohi		2 bdls
File registers		6 v
Vernacular volumes		3 v

WESTERN RAJPUTANA STATES AGENCY RECORDS

Western Rajputana States Agency files	1840–1947	32 v, 15 bdls
Miscellaneous receipt and issue registers	1839–73	48 v
Correspondence receipt and issue registers —A.G.G.	1832–73	53 v
Registers and miscellaneous volumes		114 v

MEWAR AND SOUTHERN RAJPUTANA AGENCY RECORDS

Mewar Residency files (English)	1837–1930	43 bdls
Boundary dispute files (vernacular), Mewar and Tonk	1864–88	297 v
Western India States Agency files	1848–81	4 v
Mewar and Southern Rajputana States Agency letter-books (vernacular)	1844–94	23 v
Kherwara Superintendency outward letter-books (English)	1826–94	20 v
Mewar Residency, agent to the governor-general, letter-books	1860–71	8 v

Index of important letters to the A.G.G. Rajputana	1860–71	8 v
Udaipur outward letter-books and Index	1841–71	18 v
Miscellaneous letter-books and Index	1842–71	17 v
Outgoing Political letter-book	1854–66	1 v
Letters despatched regarding Sindhia's ceded districts of Jawad and Nimach	1857–63	1 v
Regimental letter-books	1853–73	7 v
Receipt and issue register	1855–7	1 v
Banswara letter-book, letters received and Index	1852–71	7 v
Partabgarh letter-books and Index	1834–54	4 v
Correspondence and Index book in regard to Doongarpur letter-book	1846–71	2 v
Kherwara Assistancy correspondence registers	1827–72	33 v
Confidential files and returns	1836–78	2 bdls
Assistant Resident Marwar records	1842–1937	6 bdls
Assistant Political Superintendent, Mewar: hilly tracts	1872–1937	1 bdl
Southern Rajputana States Agency records	1828–1920	23 bdls, 3 v
Mewar and Southern Rajputana States Agency records	1908–47	23 v, 66 bdls

WESTERN INDIA AND GUJARAT STATES AGENCY

The Western India and Gujarat States Agency comprised all states in the Kathiawar and Gujarat region. It was formed in 1944 on the amalgamation of the Western India States Agency with the Baroda and Gujarat States Agency. The resident was assisted by three political agents: (1) for Eastern Kathiawar and Sabarkantha; (2) for Western Kathiawar, and (3) for the Gujarat States Agency. The predecessor agencies and residencies of the Western India and Gujarat States Agency included the following:

(1) WESTERN INDIA STATES AGENCY (RESIDENCY FROM 1937)

This agency was established in 1924 and placed in direct relationship with the Government of India. It included the former Kathiawar Political Agency, the Cutch Agency, and the Palanpur (Banaskantha) Agency, which had all been previously under the Government of Bombay. In 1933 Palanpur was handed over to the Rajputana Agency, and Mahikantha Agency (except Danta) became part of the Western India States Agency.

Banaskantha (minus Palanpur) and Mahikantha Agencies then amalgamated to form the subordinate Sabarkantha Agency. The resident was assisted by three subordinate political agents: (1) Eastern Kathiawar (comprising the old Prants of Gohilwad and Jhalawad); (2) Sabarkantha (Banaskantha and Mahikantha until 1933); (3) Western Kathiawar (comprising the old Prants of Halar and Sorath). The following states were in direct relations with the resident: Bhavnagar, Cutch, Dhrangadhra, Dhrol, Gondal, Idar, Jafarabad, Junagadh, Limbdi, Morvi, Nawanagar, Palitana, Porbandar, Radhanpur, Rajkot, Vijayanagar, Wadhwan, and Wankaner. The following states were in political relations with the political agent, Western Kathiawar Agency: Bilkha, Jetpur, Jasdan, Khirasra, Kotda-Sangani, Malia, Manavadar, Thana Devlia, Virpur, and Wadia. The following states were in political relations with the political agent, Eastern Kathiawar Agency: Bajana, Chuda, Lakhtar, Lathi, Muli, Patdi, Sayla, and Vala. The following states were in political relations with the political agent, Sabarkantha Agency: Amliyara, Ghodasar, Ilol, Katosan, Khadal, Malpur, Mansa, Mohanpur, Pethapur, Punadra, Ranasan, Sudasna, Tharad, Varsora, Varahi, and Vav.

(2) KATHIAWAR POLITICAL AGENCY

The first political agent in Kathiawar was appointed in 1820, although the proper functioning of the agency began only in 1822. In 1857 the agency was divided into two divisions, under two assistants, and in 1865 into four administrative divisions (Prants)—Jhalawar, Halar, Sorath, and Gohilwad Prants—under assistant political agents. In 1902 the political agent in Kathiawar was redesignated agent to the governor and the four assistants became political agents. In 1922 the number of agents was reduced to two, each being in charge of two of the Prants. In 1924 the agency was placed in direct relations with the Government of India and, with the Cutch and Palanpur Agencies, became the Western India States Agency.

(3) CUTCH AGENCY

The Cutch Agency was established in 1815 and was under the political superintendence of the Government of Bombay until 1924 when the agency was placed in direct relations wtih the Government of India and, with the Kathiawar and Palanpur Agencies, became the Western India States Agency. However, the Cutch Agency was abolished in 1925, and Cutch state was placed in direct relations with the resident, Western India States Agency.

(4) PALANPUR AGENCY (BANASKANTHA AGENCY, 1925–33)

British connections with Palanpur dated from 1809, and with the other states in the agency from 1813 (Radhanpur), 1819 (the remaining states, except Kankrej), and 1819/20 (Kankrej—part of the Mahikantha Agency until 1844). From 1817 to 1874 the task of administration of Palanpur state was controlled by a political superintendent. The agency was under the political superintendence of the Government of Bombay until 1924, when it was placed in direct relations with the Government of India and, with Kathiawar and Cutch Agencies, became the Western India States Agency. In 1925 the name of the agency was changed to Banaskantha, and in 1933 the State of Palanpur was transferred from the Banaskantha Agency to the Jaipur Residency, and in 1934 to the Western Rajputana States Agency. The Banaskantha Agency was then (1933) amalgamated with the Mahikantha Agency to become the Sabarkantha Agency, still subordinate to the Western India States Agency.

(5) MAHIKANTHA AGENCY

The Mahikantha Agency was established in 1820 and remained under the political superintendence of the Government of Bombay until 1933, when it was placed in direct political relations with the Government of India. Except for Danta state it was then amalgamated with the Banaskantha Agency to become the Sabarkantha Agency in the Western India States Agency. Danta state was transferred to the Jaipur Residency, and in 1934 to the Western Rajputana States Residency. Kankrej was part of the Mahikantha Agency from 1820 to 1844 when it was transferred to the Palanpur Agency. The most important state in the Mahikantha Agency was Idar, and the political agent had three assistants.

(6) SABARKANTHA AGENCY

The Sabarkantha Agency was a subordinate political agency within the Western India States Agency, formed in 1933 by the amalgamation of the Mahikantha Agency and Banaskantha Agency (except for Palanpur state). When in 1944 the Western India States Agency was amalgamated with the Baroda and Gujarat States Agency, Sabarkantha was placed with Eastern Kathiawar under one subordinate political agent in the new Western India and Gujarat States Agency.

(7) BARODA AND GUJARAT STATES AGENCY

The Baroda and Gujarat States Agency was established in 1933 when the Baroda Residency was enlarged with the States of Balasinor, Bansda, Bariya,

Cambay, Chhota Udaipur, and the Rewakantha Agency. In 1937 the agent to the governor-general for the Gujarat States and resident at Baroda became the resident for Baroda and the Gujarat States, and in 1944 the residency was amalgamated with the Western India States Agency to become the Western India and Gujarat States Agency. There was one subordinate political agent in charge of the Gujarat States Agency, with headquarters at Baroda.

(8) BARODA RESIDENCY

The Baroda Residency was established in 1802 and abolished in 1830 when the resident was appointed political commissioner in Gujarat residing at Ahmedabad (this office was abolished in 1844). However, the Baroda Residency was revived in 1835. Until 1854 it was under the charge of the Government of Bombay, but in that year it was transferred to the Government of India. In 1861 the residency was re-transferred to the Government of Bombay, but in 1874 control again went to the Government of India, and the designation of the resident was changed to agent to the governor-general and special commissioner at Baroda. In 1899 the agent was re-designated resident at Baroda. In 1933 the jurisdiction of the Baroda Residency was enlarged with the states of Balasinor, Bansda, Bariya, Cambay, Chhota Udaipur, and the Rewakantha Agency, and its designation was changed to Baroda and Gujarat States Agency.

(9) REWAKANTHA AGENCY

The Rewakantha Agency was established in 1826, abolished in 1829, and revived in 1842. The agency was subordinate to the governor of Bombay and eventually included sixty-one separate states. In 1933 the agency came under the political control of the Government of India and was joined to the Baroda Residency to form the Baroda and Gujarat States Agency. This agency in 1944 became part of the Western India and Gujarat States Agency, and the work of superintending the Rewakantha states fell to the political agent for the Gujarat States Agency, in subordination to the resident, Western India States Agency.

BOMBAY GOVERNMENT RECORDS (*these records are to be returned to the Bombay Government*)

Kathiawar

Index	1922–32	1 v
Correspondence	1820–1925	1,453 v
Confidential records	1902–24	7 boxes

Cutch

Index	1820–57	1 v
Correspondence	1831–1923	191 v

Mahikantha

List of records	1820–1913	4 v
Correspondence	1836–1933	178 v

Palanpur

Correspondence	1858–78	106 v

WESTERN INDIA STATES AGENCY RECORDS (*including records of predecessor and successor bodies*)

Index	1808–1940	97 v
List and index of outward and inward correspondence	1808–42	2 v

Government Books. These volumes contain the correspondence of the Kathiawar Political Agency (cr. 1820). The volumes before 1820 contain correspondence with the Gaekwar, and relate to this region

	1807–1908	1,749 v
Huzur Accounts Office: correspondence	1912–26	7 v
Administration: correspondence	1909–30	90 v, 1 box
Air Survey: correspondence	1927–9	2 v
Appeals	1930–3	33 v, 1 box
Books, Acts and Publications: correspondence	1919–30	8 v, 1 box
Boundary: correspondence	1924–30	5 v
Education: correspondence	1909–29	73 v, 1 box
Epidemics: correspondence	1918–29	7 v, 1 box
Establishment: correspondence	1918–30	12 v, 5 boxes
Famine: correspondence	1917–29	18 v
Female Training College: correspondence	1920–6	6 v
Finance	1909–33	43 v, 1 box
Foreign Service and Establishment: correspondence	1919–24	2 v
General: correspondence and index	1909–33	383 v, 2 boxes
Judicial: correspondence and index	1909–33	324 v, 1 box
Male Training College: correspondence	1917–26	7 v
Marine: correspondence	1909–30	21 v, 1 box
Medical: correspondence	1917–30	17 v, 1 box
Military: correspondence	1909–29	27 v
Plague: correspondence	1910–29	17 v, 1 box

Police: correspondence	1917–29	20 v, 1 box
Political: correspondence	1909–30	200 v, 1 box
Political miscellaneous: correspondence	1909–30	62 v, 1 box
Public Works: correspondence	1909–33	69 v, 1 box
Rajkumar College, Rajkot: correspondence	1917–30	17 v, 1 box
Revenue: correspondence and index	1909–33	486 v, 4 boxes
Railway: correspondence	1909–30	106 v, 1 box
Tribute: correspondence	1820–1930	10 v
Vaccination	1919–30	7 v
Veterinary: correspondence	1918–27	5 v
War: correspondence	1919–29	14 v
Treasury Papers	1854–1916	46 v
Confidential papers relating to Kathiawar, Junagadh and Mangrol	1818–1919	3 boxes
A Branch (Appeals, Extradition, Rules and Acts, Records etc.)	1934–52	69 v, 19 boxes and 1,414 bdls
A.I.S. Branch: correspondence	1942–6	1 box
D Branch (Railways, Customs, Famine, Marine, Administration, Police, War Contributions etc.)	1933–50	249 v, 107 boxes, 15 bdls
D and E Miscellaneous branch: correspondence	1945–50	3 boxes
E Branch (Establishment, Appointment and Transfer, Succession etc.)	1933–50	170 v, 60 boxes
F Branch (P.W.D., Museums, Motor Vehicles etc.)	1926–53	78 v, 21 boxes
G Branch (Education, Public Health, Births and Deaths, Arms and Ammunition, Release of Convicts etc.)	1931–49	110 v, 44 boxes
H Branch (Visas and Passport Regulations)	1938–42	8 v, 1 box
M Branch		3 boxes
Confidential Branch (including 'War')	1914–53	32 v, 28 boxes, 11 bdls
Deputy Regional Commissioner's Office		3 v, 4 bdls
Appeals	1865–1948	76 v, 374 bdls, 1 box
Officer on Special Duty: correspondence	1947	1 bdl
Passport	1916–48	9 v, 5 bdls
Police	1927–53	28 v, 19 bdls
Palitana Political Cases	1886–90	5 bdls, 1 v
P.W.D. Superintending Engineer's Office	1853–1900	21 bdls

Railway (B.G.J.P.)	1879–1911	36 bdls, 12 v
Register, Office Orders	1872–1943	23 v
Standing Orders: files		13 v
Registers of inward letters	1850–1949	89 v
Registers of inward (and outward) miscellaneous letters	1851–1954	62 v
Outward letter-books	1851–71	5 v
Registers	1940–54	19 v
Annual reports	1890–4	4 v
Consolidated Local Fund	1909–29	4 v, 1 bdl
Group Liaison Officer	1946–8	3 v
Agreements		1 box, 1 bdl
Vernacular records		341 v, 46 boxes, 1 bdl
Central Record Office	1913–52	8 v, 6 bdls

GOHILWAD PRANT

A division of the Kathiawar Political Agency. It was amalgamated with Jhalawad Prant in 1924 to form the Eastern Kathiawar Agency, a subordinate agency within the Western India States Agency.

Correspondence and list of volumes	1858–1922	297 v

JHALAWAD PRANT

A division of the Kathiawar Political Agency. It was amalgamated with Gohilwad Prant in 1924 to form the Eastern Kathiawar Agency.

Correspondence and Index	1863–1922	479 v

EASTERN KATHIAWAR AGENCY

Correspondence	1923–44	1,118 v
Branches	1941–7	10 bdls

HALAR PRANT

A division of the Kathiawar Political Agency. It was amalgamated with Sorath Prant in 1924 to form the Western Kathiawar Agency.

Correspondence, Index and register	1866–1922	507 v

SORATH PRANT

A division of the Kathiawar Political Agency. It was amalgamated with Halar Prant in 1924 to form the Western Kathiawar Agency.

Correspondence and Index	1863–1922	510 v

WESTERN KATHIAWAR AGENCY

Correspondence and Index	1923–44	946 v
Branches	1934–47	37 bdls
Registers	1926–44	8 v
Kachcha volumes	1936–43	8 bdls

BARODA RESIDENCY

Correspondence		47 bdls, 5 v
War	1914–18	5 bdls
	1939–45	25 bdls
A.G.'s Office, ex-Baroda State		1 bdl
Registers	1908–45	5 v
Baroda–Junagadh Boundary Dispute		7 v, 2 bdls

GUJARAT STATES AGENCY

Correspondence and passport register	1945–8	4 v, 3 bdls

SABARKANTHA AGENCY

Files	1935–44	3 bdls

MAHIKANTHA AGENCY

Correspondence etc.	1820–1933	95 v, 10 boxes, 4 bdls

BANASKANTHA AGENCY (PALANPUR AGENCY UNTIL 1925)

Correspondence etc.	1817–1930	177 v

REWAKANTHA AGENCY

Correspondence	1822–1913	29 v

CUTCH AGENCY

Index	1813–1921	1 v
Lists of correspondence	1858–1924	2 v
List of Ciras cases decided	1928–9	1 v
Correspondence etc.	1813–1929	145 v
Cutch–Morvi Boundary Dispute	1862–1945	8 v, 47 bdls
Gondal–Junagadh Gir case		4 bdls (vernacular)

MISCELLANEOUS VOLUMES

155 v

IV

NATIONAL ARCHIVES OF INDIA
PRIVATE PAPERS

The National Archives has collections of private papers both in western and in oriental languages. These are constantly being added to. Its western languages collections include a number of single items from private sources. Its minor collections of private papers include 43 documents which are copies and English translations of original Persian correspondence from the East India Company to the Peshwa Darbar during the regime of Sawai Madharao Peshwa; manuscript poems and letters of Mrs Sarojini Naidu; letters from Sir Bampfylde and Lady Fuller to G. P. Mathur and his daughter 1930–48; and 50 letters from the papers of V. Krishnaswami Aiyer. There are major collections too.

Major western language collections include

Macartney papers	1776–98	115 docs
Tyabji papers	1871–1905	15 f, 9 v
Khaparde papers	1879–1938	47 v, 14 f
Gokhale papers	1889–1915	68 f

Gandhi papers [An ever-enlarging collection, to be deposited in the Gandhi Smarak Nidhi]

Jayakar papers	1905–55	
Correspondence		915 f
Newspaper cuttings		258 v
Diaries		60 v
Coyajee papers	1910–40	11 f, 4 notebooks. Approx. 40 small diaries
Bhopal papers		Includes several hundred English letters
Khare papers	1935–60	165 docs
Naoroji papers		11 bdls
Tandon papers		302 f, 6 bdls

Oriental language collections include the Inayak Jang collection relating to the administration of the Deccan. (A detailed catalogue is in preparation.)

1685–1774   1, 35, 931 docs

v

NATIONAL ARCHIVES OF INDIA
NEWSPAPERS

The National Archives of India does not have a newspaper collection: there is one in the National Library of India, Calcutta. It has, however, an incomplete set of the reports on native newspapers, which were compiled by the Home Department and consisted of abstracts or summaries in English of vernacular newspapers. These reports have been microfilmed and the gaps filled by microfilming copies borrowed from other repositories: with the microfilm the set is therefore complete.

REPORTS ON NATIVE NEWSPAPERS

ORIGINAL VOLUMES		376 v
Bengal Presidency	1863–1911 (with gaps)	
	1920–7 (with gaps)	88 v
East Bengal and Assam	1907–11 (with gaps)	8 v
Bombay	1868–1911 (with gaps)	
	1920–7 (with gaps)	91 v
Central Provinces, Ajmer–Merwara, Central India, Burma etc.	1896–1911; 1921–7 (with gaps)	26 v
Madras	1872–1911 (with gaps)	approx. 30 v
Punjab	1864–1911; 1920–6 (with gaps)	62 v
North-West Province, Oudh, and Central Province	1864–1911 (with gaps)	41 v
Ajmer–Merwara, Rajputana etc.	1895, 1896	2 v
Burma	1908, 1909	2 v
Native Press	1875	1 bdl (not microfilmed)
India Department of Thagi and Dakaiti, report of native newspapers	1898, 1899, 1900, Jan.–June 1901	4 v

MICROFILMS		
		229 reels (19,315 feet)
Bengal	1863–1929	56 reels
Madras	1872–1926, 1929–36	37 reels

Bombay	1868–1932	75 reels
Punjab	1864–75, 1877–1911	27 reels
U.P.	1890–1917	22 reels
Eastern Bengal and Assam	1907–11	4 reels
Central Provinces, Ajmer–	1896–1911, 1921–2,	8 reels
Merwara, Central India, Burma	1924–7	

PUBLICATIONS OF NATIONAL ARCHIVES OF INDIA

A. PRINTED AIDS TO REFERENCE

Handbook to the records of the Government of India in the Imperial Record Department 1748–1859 (Calcutta, 1925)

Guide to the records in the National Archives of India (in progress) Part I *Introductory* (New Delhi, 1959)

J. T. Wheeler, *Memoranda on the records in the Foreign Department of the Government of India* (Calcutta, 1865)

J. T. Wheeler, *Memoranda on the records in the Home Department and in the General Treasury* (Calcutta, 1868)

G. W. Forrest, *Report on the records of the Military Department* (Calcutta, 1891)

H. Scott Smith, *Calendar of Indian state papers: Secret series, Fort William 1774–1775* (Calcutta, 1864)

Calendar of Persian correspondence (receipts and issues) 1766–1777 (Calcutta, 1907)

Calendar of Persian correspondence...(Calcutta/New Delhi, 1911–) (in progress), 13 vols.

I	1759–67 (1911)	VIII	1788–9 (1952)
II	1767–9 (1915)	IX	1790–1 (1949)
III	1770–72 (1919)	X	1792–3 (1959)
IV	1772–5 (1925)	XI	1794–5 (in progress)
V	1776–80 (1930)	XII	1796–7 (in progress)
VI	1781–5 (1938)	XIII	1798–9 (in progress)
VII	1785–7 (1940)		

Lists of original treaties, engagements, etc. transferred from the Foreign Department to the Imperial Record Office (Calcutta, 1901–8), 3 vols.

Lists of the records of the Government of India preserved in the Imperial Record Office (Calcutta, 1904–10), 10 vols.

| Foreign Department | 1716–1888 | 3 v |
| Military Department | 1774–1858 | 3 v |

Finance Department	1806–1908	1 v
Home Department	1749–1892	2 v
Public Works Department	1850–94	1 v

Abstract hand-list of the post-Mutiny records of the Government of India in the Imperial Record Department (corrected up to 1 September 1938) (New Delhi, 1939)

List of treaties, engagements and sanads in the custody of the Imperial Record Department (Simla, 1941)

Press-list of ancient documents preserved in the Imperial Record Room...: Public Department 1748–1800... (Calcutta, 1898–1922), 18 vols.

Press-list of copies of ancient documents obtained from the India Office: Public Department (Calcutta, 1921–2) 2 vols.

Press-list of records belonging to the Foreign Department... (Calcutta, 1917–) (in progress)

series I	Select Committee	1756–74 with index
series II	Secret and Separate Branch	1761–1811 (unpublished)
series III	Secret Department	1763–75 (1776 onwards in progress)
series IV	Secret Department of Inspection	1770–87 with index

Press-list of the copies of Persian correspondence (receipts) 1769–1801 (Calcutta, 1904)

Press-list of Mutiny papers (Calcutta, 1921)

Press-list of Bengal and Madras papers 1746–1785 (Calcutta, 1902)

Descriptive list of Mutiny papers in the National Archives of India, Bhopal: vol. I (New Delhi, 1960), vol. II (New Delhi, 1963) (in progress)

Index to the press-list of ancient documents belonging to the Public Department... (Calcutta, 1910–16), 2 vols.

I	1749–59
II	1760–9

Index to the press-lists of the Public Department records 1748–1800 (Calcutta, 1924)

Index to the Land Revenue records 1830–1859 (New Delhi, 1940–2), 2 vols.

I	1830–7
II	1838–59

Index to the Foreign and Political Department records, 2 vols.

I	1756–80 (New Delhi, 1957)
II	1781–3 (in progress)

B. LIST OF PUBLICATIONS ISSUED UNDER THE
PUBLICATIONS PROGRAMME OF THE NATIONAL
ARCHIVES OF INDIA LAUNCHED IN 1942

SCHEME I

Fort William–India House Correspondence (1748–1800)
I, Public Department, 1748–56, editor: Dr K. K. Datta (New Delhi, 1958);
II, Public Department, 1757–9, editor: Dr H. N. Sinha (New Delhi, 1957);
III, Public Department, 1760–3, editor; Dr R. R. Sethi (New Delhi, 1968);
IV, Public Department, 1764–6, editor: Prof. C. S. Srinivasachari (New
Delhi, 1962); V, Public Department, 1767–9, editor: Dr N. K. Sinha (New
Delhi, 1949); VI, Public Department, 1770–2, editor: Dr Bisheshwar
Prasad (New Delhi, 1960); IX, Public Department, 1782–5, editor: Dr B. A.
Saletore (New Delhi, 1959); XIII, Public, Separate and Law Departments,
1796–1800, editor: Dr P. C. Gupta (New Delhi, 1959); XV, Foreign and
Secret Departments, 1782–6, editors: Prof. C. H. Philips and Dr B. B.
Misra (New Delhi, 1963); XVII, Foreign, Political and Secret Depart-
ments, 1792–5, editor: Prof. Y. J. Taraporewala (New Delhi, 1955).

SCHEME II

Selections from English records published by the National Archives of
India.
Indian Travels of Thevenot and Careri, editor: Dr S. N. Sen (New Delhi,
1949).
Browne Correspondence, editor: K. D. Bhargava (New Delhi, 1960).

SCHEME III(*a*)

Records in Oriental languages published by learned institutions other than
the National Archives of India.
(1) *Prachin Bangala Patra Sankalan* (Bengali letters with their English
synopses), 1779–1820, editor: Dr S. N. Sen (Calcutta, 1942).
(2) *Telugu Documents*, editor: Prof. G. J. Somayaji (Waltair, 1957).
(3) *Prachin Hindi Patra Sangrah* (Collection of Old Hindi Letters), vol. I,
editor: Dr D. Varma (Allahabad, 1959); vol. II (in progress).
(4) *Sanskrit Documents, 1778–1857*, editors: Dr S. N. Sen and Dr U.
Misra (Allahabad, 1951).
(5) *Persian Akhbars*, vol. I, editor: Dr P. Saran (New Delhi, 1968).

SCHEME III(*b*)

Selections from English records published by other institutions.
(1) *Selections from Orme Manuscripts*, editor: Prof. C. S. Srinivasachari
(Annamalainagar, 1952).

(2) *Punjab Akhbars, 1839–40*, editor: Dr Ganda Singh (Amritsar, 1952).
(3) *Elphinstone Correspondence, 1804–8*, editors: Dr R. M. Sinha and Dr
A. Avasthi (Nagpur University, 1961).
(4) *Selections from Ochterlong Papers, 1818–25*, editors: Dr. N. K. Sinha
and Dr A. R. Dasgupta (Calcutta, 1964).

C. SELECTIONS, EXTRACTS AND *IN EXTENSO* OFFICIAL PUBLICATIONS

Selections from the records of the...Foreign Department: succession to
Muhammudan States, Jowrah, 1825–1829 (Calcutta, 1865)

J. Long, *Selections from unpublished records of government for the years 1748*
to 1767 inclusive, relating mainly to the social condition of Bengal...
I (Calcutta, 1869)

T. C. Plowden, *Précis of a portion of the correspondence etc. relating to the*
affairs of Mysore, 1799–1878, with appendices (Calcutta, 1878)

G. W. Forrest, ed. *Selections from the letters, despatches and other state*
papers preserved in the Foreign Department...1772–1785 (Calcutta,
1890), 3 vols.

G. W. Forrest, ed. *Selections from the letters, despatches and other state*
papers preserved in the Military Department...1857–1858 (Calcutta,
1893–1912), 4 vols.

S. C. Hill: *An abstract of the early records of the Foreign Department:*
part I, 1756–1762 (Calcutta, 1901)

W. K. Firminger, ed. *Proceedings of the Select Committee 1758* (Calcutta,
1914)

Kabul papers 1839–1859 (Calcutta, 1919)

Jagir statements 1847–1857 (Calcutta, 1919)

Selections from Educational records (Calcutta, 1920–2; reprinted New Delhi,
1965); I, H. Sharp, ed. 1781–1839; II, J. A. Richey, ed. 1840–1859

Selections from Educational records (new series) (in progress) I, *Educational*
Reports, 1859–71 (New Delhi, 1960); II, *Development of University*
Education, 1860–87 (New Delhi, 1963)

Bengal and Madras papers 1671–1785 (Calcutta, 1st ed. 1892–3; 2nd ed.
1928)

D. ADMINISTRATIVE AND OTHER PUBLICATIONS, INCLUDING THOSE OF THE INDIAN HISTORICAL RECORDS COMMISSION

Annual report of the National Archives of India (1891–), annual
Indian archives, vols. I–XVI (1947–), quarterly/annual/biennial
Bulletin of research theses and dissertations: nos. 1–3 (1955–)
List of the heads of administrations in India and of the India Office in England corrected up to 1 October 1938 (New Delhi, 1939)

BROCHURES, PAMPHLETS, etc.

Indian Historical Records Commission: *Proceedings,* I–XXXVI (1919–)
Sepoy recruitment in the old Madras Army, by H. H. Dodwell (Calcutta, 1922)
Manual of rules regulating access to archives in India and Europe (1940)
Indian Historical Records Commission: a retrospect 1919–1948 (Delhi, 1948)
Resolutions of the...Commission 1919–1948 (Delhi, 1949)
Proceedings of the National Committee of Archivists of India: I–II (New Delhi, 1956–9)
Index to papers read at the...Commission sessions 1920–1956 (New Delhi, 1956)
Inspection reports of the Director of Archives on the central and state records in the custody of the state governments, I (New Delhi, 1957)
Report of the Committee on Archival Legislation (New Delhi, 1962)
An Introduction to National Archives (New Delhi, 1st ed. 1958; 2nd ed. 1962)
Archives and records: what are they? (New Delhi, 1st ed. 1960; 2nd ed. 1961)
Indian Seals (problems and prospects) (New Delhi, 1960)
Diplomatic of Sanskrit copper-plate grants, by B. C. Chhabra (New Delhi, 1961)
Repair and preservation of records (New Delhi, 1st ed. 1959; 2nd ed. 1967)

ANDHRA PRADESH

State Archives, Government of Andhra Pradesh, Tarnaka,
Hyderabad-7
Officer in charge: Director
Authority: Secretary, Education Department, Government
of Andhra Pradesh, Hyderabad

RULES OF ACCESS

Applications to consult the records should be addressed to the Director, State Archives. Conditions of access are regulated by the government, but in general records over forty years old are open for consultation.

THE STATE OF ANDHRA PRADESH

The Deccan became a province of the Mogul empire in 1687. The Emperor appointed Chin Qulich Khan viceroy of the Deccan in 1713 and as Asaf Jah I he founded the dynasty of the Asaf Jahi rulers of Hyderabad in 1724. They ruled a vast territory until they lost Khandesh and the Carnatic and other areas in the north and south. Between 1759 and 1800 Masulipatam, the Northern Circars, the Guntur Circar and the districts of Cuddapa, Kurnool and Bellary were ceded by treaty to the East India Company. In 1853 a new treaty was concluded whereby the British agreed to maintain an auxiliary force, the Hyderabad Contingent, financed by the assignment in trust to them of Berar, Dharaseon and the Raichur Doab. Later these areas were restored to the Nizam except Berar, until in 1902 the Nizam's sovereignty over Berar was reaffirmed and the Treaty of Assignment replaced by a perpetual lease. For several decades until 1933 the Residency Bazars, a part of Hyderabad city, was administered by the British Resident, and in 1945 Secunderabad, a British cantonment near the capital, was restored to the Nizam. Hyderabad State acceded to the Indian Union in 1950. In 1953 the state of Andhra was formed from the Telugu-speaking districts of Madras. In November 1956 the state of Hyderabad was divided into Telengana, Maharashtra and Kannada areas according to the languages spoken, and the Telegu-speaking (Telengana) area added to Andhra to form the new enlarged state of Andhra Pradesh. The Marathi- and Kannada-speaking regions were merged with the contiguous territories speaking the same language in the Maharashtra and Mysore states. The capital is Hyderabad.

ADMINISTRATIVE CHANGES IN ANDHRA PRADESH

As a province of the Mogul empire the Deccan was administered by a *subadar* (governor) who was a *de facto* ruler responsible for the entire civil and military administration of the province. Justice was administered according to local custom and Muslim law, and village *panchayats* looked after the interests of the villages. The *subadar* was assisted by the *kotwal* (police officer), *foujdar* (court official), *qazi* (magistrate), *amil* (revenue collector), *shiqdar* (revenue official), *muqaddam* (village headman), *patwari* (village accountant) and other officials. The *diwan* (prime minister) was the highest executive. As the administrative machinery became outmoded the then *diwan*, Sir Salar Jung I (1853–83), instituted modern reforms. He created the secretariat offices under the charge of secretaries and a *sadr-ul-Maham* (member with a portfolio) looked after the affairs of the secretariat offices under him. In 1864 a Board of Revenue was set up and the state divided into *zilas* (districts) under *taluqdars* (district collectors). In 1867 these districts were grouped into divisions, each under a *sadr taluqdar*. In 1884 the Nizam created a purely advisory Council of State from members of the state's nobility and replaced it in 1893 with a Cabinet Council for dealing with executive matters and a Legislative Council for framing laws. Non-officials were for the first time associated with the law-making Council. In 1919 the Nizam replaced the Cabinet Council with an executive Council which continued to function until the state acceded to the Indian Union.

ARCHIVES ADMINISTRATION IN ANDHRA PRADESH

The *Dafter-i-Diwani* formerly dealt with all matters pertaining to the civil and military administration of four *subas* (divisions) of the Deccan, namely Aurangabad, Berar, Bijapur and Burhanpur, and the *Daftar-i-Mal* of the *subahs* of Hyderabad and Bidar. When the administration of Hyderabad was reorganized during the time of Sir Salar Jung I, these two offices were gradually divested of their executive powers and were left with the functions of record keeping, issuing sanads relating to land grants, and verifying sanads in cases of dispute. In 1894, the *Dafter-i-Diwani*, retaining the same name, was converted into a State Record Office, and in time it acquired the records of subsidiary *daftars* as they became defunct. In 1950 the name was changed to Central Record Office. With the establishment of Andhra Pradesh in November 1956 the control of the Central Record Office, Hyderabad, and of the records of the state of Andhra, passed to the new state government. The Andhra Record Office was transferred from Kurnool and merged with the Central Record Office at Hyderabad in March 1957. The name was changed to State Archives in 1962.

NATURE AND EXTENT OF HOLDINGS

The *Dafter-i-Diwani* and *Daftar-i-Mal* which were created about the year 1721 form the nucleus of the State Archives. These form part of the Asafia records, that is, records of the *daftars* set up under the Asaf Jahi rulers of Hyderabad, which were recovered from the descendants of the hereditary *daftar* holders. The Mogul records of the former Deccan viceroyalty were found in Arak Fort in Aurangabad in 1916 and contain valuable information for the period 1628–1706, particularly about the military administration of the reigns of Shah Jahan and Aurangzeb. A few hundred documents in Persian, mainly *farmans* of the Bahmanis (1347–1526), Adil Shahis (1489–1686), Qutb Shahis (1512–1687) and other rulers of the Deccan do not form part of a series. With the creation of the state of Andhra and other territorial changes affecting Madras in 1953, the post-1920 records of undivided Madras were apportioned accordingly.

Secretariat and Board of Revenue records, if they were in separate files and related exclusively to Andhra or Mysore, were transferred to those states. Records of common interest remained in Madras, but typed copies from August 1947 to 1952 were sent to Andhra or Mysore as were district records in those areas incorporated in Andhra or Mysore. All pre-1920 records remained in Madras. Thus A.P. State Archives holds, besides the secretariat records of Hyderabad State for 1853–1956, the secretariat records of the composite Madras State which relate to Andhra for 1920–52. The gaps in these records are gradually being filled. A reference library containing valuable printed and manuscript material is attached to the archives. There are 574 manuscript books in Persian, Arabic and Urdu which have been catalogued with descriptive notes in two volumes under the headings History (Afghanistan, Qandahar, Persia and India, pre- and post-Islamic period), Biography, Geography of the Eastern countries, Law, Grammar and Dictionaries, Ethics and Mysticism. There are also some palm-leaf manuscripts in Telugu.

AIDS TO REFERENCE

All the collections are catalogued, the records being entered in registers in which serial numbers, dates and titles are shown. The cataloguing of the Mogul records is still in progress. Publication of repository lists of the records is planned. The Andhra records have printed indexes. A guide to the archives is in the final stages of printing. This guide contains a description of the documents, their series, an assessment of the quantity of the holdings and the historical and administrative background of the state.

PUBLICATIONS

Nine volumes of selections from Marathi and Persian records of the Mogul and Asaf Jahi rulers of Hyderabad with English translations or summaries have been published since 1950.

HOLDINGS

State Archives, Tarnaka, Hyderabad–7

Serial number			Shelving (running feet)
1	Daftar-i-Salatin-i-Mughlia	1634–1706	196
2	Family collections		
a	Rajendra (Gangakhed) collection Political correspondence, military despatches, sanads, ahkams and other papers. Classification in progress		
	In Persian		28
	In Marathi		140
b	Salar Jung collection. Classification in progress		28
	Several members of this family held the post of prime minister. Papers cover the period from Mir Alam (1804–8) to Salar Jung III, with most relating to Salar Jung I (1853–83).		
c	Panchakki collection	1712–1824	28
	Correspondence between Mahmud Shah Musafir, a successor of the noted saint of Panchakki Darga in Aurangabad, Baba Shah Musafir, and his disciples. In Persian and Marathi (Modi script)		

		No. of documents
d	S.S. Khusro collection	
	Documents relating mainly to the grants made to the family of Khwaja Bandehnawaz of Gulbarga and some correspondence of his family. These documents include papers of Bahmani, Adil Shahi, Qutb Shahi, Mogul and Asaf Jahi rulers of the Deccan, and cover the period 1422 to 1900. Classification in progress	930
e	Mir Alauddin Hussain collection:	
	Papers relating to the reign of the Mogul Emperor Aurangzeb, the later Moguls, and Asaf Jahi rulers, covering the period 1673–1784. Classification in progress	34

f Muhammad Moinuddin collection:
Mogul and Asaf Jahi documents in Persian covering the   13
period 1786–1806. Classification in progress
g Hamid Siddiqi collection:
Persian, Urdu and English documents comprising ad-   1,589
ministrative documents as well as correspondence of
nobility, covering the period from Shah Jahan to the
seventh Nizam, i.e. 1669 to 1948. Classification in progress
h Moinuddin Ali Khan collection:
Persian documents relating to titles and ranks of the   17
nobility, 1759 to 1896. Classification in progress
i Ghiyas Siddiqi collection:
Persian documents mainly relating to grants in Kalyan,   14
from 1562 to 1842. Classification in progress
j Yafai collection:
Persian documents including Farmans, Parwanas, Chaknamas,   167
Istishhad etc., from 1534 to 1889. Classification in progress
k Agarwal collection:
Parwanas dastaks and petitions from 1772 to 1821.   7
Classification in progress
3 Records of old *daftars* (Asafia records)
   a *Daftar-i-Diwani*

Persian	1721–1895	616
Marathi	1760–1846	60

   b *Daftar-i-Istifia*   1715–1858   84
Prepared and maintained duplicate copies of sanads.
   c *Daftar-i-Mal*   1725–1918   2,976
Transacted all the civil and military business of the *subas*
of Hyderabad and Bidar.
   d *Daftar-i-Mawahir*   1767–1956   94
Controlled the manufacture of seals and badges for use in
government offices and by the nobility
   e *Daftar-i-Manasib-U-Khitabat*   1720–1948   21
Concerned with the conferring of titles, honours and ranks
   f *Daftar-i-Mulki*   1843–1927   560
Dealt with all administrative matters and political correspondence between the *nizams* and the British government
from 1843 to 1912.
   g *Daftar-i-Bakshigiri*   1756–1931   252
Dealt with administrative matters and payments relating
to the irregular forces raised by the feudal nobles.

h	Daftar-i-Darul Insha	1771–1919	42

The *Peshi* (personal) office of Nawab Nizam Ali Khan,
which dealt with foreign and political affairs of the state.

i	Dafter-i-Munshikhana	1847–1918	757

Created by Salar Jung I, it functioned as the Revenue
Department and controlled the *taluqdars* (district
collectors).

j	Daftar-i-Qanungoi	1807–1929	126

Settlement of the boundaries of lands and villages.

k	Daftar-i-Peshkari	1798–1941	84

Kept records of the original drafts and orders of the period
of the Peshkars, Raja Chandu Lal and Raja Ram Baksh.

l	Khazana-i-Amira	1852–1920	690

Dealt with financial transactions of the state.

m	Sadarat-ul-Aliya	1758–1962	237

Dealt with religious endowments and religious affairs.

n	Nazm-i-Jamiat	1875–1954	690

Army headquarters of the irregular forces of the state, set
up in the process of centralization under Salar Jung I to
supervise and control the establishments of the feudal
lords.

o	Muntakhabajat	1861–1962	126
p	Shorapur papers	1767–1856	—
4	Secretariat records		5,830
a	Hyderabad State	1846–1956	
b	Andhra Districts of the Madras State	1920–53	
c	Andhra State and Andhra Pradesh	1953–6 1956–60	
d	Farmans	1910–48	
e	Board of Revenue (Hyderabad)	1895–1949 (with gaps)	
f	Board of Revenue (Andhra)	1927–55	
5	Strong Almirah documents	1917–59	30
6	Confidential records	1937–53	60
7	Survey records		2,386
a	Administrative field books	1861–78	
b	Original measurement books	1895, 1903, 1922, 1925	
c	Mounted and unmounted litho maps	1861, 1903, 1925	
d	Traverse records	1861, 1903–25	

PUBLICATIONS

State Archives (formerly Central Record Office, Hyderabad)

Kitab-i-Daftar-i-Diwani-Wa-Mal-Wa-Mulki (1938). Facsimiles of old Persian documents relating to the grant of land, cash etc.

Chronology of modern Hyderabad 1720–1890 (1954). Translated into English from the original Persian, with indexes of names and places and genealogical trees of the *nizams* and their nobles.

Diplomatic correspondence between Nizam Ali Khan and the East India Company 1780–1789 (1958). Translated and summarized into English from the original Persian.

News-letters of Nawab Mir Nizam Ali Khan 1767–1799 (1955). Intelligence reports sent by the agents of the *nizam* from various *darbars* and neighbouring states.

Selected Waqai of the Deccan 1660–1671 (1953). Selection of *waqai* (newsletters) and *roznamachas* (daily news) with foreword, preface, introduction, summaries and descriptive notes in English. They provide information on the early period of Aurangzeb's reign.

Selected documents of Shah Jahan's reign 1634–1658 (1950). In Persian with English preface, summaries and descriptive notes.

Poona Akhbars, I–III, 1773–1794 (1953, 1954, 1956). A collection of Marathi *akhbars* (newsletters) narrating the happenings at the Maratha court at Purandhar and Poona. English prefaces, summaries, glossaries and indexes of persons and place names.

Sanpuri Bakhar 1689–1776 (1950). A brief Marathi chronicle, writer unknown, starting with the execution of Chatrapati Sambaji in 1689. In Marathi with English summary.

Selected documents of Aurangzeb's reign 1659–1706 (1958). In Persian with English summary, introduction and index.

Farmans and sanads of the Deccan sultans (in the press). *Farmans* and sanads of the Bahmani, Barid Shahi, Adil Shahi and Qutub Shahi kings, in Persian with English summaries.

The freedom struggle in Hyderabad: a connected account, I–IV, 1800–1857 (1956), 1857–1885 (1956), 1885–1920 (1957), 1921–1947 (1966).

ASSAM

Secretariat Record Office, Shillong
Officer in charge: Keeper of Records
Authority: Secretariat Administration Department,
Government of Assam, Shillong

RULES OF ACCESS

All non-confidential records up to 1901 are open for bona fide research purposes, and excerpts from these records are generally released without scrutiny. Non-confidential records up to 1935 can also be consulted with the special permission of the department concerned. Typed copies of extracts from records are supplied on payment of search and transcription fees. Applications for permission to consult the records should be addressed to Keeper of Records, Assam Secretariat Record Office, Shillong.

THE STATE OF ASSAM

Assam came under British rule at the close of the first Burmese War and was attached to Bengal for administrative purposes. In 1833 Upper Assam was formed into a separate principality and made over to Raja Purandar Singh on certain conditions, but in 1839 he was deposed due to mis-government and the entire province again came under direct British administration.

In 1874 Assam was detached from Bengal and made a separate chief commissionership. On the partition of Bengal in 1905 it was united to the eastern districts of Bengal under a lieutenant governor, but from 1912 the chief commissionership was revived and in 1921 a governorship was created. On the partition of India almost the whole of the predominantly Muslim district of Sylhet was merged with Eastern Bengal (Pakistan). Dewangiri in North Kamrup was ceded to Bhutan in 1951. The Naga Hills district of Assam and the Tuensang Area of the North-East Frontier Agency became the separate state of Nagaland in December 1963, with headquarters at Kohima. The North-East Frontier Agency is administered by the governor of Assam, acting as the agent of the president, through an adviser whose status corresponds to that of a commissioner. It includes the Kameng, Subansiri, Siang, Lohit and Tirap divisions. The capital is Shillong.

ARCHIVES ADMINISTRATION IN ASSAM

The Assam Civil Secretariat Record Office was established in 1874 and placed in the charge of a registrar. In 1929 a separate records building was constructed, an important step towards better preservation of records. In 1953 the office was placed under a full-time keeper of records. The Regional Records Survey Committee, since its reconstitution in 1955, has surveyed records of the several District Record Rooms and prepared lists of records deserving permanent preservation with a view to their transfer to the custody of the Secretariat Record Office.

NATURE AND EXTENT OF HOLDINGS

Holdings occupy 5,000 cubic feet and are in two parts, the 'old records' mainly of the period 1826–74, and those records accruing since 1874. When Assam was finally reconstituted in 1912, a large portion of the records of the Eastern Bengal and Assam Secretariat was transferred to Assam. With Partition certain records went to East Pakistan. On the abolition of the post of commissioner of divisions in 1947 the non-current records of that office were transferred to the Secretariat Record Office, and on an average 12,000 files are deposited annually by the various government agencies. Certain Government of India records are also housed in the same building. However, for political reasons the Manipur Agency records and North-East Frontier Agency records were transferred from the custody of the state government to the office of the adviser and certain records relating to the Assam Rifles transferred to the Assam Rifles headquarters.

OTHER COLLECTIONS

Of the collections still held elsewhere mention may be made of the records of the Court of Wards, the Abhayapuri Estate and the District Record Rooms. The holdings of the Record Room at Dhubri, for example, date from 1793, relate to Goalpara, Gare Mahal, Eastern Duars, Bhutan, Cooch Behar, Rangpur and Dinajpur, and include letters and reports exchanged between the collectors, commissioners and political agents.

AIDS TO REFERENCE

Published guides include Dr S. K. Bhuiyan's *Preliminary report on the old records of the Assam Secretariat* (1951), a precursor of K. N. Dutt's *Handbook to the old records of the Assam Secretariat* (1959). There is also a press list of pre-1874 files and an index to pre-1874 files while an exhaustive index to the volumes of pre-1874 records is under preparation. Amalgamated indexes to government proceedings from 1874 are printed annually.

HOLDINGS
Assam Secretariat Record Office, Shillong

I 'Old records' 1823–74
  1 Letters received from Government
  2 Letters issued to Government of Bengal, entered in copy books
  3 Letters issued to Government, rough drafts
  4 Letters received from Board of Revenue for the Lower Provinces
  5 Letters issued to Board of Revenue
  6 Letters to Board of Revenue, rough drafts
  7 Letters received from District Officers
  8 Letters issued to District Officers
  9 Letters received from miscellaneous quarters like Manipur, Rangpur, Accountant-General, Military Board, Marine Board, Medical Board, Commandant of Assam etc.
  10 Letters issued to miscellaneous quarters
  11 Letters issued to districts, rough drafts
  12 Miscellaneous circulars 1861–8, diary book 1857–9, précis 1871–2
  13 Miscellaneous papers including Mr Vallente's Notebook, Captain Jenkins' 'Journal of a Tour in Upper Assam', 1838
  14 Assam Commissioner's files
II Records transferred to Assam on the formation of the chief commissionership in 1874
  1 Government of Bengal   1788–1874
  2 Board of Revenue, Lower Provinces 1774–1874
  3 Commissioner of Dacca   1824–74
  4 Commissioner of Cooch Behar   1867–74
III Proceedings of the Chief Commissioner 1874–1905
  1 Foreign Department
  2 Finance and Commerce Department
  3 Military Department
  4 Home Department
  5 Revenue and Agriculture Department
  6 General Department
  7 Judicial Department
IV Proceedings of Lieutenant Governor of East Bengal and Assam 1905–11
  1 Revenue Department
  2 Political Department
  3 Appointment Department
  4 Municipal Department

5 Education Department
6 Finance Department
7 General Department
8 Judicial Department
v Proceedings of the Chief Commissioner 1912–20
  1 Political Department
  2 Appointment Department
  3 Municipal Department
  4 Education Department
  5 Judicial Department
  6 General Department
  7 Finance Department
  8 Revenue Department
vi Proceedings of the Government of Assam, 1921–47
  1 Home Department
  2 Appointment Department
  3 Finance Department
  4 General and Judicial Department
  5 Local self-government
  6 Education Department
  7 Medical Department
  8 Revenue Department
  9 Confidential Department   1936–47
 10 Budget Department   1942–7
 11 Finance (Miscellaneous) Department 1942–7
 12 Transport Department   1942–7
 13 Supply (A and B) Department   1942–7
The details about the records after 1947 are not given because some of the series are not complete.

Government of India records
(*Secretariat Record Office, Shillong*)

1 Manipur Agency records, records of Cooch Behar and Tripura from 1874
   Include 400 volumes of mixed records of earlier years and 319 confidential files 1933–52. In the custody of the Office of the Adviser (NEFA Administration).
2 Khasi State records   from 1874
3 Records relating to the tribal areas   from 1874
   491 bundles. Classified 'A', 'B', 'C', according to importance, and the 'A' records printed. Printed indexes from 1890.

4 Records relating to the Assam Rifles from 1874
   In the custody of the NEFA Administration and Assam Rifles headquarters.
5 Miscellaneous (titles, honours, durbars etc.)   1870–1949
   145 bundles.

BIHAR

State Central Archives, Old Secretariat Buildings, Patna
Officer in Charge: Record Keeper, responsible to Director of Archives
Authority: Under Secretary, Political Department, Government of Bihar, Patna

RULES OF ACCESS

Bona fide research students are allowed access to pre-1901 records. Excerpts from non-confidential records more than fifty years old are not subject to scrutiny.

THE STATE OF BIHAR

In the sixteenth century the Afghan-dominated kingdom of Bihar became part of the Mogul empire. In return for the East India Company's support against his enemies, the Emperor Shah Alam in 1765 granted the British the *diwani* or right to collect revenue from Bengal, Bihar and Orissa. Bihar was administered as part of the Bengal presidency outside the ceded territories until 1912 when, with parts of Orissa and Chota Nagpur forming one of its divisions under a commissioner, it became a separate province administered by a lieutenant governor with an executive council. By an act of 1919 Bihar and Orissa was given a governor. The Orissa division, with portions of the Central Provinces and Madras, was constituted a separate province in April 1936. Bihar received certain areas from the Purnea district and the Purulia subdivision of the Manbhum district from West Bengal and in May 1948 the administration of the states of Saraikella and Kharswan from Orissa. The state now contains the two ethnic areas of Bihar and Chota Nagpur. The capital is Patna.

ARCHIVES ADMINISTRATION IN BIHAR

The Civil Secretariat Record Room, Bihar, was established in 1861 and reorganized in March 1954 to become the State Central Records Office.

Records of historical interest lying in the offices of the Board of Revenue and district and divisional offices are being centralized at Patna and already many important series and collections have been transferred. The office also attends to the needs of departments, the preservation and re-habilitation of records, research and publication. Some highly valuable collections still remain in the private custody of the scions of the houses of the landed aristocracy of Bihar. Many of the old *zamindari* had *mahafiz-khana* modelled on the district record rooms. Some of these collections have been investigated by the Regional Records Survey Committee. Two examples are the Darbhanga Raj Records Office, which holds Persian records from the time of Akbar until 1860 and scientifically arranged and well-preserved English records from 1860 contributing to the history of north Bihar, and the Bettiah Raj records relating to the northern half of the Champaran district. The Records Office is now known as the State Central Archives.

NATURE AND EXTENT OF HOLDINGS

Records pertaining to the earlier administration of the areas now incorporated in Bihar are held by West Bengal although printed copies of relevant records have been received from the Bengal Government. Among the acquisitions by Patna from district and divisional offices have been many hundreds of volumes of pre- and post-Mutiny English records and correspondence as well as Persian documents of the Mogul period. Centralization is still going on. A library of over 2,000 old and rare books, official publications and some revenue account books is attached to the office.

AIDS TO REFERENCE

Records transferred by the secretariat are accompanied by printed indexes from which consolidated indexes are compiled. District and divisional records are described in *A hand book of the Bihar and Orissa provincial records 1771–1859* (1933), although with the transfer of many of these records to Patna it is no longer a guide to location. In addition, the Chota Nagpur records are press listed, a *Catalogue of Patna Commissioner's English records, 1813–1853* has been published and a pamphlet describing the records of the Purnea and Saran collectorates was issued by the Bihar Regional Records Survey Committee in 1959.

PUBLICATIONS

As a result of a systematic publication programme five volumes based on original records have appeared, two more are to be published shortly and further works are under compilation.

HOLDINGS
State Central Records Office, Patna

I Archival collections. 'A' and 'B' proceedings, proceedings volumes, registers of correspondence etc.

Secretariat records	1859–1959

All departments of government except the Public Works Department.

Patna commissioner's records	1811–1900
Chota Nagpur commissioner's records	1795–1900
Bhagalpur commissioner's records	1832–1900
Bhagalpur collectorate records	1770–1900
Monghyr collectorate records	1812–1900
Purnea collectorate records	1775–1874
Hazaribagh collectorate records	1833–1876
Champaran collectorate records	1837–1905
Muzaffarpur collectorate records	1782–1869
Gaya collectorate records	1842–1905
Shahabad collectorate records	1781–1800
Ranchi collectorate records	1837–1900
Chaibassa collectorate records	1837–1900

II Special acquisitions

Persian *firmans* and *sanads* of the Mughul period	
Records relating to Mahatma Gandhi in Champaran	1917–18
Records on Freedom Movement in Bihar	
Rare government publications of the early period	

III Gazettes

Calcutta Gazette	1832–1956
Gazette of India	1864 to date
Bihar Gazette	1912 to date

IV Electoral rolls   1956–62

ADDITIONAL PUBLICATIONS

K. K. Datta, ed. *Unrest against British rule in Bihar 1831–1859* (1957)

K. K. Datta, ed. *A selection from the correspondence of Patna Judge-Magistrate records, 1790–1837* (1954)

Some farmans, sanads and parwanas 1578–1802 A.D. (1962)

Select documents on Mahatma Gandhi in Champaran, 1917–18 (1963)

Hand books on Bhagalpur Collectorate records (to be published shortly)

Bhagalpur Commissioner's Judicial records 1793–1805 (to be published shortly)

DELHI

Chief Commissioner's Office, Delhi

Delhi was part of Punjab province until October 1912, when the enclave was created a separate province under a chief commissioner. In 1915 a tract of land from the United Provinces was added to the Delhi Province. The office holds only post-Mutiny papers as the pre-Mutiny records were destroyed. There is little political material, but much on Delhi city throughout the nineteenth century. The surviving Delhi Residency records are stored in the West Pakistan Government Record Office, Lahore. The Mutineers' papers were transferred to the Imperial Record Department (National Archives of India) and appear in *A Press list of the Mutiny papers 1857* (1921). The holdings are not catalogued.

GOA

Historical Archives of Goa (*Purabhilekh Sangrahalaya*), Panjim, Goa
Officer in charge: Director

RULES OF ACCESS

Research scholars are allowed access to the records after receiving permission from the government. The Archives has a small microfilming machine and a microfilm recorder, and microfilms of documents can be supplied after authorization from the government. Applications should be addressed to the Director.

THE TERRITORY OF GOA

Vasco da Gama landed at Calicut in the kingdom of Zamorin on the west coast of India in May 1498 and the Portuguese captain of fleet occupied Anjediva in 1505. The island of Goa was taken by the Portuguese from the Bijapur rulers in 1510 and Diu and Damão obtained from the Gujarat sultans in 1534 and 1559. The seat of the Portuguese Government in Indian and South-east Asian waters was moved from Cochin to Goa in 1530. Goa was made a centre of Jesuit activities, and from there the Portuguese maintained a monopoly of eastern trade for 100 years. Furthermore, the trade of the Vijayanagar empire of south India with neighbouring countries, especially Persia, passed through Goa. Malacca and the Portuguese establishments in Ceylon and Burma passed to Holland in the early seventeenth century, Mozambique was separated from Goa in 1750 and Timor and Macao in 1800. As Portuguese power declined, only Goa remained to them of their Estado da India. They evacuated these territories in December 1961 and Goa is now administered as a territory of the central government of India.

ARCHIVES ADMINISTRATION IN GOA

The previous records of the Portuguese State of India were in 1595 organized into an archives office, the *Torre do Tombo do Estado da India*, by the learned Portuguese historian of Asia, Diogo do Couto, who was appointed the first *guarda-mor* (record keeper). The office was attached to the office of the Portuguese viceroy of India and formed part of the secretariat. The name was changed in 1930 to *Arquivo Geral e Histórico do Estado da India* and in 1937 to *Cartório do Governo Geral do Estado da India*. By 1952 it had developed into a separate directorate, the *Arquivo Histórico do Estado da India*, and was renamed *Purabhilekh Sangrahalaya* (Historical Archives of Goa) when it passed under Indian control. Under Portuguese administration the records of Goa, Damão and Diu were not centralized. Substantial collections were held in the offices and archives of the Director of Civil Administration, the Director of Treasury Services, the municipal *câmara* of Goa (52 volumes, 1517–1728 and 1744–99), municipal *câmara* of Damão (15 volumes, 1736–1878), the Keeper of the Civil Register (birth and baptismal records), the Patriarchal Palace of Goa, the Santa Casa da Misericordia of Goa (157 volumes, 1466–1924) and the Biblioteca Nacional Vasco da Gama. Since the accession of Goa to India a survey of archives scattered over Goa, Damão and Diu has been made and records from various offices will now be centralized at Panjim. These may prove to be very numerous. The offices have already supplied lists of their records and some have now been transferred. No records were removed by the Portuguese authorities, but microfilms of the correspondence between the governor general at Goa and the government of Portugal (*Monções* and *Cartas patentes*) are held at Lisbon.

NATURE AND EXTENT OF HOLDINGS

The archives of Goa cover primarily the period 1600–1900 although there are valuable records dating from 1510. At present there are some 1 crore (1,00,00,000) documents and 20,000 volumes, but after the centralization of all records at Panjim these quantities may be increased to 5 crores loose documents and 1 lakh (1,00,000) bound volumes. As Goa's sphere of influence during the period of European expansion in Asia and Africa extended to Burma, Ceylon, Malacca, Macao, China, Japan, Manila, Timor, Ormuz, Mozambique and Brazil the early archives have an importance which extends far beyond the confines of Goa. The archives are also rich in material relating to the Vijayanagar empire, the Deccan sultanates, Haidar Ali and Tipu Sultan and, later, the Maratha empire. The Marathi/Modi account books of the *communidades*, village communities held as joint property by several families, provide excellent source material for economic history.

AIDS TO REFERENCE

Two guides to the records have been published, an *Index alfabetico, chronologico e remissivo* (1811) and P. S. S. Pissurlencar's *Roteiro dos arquivos da India Portuguese* (1955), an alphabetical list of which the list of holdings below is mostly a brief summary. Some of the correspondence between the governor general at Goa and the Government of Portugal (*Monções* and *Cartas Patentes*) appears in *Boletim da Filmoteca Ultramarina Portuguesa* (19 volumes, still in progress) published at Lisbon by *Centro de Estudos Historicos Ultramarinos*. There are two catalogues of the holdings of the Biblioteca Nacional Vasco da Gama by J. A. Ismael, *Catalogo dos livros do assentamento da gente de guerra que veio do Reino para a India desde 1731–1811* (Nova Goa, 1893) and *Catalogo dos livros opusculos e manuscritos pertencentos a Biblioteca, Nova Goa* (1907).

HOLDINGS

Historical Archives of Goa, Panjim, Goa

	Approximate dates	Volumes
Acórdãos e assentos da câmara de Goa	1535–7; 1572–83;	14
(decrees and determinations of the	1592–1723; 1765–93;	
câmara of Goa)	1823–36	
Administração fiscal (fiscal administration)	1847–8; 1851–80	24
Administração civil (civil administration)	1858–1951	836
Administration of Bardês	1851–80	11
of the island of Goa	1851–80	10
of Salsette	1851–80	9
Aforamentos (rented lands)	1616–1889	73
Agência Portuguesa em Bombaim (Portuguese Agency in Bombay)	1841–64	3
Agriculture	1782	1

Alfândegas (customs-houses)	1593–1887; 1902	2,450
Alvarás e provisões de Sua Magestade (charters and provisions of His Majesty)	1593–1781	7
Almotaçaria (estimates)	1791–1854	16
Anais históricos (historical annals of the *câmara* of Goa)	1787–1849	1
Assentos e juramentos (determinations and judgements of the *câmara* of Goa)	1640–8; 1674–5; 1683–93; 1765–93	4
Arsenal of Goa	1779–98; 1805–53; 1869–70	19
Baçaim	1610–1739	12
Bambolim	1731–59	2
Bandorá	1622–1735	2
Bengal Mission, registration of baptisms	1665–1791	1
Bens nacionais (national possessions)	1844–79	11
Botiqueiros (merchants)	1736–8; 1765–7	2
Câmaras		
of Bardês	1851–9	1
Cacorá	1842	1
Damão	1851	1
Diu	1851	1
Embarbarcém	1766–1843	2
Island of Goa	1851–79	3
Salsette	1691–1720; 1780–1810; 1851–79	4
Orders of the Secretary General to the Presidents of the municipal *câmaras*	1847–8	1
Canará (Kanara) correspondence	1698–1720; 1747–69	2
Capelas (chapels)	1715; 1723–1832	4
Carta Constitucional (oath of the Constitutional Charter)	1842	1
Cartas e ordens (orders and rights issued to Portuguese officers in or proceeding to India)		
Secretary General	1609–1865	127
Fazenda (treasury)	1624; 1642–67; 1678–81; 1729–31	4
Cartas patentes	1550–62	1
Cartas patentes e provisões	1561–2; 1565–7; 1569–82	3
Cartas patentes e alvarás	1557–68; 1596–1601; 1611–1875 with gaps	272

Cartas patentes, provisões e alvarás	1593–1743; 1753–4; 1775–97; 1799–1836	38
Cartas régias e provisões	1726–52	1

Cartazes (Safe conducts. Correspondence relating to Portugal's claim to exclusive rights over navigation in eastern waters and including volumes about British, Dutch, French and Danish ships which visited India between 1700 and 1870.)

	1704–82; 1792–1817	8
Casa da moeda (Mint)	1830	1
Castigos (register of punishments inflicted on the soldiers of the 2nd Battalion of Cadadores)	1843–60; 1864–71	6
Catecúmenos (converts under pre-baptismal instructions at Betim)	1701–1861	146
Ceilão Mission coffers	1807–38	1
Certidões (certificates)	1602–1828; 1857–84	8
Chancelaria (Chancery)	1656–1854	30
Chaul	1591–1612; 1663–73; 1734–40	3
City of Goa	1777–82	2
Colleges of S. Agostinho, Bom Jesus, Sam Bõaventura, Chorão, S. Domingos, S. José, S. Paulo, Pópulo, Rachol, S. Tomás	1553–1876	110

Comunidades (Account books of village communities held as a joint property by many families)

das Novas Conquistas ('New Conquests', the northern coastal and inland regions)	1761; 1766–1907	3,271
das Velhas Conquistas ('Old Conquests', the coastal region around Panjim)	1595–1602; 1629; 1638; 1664–5; 1670; 1677; 1683; 1687; 1695; 1771–2; 1811; 1871–80	19
de Cotigão	1858–80	1
das Ilhas do Goa	1582–1828	255
de Salcete (Salsette)	1631–1800	100
Conciliações (conciliations)	1864–70	38
Condecorações (badges and insignias of Orders of Knighthood)	1845–77	1
Confidências (confidential, Secretary-General)	1844–70	1

Confisco (confiscations)	1705–1892	245
Confrarias (brotherhoods)	1682–1725; 1778–1844;	7
	1854–71	
Congregaçõa (brotherhoods) *dos Agos-*	1605–82; 1690–1835	24
tinianos, S. Domingos, Oratorianos, India		
Oriental		
Conselho de Distrito (District Council)	1850–60	1
Conselho do Estado (State Council)	1618–1740 with gaps;	11
	1770–85	
Conselho de Fardamento (Uniform	1855–7	1
Council)		
Conselho de Fazenda (Treasury Council)	1613–1781	59
Conselho do Governo	1822–77	12
Conselho de Guerra (War Council)	1867–72	1
Conselho de Justiça (Justice Council)	1845–53	1
Consultas do serviço de partes	1614–80; 1688; 1701;	12
(consultations regarding the service in	1717–32; 1736; 1742	
that division)		
Contas diversas (miscellaneous accounts)	1655–1857	8
Contadoria Geral (Accountant-General)	1821–44; 1847–63	5
Contratos (contracts)	1843–4; 1871–82	2
Convento de Santo Agostinho, Santa	1560–1893	237
Bárbara, S. Bõaventura, Bom Jesus,		
N. Sra de Bom Sucesso, Cabo, S.		
Caetano, Carmo, Santa Cruz dos		
Milagres, Damão, Dio, S. Domingos,		
Espírito Santo, S. Francisco, S. João		
de Deus, Madre de Deus, Santa		
Mónica, Pilar		
Conventos extintos (extinct convents)	1560–1885	177
Cristandade (Christianity)		
Laws	1562–1843	1
Provisions	1513–1840	1

These codes contain a register of the various laws for the purpose of propagating the Catholic religion in parts of India. Indexed *Roteiro*, pp. 61–95.

Correspondência para o Reino	1763; 1765–9;	124
(correspondence to the realm)	1773; 1776–87	
Cumbarjua factory	1734–51; 1785–96;	20
	1800	
Damão	1592; 1770–1885	83

Damão, Diu and Macao correspondence	1838	1
Degredados (Exiles to Mozambique, Timor, Diu, Royal Arsenal of Goa, Powder Battery of Goa, also from Goa to Mozambique)	1828–34; 1881–92	5
Diu	1591–7; 1698–1888	163
Diplomas de nomeação (appointment diplomas)	1847–73	5
Dízimos (Tithes)	1683–5; 1752–4; 1758–63; 1768	4

'Historical memorial on the establishment of agrarian tithes...Goa, Bardes and Salcete.' Of great interest to the economic history of Goa. Indexed *Roteiro*, pp. 101–2.

	1793	1
Efeitos (terms of receipts of effects)	1774–50 [*sic*]	1
Embaixada á China (embassy in China)	1669	1
Erário Real (royal purse)	1765–70; 1817; 1829	3
Escravos (slaves)	1682–1759; 1855	10
Escrituras públicas (public contracts)	1753–1898	542
In Marathi	1776–1867	359
Estanco Real (royal archives)	1686–93	1
Estrangeiros (foreign relations, mainly with Burma, French India)	1815–92	27
Fazenda (treasury)	1712–1902	139
Feitorias (factories) Indexed *Roteiro*, pp. 112–16	1667–84	1
Baçaim	1701; 1722–5; 1728–9	3
Chaul	1680–1736	1
Diu	1686–1704; 1743–73; 1781; 1796–8; 1807–10; 1842–85	16
Goa	1722; 1735–1852	13
Mangalor	1741; 1763; 1769; 1770	4
Sião	1769–1821; 1841	4
Sofala	1740	1
Surat	1781–1821; 1827–9; 1841	18
Feitores (factories agents)	1710; 1764; 1771; 1773; 1879–80	5
Feitoria (factories). Indexed *Roteiro*, pp. 151–7	1717–1835	170

Fianças (securities)	1626–30; 1635–60; 1761	4
Forais (registers of duties paid to the king)		
Island of Goa	1517; 1567	3
Bardês	1647; 1771; 1800	7
Salsette	1567; 1622–94; 1880	9
Description of contents, *Roteiro*, pp. 117–19		
Foros (tribunals)	1682–1723; 1770–92; 1819; 1868–88	11
Fortalezas (fortresses)	1545–1694	4
Gerais (general volumes)	1843–79	12
Gãocares (village heads responsible for the collection of government taxes)	1770	1
Homenagens (respects, homages)	1638–40; 1656–1737; 1744–1805; 1842–77	8
Hospital Real Militar (Royal Military Hospital)	1777; 1830, 1835; 1838; 1886	6
Imprensa nacional (National press)	1835–9; 1849–62	3
Inquisition	1782–1832	4
Inventories	1759–1862	2
Japan	1576–1769	4
Jesuits	1664; 1684–1806; 1845–6	46
Juntas	1762–70; 1874–86	11
Justice	1779; 1837–74	15
Licenças (liquor and tobacco licences)	1840–6	3
Livros azul, morato, vermelho, verde (blue, mulberry, red and green books)	1544–1873	10
Macao (includes correspondence with Japan, China, Manila and Timor)	1677–1861	119
Maim	1835	1
Malabar	1759–60	4
Marata (examination in Marathi language)	1875	1
Marathi-Modi correspondence	1650–1850	8,000 loose papers

(correspondence between Portuguese viceroys of Goa and Maratha rulers from Satara Kholaphur, Sawantvaddi and Poona Court, Sunda kings of Canara etc.)

Memorials	1828–1863	39

Merces, merces gerias (grants of land, local title and other privileges in return for services to the state)	1607–1883	61
Militia	1763–1894	1,063
Missões (missions)	1665–1791	7
Mozambique	1675–9; 1709–40; 1749–1884	22

Moncões do Reino (monsoon papers. This, the largest series, contains reports and letters sent to Portugal, including many reports from Brazil, China, Japan, and other parts of the Portuguese empire, so-called because the Royal Mail was sent annually before the start of the south-west monsoon. *Index alfabetico* contains a brief index compiled in 1810).

	1557–1914	600
Nagar-Aveli	1783	1
Namoxins (assigned property)	1630; 1646; 1737–40; 1759; 1762–1857	10
Norte province	1686–96; 1715–20	3
Noviciado de Chorão (novitiates of Chorão)	1714–1842	11
Ordens régias (palace orders)	1630–45; 1660–6; 1676–1868	86
Paço, Mesa do (palace table)	1774–8	1
Padrõado (patronage)	1845–6	1
Passaportes (passports)	1783–1803; 1817–1908	29
Pensões (pensions)	1698–1838	20
Pensões de Sendi (Xendi tax, on a Hindu religious symbol)	1758; 1768	2
Perném	1749–65; 1852	5
Porta (entrance)	1809–80	153
Portarias (determinations)	1735–8; 1750–1899	55
Posses (possessions)	1710–20; 1733–46; 1788–1844; 1877–87	5
Prasos da Coroa (rented land grants)	1774–1830; 1857	11
Prefeitura (prefecture)	1835	1
Processos judiciais (judicial processes)	1592; 1722–1852	17
Professores primários (principal teachers)	1852–64	1
Provedoria. Indexed *Roteiro*, pp. 157–60	1720–1839	101
Provisões, alvarás e regimentos. Indexed *Roteiro*, pp. 161–88	1515–98	2
Provisões		
Cristandade (Christianity)	1515–1843	2

Vice-Reis (viceroy)	1600–12; 1621	3
Estanco do Tabaco (tobacco post)	1686–93	1
Fazenda (treasury)	1688–99; 1757–59	2
Diu	1731–40; 1780–1801; 1806–19; 1830–3; 1841–61; 1867	14
Régias (royal)	1766–1825	1
Damão, Diu, Macao, Mozambique, Solor and Timor etc.	1769–1846	10
Erário Real (royal purse)	1765–70; 1791–1829	5
Governo provincial	1786–1837	1
Casa de moeda (Mint)	1834–41	1
Other	1626; 1669; 1687–91; 1718; 1726–52	5
Provisões, alvarás e cartas patentes	1558–93; 1716–29; 1768–71	4
Quilimane	1742	1
Rachol	1793–1853	1
Ranes (Rajas) de Sanquelim	1746–97; 1856–9	2
Relaçao de Goa (report on Goa)	1526–1835; 1869–84	5
Regedorias (civil magistracies)	1847–98	1
Regimentos (rules of the Office of Accounts). Indexed *Roteiro*, pp. 191–2	1554–1731	1
Regimentos	1568; 1589; 1595; 1626; 1675; 1746–64; 1804; 1833	10
Regimentos e instruções	1564–1666; 1684–1869	25
Regimentos e regulamentos Indexed *Roteiro*, p. 194	1830–9	1
Reis vizinhos (correspondence with Haidar Ali and Tipu Sultan, the smaller dynasties of Kanara and the Maratha naval chiefs)	1619–1753; 1770–1842	22
Vice-reis e governadores (viceroys and governors). Indexed *Roteiro*, pp. 195–9	1604–1837	1
Rendas do Estado (revenues of the state)	1591–1838; 1882–7	20
Registos gerais (general registers) Senate of Goa	1570–92; 1609–23; 1629–31; 1640–59; 1675–80; 1688–97; 1708–16; 1724–33;	31

	1741–54; 1765–75; 1777–1804; 1816–76	
Senate of Diu	1606–43; 1715–43; 1758–1828	12
Treasury	1769–86; 1790–1855	33
Secretary-General	1802–1904	53
Repartição de Gabinete (Cabinet office)	1899–1958	165
Requerimentos (requisitions)	1729–72; 1775–80; 1783–1904	72
Saguates (gifts)	1598; 1688	2
Sal e abcari (salt and excise duty)	1880	1
Sapais de Chorão (station in the market place for the collection of municipal taxes)	1843–9	1
Secretary-General	1688–1904	204
Segredo (secret negotiations with the kings of Ceylon during the transition from Portuguese to Dutch rule)	1635–47; 1711–15	2
Selo (stamp)	1815–18; 1841–9	2
Seminary of Chorão	1685–1715; 1738–62; 1772; 1784; 1793; 1796–1845	15
Seminary of Rachol	1790; 1796–1855	12
Senado de Goa (senate of Goa)		
Acórdãos e assentos (determinations and decrees)	1535–7; 1572–83; 1592–1723; 1765–93; 1765–93; 1823–36	15
Almotaçaria (estimates)	1768; 1791; 1797; 1799; 1806; 1808–49; 1851–4	19
Alvarás e provisões (briefs and provisions of His Majesty)	1593–1781	3
Anais (annals)	1787–1849	1
Assentos e juramentos (determinations and judgements)	1640–8; 1674–93; 1765–93	5
Bandos (edicts)	1707–69; 1777–1829	2
Cartas, alvarás e provisões	1623–54; 1733–40; 1757–1847	7
Cartas do governo	1668–75; 1713–1871	13
Cartas patentes	1596–1603; 1612–22; 1644–6; 1660–4; 1680–8	8

17   LGA

Cartas Régias (royal charters)	1529–1611; 1630–1756	5
Capela (chapel) *de Santa Catarina*	1740–3; 1810–66	2
Chancelaria (chancery)	1772–1834	3
Termos de conciliações (conditions of conciliation)	1838	1
Correspondência diversa (miscellaneous correspondence)	1676–1708; 1859–1909	3
Fianças (guarantees)	1643–5; 1695–1721; 1770–9; 1817–18	4
Juizes (judgements)	1803–38; 1854–99	5
Marcas de ourives (gold- and silver-smith marks)	1777–1834	1
Termos das obras (terms of labour)	1654–5; 1770–3; 1791–1854	6
Arrematação das rendas (auctions to collect revenues)	1650–1756; 1766–1816; 1836–79	12
Bens (possessions)	1764–87	1
Diversos oficios (various offices)	1776–90; 1822–53	5
Venda do papel selado (sale of sealed documents)	1742–1813; 1820–38	3
Vária (miscellaneous)	1565–72; 1623–6; 1773–1877	23
Sermões (sermons)	1695	1
Serviços (duties)	1751–1838	5
Sul	1760	2
Sundém (negotiations of the House of the King of Sundem)	1838	1
Telegramas (in English)	1859–61	1
Tesouraria geral (treasure-house general)	1777; 1793; 1825–6	4
Testamentos (wills)	1709–1835	44
Timor	1769–1831; 1838; 1857–66	12
Tombos (archival registries: various)	1553–62; 1566–8; 1572; 1591; 1835; 1842–54	24
Tratados da India (treaties)	1571–1856	5
Vários (various)	1667–1877; 1880	5
Vassalagem (vassalage)	1746–97	1
Vencimentos (salaries of ecclesiastical and civil functionaries)	1770–1; 1775–1804; 1844–6	4
Vias de sucessão (means of succession)	1742–1458	2

POST ACCESSION ADDITIONS

'Misericordia' of Goa	1736–1866	21 v
General Secretariat Office	1870–1951	266 v
Municipality of Damão	1746–1884	8 v
Commercial Institute	1917–1928	44 v
Village Communities	1750–1916	284 v
Damão	1782–1833	3 v
'Fazenda' of Diu	1773–1912	106 v
'Adjunto' of Diu	1798–1916	52 v
Government of Diu	1818–1947	72 v
Customs	1781–1926	61 v

GUJARAT

Baroda Record Office, Baroda
Officer in charge: Superintendent of Records
Authority: Chief Secretary to the Government of Gujarat,
General Administration Department, Sachivalaya,
Ahmedabad-15

RULES OF ACCESS

The rules are still the same as those governing access to the records of the Secretariat Record Office, Bombay, Maharashtra. Applications for permission to consult the records are addressed to the chief secretary to the Government of Gujarat through the superintendent of records, Baroda, and must contain particulars of identification, purpose of research and a recommendation. Proof of a person's bona fides may be requested. Permission to consult the records, which are generally open up to 1916 and beyond that time in special circumstances, remains valid for one year after a signed undertaking by the applicant to deposit with the record office one copy of any published work, or one typed copy of any thesis, based on the records. Excerpts are subject to scrutiny.

THE STATE OF GUJARAT

The British established their first trading post in India proper at Surat in 1612. It became the headquarters of the East India Company in Western India until the seat of the presidency was transferred to Bombay in 1708. The province of Gujarat (Baroda) was wrested from the Mogul empire by the Marathas under Damaji Gaikwad in the early eighteenth century, and they remained in control first as feudatories of the Peshwa and then, from 1817, of the British Government at Bombay. The fourteen states of the Baroda and Gujarat Agency amalgamated with the Western India Agency in 1944, and all were merged with Bombay State, the heir to the Bombay presidency, in May 1949. Saurashtra, constituted in 1948 from a merger of 222 former Indian states including Rajkot, and Kutch, an area administered by the central government from 1948, were also united with Bombay State in 1956. Gujarat was formed on 1 May 1960 from the north and west (predominantly Gujarati-speaking) portion of Bombay State, namely the districts of Ahmedabad, Mahals, Baroda, Dangs, Surat, Rajkot, Bhavnagar and certain parts of West Khandesh, together with the former states of Saurashtra and Kutch. The state now consists of the seventeen districts of Surat, Dangs, Sabarkantha, Banaskantha, Mehsana, Ahmedabad, Kaira, Panch Mahals, Baroda, Broach, Jamnagar, Rajkot, Surendranagar, Bhavnagar, Junagad, Amreli and Kutch. The building of a new capital has been proposed, about 10 miles from the present capital of Ahmedabad.

ARCHIVES ADMINISTRATION IN GUJARAT

Since the creation of the state of Gujarat no central records repository has yet been established. However, the Baroda Record Office, formerly the record department of the princely state of Baroda and then a subordinate office of the Director of Archives, Bombay, falls within its territory and remains the principal repository administered by the Gujarat Government.

NATURE AND EXTENT OF HOLDINGS

Under the regime of the former state of Baroda, the Baroda Record Office had been one of the more organized archival repositories in India. Records from nearly all departments of state, including the secretariat departments, were classified and held there, the various departments adhering to uniform rules, published in 1902, on the preservation or destruction of records. A spacious building, planned and equipped to allow the most scientific methods of preservation then in practice, was built in 1913. An unprecedented influx of records took place just before the merger of Baroda into the state of Bombay in May 1949, including records scheduled for destruction and the holdings of such agencies as the *Jakat Naka*, the former Baroda state forces, the vernacular records of the Baroda Residency and the Crown Representative's records from the Mahikantha and Banaskantha agencies received from the Regional Commissioner, Rajkot. The yearly acquisition of departmental records ceased in 1949. Under the administration of the director of archives, Bombay, no basic change took place.

Holdings total 48,784 rumals (bundles) and 14,438 files, including 3,000 rumals of historical records, housed in three buildings which comprise nine units with an area of 3,100 sq. ft. each, two units of 1, 496 sq. ft. each, and five smaller units. Certain series relating to Surat and Gujarat states are held in the Secretariat Record Office, Bombay, Maharashtra. The Gujarat Agency records, acquired by Bombay in 1949, have been lodged with the National Archives of India (q.v.).

AIDS TO REFERENCE

Handwritten inventories or indexes are held in the office for nearly all the records housed there. In addition a *Persian catalogue, being a list of the Persian documents in the Baroda Record Office* has been published.

PUBLICATIONS

A publications programme based on the Baroda records was inaugurated in 1934 when the first volume in the series 'Historical selections from Baroda state records' was published. The series was continued under the administration of the director of archives, Bombay, and the present Gujarat administration. In addition, a selection of English documents from the records of the British Residency at Baroda has been edited and published by the History Department of the Maharaja Sayaji Rao University of Baroda with the title *Gaikwads of Baroda, Sayaji Rao II, 1821–1830.*

HOLDINGS

Baroda Record Office, Baroda

1	*Huzur* Central Office	1874/5–1948/9
2	*Huzur* Political Office	1874/5–1948/9
3	*Huzur Kamdar* Office	1889/90–1948/9
4	Baroda Residency	1770–1947
5	Crown Representative records (Regional Commissioner, Rajkot)	1874/5–1943
6	*Sarsuba* Office	1863/4–1948/9
7	*Barkhali* and *Giras* Office	1871–1946/7
8	Revenue records	
	a *Suba* Office	1874/5–1918/19
	b *Taluka* records	1655/6–1883/4
9	Accountant-general's Office	1855/6–1945/6
10	Military records (*Senapati* Office)	1821/2–1935/6
11	*Sahakari Adhikari* (Co-operative Department)	1905/6–1946/7

12	*Huzur* Public Works Department	1928/9–1946/7
13	Survey and Settlement Department	1891/2–1946/7
14	Furniture factory	1931/2–1946/7
15	*Dhara Sabha*	1916/17–1948/9
16	Income tax and sales department	1943/4–1946/7
17	Director of Civil Supplies	1942/3–1948/9
18	Legal Remembrancer's Office	1903/4–1946/7
19	Privy Council Office	
20	Department of Agriculture	1888/9–1946/7
21	State Record Department	1893/4–1949
22	Aerodrome	Nil
23	*Jakat Naka* records	1884/5–1946/7
24	Baroda City Municipality	1879/80–1904/5
25	Historical records	from 1728

    a   *Daftars* regarding *Devastans*, the *Dakshina* given in the month of *Srawan* and other charities

    b   Regarding the affairs of *hakdars*, *asamdars*, pensioners, members and sons-in-law of the Gaikwad family, *mankaries* of the Maharaja, *vatandars*, tributary princes and holders of *inami* villages and recipients of *kothalisath*

    c   About the *paga Siledar*, corps *Sibandi*, Contingent Horse and Disciplined Troops

    d   *Makhalasis* and *daftars* (books in which letters and other papers are registered)

    e   Account books such as *keerds* (ledgers) and *khatawanis* both of cash and kind

    f   Records of the transactions with the bankers, *daftars* regarding *dumala* and *inam* villages etc.

    g   *Daftars* of the *karkhanas* of the state, regarding Public Works Department and government buildings

    h   *Daftars* regarding marriages, naming ceremonies, observances on the *Nagpanchami*, *Divali* or *Dasera*, death anniversaries and funerals and other rites

    i   *Daftars* of the criminal and civil courts, also those containing various deeds and papers regarding compensation etc.

    j   Accounts of the *mahals*. Accounts regarding *nemnooks* and *inams* from these *mahals*. Lists and survey registers of the villages in each *mahal*

    k   Copies of the orders issued on the *Huzur* Treasury inward and outward registers, *daftars* of the *Huzur Kamdar Bhaskarrao Vithal* and *Arjiwala*

1 Political *daftars* containing correspondence with the Residency, treaties and engagements with the British and other governments etc.

ADDITIONAL PUBLICATIONS
Baroda Record Office, Baroda
Historical selections from the Baroda records (old series). 7 vols.

1	1724–68 (1934)	5	1813–20
2	1769–89	6	1793–1800
3	1790–8	7	1819–25 (1943)
4	1799–1813		

Historical selections from the Baroda records (new series). 3 vols.
1 (8) 1826–35 (1955). 2 (9) *Disturbances in Gujarat 1857–1864* (1963).
10 *Selections from Shastri Daftar 1799–1839.*

JAMMU AND KASHMIR

State Archives Department, Srinagar
Officer in charge: Director of Archives
Authority: Ministry of Education, Jammu and Kashmir

RULES OF ACCESS

All pre-1925 records are open to bona fide research scholars other than certain records declared to be privileged. Access is governed by rules sanctioned by the government and applications to consult the records should be addressed to the director of archives.

THE STATE OF JAMMU AND KASHMIR

For many centuries Kashmir was ruled by Scythian Hindu rajas who were succeeded by Tartar and Muslim princes. In 1588 the country was conquered by Akbar and became part of the Mogul empire. After a period of Afghan rule it was annexed to Ranjit Singh's Sikh kingdom of the Punjab in 1819, as was Ladakh in 1833. Disturbances in the kingdom after the death of Ranjit Singh in 1839 led to intervention by the British, and Kashmir was assigned to Maharaja Gulab Singh of Jammu by the Treaty of Lahore in 1846. He consolidated Jammu and Ladakh into one state and the reign of the Dogra maharajas continued until 1952. The ruling maharaja acceded to the Indian union in 1947, but the accession was disputed by Pakistan and the matter brought before the United Nations.

ARCHIVES ADMINISTRATION IN JAMMU AND KASHMIR

A Central Records Office under a director of records was first organized in 1928 and developed into the State Archives Department. The records are held in three repositories, each under the charge of a provincial superintendent. These are the State Archives Repository, Jammu; the State Archives Repository, Srinagar; and the State Archives Repository, Leh, Ladakh. A Regional Records Survey Committee was set up in 1955 to locate and arrange for the preservation of important historical documents. Already some 3,000 manuscripts, paintings and curious and rare publications in Sanskrit, Sharda, Hindi, Arabic, Persian, Urdu and English have been located, on such subjects as history, religion, philosophy, grammar, fiction, poetry and drama. Some 500 of these manuscripts have been acquired by the State Archives Department and are held at Srinagar.

NATURE AND EXTENT OF HOLDINGS

Government records cover the period 1724–1960. There are reference libraries at Srinagar and Jammu which contain some 20,000 published items. A map section, modelled on the National Archives of India map section, has collected 1,500 maps which are housed at Srinagar, while a considerable number of survey maps are housed at Jammu.

AIDS TO REFERENCE

All secretariat records before 1950 have been indexed and twenty-two of these index volumes published. Most records have also been listed chronologically. All files are entered both serially into accession registers and into block registers.

HOLDINGS

State Archives Department, Jammu and Kashmir

1 Archives
   1 Individual documents in Turkish, Tibetan and
     other languages
   2 Persian records   1724–1892
   3 *Kitab Navisi* registers   1847–1927
   4 Old English records   1868–1921
   5 Late His Highness's confidential records   1885–1925
   6 State Department records   1885–1942
   7 Vernacular records   1889–1921
   8 Secretariat records   1889–1960

   9 Council proceedings   1922–6
  10 Military records   1922–43
  11 His Highness's orders   1926–47
  12 Council and Cabinet orders   1934–60

II Map section, Srinagar
   1 Historical maps on cloth and hand-made paper
   2 Language maps
   3 Railway maps
   4 Physical and political maps
   5 Survey and boundary maps
   6 *Mujamali* (revenue) maps
   7 Maps showing mines, minerals, canals etc.
   8 Tourist maps

III Printed publications in the reference libraries, Srinagar and Jammu
   1 *Administration reports*   1872–1960
   2 *Jammu and Kashmir gazettes*   1889–1960
   3 *Punjab gazettes*   1925–34
   4 *Government of India gazettes*   1925–55
   5 *Census of India*   1891–1941
   6 Jammu and Kashmir *Military civil lists*   1893–1942
   7 Jammu and Kashmir *Budgets*   1893–1960
   8 Combined *Civil lists* for India   1941–2
   9 Jammu and Kashmir *Praja Sabha debates* 1934–60
  10 Treaties, engagements and sanads   1892–1931
  11 Book collection on history, law and other subjects

PUBLICATIONS

Published indexes to the Jammu and Kashmir Secretariat records.
Index of Persian records 1724 to 1892
Index of vernacular records 1889 to 1913
Index of old English records 1868 to 1912
General Department Period Group 1922 to 1940
Chief of the Staff, Jammu and Kashmir State Forces 1923 to 1942
General Staff Officer 1913 to 1941
Adjutant Quarter General 1902 to 1942
Adjutant-General's indexed records 1891 to 1925
Commander-in-Chief's records 1891 to 1939
Army Council records 1925 to 1929
Army Council resolutions 1925 to 1929
Scholarship Selection Board 1922 to 1940

Scholarship Selection Board Permanent Group
Publicity Department records 1916 to 1938
Political Department records 1922 to 1940
Commands of His Highness the Maharaja Bhadur 1932 to 1943
Customs Department Permanent Group 1890 to 1940
Customs Department Period Group 1896 to 1931
General Department, Chief Secretariat 1922 to 1940
Political Department records 1940 to 1950
Irrigation Department records
Public Works Department records

KERALA

Kerala State Archives, Secretariat, Trivandrum
Officer in charge: Director of Archives
Authority: Education Department, Government of Kerala,
Trivandrum

RULES OF ACCESS

Permission to allow access to the records for bona fide research is granted by the government.

THE STATE OF KERALA

Contacts between the Hindu kingdoms of the Malabar coast and countries to the west extend back to the fifth century A.D. when Syrian refugees arrived there and converted to Christianity a number of high-class Hindus. However, the kingdoms remained isolated from the encroachments of the Mogul and Maratha powers until the eighteenth century when all but Travancore (capital Trivandrum) fell to Haidar Ali and his son Tipu Sultan. From the sixteenth century the Portuguese had trading relations with the Zamorin of Calicut (capital Kozhikode), and with Cochin (capital Ernakulam), where they established a factory and enlarged the Christian community. The Portuguese were supplanted first by the Dutch and then by the English, who made a treaty to protect the Raja against Haidar Ali in return for an annual subsidy. In July 1949, Travancore and Cochin united to form the state of Travancore-Cochin, which was renamed Kerala under the States Reorganization Act of 1956. By this act, four taluks of the Trivandrum district and a part of the Shencottah taluk of Quilon district were ceded to Madras, and the Malabar district and the Kasaragod taluk of South Kanara were received from Madras. The Laccadive, Minicoy and Amindivi Islands became a centrally administered area. The capital of Kerala is Trivandrum.

ARCHIVES ADMINISTRATION IN KERALA

The Kerala State Archives was in 1962 established to survey, collect and maintain archives and manuscripts in both public and private custody. An advisory committee presided over by the chief minister controls the department which is attached to the Education Department of the secretariat. The secretary to the government Education Department, is ex-officio director of archives. The Regional Records Survey Committee of Travancore-Cochin, constituted in 1951, was expanded upon the formation of Kerala. The committee has made proposals for a publications programme. The records of Kerala are held at repositories in Trivandrum, Ernakulam and Kozhikode.

Central Record Office, Fort, Trivandrum

NATURE AND EXTENT OF HOLDINGS

Formerly the Huzur Central Record Office of the state of Travancore, this repository has two sections, vernacular records and English records.

The vernacular records relate mainly to the state of Travancore prior to 1908 (1083 M.E.) and occupy 1500 running feet of shelving. Many of the earlier records, both cadjan and paper, are written in Malayazhma, a script popular until the nineteenth century, but the Tamil and Malayalam scripts are used in later records.

The English records occupy 10,000 running feet of shelving, some 45 lakhs of files, each file comprising 20 to 30 folios. Of these, about 15 lakhs are pre-merger records, the earliest dated 1825. The land records are of great historical value. After the unification of Travancore-Cochin, records of the Cochin government from 1897 (1072 M.E.) were brought to Trivandrum, and old records of the district and taluq offices relating to the revenue administration of the districts are also kept in the Central Record Office. Printed copies of some of the records are available and the *Sri Chitra Huzur Central records series* was published in two volumes. The office also preserves government publications and other published documents.

AIDS TO REFERENCE

Records are held in bundles, classified and numbered as prescribed in the Kerala secretariat office manual. Files of the erstwhile Travancore state prior to 1903 are held under the cover system. There is no handbook to the records, but descriptive lists and some indexes in Malayalam assist research.

Central Record Office, Ernakulam

NATURE AND EXTENT OF HOLDINGS

Formerly the State Record Office of the state of Cochin, this office holds the paper records of the Cochin Government prior to 1897, miscellaneous correspondence between the rulers and officials of the East India Company, letters of the residents and diaries of the diwans, as well as earlier cadjan records, a collection of seals, maps, proclamations from 1818 to 1825 and books and manuscripts of historical interest. *Letters from the rajas of Cochin to Batavia* was published in 1946.

AIDS TO REFERENCE

There is no handbook to the records, but old indexes assist research.

Kozhikode Collectorate, Kozhikode

NATURE AND EXTENT OF HOLDINGS

In this office there are cadjan and paper records dating from 1835 which relate to the Malabar district which formerly belonged to Madras. In addition there are about 200 files relating to the Laccadive and Minicoy Islands. Some of these records have been transferred to the administration office, Kozhikode.

HOLDINGS

Central Record Office, Trivandrum

CADJAN RECORDS	1742–1873

These total 11,000 cadjan *churunas* (bundles) each of 500 to 1,000 leaves.

1 Land records		
	a *Ozhuhu*—pre-settlement	1802–37
	b *Pathivinpadi Anuvu*—pre-settlement	1837
	c *Vilangiper*	1818–31
	d Revenue miscellaneous	
2 Administrative		
	a *Jamabandi* orders	1844–73
	b *Neetus* (royal commands)	1756–1873
	c *Huzur Rayasom* (government orders)	1759–1912
	d Boundary disputes	1755–1865

e	*Thirattus* (accounts)	1777–1876
f	Judicial	1814–74
g	Huzur Treasury	1799–1873

PAPER RECORDS 1812–1910

20,464 volumes, 9,000 bundles and 300 single sheets.

- *a* *Jamabandi Rayasom*
- *b* *Jambandi* accounts
- *c* Huzur *Rayasom*
- *d* Huzur Settlement
- *e* Huzur Public Works Department
- *f* Judicial (Sirkar Vakil's Department)
- *g* Sanitary Department
- *h* Excise Department
- *i* Police Department
- *j* Education Department
- *k* Huzur Treasury
- *l* Palace
- *m* Settlement—miscellaneous
- *n* Land acquisition
- *o* Indian medicines
- *p* Gazettes
- *q* Royal commands
- *r* Settlement Central Office
- *s* Registers and records relating to revenue settlement   1883–1911
- *t* Appeal petitions and other papers relating to settlement   1885–1906
- *u* Copies of government communications
- *v* Miscellaneous papers etc.

OTHER RECORDS OF HISTORICAL IMPORTANCE

1 Charts etc.

These show various ancient forms of characters in Malayalam, Tamil and Malayazhma.

2 Historical collections of Sir T. Madhava Rao

Collected during the course of his compiling a history of Travancore.

- *a* Treaties with Cochin, the Dutch East India Company etc.   1763–1805
- *b* Administrative organization of the state of Travancore   1763–1805
- *c* Reforms
- *d* Revenue receipts and expenditure
- *e* *Keralolpathi*

3 Records showing sign manuals of the various sovereigns   1729–1924
4 Records with signatures of the diwans   1789–1877
5 Records relating to certain state ceremonies etc.
6 Settlement records of the tenth and eleventh centuries
7 Some royal proclamations
8 Dalawa Ramayyan family records

Central Record Office, Ernakulam

BAMBOO SPLITS   1630–90   20

COPPER PLATES   1625–75   16

CADJAN RECORDS
1 *Churunas* dealing with land   1818–1905   over 2,000
2 *Grandhas* dealing with *devaswoms*   1525–1891   72
3 Loose *cadjan* leaves   1525–1772   about 10,000

PAPER RECORDS
1 Files
   1st series   1684–1797
   2nd series   1791–1840
   3rd series   1812–69
   Diwan's D.O. Correspondence   1896–1937
   Kooduthal-Kuravu account files   1900–07
   Rayasam files
   Persian letters   1827–50
2 Bound volumes   over 10,000
   a   Letters of the British resident   1814–95
   b   Diaries of the diwans   1814–97
   c   *Theetoorams* (royal commands)   1818–98
   d   Malayalam diaries   1814–32
   e   *Jamabandi* orders   1856–98
   f   Police orders   1838–97
   g   *Proverthy Therattus*   1893–1908
   h   *Taluk Therattus*   1875–97
   i   *Rayasom* orders   1855–97
   j   Market rates   1885–1902
   k   *Maramat* accounts   1867–96
   l   *Chowkey* orders   1858–89
   m   Bill books   1858–97
   n   Miscellaneous books   1819–97
3 Batavia diary (printed)   1661–81
4 Treaties (copied)   1663–1806

5 Portuguese and Dutch letters   1768–1790
6 Selected letters of the Cochin ruler and Batavia (printed)
7 MS copies of agreements and lease deeds between the former Cochin
   Sircar and European companies
8 Hukmnamas etc. and Cochin rulers   from 1812
9 Cochin administrative records   1896–1935
10 Cochin administrative reports   from 1866
11 Survey records   about 4,000
                                             items

MADHYA PRADESH
(including National Archives of India, Regional Office, Bhopal)

Records and Library Branch, General Administration Department, Government of Madhya Pradesh, Bhopal Authority: Chief Secretary to Government, Madhya Pradesh, Bhopal

RULES OF ACCESS

Applications to consult and queries concerning the secretariat records should be addressed to the Secretary to the Government of Madhya Pradesh, General Administration Department, Bhopal.

THE STATE OF MADHYA PRADESH

On the death without an heir of the Maratha raja at Nagpur in 1853, his territories were declared to have lapsed to the paramount power. Nagpur province was administered by a British commissioner until 1861 when it was amalgamated with the Saugor and Nerbudda territories to form the Central Provinces, administered by a chief commissioner. Nimar was transferred to the newly formed unit in 1864 and in 1903 the administration of Berar, formerly one of the Hyderabad Assigned Districts, was transferred to the chief commissioner of the Central Provinces. In 1920 the chief commissioner was replaced by a governor. In 1937 Berar became part of the Central Provinces which was renamed the Central Provinces and Berar. After Independence, 14 states in the former Chhattisgarh Agency and Makrai state in the Central India States Agency were integrated with the province, which in January 1950 was named Madhya Pradesh. Madhya Bharat was formed in May 1948 by the integration of twenty-five states of the former Central India States Agency, with the Maharaja of Gwalior as *rajpramukh* and the rulers of Indore, Dhar and Khilchipur as senior and junior *up-rajpramukhs*. The United State of Vindhya Pradesh was formed in April 1948 from 35 former princely states of Bundelkhand and Baghelkand with the Maharaja of Rewa as *rajpramukh*. In 1950 fifteen of these states were wholly or substantially transferred to Uttar Pradesh, and Khaniadhana to Madhya Pradesh. The remaining Vindhya Pradesh became a centrally administered area, then a part 'C' state headed by a chief commissioner, and a lieutenant-governor's province in 1952. The present state of Madhya Pradesh was formed in November 1956 from the seventeen Hindi-speaking districts of the previous state of that name, to which were united the states of Bhopal, Vindhya Pradesh, Madhya Bharat excepting the Sunel enclave of the Mandsaur district, and the Sironj subdivision of the Kothah district of Rajasthan. The eight Marathi-speaking districts of old Madhya Pradesh were transferred to the then Bombay State, now Mahrashtra. The capital is Bhopal.

ARCHIVES ADMINISTRATION IN MADHYA PRADESH

Secretariat records are held in five repositories, at Bhopal, Nagpur, Indore, Gwalior and Rewa. Records of administrative formations below secretariat level are kept in records rooms attached to the offices of origin and specific enquiries concerning them should be addressed to the Secretary to Government, General Administration Department. Records of some of the princely states now integrated with Madhya Pradesh are still held in the record rooms of the *tehsildars*, collectorates and subdivisional offices. As a result of an offer from the erstwhile government of Bhopal to hand over all its historical records to the central government as a gift, the National Archives of India opened a regional office at Bhopal in 1954. Since these records will in due course be transferred to the Government of Madhya Pradesh they are listed here for convenience. Of the remaining records, the secretariat records were transferred to the Secretariat Record Room, Bhopal, other records to the relevant government departments of Madhya Pradesh, and the Central Records Office of former Bhopal then closed.

OFFICERS IN CHARGE

Secretariat Record Room, Bhopal: Records Officer, General Administration Department (Records Branch), Bhopal.

Record Room, Nagpur: Record Keeper, Old Secretariat Building, Nagpur.

Record Room, Indore: Inspector of Offices and Records, Indore.

Record Room, Gwalior: Inspector of Offices and Records, Gwalior, and the Registrar, Historical Section, Gwalior.

Record Room, Rewa: Inspector of Offices and Records, Rewa.

National Archives of India, Regional Office, Bhopal: Keeper of Records.

NATURE AND EXTENT OF HOLDINGS

Secretariat records pertaining to the administration of the Central Provinces from its formation in 1861 until 1919 are held at Nagpur along with records pertaining to Berar and to the various incorporated districts before that date. Vindhya Pradesh records for 1948–56 are held partly at Rewa and partly at Bhopal. Records of the former Central Records Office, Bhopal, now in the custody of the National Archives of India are listed on pp. 276–8. Of the remaining Bhopal records, the secretariat records are held at Bhopal, the jaghir and miscellaneous revenue, and *faujdari* records for 1914–56 are held by the relevant government departments. At the time of the States Reorganization in 1956, all records for the years 1920–56 of the eight Marathi districts of old Madhya Pradesh transferred to Bombay State were handed to Bombay. Files of common interest to both states were duplicated and the originals held in Madhya Pradesh, where they are housed at Bhopal. Madhya Bharat records of 1949–56 are housed at Bhopal, but records of the merged states before that date have not yet been centralized and remain in the custody of the district officials in whose jurisdiction the former states are situated, apart from the accountant-general's record at Indore. The former State Record Office, Rajgarh, for instance, holds records of the rulers from 1740 to 1900 and Persian and Urdu letters received from the Bhopal Agency.

AIDS TO REFERENCE

In general records are organized under general subject head indexes for all departments, followed by distinct catalogues of records falling under permanent and ephemeral categories. As chronological registration of all important closed records thus takes place automatically, there are no descriptive catalogues. The Central Provinces secretariat records (at Nagpur) are indexed under major topics or bound together according to subject up to 1892 and are arranged by department with case file registers and indexes for each department thereafter. Secretariat records from 1920 to date of old and new Madhya Pradesh (at Bhopal) are arranged by year and department, with correspondence registers, case file registers and printed index registers for all years.

PUBLICATIONS

Selections from the Nagpur Residency records, volumes 1–5 covering the period 1799–1842, appeared between 1950 and 1955. About two more volumes are planned to bring the period up to 1858.

HOLDINGS
Secretariat Record Room, Bhopal

		Shelving (running feet)
1 Former Mahakoshal	1920–56	4,352
2 Former Bhopal	1914–56 ⎫	
3 Former Madhya Bharat	1949–56 ⎬	1,170
4 Former Rewa	1949–56 ⎭	
		———
		5,522
Secretariat records of old and new Madhya Pradesh (including those of common interest to Maharashtra)	1920–56	

Record Room, Old Secretariat Building, Nagpur

I Prior to 1861
   1 Nagpur Residency records. Some indexed   1798–1854
   2 Saugor and Nerbudda territories. Indexed   1848–61
   3 Jubbulpore Division. Indexed   1806–57
   4 Chhattisgarh Division. Indexed   1854–8
   5 Old vernacular records. Indexed
     a Bhonsla Estate   1814–85
     b Shah Garha State   1810–60
     c Bijey Ragho Garha Estate   1818–60
   6 Records of 11 districts from their annexation until the formation of the Central Provinces in 1861: Betul, Chanda, Chhindwara, Damoh, Hoshangabad, Jubbulpore, Mandla, Nimar, Saugor, Seoni, Narsinghpur.
   7 Miscellaneous records transferred from Bengal
II Central Provinces Secretariat internal records   1861–92
   1 Bundle correspondence generally indexed under major topics such as 'Settlement', 'Mutiny'   1861–74
   2 Compilations—correspondence on major subjects removed from bundles and bound together by subject   1870–5, 1879–86
III Central Provinces 1892–1919

When in 1892 the C.P. secretariat was divided into departments, the records were also so organized, with indexes for each department. There are case file registers to the original documents and some have been printed as proceedings without indexes.

1 Appointments	5 Commerce and Industry	9 Local Self-government
2 General	6 Agriculture	10 Judicial
3 Police	7 Forest	11 Home
4 Military	8 Revenue	12 Foreign

Record Room, Indore

		Shelving (running feet)
1 Holkar State Secretariat records	1849–1948	8,192
2 Holkar State Revenue record including jaghir and *Inam* Branch record	1763–1948	5,078
3 Holkar State Huzur *Chitnisi* record	1749–1947	1,125
4 Holkar State Huzur *Fadnisi* record		11,175
5 Accountant-general's record comprising the records of covenanting states of Madhya Bharat	1795–1949	15,030
		40,600

The extent of the records, particularly of items 4 and 5, will be considerably reduced at the weeding of ephemeral records.

Record Room, Gwalior

Gwalior State records, all departments	1843–1948
Fadanvisi records and *Dakhla* papers	1780–1942 (samvat 1837–1999)

Accountant-general's record
A major portion of these records have been eliminated.
Historical Section

1 *Khasigiwale* records	1776–1869
2 Chamber of Princes	1940–7
3 *Munshi* raja	1776–1869
4 *Dastaries* and *Parcha Akhbars*	1792–1853, 1811–32
5 War records	1914–41
6 Indore Huzur Office and household records	1830–1904
7 Kurwai State Bank records	1924–34

Record Room, Rewa

Holdings total 17,000 running feet.
1 Former Rewa State Secretariat, Rewa
2 Former offices of the commandant, Vindhya Pradesh
3 Former Vindhya Pradesh State accountant-general, Rewa
4 Former regional commissioner's office, Nowgong
5 Vindhya Pradesh Secretariat records 1948–56. A part of these records have been transferred to Bhopal.

National Archives of India, Regional Office, Bhopal

Daftar Insha (private secretariat)	1846–1907	8,081 v
		14,058 f. approx.

BHOPAL STATE SECRETARIAT

a	Private Secretariat		
b	P.D.W. Secretariat		
c	Judicial Secretariat		
d	Moin-ul-Mahami (Revenue Secretariat)	1908–15	125 v
e	Chief Secretariat		21,047 f
f	Financial Secretariat		
g	Military Secretariat	1908–19	
Mutiny Papers			89 v
			500 f. approx.
Daftar Tanzimat (Legislative Department)	1843–44 to 1914	57 v
		1,547 f
Daftar Vakalat (Political Department)	1851–1948	319 v
		13,965 f
Daftar Tarikh	Pre-1913 various years, 1913–31	646 v
		481 f
Wazarat Mal (First Minister's Office)	1897–1907	11 bdls
Niabat Mal (Revenue Minister's Office)	1890–1908	420 f
Twenty Years Settlement		3,273 v
		10,000 f. approx.
Jaghir sanads	Various years	976 f
Salana-daran (annuitants)	1845–1921	1,116 f
Daftar Chaudhrat	1843–4 to 1925–6	620 f. approx.

Kutub Had Bast Dehat	1845–60	30 v
Volumes giving names of Bazars and Mohallahs of Bhopal State	1850–87	33 v
Daftar Huzur (accounts etc.)	Not arranged chronologically	4,547 bdls
State Treasury	Not arranged chronologically	46 bdls
Daftar Toshak Khana	1908–15	88 v and 464 f.
Collectorate and tahsils	Not arranged chronologically	105 bdls
Maps and plans		4,000 approx.

MISCELLANEOUS OFFICES

Jaghirat, census etc.	Not arranged chronologically	15 bdls
Wazaief	Not arranged chronologically	25 bdls
Education Department	1864–1925	184 f
Military Headquarters	1908–14	151 v
Hamidia Library	1906–28	37 v and 62 f
Municipal Board	1908–24	90 v and 464 f
Farash Khana	Not arranged chronologically	1 bdl
Unanai Shafa Khana	Not arranged chronologically	1 bdl
State Press	Not arranged chronologically	8 bdls
Forest Department	Not arranged chronologically	10 bdls
Customs and Excise Department	Not arranged chronologically	4 bdls
Chief Engineer's Office	Not arranged chronologically	7 bdls
Copies of letters and correspondence between the Political Agent, Bhopal State, and the Resident at Indore	1817–59	1 v
Ahdnamajat (agreements)		8 v
Acts and Rules of Bhopal State and British Government (some on parchment bearing seals of the Nawab of Bhopal)	1852–1944	520 v

Administration Reports		733 v
Civil Lists	1912–47	211 v
Gazettes		26 v

MADRAS

Madras Record Office, 6 Gandhi-Irwin Road, Egmore,
Madras 8
Officer in charge: Curator
Authority: Chief Secretary to Government, Public (General-
M) Department, Fort St George, Madras-9

RULES OF ACCESS

Records over fifty years old are available for consultation by bona fide research students, including previously restricted confidential records such as the Vellore Mutiny papers. The Curator disposes of all applications and scrutinizes extracts taken from the records. To consult more recent records special permission from the government is required, although general information publications on current records are available. If one is unable to call in person information can be extracted on payment of a search and transcription fee.

THE STATE OF MADRAS

The British established a trading station at Peddapali (now Nizampatam) in 1611, and then at Masulipatam. In 1639 they were permitted to make a settlement at the present site of Madras, founding Fort St George. By 1801 the whole country from the Northern Circars to Cape Comorin apart from the French and Danish settlements was under British rule. The presidency was constituted an autonomous province on 1 April 1937. After Independence the Indian states of Pudukottai, Banganapalle and Sandur were absorbed. The state of Andhra was created in 1953 from the undisputed Telugu-speaking area of Madras. Under the States Reorganization Act, 1956, the Malabar district and Kasaragod taluk of South Kanara were transferred to Kerala; the South Kanara and Kollegal taluk of the Coimbatore district transferred to Mysore; the Laccadive, Amindivi and Minicoy Islands constituted a centrally administered territory; and four taluks of the Trivandrum district and the Shencottah taluk of Quilon were transferred from Travancore-Cochin to Madras.

ARCHIVES ADMINISTRATION IN MADRAS

Madras was the first Indian state to organize a central record office. The secretariat records were centralized in Fort St George in 1806 under a record keeper, and a separate office established in 1909. The building at Egmore consists of an administrative block and nine record blocks containing 160,000 cubic feet of stack area. To ensure safety during the war the East India Company records were held at Palamer and other holdings at Chittoor from 1942 to 1950. The office supervises non-current series still held with other departments or in regional record repositories.

NATURE AND EXTENT OF HOLDINGS

Holdings total some 47,332 running feet. They include all records of all departments of the secretariat 1670–1958, confidential and non-confidential, the records less than three years old being regarded as current; Board of Revenue and Survey Office records from the beginning, those of the last ten years regarded as current; the records of district collectors from earliest times to 1857, thereafter the records being held in the collectorates; records of defunct departments; records of the merged states of Sandur, Banganapalle and Pudukkottai; and passport records of the Mysore, Hyderabad and Madras State Residencies prior to 1953. Dutch and Danish records are on quasi-permanent loan from the central government, which also handed over the Tanjore Raj records in 1950. Some 206,077 books published in Madras State since 1867, formerly housed in the office of the Registrar of Books, have been transferred, as will be the records of the High Court 1800–1900. Records relating to areas formerly administered by Madras and now included in Andhra Pradesh or Mysore were apportioned thus: all pre-Mutiny records remained in Madras; secretariat and Board of Revenue records subsequent to 1920, held in separate files and relating exclusively to Andhra or Mysore, were transferred; original records of common interest remained in Madras but typed copies of those after August 1947 were transferred; post-Mutiny district records held in the districts were transferred along with the areas transferred.

AIDS TO REFERENCE

Every series is catalogued. There is a printed catalogue of pre-Mutiny records and of post-Mutiny manuscript records. Secretariat and Board of Revenue records possess printed indexes prepared by the departments sent along with them. Listing of the Persian records began over thirty years ago, was abandoned in 1924, but taken up again in 1960 for publication. Other printed aids to reference include *Calendars for 1740–65*, 3 vols.; *Guides to the District records 1682–1835*, 40 vols.; *Press lists* of all series 1670–1800, 36 vols.; *Calendars for the Revenue records 1765–1800*; *Catalogue of the Danish records* (1954); *Press list of ancient Dutch records 1657–1825*; *Supplementary catalogue of the Dutch records (1954)*; *Press lists of ancient records in Fort St George 1672–1800*; *Supplementary catalogue* of old records accessioned since 1916; and *A guide to the records preserved in the Madras Record Office* (1936).

PUBLICATIONS

Publications are listed in the *Catalogue of Madras Record Office Publications* (1942, repr. 1954). Over 300 volumes cover records from 1670 to 1750 and some for the period after, including *in extenso* publications of all the main series for the period 1751–65, calendars of the military country correspondence 1750–65 and revenue records 1765–1800, and selections from records including the Judicial Department 1800–57.

HOLDINGS

Madras Record Office

			Volumes	Bundles
1	Records up to 1856 (East India Company's period)			
	1 Public	1670–1856	3,468	1,000
	2 Military	1752–1856	3,141	1,400
	3 Revenue	1764–1856	1,137	610
	4 Secret	1785–1850	352	161
	5 Judicial	1795–1856	824	361
	6 Political	1769–1856	728	379
	7 Financial	1807–56	303	150
	8 Commercial	1787–1848	149	—
	9 Law	1806–56	59	16
	10 Foreign	1814–50	149	—
	11 Ecclesiastical	1816–56	174	98
	12 Marine	1838–56	139	70
	13 Public Works	1843–56	146	97
	14 Financial Railway	1853–6	40	40
	15 Petition	1815–56	76	—
	16 Receipt registers of Military and Judicial Departments	1841–56	430	—
	17 Board of Revenue	1781–1856	3,484	6,350
	18 High Court Sessions records	1840–56	—	135

			Volumes	*Bundles*
19	Records of the Registration Department	1760–1856	550	—
20	Surgeon-general's records	1787–1856	33	—
21	Army records	1761–1856	255 cases	
22	Mayor's Court records	1689–1813	541	—
23	Madras Mint records	1744–1856	712	—
24	Sinking and Native Fund records	1799–1836	63	—
25	Native Pension Fund records	1810–31	24	—
26	Coroners' Pension Fund records	1818–56	146	—
27	General Territorial Political ledgers and journal of Fort St George	1678–1856	247	—
28	Collectorate records (including Bellary Collectorate)	1767–1904	9,001	105
29	Merged state records	1787–1857	—	4
30	Sheriffs' records	1799–1856	191	—
31	Church records	1739–1856	26	—
32	Dutch and Danish records	1657–1845	1,763	—
33	Tanjore Raj records	1738–1856	—	320
34	Marathi records	—	268	—
35	Persian records	1749–1802	384	455

II Records subsequent to 1856 (post East India Company's period)

			Volumes	*Bundles*
1	Public	1857–1958	21	3,636
2	Political	1857–1936	309	1,095
3	Military	1857–1907	477	4,992
4	Revenue	1857–1958	43	8,874
5	Revenue (special War)	1918–20	—	68
6	Revenue Special	1918–20	—	37
7	Development	1922–52	—	1,209
8	Judicial	1857–1920	121	3,990
9	Judicial and Public Police	1921–36	—	114
10	Judicial (magisterial)	1923–4	—	11
11	Law (general)	1921–36	—	629
12	Law (registration)	1921–36	—	49
13	Finance	1857–1958	11	3,155
14	Finance (pension)	1857–1942	—	1,587
15	Finance (books)	1901–6	—	24
16	Finance (code)	1926–7	—	6
17	Finance (separate Revenue and central subjects)	1916–25	—	101

		Volumes	*Bundles*
18 Ecclesiastical	1857–1935	16	366
19 Public Works	1857–1958	24	6,073
20 Public Works (irrigation)	1877–1925	—	1,447
21 Public Works (railways)	1857–1925	—	1,231
22 Finance (railways)	1857–65	50	45
23 Education	1861–1958	—	2,051
24 Local and municipal	1885–1935	—	5,019
25 Local Administration	1936–58	—	773
26 Home (miscellaneous)	1916–21	—	98
27 Home	1936–58	—	1,410
28 Home (passport)	1945–58	—	433
29 Medical	1916–20	—	54
30 Public Health	1921–58	—	1,367
31 Legislative	1858–1935	—	466
32 Legal	1936–53	—	1,131
33 Law	1953–5	—	16
34 Food	1946–8	—	53
35 Food and agriculture	1949–58	—	293
36 *Firka* development	1947–50	—	21
37 Rural Welfare	1950–3	—	45
38 Industries, Labour and Co-operation	1953–8	—	223
39 Education, Health and Local Administration	1953–5	—	225
40 Marine	1857–1935	16	366
41 Petition	1857–91	104	—
42 Army records	1857–98	102 cases	
43 Surgeon-general's records	1857–8	2	—
44 Madras Mint records	1857–76	193	—
45 Coroners' records	1857–89	283	—
46 General Territorial Political Ledgers and journal of Fort St George	1857–8	3	—
47 Board of Revenue	1857–1951	1,324	14,156
Inam records	1858–1945	—	858
48 Records of Irrigation Development Board	1931–51	—	11
49 Land complaint files	Prior to 1920	—	161
50 Settlement registers	1865–1903	1,850	—
51 High Court Session records	1857	—	10

		Volumes	Bundles
52	Collectorate records, including volumes relating to pre-1857 period	1857–1906	186	—
53	Records of Registration Department	1857–76	221	—
54	Sheriffs' records	1857–1920	305	—
55	Records of the Receiver of the Carnatic Property	1857–77	82	—
56	Church records	1857–82	11	—
57	Records created by committees	1947–60	—	46
58	Survey records	1859–1942	—	15,773
59	Maps and plans	1765–1884	—	1,435
60	Patents and specifications	1857–1960	—	237
61	Tanjore Raj records	1857–73	—	80
62	Strong Almirah documents	1765–1959	—	425

ADDITIONAL PUBLICATIONS

Madras Record Office

I *a* Public Department records

Diaries and consultations 1672–1760	90 v
Despatches from England 1670–1758	61 v
Despatches to England 1694–1751	over 18 v
Country Correspondence 1740–51	4 v
Letters from Fort St George 1699–1765	40 v
Letters to Fort St George 1681–1765	45 v
Manilha consultations 1762–4	10 v
Private diary of Ananda Ranga Pillar 1736–61	12 v

b Military Department records

Diaries and consultations	5 v
Country correspondence	6 v

c Political Department records

Country correspondence 1800–4	5 v

II Mayor's Court records

Minutes of proceedings 1689–1746	10 v
Pleadings 1731–45	7 v

III Baramahal records

Baramahal records: Section 1, 3–7, 15–19, 21–22 (1907–)

IV Factory records 1682–1751

Anjengo consultations	3 v
Fort St David consultations	42 v

Letters from Fort St David	3 V
Letters to Fort St David	4 V
Tellicherry consultations	20 V
Letters from Tellicherry	8 V
Letters to Tellicherry	12 V
v Dutch and Danish records	17 V

vi District handbooks replacing the old District gazetteers
Handbook of Madurai district (1958)
Handbook of the Tanjore district (1957)
Handbook of South Arcot district (1962)
vii Other
Administration reports, to 1940–1; resumed 1944–5

MAHARASHTRA

*Secretariat Record Office, Elphinstone College Building,
Bombay 1
Officer in charge: Director of Archives
Authority: General Administration Department, Government
of Maharashtra, Bombay*

RULES OF ACCESS

Applications for permission to consult the records are addressed to the director of archives and must contain particulars of identification, the purpose of research and a recommendation. Proof of a person's bona fides may be requested. Permission to consult the records, which are generally open up to 1916 and beyond that time in special circumstances, remains valid for one year after a signed undertaking by the applicant to deposit with the Secretariat Record Office one copy of any published work or a typed copy of any thesis based on the records. Excerpts are subject to scrutiny.

THE STATE OF MAHARASHTRA

By a *farman* issued by the Mogul emperor in 1613, the British were allowed to establish their first trading post in India proper at Surat. It became the headquarters of the East India Company in Western India until the depredations of the Marathas forced them in 1708 to move the seat of the presidency to Bombay. Bombay, a Portuguese possession since 1530, had come to Charles II of England as part of his wife's dowry and he had made it over to the Company in 1668, giving them full rights of administration, justice and coinage. After the collapse in 1817 of the Maratha confederacy which was centred on the peshwa and his secretariat at Poona, the whole of the peshwa's dominions with the exception of Satara became part of the Bombay presidency, although certain small Maratha states including Kolhapur retained their separate existence. The coast from Goa to Bombay was taken over by Bombay in 1820. The province of Sind (now in West Pakistan) was separated from the presidency in 1936. After Indian Independence, the states of the former Western India Agency, the Baroda and Gujarat Agency and Kolhapur and the related Deccan states were added to Bombay State, the heir to the Bombay presidency. By the States Reorganization Act of 1956 further territories were united to Bombay State, including Kutch and the Union of Saurashtra, eight Marathi-speaking areas of Madhya Pradesh (Vidarbha) and the Marathi-speaking areas of Hyderabad (Marathwada), while the Kannada-speaking areas of Belgaum, Bijapur, Kanara and Dharwar were transferred from Bombay to Mysore, and the Abu Road *taluka* to Rajasthan. Maharashtra was created in May 1960 from the southern and eastern districts of Bombay State, including Ahmednagar, Aurangabad, Bhandara, Bhir, East Khandesh, Satara and parts of Thana and West Khandesh. The remainder of Bombay State which includes Surat, Saurashtra and Kutch was named Gujarat. The capital is Bombay.

ARCHIVES ADMINISTRATION IN MAHARASHTRA

The Secretariat Record Office of the Bombay presidency was established in 1821. When the states of Kolhapur and Baroda were merged with Bombay State their records were placed under the supervision of the Director of Archives, Bombay, although they remained in their former repositories. Supervision of the Baroda records ceased when in 1960 Baroda passed to the new state of Gujarat. The director of archives is also responsible for the preservation and publication of the records of the Alienation Office, Poona, and of district and divisional offices.

NATURE AND EXTENT OF HOLDINGS

The holdings of the Bombay Secretariat Record Office total some 41,000 linear feet of shelving and date from 1630. After 1919 all records of the Central Provinces government were duplicated and divided between the present Madhya Pradesh and Maharashtra governments. Agency and other records formerly held at Bombay which relate to areas now incorporated in Gujarat have remained in Bombay.

AIDS TO REFERENCE
A Handbook of the Bombay government records by A. F. Kindersley was published in 1921. *Descriptive catalogue of the diaries of the Secret and Political Department*, vol. I, *1755–1820* has appeared and a second volume is under preparation. Press lists cover the period 1646–1760. Indexes are listed in the Holdings list with the collections to which they pertain.

PUBLICATIONS
A number of series of selections from the records have been published and are still in progress. However the series 'Historical selections from Baroda State Records' has ceased.

Record Office, Kolhapur
Officer in charge: Superintendent of Records, responsible to the Director of Archives, Bombay

NATURE AND EXTENT OF HOLDINGS
The office holds the administrative records of Kolhapur from 1840, the pre-1870 records of the Kagal *jaghir*, and of Kurundwad state, 8 rumals of records of the Himmat Bahadur *jaghir* and 6 rumals of the records of Sarlaskar covering the period 1798–1881. Although the collector has charge of the revenue records and the district judge of the judicial records, they are also housed in the Kolhapur Record Office. A guide to the records is under preparation.

Alienation Office (*Peshwa* Daftar), *Poona*

ADMINISTRATIVE AUTHORITY
Settlement commissioner and director of land records. The director of archives, Bombay, is responsible for the preservation of the records.

NATURE AND EXTENT OF HOLDINGS
The records of the Peshwa *daftar* date from 1729 and number about 350,000 papers kept in 35,000 bundles. The majority of these records, written in Marathi, Modi script, are account papers, village, district and provincial accounts, budget estimates and audited accounts of the peshwa's dominion. About 350 bundles contain letters and despatches which passed between the peshwa or his deputies and his envoys at foreign courts, generals and diplomats. Some recent acquisitions are the records of Aundh, Budhgaon and Phaltan, Sangli; two bundles of Brahmanal records from

the collector, South Satara; the *Parwardhan daftar* of the raja of Miraj, and some old records of the states of Palanpur, Sawantwadi and Janjira. Documents relating to the divisions and districts which formed the dominions of the peshwa are kept separately and are tied into numbered bundles according to their contents and the year, with the general contents marked on the outside. The bundle number refers to the general register in which the contents are entered at length. A catalogue of the *Shahu daftar* is under preparation. English records are listed on p. 292.

HOLDINGS

Secretariat Record Office, Bombay

1 Pre-1820 records

Secret and Political Department

		Volumes
Diaries		
Combined	1755–1808	260
Secret Department	1809–20	58
Political Department	1809–20	180
Outward order books		
Combined	1778–1814	57
Secret Department	1814–52	46
Political Department	1815–60	152
Minute books (vols.)		
Combined	1755–1813	27
Secret Department	1813–69	57
Political Department	1813–62	105
Hon. Court's inwards		
Secret Department	1744–1847	17
Duplicates	1783–1873	25
Political Department	1794–1873	152
Duplicates	1796–1862	97
Hon. Court's outwards		
Combined	1794–1814	14
Secret Department	1815–65	151
Duplicates	1822–8	1
Political Department	1815–1918	376
Duplicates	1896–8	19
Table of contents	1841–7	6
Indexes		
Secret Department	1821–61	47
Political Department	1821–59	61

Finance Department
Diaries	1811–20	30
Outwards or order books	1813–30	26
Minute books	1813–59	48
Hon. Court's inwards	1808–50	19
Duplicates	1808–85	59
Hon. Court's outwards	1807–67	38
Duplicates	1807–85	24
Indexes	1821–63	43

Judicial Department (Home Department)
Diaries	1795–1820	129
Outward order books	1813–42	94
Minute books	1813–61	86
Hon. Court's inwards	1814–60	34
Duplicates	1814–86	59
Hon. Court's outwards	1803–63	93
Duplicates	1803–69	95
Indexes	1821–1920	181

Public Department
Diaries	1720–1820	439
Outwards or order books		
Public Department	1766–1820	187
General Department	1821–39	68
Minute books		
Public Department	1790–1820	55
General Department	1821–60	49
Hon. Court's inwards	1681–5	1
Public Department	1742–1858	74
Duplicates	1743–1885	74
Hon. Court's outwards		
General Department	1746–1868	118
Duplicates	1796–1895	49
Indexes	1821–60	40

Commercial Department
Diaries	1786–1820	152
Outwards or order books	1813–30	30
Minute books	1813–36	24
Hon. Court's inwards	1787–1833	19
Duplicates	1794–1833	22
Hon. Court's outwards	1788–1833	24
Duplicates	1796–1820	14

Indexes	1822–8	6
Ecclesiastical Department (established 1817)		
Minute books	1847–60	14
Hon. Court's inwards	1816–73	19
Duplicates	1816–42	5
Hon. Court's outwards	1817–73	15
Duplicates	1820–95	5
Indexes	1847–74	38
Marine and Forest Department		
Diaries	1818–20	15
Outwards or order books	1818–34	34
Minute books	1818–60	43
Hon. Court's inwards	1798–1866	66
Marine Department	1841–58	7
Duplicates	1798–1867	59
Marine Department	1841–58	7
Forest Department	1867–	1
Hon. Court's outwards	1818–87	48
Duplicates	1818–95	67
Forest Department	1861	1
Mint Department		
Minute books	1830–6	6
Hon. Court's outwards	1829–35	2
Steam Department		
Minute books	1837–9	3
Hon. Court's outwards	1838–9	2
Duplicates	1838–9	2
Indexes	1838–9	2
Revenue Department		
Diaries	1779–1820	165
Outwards or order books	1813–30	47
Minute books	1813–59	88
Hon. Court's inwards	1787–1851	24
Duplicates	1795–1885	77
Hon. Court's outwards	1796–1867	80
Duplicates	1796–1885	53
Indexes	1820–63	62
Factory and Residency records		
Surat factory		
Diaries of Chief in Council	1659–1809	48
Diaries of Chief in Council	1719–99	99

Judicial and judicial proceedings	1796–1804	4
Diaries of the Commercial Board	1795–1809	10
Latty records	1792–1804	57
Outwards or order books	1630–1700	4
Inwards or letter books	1646–1701	1
Records in Dutch		30

Broach factory
Diaries	1772–83	16

Commercial Residency Northward (Surat, Broach, Cambay and Kattywar)
Diaries	1774–1835	141

Karanja Residency
Diaries	1775–1802	28

Balapur factory
Diaries	Oct. 1780–Dec. 1781	1

Thana factory Diaries
Proceedings of Chief and Council	1776–1817	57
Proceedings of Court of Sessions	1801–2	1
Outwards or order book	1780–2 } 1793–8 }	1
Inwards or letter books, minutes	1781–92	1

Kalyan Residency
Diary	23 Feb.– 17 Dec. 1781	1

Poona Residency
Outwards or order books	1798–1819	38
Inwards or letter books	1812–19	61

Raree Residency
Record of operations against Khem Sqwant Bhonsle	29 Apr.– 4 Oct. 1766	1

Bankot (Fort Victoria) Residency
Diaries	1757–1809	9

Bankot factory
Diaries	1756–1814	7

Karwar factory
Diaries	1751–2	1
Outwards or order books	1720–2	1

Malabar Commercial Residency
Diaries	1793–1818	4
Letter books	1793–1818	1
Books of miscellaneous entries	1796–1813	2

Sind factory		
Diaries	Aug. 1762–	1
	July 1764	
Mokha factory		
Diaries	Dec. 1722–95	4
Mokha Residency		
Diaries	1820–8	9
Basra factory		
Diaries	1763–77	11
Outwards or order book	1725	1
Basra Residency		
Diaries	1766–1811	9
Bushire Residency		
Outwards or order books	1789–98	1
Gombroon factory or Residency		
Diaries	Aug. 1741–	7
	Aug. 1757	
Outwards or order books	1744–5	1
Inwards or letter books	1743–4	1
Diego Garcia Island		
Diaries	1786	1
Bantam factory		
Inwards or letter books	1679–83	1
II Post-1820 records		
Secret and Political Department		
Volumes	1821–1911	15,791
Files and compilations	1912+	53,370
Indexes		97
Judicial Department		
Volumes	1821–1911	11,082
Files and compilations	1912+	74,967
Indexes		260
General Department		
Volumes	1821–1911	7,532
Files and compilations	1912+	54,720
Indexes		39
Education Department		
Volumes	1855–1911	2,633
Files and compilations	1912+	31,290
Public Works Department (including Railways and Irrigation)		
Volumes	1844–1911	6,883

Files and compilations
Revenue Department

Volumes	1821–1911	18,852
Files and compilations	1912+	127,260
Indexes		62

Finance Department

Volumes	1821–1911	3,645
Files and compilations	1912+	37,590
Indexes		43

Miscellaneous

Maps	6,959
	approx.
Key books	357
Volumes and compilations lists	503
Gujarat State Region records	
Bound volumes	1,095
Files	10,166
Janjira records	757

Alienation Office (Peshwa Daftar), Poona

English files		*Files*
Inam Commission records		4,821
Commissioner, C.D. records relating to Alienation and *Sardars*	1818–87	844
Agent for the *Sardars* records	1826–45	1,009
Deccan Commissioners records	1817–26	508
Satara Residency records	1818–48	150
Poona Residency records	1785–1818	26
Old files from the Ratnagiri Collector	1821–37	52
Files from Kolaba Collector	1840–4	12
Loose bundles not listed		60
Total		7,482

Printed books and selections from government records.

ADDITIONAL PUBLICATIONS

Secretariat Record Office, Bombay

'English records of Maratha history': J. Sarkar and G. S. Sardesai, eds. *Poona Residency correspondence*, vols. 1–9 (1936–43); vol. 10, *Treaty of Bassein and war of 1803–1804 in the Deccan* (1951); vol. 11, *Poona affairs.*

Elphinstone's Embassy 1811–1815 (1950); vol. 12, *Poona affairs*. *Elphinstone's Embassy 1816–1818* (1953); vol. 13, *Daulat Rao Sindhia and north Indian affairs 1810–1818* (1952)

'Persian records of Maratha history', ed by P. M. Joshi: vol. 1, *Delhi affairs 1761–1788; newsletters from Parasnis collection* (1953); vol. 2, *Sindhia as Regent of Delhi 1787 and 1789–91* (1954). Newsletters of the Lalsot campaign from the Salar Jung manuscripts, Hyderabad, and newsletters from the Parasnis collection, Bombay

'Historical selections from the Baroda State records' (old series): vol. 1, 1724–68; vol. 2, 1769–89; vol. 3, 1790–8; vol. 4, 1799–1813; vol. 5, 1813–20; vol. 6, 1793–1800; vol. 7, 1819–25

'Historical selections from the Baroda State records' (new series): vol. 1, 1826–35 (1955); vol. 2 (in press)

'Selections from the Peshwa Daftar' (old series):

Miscellaneous papers 1699–1817 (1933)

'Selections from the Peshwa Daftar' (new series): vol. 1, *Expansion of Maratha power 1707–1761* (1957); vol. 2, *Revival of the Maratha power 1761–1772*

'Selections from the Parasnis collection': J. Sarkar, ed. *The Persian akhbars or Delhi news-letters 1770–1787*

Source material for a history of freedom movement in India (collected from Bombay Government records), vol. 1, 1818–85 (1957); vol. 2, 1885–1920 (1958)

Annual reports

MANIPUR

Formerly a feudatory state under the political control of the governor of Assam, the administration of Manipur was taken over by the Government of India, through a chief commissioner, 15 October 1949. Capital Imphal.

The Secretariat Record Room, under an assistant secretary, holds no record prior to 1891. There are 701 files in the following groups:

Political Agent	1891–1947
Dominion Agent	1947–9
Manipur State Durbar and Council	1907–46
Chief Commissioner's records	1950–

Revenue and Judicial records are housed in a separate building under the custody of the chief secretary and the judicial commissioner.

Records of other departments are held with the department concerned.

MYSORE

General Records Section, Mysore Government Secretariat Record Office, Vidhana Soudhana, Bangalore
Officer in charge: Superintendent
Authority: Chief Secretary, through the Additional Deputy Secretary to Government, General Administration Department, Bangalore

RULES OF ACCESS

All records relating to the period before and including 1925 may be made available to any authentic research scholar whenever such a request is accompanied by the necessary credentials. Applications should be addressed to the chief secretary through the departmental head in a university with the recommendations of the professor concerned, or through the head of other educational institutions. Applications from aliens must be accompanied additionally by a certificate of authenticity from the Indian diplomatic or consular representatives in their country of origin. Each application to examine the records personally will be considered on its merits by the chief secretary, and in accordance with the rules drawn up by the departments to which the records belong. All copies, extracts and notes must be legible and are subject to the scrutiny of the chief secretary. Research on behalf of scholars unable to visit the office in person may be undertaken on the payment of a fee. One or two copies of any published works utilizing the records must be deposited free of charge immediately after publication. The complete rules regulating access are set out in the General Administration Department's document no. GAD 5 RHR of 20 June 1960.

THE STATE OF MYSORE

Mysore remained independent under its Hindu rulers from the fall of Vijayanagar until 1759 when the reigning raja was deposed by one of his captains, Haidar Ali. Haidar and his son Tipu Sultan extended the boundaries of the state until the fall of Tipu at Seringapatam in 1799 when Lord Wellesley partitioned the territories and restored the Wadiyar family to the old Mysore state, although on terms of subordination to the British. The conduct of the maharaja and a rising in Bednur in 1830 led to the resumption of administration by a British commissioner and four divisional superintendents in 1831. By 1862, when the state was redistributed into three divisions, the former patriarchical administration was replaced by the regulation system introduced into all departments. The number of departments and agencies gradually increased and in 1869 the designation 'superintendent' was replaced by 'commissioner' and the head of the administration was called the chief commissioner. The restoration or 'rendition' of Mysore to a Wadiyar ruler in 1881, the cantonment area of Bangalore remaining with the British for military purposes, little changed the administration although further departments were established and the diwan became the executive head and president of the council of three members. With Independence in 1947 Mysore acceded to the Union with the maharaja as *rajpramukh* and later governor. The state of Coorg had come under British control in 1834 when the reigning raja was deposed. In 1881 the resident in Mysore became chief commissioner of Coorg but from July 1940 a separate chief commissionership was established with headquarters at Mercara. In 1947 it became a centrally administered state. By the States Reorganization Act, 1956, the Kannada-speaking people of five states were brought together to make the present state of Mysore. To the old Mysore and Coorg were added the Bijapur, Kanara, Dharwar and part of the Belgaum districts of Bombay, most of the Gulbarga, Raichur and Bidar districts of former Hyderabad and the South Kanara district and Kollegal taluk of the Coimbatore district of Madras. The capital is Bangalore.

ARCHIVES ADMINISTRATION IN MYSORE

The records of all the departments of the Mysore Government secretariat are deposited in the General Records Section of the secretariat. The section is divided into seven subsections. The current records, which cannot be shown to any unauthorized persons, comprise original 'A' and 'B' file collections, proofs and originals of letters and notes of completed registers. Non-current records are those more than 35 years old. Historical records are those so declared from time to time by the government from among the non-current records and these may be thrown open for the inspection of scholars. Separate again are the confidential records of the General Administration Department and of the Home Department. In spare copies are held all printed documents such as 'A' collections (printed), proceedings of government, notifications, monthly volumes and indexes and government publications. There is also a multigraph section and a bindery. Collections are kept in labelled bundles arranged according to department in annual series in order of subject. Printed copies are made of 'A' collections. The current records are divided into those scheduled for destruction after a specified period and those worthy of permanent preservation.

OTHER COLLECTIONS

The holdings of the Record Room of the deputy commissioner, Coorg, are a valuable source for historical information and the Regional Records Survey Committee has suggested their transfer from Mercara to the Secretariat Record Room at Bangalore for better preservation.

AIDS TO REFERENCE

Manuscript registers of indexes in English for all records 1863/4–July 1892 are available separately for receipts and issues. From July 1892 onwards there is a regular index which forms part of the monthly proceedings except for the years 1904–6, for which period a consolidated index to the register of file headings of all departments and branches is available. In addition there is a selection of important papers from the proceedings of government 1834–91, a consolidated index to government orders April 1891–June 1915 and monthly printed proceedings volumes from March 1873 onwards. Those vernacular records which have been preserved are listed and a catalogue of important printed compilations has been printed.

HOLDINGS

General Records Section, Mysore Government Secretariat Record Office, Bangalore

I Records prior to 1799

These are mostly in the vernacular, either Maharathi, Persian or Kannada, relating principally to the *inamti* accounts.

II Records 1800–92

Receipts and issues are held separately by year with their registers.

Pre-rendition period 1831–81
(From and to) Nandidroog Division
Asthagram Division
Nagar Division
Accountant-general
Military miscellaneous
Civil miscellaneous
Collectors, magistrates
Survey Department
General Department   1879–80
Resident in Mysore
Conservator of Forests

Government of India
Government of Madras
Government of Bombay
Medical Department
Deputy Commissioner   1879–81
Municipal   1879–81
Director of Public Instruction
Department of Public Works
Judicial Commissioner
Old Residency records
Muzrai Department
Old *firiyad* registers
Post-rendition period 1881–92
    (From and to) Deputy Commissioners of the districts of Tumkur,
      Mysore, Hassan, Shimoga Kadur and Chitaldurg and the sub-
      divisions of French Rocks and Hassan
    Chief Judge
    Public Works Department
    Department of Railways
    Education Secretary
    Military Department
    Forest Department
    Revenue and *Inam* Survey Department
    Registration and Stamp Department
    Controller to the State
    Anche Department
    Firiyad miscellaneous
    Public miscellaneous
    Private
    Legislature files
    Political Pension files
    Confidential files
    Local Boards
    Petitions
III   Records 1892–1903
Arranged in closed files formed by different departments of the secretariat.
IV   Records 1903 onwards
Arranged in files according to subject and branch.
    Land Revenue   1821–56
    Land Survey   1858–1956
    Muzrai   1846–1956

Separate Revenue	1895–1918
General miscellaneous	1799 (1 bundle), 1831–1956
Medical	1831–1956
Sanitary	1862–1925
Public Health	1926–56
Pension and salary	1918–56
Census	1901–56
General finance	1845–1956
Salary and allowances	1851–1956
Banking	1877–1914
Military	1941–56
Police	1874–1956
Courts	1835–1956
Agriculture	1837–1956
Forest	1875–1956
Legislature	1860–1956
Registration	1864–1956
Industries and commerce	1872–1956
Municipal	1859–1956
Local boards	1837–1956
Education	1851–1956
Electrical	1943–56
Public Works Department	1943–56

v Records received from Madras, Bombay and Hyderabad consequent upon territorial reorganization

Records relating to integrated districts

Bombay secretariat records	1933–56
Hyderabad secretariat records	1948–56
Madras secretariat records	1920–56
Madras Board of Revenue	1920–45
Madras Government proceedings volumes	from 1857
Reprints from the records of Fort St George	1670–1750
Madras Gazette	from 1833
Bombay Gazette	1956
Index to the Madras records	
Bombay, Hyderabad and Coorg codes	

vi Miscellaneous series

Records of the heads of departments	up to 1881
Mysore Residency records	1881–1947

These records belonging to the Government of India relate to the administration of the former civil and military station in Bangalore. They consist of 322 bundles of 'A' proceedings, 68 bundles of 'B' proceedings and 10 miscellaneous bundles.

VII Printed records

Government orders (proceedings) from March 1873

Arranged by year up to 1892 and by year and issuing branch after that date.

Monthly proceedings volumes

Administration reports from 1866

Gazettes of Madras

Gazettes of Bombay

Gazettes of India

Survey and other maps

ORISSA

Orissa State Archives, Bhubaneswar-1
Officer in charge: Assistant Director, Archives
Authority: Director of Cultural Affairs, Government of
Orissa, Bhubaneswar

RULES OF ACCESS

The use of archives by bona fide research students has been restricted to date, in general only the pre-Mutiny records being made available for research.

THE STATE OF ORISSA

Orissa, ceded to the Marathas by Alivardi Khan in 1751, was conquered by the British in 1803. Two commissioners were appointed in 1804 to administer the province and in 1805 it was designated the district of Cuttack and placed in the charge of a collector, judge and magistrate. In 1828 the area was split into the three regulation districts of Cuttack, Balasore and Puri, and non-regulation tributary states administered by their own chiefs under the aegis of the British Government. One of these states, Angul, was annexed in 1847 and with the Khondmals, ceded in 1855–6 by the tributary chief of Baudh State, was constituted a separate non-regulation district. In 1905 Bamra and Rairakhol (the Sambalpur Garhjat) were transferred to Orissa from the Central Provinces and the states of Gangpur and Bonai from Chotanagpur Division. These districts formed an outlying tract of the Bengal presidency until 1912, when they were transferred to Bihar, constituting one of its divisions under a commissioner. The Orissa area had long been divided between Bihar, the Central Provinces and Madras, but the Orissa division was constituted a separate province on 1 April 1936, with portions of the Central Provinces and Madras transferred to it. The Eastern States Agency, with a resident at Calcutta and political agents at Sambalpur and Raipur in relationship with Cooch Behar (West Bengal), Tripura and Mahurbhanj, ceased to function on 19 August 1947. The rulers of twenty-five Orissa states surrendered authority on 1 January 1948, on which date the provincial government took over. The administration of Saraikella and Kharswan was transferred to Bihar in May 1948. Mahurbhanj State was absorbed on 1 January 1949. The capital is Bhubaneswar.

ARCHIVES ADMINISTRATION IN ORISSA

When a Research Section of the Education Department was established in 1950, the State Museum and the State Archives, created temporarily in 1946, were amalgamated with it. The archives became an independent institution in January 1960, its development provided for under the five-year plans. From November 1962 it was placed under the Cultural Affairs Department and the curator designated assistant director. The archives will be housed in the new secretariat building at Bhubaneswar and, with the Museum, hold all those non-current records which are at present scattered in the district offices, the secretariat record room and the revenue record rooms of the various collectorates, commissioners' offices and the Board of Revenue.

AIDS TO REFERENCE

A *Guide to Orissan records* under the 'Orissan record series', containing calendars of 'A' and 'B' papers with subject index and glossary, is being published and already three volumes have appeared. Two *Bulletins* explain the functions of the State Archives and an old guide is K. P. Mitra's *Handbook of the Bihar and Orissa provincial records*.

PUBLICATIONS

Under the 'Orissan record series' it is also planned to publish *in extenso* some important records. A bulletin, *Orissa in 1869–70*, was compiled from old newspapers.

HOLDINGS
Orissa State Archives, Bhubaneswar

1 Judicial Department		
Cuttack collectorate	1805–61	108 v
Balasore collectorate	1820–74	69 v
2 Salt Department		
Cuttack collectorate	1805–66	61 v
Balasore collectorate	1821–64	48 v
3 *a* Revenue Department		
Cuttack collectorate	1803–70	382 v
Balasore collectorate	1803–99	241 v

Comprising 226 vols. Revenue, 12 vols. Customs, 1 vol. Marine, 2 vols. Treasury transactions

b Mahalwari Khewat		
Balasore collectorate		116 v
Mahalwari Kabuliyat		
Balasore collectorate		68 v
Indexed 1897–1926		41 v
4 *a* Oriental records, Mogul,		
Maratha and British		1,442
b Robkari records	1836–1914	1,652 bdls

Relating to rent suits, mutation cases etc., in Persian, Oriya, English and Bengali.

Indexes		74 bdls
5 Old newspapers	1869–1933	59 v with some gaps
6 *Fort St George Gazette*	1832–1936	693 v
7 Old maps and sketches, contemporary		160
Jhana and district maps		
8 Old palm-leaf paintings and MSS		44
9 Old coins		42

PUNJAB (INDIA)

Punjab State Archives, Moti Bagh Palace, Patiala
Officer in charge: Director of Archives
Authority: Secretary to Government, Punjab, Department of
Education

RULES OF ACCESS
In general, records over fifty years old are available for consultation. Microfilming and photographic facilities are placed at the disposal of bona fide research students.

THE STATE OF PUNJAB
The Punjab was part of the Mogul empire, but as Marathas and Muslims fought for possession of the territory central authority gradually weakened and permitted the rise of Sikh power throughout the area. Amar Singh founded Patiala state in 1767, Lahore fell to Ranjit Singh in 1799, Amritsar in 1802 and Ludhiana in 1806. However the break-up of the Sikh kingdom after the death of Ranjit Singh led the British to annex the Punjab in 1849. It was placed under a board of administration, under a chief commissioner in 1853 and, with Delhi territory, under a lieutenant-governor in 1859. The North-West Frontier area was detached in 1901, the Delhi province in 1911, and the Punjab was constituted an autonomous province in 1937. After Independence the province was partitioned between India and Pakistan, the Lahore, Rawalpindi and Multan divisions which comprised West Punjab becoming part of West Pakistan and East Punjab becoming the state of Punjab (India). Of the forty-five former Indian states and estates having political relations with the crown representative through the resident at Lahore, thirty were merged to form the centrally administered territory of Himachal Pradesh, Tehri-Garhwal was added to Uttar Pradesh, and eight were united in 1948 to form the Patiala and East Punjab States Union (P.E.P.S.U.): Patiala, Kapurthala, Malerkotla, Faridkot, Nabha, Jind, Nalagarh and Kalsia. Punjab (India) and P.E.P.S.U. were united on 1 November 1956. In 1966 Punjab was divided into the two states of Punjab and Hariana; the new capital, Chandigarh, became the joint capital.

ARCHIVES ADMINISTRATION IN PUNJAB

After Partition the parent organization for Punjab archives remained at Lahore. A Punjab (I) Record Office was established in 1948 with provisional headquarters at The Manse (formerly St Andrew's Church), Simla and early in 1959 moved to Patiala. It is planned eventually to establish the State Archives at the new capital of Chandigarh. In addition to the preservation of archives the office assumed certain related responsibilities regarding cultural relics, historical materials and such secondary source materials as government publications, and the director of archives is a joint post with that of the curator of the Punjab Government Museum. The Office of Old Records, Qila Mubarik, Patiala, had been established in the early nineteenth century and became part of the Archives of P.E.P.S.U., established in 1948, as were the records of the other constituent states. The Regional Record Survey Committee of P.E.P.S.U. was dissolved after the integration of Punjab and P.E.P.S.U. and its duties taken over by the State Archives. A separate Archives for Hariana has yet to be established.

NATURE AND EXTENT OF HOLDINGS

The nucleus of the collection is that portion of the records of the Lahore Secretariat Office apportioned to India at Partition. The records were divided according to primary interest, or on a fifty-fifty basis in the case of shared interest, having regard to the integrity of series. The bulk of the English series remained at Lahore, but many of these have been microfilmed for the Punjab office from among the concurrent records available at the National Archives of India. To the Lahore records have been added the collections from within the newly created state, and the archives of P.E.P.S.U., of which the files and registers of the constituent states total some 18 lakhs. The records of the former state of Patiala date from 1761 with some earlier material for the period 1748–58. The use of the attached reference library containing over 20,000 items is restricted to government agencies and bona fide scholars.

AIDS TO REFERENCE

Registers and catalogues exist for the records of Patiala and a *Handbook of the Patiala Union records* was published about 1954. A descriptive catalogue of all the Punjab records is under preparation and the English files are being press listed.

PUBLICATIONS

A publication programme was undertaken by the Punjab Record Office from its inception.

HOLDINGS
Punjab State Archives, Patiala

1 Records of the erstwhile Punjab
  Khalsa Durbar records   1811–March 1849   Nearly 2,50,000 loose
                                                    sheets in 132 rolls
These include 44 volumes of correspondence between Ranjit Singh and the
Ludhiana and Ambala agencies. Catalogued: vol. 1 (1919); vol. 2 (1927).
2 Divisional records
   a Commissioner of Ambala before 1900   1,000 bdls
Revenue, Judicial, Military, Political, P.W.D. and General departments.
   b Commissioner of Ambala 1900 onwards   26 boxes
Manuscript press lists of the English files.
   c Commissioner of Jullundur, and Administrator of Simla, Gurdaspur
and Karnal
Include '*Haquiqat-i-Hal-i-Deh Subah Delhi*' (Facts about villages in
Delhi province), 1828–1900, 6 vols. acquired from Karnal district headquarters.
   d Delhi and Hissar Division, 1822–1916
3 District records including   1820–1931   21,000 *mislat*
                                              (original case files
                                            in Urdu)
Primary source material about Karnal, Ambala, Gurgaon, Simla and the
British administration of the Cis-Sutlej, also some records from the
district offices of Ludhiana and Karnal.
4 Mian Chatar Singh   1837–99   60 documents
  collection
Papers of jaghir disputes between Gulab Singh and the descendants of his
brother Dhyan Singh in Persian.
5 East Punjab Government   1947–9   39 bdls
Liaison Agency records
About evacuation and other problems of Partition.
6 Rai Inderjit Singh   1809–49   over 4,000
Bhandari family papers   documents
The Bhandari family were envoys of the Lahore Durbar in the Cis-Sutlej
territories.
   a Political correspondence   1813–67   763 letters
To and from members of the family in their capacity as *vakils*.
   b Miscellaneous letters by *Dak*   167 letters
Mostly private correspondence.

c Letters and office orders   1808–59   1,872 letters
By the maharajas, with memoranda by other notables.

d Grants, deeds, petitions   over 50 documents

e Diary of Major Broadfoot   1 Mar.–31 July
    to the governor-general;   1845
    muqqadamat nos. 35–9

f Diary of Ranjit Singh to   March 1830–May
    two officials   1831

g Military organization,
    draft treaties

7 Historical materials col-
    lected by the Punjab
    Regional Survey Committee

8 Records of the British   1823–46
    agencies in the Punjab

9 *Punjab government gazettes*   1857–1947
    Complete set

10 Baba Prem Singh of Hoti Mardan collection   2,000 objects
    Manuscripts, paintings and rare publications

11 Records of the Constituent states of P.E.P.S.U.
    and the Union

    1 Faridkot state   1901–48
    2 Jind state   1859–1948
    3 Kalsia state   1907–48
    4 Kapurthala state   1848–1948
    5 Nabha state   1822–1948
    6 Nalagarh   1823–1948
    7 Malerkotla   1823–1948
    8 Patiala state   1708–1948
    9 *Narendra Mandal* (Chamber of Princes)
   10 P.E.P.S.U. Education and   1948–56
        Civil Supplies records

PONDICHERRY

Founded by the French in 1674, Pondicherry was captured by the Dutch
in 1693 although restored to the French in 1699. On three occasions it was
captured by the English and subsequently restored to the French, being
in English hands 1761–5, 1778–85 and 1793–1814. Administration was
transferred to India on 1 November 1954, a chief commissioner having the

powers of the former French commissioner but under the direct control of the Union Government. The future and representation of Pondicherry remains to be determined.

Under the terms of Article 33 of the 'Agreement between the Government of India and the Government of France for the settlement of the question of the future of the French Establishments in India' the Pondicherry records of 'historical' importance were to be the property of the French Government, while the 'administrative' records were to be retained by the Government of India. With the departure of the French from Pondicherry the archives were removed en bloc to Paris. After representations by the Indian Government France agreed to give India photocopies of these records. The records will first be arranged and catalogued, then a copy of the complete catalogue sent to the Government of India to enable them to select documents of Indian interest which are to be photocopied.

RAJASTHAN

Rajasthan State Archives, General Records Building, Bikaner
Officer in charge: Director of Archives

RULES OF ACCESS
A research room capable of accommodating sixteen scholars is attached to the archives. Inquiries should be addressed to the Director of Archives.

THE STATE OF RAJASTHAN
Rajasthan was formed in 1949 by the merger of twenty-two former Indian states of Rajputana. By the States Reorganisation Act, 1956, the former chief commissioner's province of Ajmer, ceded to the British by the Maharaja of Gwalior after the Pindari War in 1818, was transferred to Rajasthan, together with the Abu Taluka of Bombay State and the Sunel Tappa enclave of Madhya Bharat. The Sironj subdivision of Rajasthan was transferred to Madhya Pradesh.

ARCHIVES ADMINISTRATION IN THE PRINCELY STATES OF RAJPUTANA
The principalities of Rajasthan had a system of record management which varied from state to state, but the practice of maintaining several archival agencies and of retaining large collections in private custody was common

to most of them. Not until the end of the nineteenth century, when first Bikaner and then some of the other states made efforts to organize central repositories, was there any attempt to integrate the various agencies. Even then, although offices were established in most states for the maintenance of civil secretariat records, most of the old documents remained uncared for in dark underground cells. None of the princely states, not even the state of Jaipur with its Historical Records Section for the preservation of old documents, threw its records open for historical research. There was variation also in the arrangement and care of records. While secretariat files were properly classified and kept on steel racks in some states like Jaipur, Jodhpur and Bikaner, in other states they were kept in *bastas* with little care for their preservation.

In Bikaner State, a General Record Office to house the revenue and judicial records of the state was established in 1896, the first move by any of the princely states of Rajputana towards the creation of a single central records repository. The office was provided with an excellent building in 1930 and the records of the *Mahakhma Khas*, Police, Court of Wards, Education, Public Works, *Devasthan*, Treasury, Municipality, Rural Reconstruction, Settlement, Village *Panchayats*, Military, Customs and Excise, Civil Supplies and Accounts departments transferred there. After the formation of Rajasthan and the consequent shifting of the secretariat records to Jaipur, the remaining General Record Offices were renamed the Deposited Records Offices. However, since the establishment of the headquarters of the Rajasthan State Archives at Bikaner, most of the historical records of all the erstwhile states of Rajasthan are being transferred there as described below.

In Jaipur State there were five record collections, those of the *Diwani Hazuri*, the *Bakhshi-khana*, the *Mustaufi Hazuri*, the *Shamlat* office and the *Mir Bakhshi*. In addition, a huge underground cell at Amer housed 'historical' documents of the seventeenth and early eighteenth centuries which in the early 1930s were sorted and cleaned and shifted to the City Palace at Jaipur. A Central Record Office was set up to house the civil secretariat records, dating from 1831, which were divided into non-current (pre-1922) and current records, but the other repositories remained outside it.

In Marwar State (Jodhpur), there were four archival agencies before the Civil Secretariat Record Office came into being. The *Dastari Darogha* had charge of *farmans*, *nishans*, sanads, *kharitas*, *kharita bahis*, sanad *bahis*, *hakikat bahis*, *munshigiri* files etc. dating from v.s. 1764 (A.D. 1707–8). The *Hazuri Daftar* records related to the grant of jaghirs, *pattas*, privileges, honours and exemptions, and to gazetted appointments after v.s. 1808

(A.D. 1751–2). The *Pardhangiri* office had similar records, but controlled by the Thakur of Pokaran, in whose custody they still remain. The *Kotwal* (City Magistrate) collection, 4,000 *patta bahis*, related to Jodhpur city. Early in this century Jodhpur State set up a Historical Research Department which made a sustained effort to collect information from the records in the custody of jaghirdars and other private agencies. In 1937 a scheme was drawn up to expand the Records Department of the civil secretariat into a Central Records Department within the secretariat, but this was not implemented until 1949 when a registrar of records was appointed and the non-current records of the Land Revenue Department, Court of Wards and *Haisiyat* Court were also placed in his charge. However, the other archival agencies still remained separate. There are no records relating to the period prior to the reign of Maharaja Ajit Singh and those up to the reign of Maharaja Man Singh are sketchy. However, from 1800 the materials are voluminous and varied.

In the chief commissioner's province of Ajmer, the records were kept in three places and their integration never attempted. The record office of the Agency, set up between 1869 and 1871, had in its custody the files of the Political, Confidential, Administration, Finance and War Branches, the Public Works Department and *Mir Munshi*'s office, and remained at Mount Abu although the headquarters of the Agency were shifted back to Ajmer in 1942. The records of the deputy commissioner's office were housed in the collectorate building and those of the commissioner, along with the semi-current and current records of the Ajmer civil secretariat, in the commissioner's office. The main series of records begin in A.D. 1818 although there are copies of *farmans* issued by the Mogul emperors and sanads issued by Daulat Rao Sindia. Two important series are the Neemuch papers dating from A.D. 1823 and the 25,000 files of settlement and revenue papers in the deputy commissioner's office.

ARCHIVES ADMINISTRATION IN RAJASTHAN

After the formation of Rajasthan, the Secretariat Record Offices in the erstwhile states were renamed Unit Record Offices and under district collectors functioned as branches of the Deposited Records Department, under the Registrar of Rajasthan Secretariat, Jaipur. All other record offices in the covenanting states were gradually brought under the control of the Unit Record Offices. In June 1955 an Archives Department was established with headquarters at Jaipur, in succession to a committee set up in 1952 to survey old records, and all records of the period prior to A.D. 1900 came under its control. This evolved into the Rajasthan State Archives, with headquarters at Bikaner (formerly at Jaipur) and twenty district archives offices at Jodhpur, Jaipur, Ajmer, Udaipur, Bikaner, Alwar, Bundi, Banswara, Bharatpur, Dholpur, Karauli, Kotah, Jhalawar, Tonk, Kishangarh, Shahapura, Sirohi, Partapgarh, Dungarpur and Kushalgarh. These have been grouped into seven circles supervised by five superintendents and two supervisors. After completion of the weeding of all ephemeral records, the non-current records of permanent value are being centralized at Bikaner. The repair and rehabilitation section of the archives also microfilms valuable documents which have become brittle with age. A library attached to the archives contains nearly 25,000 publications.

NATURE AND EXTENT OF THE HOLDINGS

The historical material preserved in Rajasthan dates from the reign of the Emperor Akbar. The wealth of material pertaining to the struggle of the Hindu kingdoms during the six centuries of Islam's fight for political domination has been virtually untouched by historians whose knowledge of the period comes almost entirely from the chronicles of the Muslim Court annalists. The bulk of the material increases throughout the later Mogul and Maratha periods while the material bearing upon the British period is virtually intact save some of the confidential files which appear either to have been destroyed or retained in private custody. The most important and best preserved collections are those pertaining to Jaipur, Bikaner and Jodhpur, while the archives of Udaipur and Kotah, and those of Alwar, Bundi and Sirohi pertaining to the later Maratha and British periods, are also of the greatest importance. Unfortunately some valuable collections still remain in the private custody of princes and the families of officials and other notables. For example, the *Pardhangiri* office records (Jodhpur State) remain in the custody of the Thakur of Pokaran. Of the Udaipur archives, all the *farmans, nishans, kharitas* and *hakikat bahis* of the period prior to the reign of Maharana Jawan Singh are in the custody of the Maharana of Udaipur, while some of the most important *bahis* are held by the families of the old *mutasaddis* and *musahibs*.

AIDS TO REFERENCE

Before proceeding with the preparation of calendars and press lists, the State Archives is classifying the records into documents of historical importance, personal papers, and unimportant documents, headed 'A', 'B' and 'C'. Only records in categories 'A' and 'B' will be preserved, together with their indexes. Already a descriptive list of Mogul *farmans, nishans* and *manshurs* has been published, and further lists and a handbook of records will appear in due course.

PUBLICATIONS

Besides the publication of lists and a handbook, the archives has undertaken to prepare a history of Rajasthan, part I of which is in the press.

HOLDINGS
Rajasthan State Archives, Bikaner

JAIPUR RECORDS

			1622–1948	10,000 bdls of approx. 1,000 papers each
1	*Farmans*	Persian	1622–1711	151 docs
2	*Nishans*	Persian	1622–1711	142 docs
3	Sanads	Persian	1638–1765	26 docs
4	*Akhbarat*	Persian	1666–1721	3,022 docs and 14,877 unlisted leaves
5	*Vakil* reports *Maharajgan*	Persian	1658–1719	1,466 docs
6	*Vakil* reports *Maharajgan*	Rajasthani	1656–1719	374 docs, including 84 undated
7	*Khatoot Maharajgan*	Persian	1658–1719	3,235 docs
8	*Khatoot Maharajgan*	Rajasthani	1644–1737	789 docs incl. 25 1 undated
9	*Khatoot Ahalkaran*	Persian	1625–1718	1,600 docs
10	*Khatoot Ahalkaran*	Rajasthani	1633–1768	475 docs incl. 68 undated
11	*Mutfarriq Maharajagan*	Persian	1665–1716	5,459 docs incl. 2,208 undated
12	*Mutfarriq Ahalkaran*	Persian	1607–1743	3,748 docs incl. 1,097 undated
13	*Kharitas*	Rajasthani	1699–2008 v.s.	2,708 docs
14	Draft *Kharitas*	Rajasthani	1719–2000 v.s.	7,314 docs
15	*Farad Kharitas*	Rajasthani	1707+	9,559 docs
16	*Farad Alkab*	Rajasthani		139 leaves
17	*Waqaya*	Rajasthani	1733–2000 v.s.	66 bdls containing 106,690 leaves
18	*Tojih Dastoor*	Rajasthani	1733–1918	76 bdls containing 92,265 leaves

19 *Pana Mahavari*	Rajasthani	1900–1945	15 bdls containing 4,640 leaves
20 Miscellaneous papers containing *Kharitas, Zanani, Tehreer, Arazdast* etc.	Rajasthani	1733–1918	108 bdls containing 16,960 docs
21 *Nawazana*		1704–1948	Assignment of villages as jaghirs etc.
22 *Nasukha Punna*		1786–1948	Rent-free lands for worship and charity
23 Sanad *Nawis*		1709–1948	*Pattas* issued to the Inamdars, Mafidars, Tankhadars etc. arranged *pargana*-wise
24 *Avarajah* and *Baqiat*		1765–1937	Accounts papers, contributions of jaghirs, realization from the jagirdars
25 *Shamlat*		1761–1948	Consolidated accounts of revenue and expenditure
26 *Adsattas*		1662–1806	Revenue registers of the villages, giving a brief sketch of the history of the village, the leading men etc.
27 *Roznamchas*		1765–1850	Tehsils' daily diaries of income and expenditure
28 *Barat*		1765–1850	Orders for payment to certain departments or troops
29 *Ikrarnama*		1604–1887	Agreements and military pacts between Rajput princes, Maratha chiefs or Pindari leaders

UDAIPUR RECORDS

		1615–1943	3,000 *bahis*
1 *Haqiqat bahis*			Personal and official activities of the Maharana of Mewar

2 *Patta bahis*	Assignment of villages or rent-free lands as jaghirs
3 *Kharita bahis*	1,000. To and from the rulers of the various states
4 *Parawana bahis*	Administrative orders
5 *Farmans* and *Nishans*	Personal archives of the Maharana of Mewar
6 Land Revenue Settlement papers	

JODHPUR RECORDS

	1764–1900	3,000 *bahis*
1 *Kotwali bahis*		Criminal cases
2 Marriage *bahis*		Interstate relations of the Rajputs cemented by matrimonial alliances
3 *Khazana bahis*		Daily income and expenditure; treasury also served the function of banks
4 *Arzi bahis*		Miscellaneous petitions, reports of the Vakils etc.
5 *Haqiqat bahis*		Personal and official activities of the rulers
6 *Kharita bahis*		To and from rulers of the various states
7 Sanad *Parawana bahis*		Administrative orders
8 *Farmans*		
9 *Kharitas*		500

KOTAH RECORDS

	From 1792	6,005 bastas, each of some 3,000 papers chronologically arranged
1 *Dowarki*		Day-to-day administration, particularly military
2 *Jamabandi*		Revenue and accounts, including revenue from the parganas of Mewar
3 *Mulki Jhadas panas* and *bahis*		Consolidated accounts of one, three, five or ten years

4 *Taliks bahis*		Orders of the Maharao or his diwan, private letters between members of the ruling family, mostly diplomatic
5 Newsletters of the *Halkaras* and the Vakil reports		Agents in the various camps of rulers, Marathas and Pindari leaders
6 *Adsattas*		
7 Secretariat	From 1876	36,373 files
a Hindi	From 1915	21,000 files
b Urdu		10,000 files
		Customs, Industries, P.W.D., Forests, Kotries, Courts, Hospitals, Army, Police, Irrigation, Cooperatives, P.O., Bhandar Shrini, Municipal
c English	1892–1948	5,000 files
		Round Table Conference, orders of the Agent of the governor-general, boundary disputes, Chamber of princes, posts and telegraph, Mayo College, interstate relations, political movements etc.
8 Gulgule Daftar	1732–1819 v.s.	6,000 docs. in 25 bdls
		Revenue collectors under the Peshwa and Sindhia; north Indian affairs of the Marathas

BIKANER RECORDS

	1604–1893	1,051 *bahis*
(Main series)	1630–1892	
1 *Talab Patta*	1809–87	52 *bahis*. Land and buildings
2 *Chitta Khatas*	1762–1870	39 *bahis*. Government orders and accounts
3 *Patta bahis*	1604–1893	120 *bahis*. Grants of lands and buildings

4 *Diwanji ki bahis*	1753–1835	196. Diwans' orders to officers and Jaghirdars
5 *Parawana*		22 *bahis*
6 *Bara Karkhana*		Household management of the Maharaja, Maharaja Kunwars and Maharanis
7 *Ranawati Sahiba ki bahis*		14 *bahis*. Jaghirs of Ranawatiji
8 *Patta bahis* of different districts and Tehsils		708 *bahis*
9 Revenue		353,530 files
10 Judicial		86,000 files
11 Districts sections in Judicial Revenue		249,424 files
12 Police		90,891 files
13 Accounts		91,891 files
14 Registers of the above departments		14,106 files
15 *Bahis*		3,000 files
16 Settlement registers and files, maps etc.		1,000 files

Court of Wards, Education, P.W.D., *Mahakhma Khas*, Treasury, Municipal board, Rural reconstruction, Civil supplies, Village *Panchayat*, *Bada Karkhana*, Military G.Q., Customs and Excise.

BIKANER SECRETARIAT RECORDS

1 Period 1896–1946	90,000 files in English approx. 39,000 files arranged chronologically
2 Period 1911–[1940 *sic*] 1914	8,961 files arranged head- and yearwise
3 Period 1914 to date	Arranged according to department
Class A (more important)	13,730 files
Class B (less important)	28,284 files

UTTAR PRADESH

State Archives, 53 Mahatma Gandhi Marg, Allahabad
Officer in charge: State Archivist
Authority: Joint Secretary to the Government of U.P. and
Director, Department of Indology, Culture and Scientific
Research, Secretariat, Lucknow

RULES OF ACCESS

Applications for permission to consult records should be addressed to the secretary to the Government of Uttar Pradesh, Lucknow. Records up to 1901 may be freely consulted. Special permission is required to consult the non-confidential records to 1935, also certain classes of restricted material such as criminal cases less than seventy years old, personal donated material less than fifty years old, and confidential records. All excerpts are scrutinized. There are photocopying, transcription and search facilities requiring payment of a fee.

THE STATE OF UTTAR PRADESH

In 1833 the Bengal presidency was divided into two parts, one of which became the presidency of Agra. In 1836 Agra was styled the North-Western Province and placed under a lieutenant-governor. The two provinces of Agra and Avadh (Oudh) were, in 1877, placed under one administrator styled the lieutenant-governor of the North-West Province and chief commissioner of Oudh. The name was changed to United Provinces of Agra and Oudh in 1902, and the lieutenant-governor became a governor in 1921. The name was shortened to United Provinces in 1935 and changed to Uttar Pradesh with effect from 24 January 1950. After Independence the states of Rampur, Banaras and Tehri-Garhwal were merged with Uttar Pradesh. The capital is Lucknow.

ARCHIVES ADMINISTRATION IN UTTAR PRADESH

The State Archives (until 1959–60 the Central Record Office under a keeper of records) existed on a temporary basis from May 1949 and was declared a permanent Department of the U.P. Government with effect from 1 April 1956. Control of the Archives was transferred from the Education Department to the General Administration Department in April 1957, then to the joint secretary to the Government of U.P. and director, Department of Indology, Culture and Scientific Research in December 1957. Owing to shortage of space in the present repository a new building at Lucknow is projected. A reference library is attached.

NATURE AND EXTENT OF HOLDINGS

The nucleus of the holdings are the archives formerly kept in the office of the Board of Revenue, consisting of over 2,000 volumes of North-West Province records 1807–58, and several thousands of files of Avadh records 1858–90. To these were added the records of the merging states, district and divisional records, and non-current judicial and departmental records. Many records were lost during 1857–8 and in subsequent fires. Unfortunately the transfer to Lucknow of large bodies of records for use in writing the history of the U.P. Freedom Movement has meant the breaking of many original district series, but in time this should be rectified.

AIDS TO REFERENCE

A summary inventory of inventories is in course of preparation. The list of holdings below was taken from the 'Summary of the holdings of the State Archives of Uttar Pradesh, Allahadab' issued by the archives in mimeograph form. Pre-Mutiny records are described in D. Dewar's *Handbook to the English pre-mutiny records in the Government record rooms of the United Provinces of Agra and Oudh* (1919), now out of print, and *Press list of pre-mutiny records—Banaras correspondence*, vols. I–III (1955–), in progress. See also *Calendar of Oriental records*, vols. I–III (1955–9); *Catalogue of State papers*, vols. I– (1956–), in progress; and *Index to the Fort William correspondence 1803–7*.

Indexes to proceedings appear in the holdings list below with the records to which they relate. The following archival aids are listed in the *Administrative reports* of the archives, 1949–54 and 1955–8.

Catalogues: Banaras records 1795–1859; Persian records of Varanasi (Banaras); records of the North-Western Provinces Judicial series 1795–1814; Mirzapur Judicial vernacular papers 1795– ; pre-Mutiny records of Agra 1807–57, Aligarh 1836–56, Etawah 1821–47, Farrukhabad 1819–58, Fatehpur 1843–57, Mainpuri 1857–8, and Meerut 1822–34.

Lists and checklists: All district and divisional series of records, improving the printed lists of R. Dewhurst; Rampur State confidential Agency records 1803–48; Rohilkhand commissioner's correspondence 1860–80; criminal and revenue files of the Land Revenue section; post-Mutiny vernacular records of the commissioner's office, Varanasi, 1858–80; English records of the commissioner's office, Agra 1858–74.

Press lists: Correspondence of Jonathan Duncan, Resident at Banaras 1776-90; Bundelkhand records.

Indexes: Revenue records 1803-74, with an alphabetical list of the files, 1857-73.

An inventory of Persian and Urdu records is in course of preparation; also a card catalogue by author, title and subject of MSS and documents acquired by the Regional Records Survey Committee, U.P.

PUBLICATIONS

A programme of three series of publications was launched in 1954: Selections from English records, Selections from Oriental records, and Miscellaneous archival publications.

Secretariat Record Room, Lucknow
Officer in charge: Assistant Secretary (General),
Secretariat Administration Department
Authority: State Archivist

NATURE AND EXTENT OF HOLDINGS

The record room is part of the administrative machinery of government. Until the new archives building in Lucknow is completed, the supervision of the state archivist over the secretariat records tends to be nominal. Records up to 1855 were written into volumes and the originals destroyed. From 1855 until 1874 abstract proceedings were entered into volumes and the originals preserved in weekly and monthly bundles. From 1874 until 1933 proceedings were classified as 'A' and printed *in extenso*, 'B' and printed as abstracts with the originals preserved in subject files, or 'C' and destroyed after routine weeding. After 1933 printing lapsed and records were kept in subject files.

HOLDINGS
State Archives, Uttar Pradesh, Allahabad

BOARD OF REVENUE

Proceedings at Fort William	1803-7	36 v
Proceedings in the Ceded and Conquered Provinces		178 v
Proceedings for Bihar and Banaras	1816-22	83 v
Proceedings in the Western Provinces	1822-9	126 v
Proceedings in the Central Provinces	1822-9	118 v

Proceedings of the Sadar Board of Revenue on Deportation	1830–2	15 v
Proceedings of the Sadar Board of Revenue, N.W.P.	1832–55	580 v
Abstract of Proceedings of the Sadar Board of Revenue, N.W.P.	1854–61	80 v
Abstract of Proceedings of Board of Revenue, N.W.P.	1874–6	65 v
Index, Board of Revenue Proceedings, Western Province	1822–9	18 v
Index, Board of Revenue Proceedings, Central Provinces	1823–9	7 v
Index, Sadar Board of Revenue Proceedings, N.W.P.	1823–9	48 v
Index, Sadar Board of Revenue Proceedings, N.W.P.	1822–34	48 v
Index, Sadar Board of Revenue on Deportation Proceedings	1831	2 v
Index, Proceedings of *Abkari* (Excise)	1829	1 v
List of special Indexes	1816–29	7 v
Index, Proceedings, Sadar Board of Revenue, N.W.P.	1790	1 v
Index, Proceedings, Board of Revenue and Sadar Board of Revenue	1862–74	108 v
Index, Proceedings, Ceded and Conquered Provinces	1807–22	26 v
Index, Proceedings, Board of Revenue, N.W.P. (Separate Revenue)	1862–74	26 v
Index, Proceedings, Bihar and Banaras	1816–22	10 v
Index, Records and Circulars	1804–85	23 v
Alphabetical indexes	1874–1918	28 v
Correspondence of Mufussil special commissioner series 1–5	1817–30	18 v
Customs Proceedings, abstracts, correspondence, circulars, memo and despatch books	1810–74	110 v, 34 f
Boards circulars	1854–93	66 v, 54 f
Receipt and Despatch registers	1831–76	80 v
Receipt and Despatch registers, Sadar Board of Revenue, Board of Revenue	1832–1907	237 v
Opium Diary and Receipt and Despatch registers	1858–1923	107 v

Misc. Revenue Dept, Opium Branch	1909–10	82 f
Petition and Revenue registers	1868–76	15 v
Camp registers	1908–13	29 v
Petition registers	1860–1908	18 v
General progress registers	1886–1908	124 v
Village statements	Various:	474 v
	post Mutiny	

Moradabad (120 v), Agra (17), Banda (19), Dehradun (3), Shahjehanpur (15), Bulandshahr (17), Mathura (7), Hamirpur (14), Muzaffarnagar (27), Aligarh (17), Mainpuri (23), Bijnor (28), Kanpur (43), Etawah (18), Azamgarh (75), Bareilly (28), Jhansi (3), Ghazipur (39), Badaun (65), Allahabad (34).

Mafi registers	1871–91	137 v
Railway	1862–1908	97 v
Weekly reports	1851–73	818 f
Shelves A–W	1838–74	310 f
Income Tax shelves	1860–72	78 f
Map shelf	1843–73	63 f
Deputy Collector shelf	1846–71	5 f
Canal shelf	1868–72	2 f
Cess shelf	1871–3	5 f
Miscellaneous	1822–1936	460 f, 215 v
Revenue Department—various	1862–82	3 files, 2 bdls
District files	1804–74	1,393 f
	(mostly	
	post Mutiny)	

Aligarh (56 f), Agra (109), Azamgarh (21), Allahabad (118), Bareilly (109), Banda (24), Basti (20), Bijnor (58), Bulandshahr (51), Badaun (17), Dehradun (27), Etah (24), Etawah (30), Farrukhabad (76), Fatehpur (17), Garhwal (2), Ghazipur (47), Hamirpur (26), Jalaun (28), Jhansi (33), Jaunpur (24), Kanpur (39), Kumaun (17), Lalitpur (25), Moradabad (36), Mirzapur (68), Muzaffarnagar (31), Meerut (65), Mathura (25), Mainpuri (26), Shahjahanpur (26), Saharanpur (49), Tarai (5), Gorakhpur (62).

N.W.P. Records, Banares, Ajmer, Kanpur	1845–73	38 f
Revenue Administrative report	1858–68	12 f
File Register, Oudh District		11 f
Family Domain of Maharaja Banares	1849–74	12 f
Avadh Records	1858–90	14,044 f

Oudh General (2,330 f), Lucknow (2,766), Rai Bareli (854), Hardoi (910), Lakhimpur Kheri (713), Barabanki (964), Bahraich (444), Unnao

(999), Fyzabad (1,113), Sitapur (573), Gonda (894), Pratapgarh (682), Sultanpur (802).

Oudh Records, abstracts	1857–64	8 f
Oudh Records, indexes, receipt and despatch registers, various	1856–90	131 v and 15 f
Oudh Circulars, revenue, records, chief commissioners	1857–85	144 v
List of Taluqdars in Oudh	1861–8	25 v
Oudh Records Assessment registers	1858–99, various	390 v

Gonda (29 v), Unnao (31), Kheri (5), Mirzapur (3), Rai Bareli (46), Fyzabad (26), Pratapgarh (26), Sultanpur (46), Barabanki (61), Lucknow (15), Sitapur (28), Bahraich (24), Fatehpur (24), Hardoi (26).

Oudh Records map register	1889–91	14 v
Oudh Records, miscellaneous, various	1859–1910	29 f

AGRA DIVISION

Pre-Mutiny Records

Customs	1808–57	21 f
Aligarh Revenue	1821–35	10 v
Agra Revenue	1829–57	18 v
Agra Judicial	1822–57	29 v
Miscellaneous	1812–57	12 v
Mainpuri Revenue	1824–57	18 v
Mainpuri Judicial	1829–57	18 v
Mathura Revenue	1833–57	11 v
Etah Revenue	1814–57	6 v
Etah Judicial	1852–7	2 v
Revenue	1829–56	8 v
Judicial	1829–56	11 v
Political	1810–57	4 v

Post-Mutiny Records

Revenue Department	1858–74	474 f
Judicial Department	1857–74	224 f
Depts I–XIII	1858–74	533 f
Miscellaneous	1854–73	8 v

FYZABAD DIVISION

	1858–90	16,274

GORAKHPUR DIVISION

Revenue, Gorakhpur Dist. incl. Basti	1807–59	130 v and 108 f
Judicial, Gorakhpur	1829–57	2 v and 7 f
Revenue, Azamgarh	1810–59	67 v and 161 f
Judicial, Azamgarh	1856	1 v and 3 f

JHANSI DIVISION

Revenue Department I–XLIV	1808–92	96 v and 1,271 f
Miscellaneous papers		18 v and 35 f
Post-Mutiny Records of different departments	1857–77	276 f

KUMAUN DIVISION

Miscellaneous letters received I–II	1814–57	113 v
Political letters received I–III	1815–59	9 v
Settlement letters received I–II	1851–8	3 v
Revenue, Judicial, Political, Settlement letters issued	1814–59	55 v

LUCKNOW DIVISION

Post-Mutiny Records	1866–91	627 f

MEERUT DIVISION

Pre-Mutiny Records	1810–12	41 f
Revenue Departments	1858–74	1,533 f
Judicial Departments	1858–74	462 f

ROHILKHAND DIVISION

Departments I–XXIV	1844–80	1,123 f

VARANASI DIVISION

Residency Records (4 categories)	1795–1871	137 v
Correspondence of Resident at Banares (Duncan Records)	1776–1810	105 v
Resident at Banares, correspondence; and settlement	1787–1853	193 f

Resident at Banares, registers	1799–1857	193 v
Resident at Banares, miscellaneous correspondence	1752–1857	197 f
Revenue (incl. supplementary)	1809–57	1,090 f
Judicial (incl. infanticide)	1821–56	114 f
Mirzapur Revenue	1830–57	1,040 f
Mirzapur Judicial	1836–60	65 f
Agency records departments I–XXXIV	1854–1916	665 f
Family domain	1859–1911	486 f
Revenue	1812–99	2,988 f
Judicial	1851–81	323 f
Miscellaneous	1861–91	224 f
Persian Records	1828–84	6,721 f
Ghazipur Revenue	1846–54	877 f
Ghazipur Judicial	1846–54	147 f
Jaunpur Revenue (incl. supplementary)	1812–57	1,576 f
Jaunpur Judicial	1831–58	2 f
Post-mutiny records index register Banares	1858–87	149 v
Miscellaneous register despatch receipt	1858–1900	48 v
List of Darbaris in Banares Division	1873–81	14 v
Index register Jaunpur	1859–81	20 v
File index register and despatch	1859–98	211 v

AGRA

Mutiny records (Urdu–Persian)	1857–74	86 f

ALIGARH

Mutiny records (Urdu–Persian)	1857–9	92 f

ALLAHABAD

Pre-Mutiny records (Urdu–Persian)	1856–1900	2,419 f

ALMORAH

Pre-Mutiny and Mutiny records (Urdu–Persian)	1839–57	42 f

AZAMGARH

Mutiny records (Urdu–Persian)	1857–91	185 f

BADAUN

(Urdu–Persian)	1858–78	76 letters

BAHRAICH

Mutiny records (Urdu–Persian)	1857	18 f

BANDA

Settlement, Miscellaneous Revenue, and Revenue records (Persian)	1834–1911	45 f

BIJNOR

Mutiny records (Urdu–Persian)	1858–9	909 f

BULANDSHAHR

Mutiny records	1857	1,576 f

ETAH

Mutiny records (Urdu–Persian)	1858–9	83 f

ETAWAH

Mutiny records (Urdu–Persian)	1858–78	11 f

FARRUKHABAD

Mutiny records (Urdu–Persian)	1857–8	178 f

FATEHPUR

Mutiny records (Urdu–Persian)	1858–66	56 f

GHAZIPUR

Revenue	1802–55	147 v
Miscellaneous records	1841–57	72 v
Settlement records	1830–52	137 v
Mutiny records (Urdu–Persian)	1857–69	79 f

GORAKHPUR

Revenue letters received	1802–57	102 v
Judicial letters received	1808–57	14 v
Revenue letters issued	1801–56	49 v
Judicial letters issued	1806–58	18 v
Miscellaneous records	1803–58	15 v

HAMIRPUR

Department XIII	1858–73	124 f
Mutiny records (Urdu–Persian)	1858–60	194 f

JALAUN

Mutiny records (Urdu–Persian)	1857	188 f
List A (Urdu–Persian)	1858–60	194 f

JAUNPUR

Mutiny records (Urdu–Persian)	1857–61	113 f

JHANSI

Mutiny records (Urdu–Persian)	1857–60	256 f

KANPUR

Mutiny records (Urdu–Persian)	1849–59	855 f

LUCKNOW

Mutiny records (Urdu-Persian)	1857–1916	1,440 f

MATHURA

Mutiny records etc. (Urdu–Persian)	1857–67	1,078 f

MEERUT

Parts I–V	1803–66	107 v

MIRZAPUR

Judicial	1830–57	99 v
Miscellaneous	1824–55	25 v
Financial	1795–1858	21 v
Revenue	1795–1857	85 v
Court of Ward	1849–59	8 v
Settlement	1833–57	116 v
Mutiny records (Urdu–Persian)	1857–60	19 f

MORADABAD

Mutiny records (Urdu–Persian)	1858–9	11 f

MUZAFFARNAGAR

Mutiny records (Urdu–Persian)	1858–80	226 f

RAI BARELI

Mutiny records (Urdu–Persian)	1858–70	19 f

RAMPUR

| Registers | 1851–1945 | 255 v |
| Records | 1805–1920 | 1,116 v |

SAHARANPUR

Revenue records	1809–58	125 v
Settlement records	1819–41	50 v
Judicial records	1805–57	59 v
Miscellaneous	1812–66	5 v
Local Agency series	1836–60	4 v

SHAHJAHANPUR

| Mutiny records (Urdu–Persian) | 1858–97 | 1,957 f |

TEHRI GARHWAL

| | 1711–1890 | 25 *bahikhatas* |
| | 1647–60 | 3 *farmans* |

UNNAO

| Unnao records (*basta* 1–19) (Urdu–Persian) | | 1,048 f |

VARANASI

Miscellaneous	1796–1835	22 v
Educational correspondence	1843–50	1 v
Judicial	1800–57	5 v
Revenue	1795–1817	8 v
Correspondence relating to Mauzas	1844–58	46 v, 153 f
Mutiny records miscellaneous (Urdu–Persian)		228 f

VARANASI STATE

Audit accounts	1920–50	120 f
Manuscripts in Sanskrit, Hindi, Marathi and Bengali etc.		8,151 MSS
Manuscripts in Urdu, Persian and Arabic		3,248 MSS

Secretariat Record Room, Lucknow

		Volume Nos.
1 N.W.P. and Agra proceedings		
1 Appointment Department	Feb. 1844–Dec. 1887	1–5

21-3

2	Foreign Department (Financial)	1847–58	6–11
3	Foreign Department (Agra Narratives)	1834–60	12–36
4	Foreign Department (N.W.P. Political)	1838–68	
5	Foreign Department (N.W.P. Proceedings General)	1845–70	37–49
6	Foreign Department (N.W.P. Proceedings Judicial)	1842–58	50–7
7	Home Department (Civil and Criminal)	1859–67	58–67
8	Foreign Department (N.W.P. Judicial —Civil)	1842–58	67–74
9	Home Department (Judicial—Civil)	1859–71	75–81
10	Home Department (N.W.P. and Oudh Judicial Proceedings)	1844	82
11	Financial Department (N.W.P. and Oudh Judicial Proceedings)	1855–1885	83–4
12	Home Department (N.W.P. and G. Judicial Proceedings)	1886–94	85–91
13	Foreign Department (N.W.P. Narrative Proceedings Judicial)	1847–58	92–3
14	Financial Department (N.W.P. and Oudh Proceedings L.S.G.D.)	1885	94
15	Foreign Department (N.W.P. Proceedings—Military Police)	1858–60	95–7
16	Financial Department (N.W.P. Proceedings—General Department Miscellaneous)	1884–5	98–9
17	Financial Department (N.W.P. Proceedings Miscellaneous Department)	1884	100
18	Home Department (N.W.P. Revenue and Miscellaneous Abstract Proceedings)	1837	101
19	Home Department (Abstract of Revenue Proceedings N.W.P. and Oudh)	1856–76	102–13
20	Financial Department (N.W.P. and Oudh Proceedings Revenue and Foreign Department)	1880–1	114–15
21	Foreign Department (N.W.P. Proceedings Revenue and Separate Revenue)	1842–58	116–24

22 Financial Department (N.W.P. Proceedings—Separate Revenue Department)	1865–85	125–7
II Oudh Proceedings		
1 Foreign Department (Oudh abstract proceedings Agency Department)	1857–8	1–3
2 Financial Department (Oudh Proceedings General Finance)	1874–7	4–7
3 Foreign Department (Oudh Proceedings General Department)	1856–71	8–27
4 Home Department	1871–6	28
5 Financial Department (Oudh Proceedings General Department Home)	1881–1872 [*sic*]	29
6 Home Department (General)	1873–4	30–1
7 Financial Department (Oudh Proceedings General Department)	1875–1874 [*sic*]	32–8
8 Foreign Department (Abstract—Judicial)	1856–61	39–43
9 Foreign Department (Abstract—Military)	1858–9	44–5
10 Foreign Department (Abstract—Political)	1856–60	46–50
11 Foreign Department (Abstract—Revenue)	1860–1	51–6
12 Abstract Proceedings of the Chief Commissioner, Oudh (Revenue Department)	1862–75	57–69
13 Financial Department (Oudh Proceedings Revenue Department Revenue Agriculture and Commerce)	1876–8	70–2
14 Oudh Revenue Proceedings	1879–90	73–5
III Proceedings from departments		
1 Revenue Department	1860–1933	
2 A and B Statement (Revenue Department)	1871–82	
3 Scarcity Department	1896–1914	
4 Oudh Revenue Department	1871–8	
5 Appointment Department	1884–1932	
6 General Department	1860–1931	

7 A and B Statement (General Department)	1876–9
8 Political Department	1860–1929
9 Agency records	1922–9
10 Medical Department	1884–1927
11 Judicial (Criminal) Department	1860–1927
12 Judicial (Civil) Department	1860–72
13 Police Department	1850–1929
14 Local Self-government Department	1884–1926
15 Finance (A) Government	1860–1936
16 Finance (B) Government	1921–40
17 Finance (C) Government	1921–30
18 Finance (D) Government	1937–9
19 Municipal Department	1873–1930
20 Miscellaneous Department	1884–1921
21 Agricultural Department	1921–35
22 Co-operative Department	1921–33
23 Revenue and Excise Department	1860–1935
24 State Revenue, Income Tax Department (assessed taxes, licences, taxes)	1860–85
25 Forest Department	1862–1933
26 Education Department	1893–1927
27 Public Health Department	1911–27
28 Legislative Department proceedings	1895–1925
29 Industries Department	1908–32
30 Miscellaneous reports etc.	1889–1909

ADDITIONAL PUBLICATIONS

State Archives, Uttar Pradesh, Allahabad

'Selections from English records' series: *Banaras affairs*: vol. I, *1788–1810*; vol. II, *1811–58*; *Henry Wellesley's correspondence 1801–1803* (1955); *Historical papers relating to Kumaun 1809–1842* (1956)

'Selections from Oriental records' series: *A calendar of Oriental records*, vol. I (1955); vol. II (1956); vol. III (1959)

Miscellaneous archival publications: *Administrative report of the Government Central Record Office, U.P., Allahabad: 1949–54* (1955); *1955–8* (1959); *Administrative Report of the State Archives, U.P. Allahabad, 1954–59; Progress Report of the State Archives, U.P. Allahabad (1959–62)*

Information Department—Publications Bureau

Freedom struggle in Uttar Pradesh: source material (Lucknow, 1957–60), vol. I, *1857–59; Nature and origin* (1957); vol. II, *Awadh; 1857–59* (1958); vol. III, *Bundelkhand and adjoining territories 1857–1859* (1959); vol. IV, *Eastern and adjoining territories 1857–1859* (1959); vol. V, *Western districts and Rohilkhand* (1960)

WEST BENGAL

West Bengal State Archives, Historical Section, 6 Bhowani Dutta Lane, Calcutta 7
Officer in charge: Director of Archives
Authority: Deputy Secretary, Department of Education, Government of West Bengal, Calcutta

RULES OF ACCESS

Persons requiring information from or copies of any records should apply in writing to the director of archives stating their occupation and the purpose for which the information or copies is required. Bona fide students should apply for a student's ticket on a prescribed form available from the director of archives. They may be allowed access to records in the custody of the West Bengal State Archives that are more than 40 years old on condition that excerpts taken from the post-1901 records are released only after scrutiny by the administrative department concerned. Each application must be accompanied by a recommendation on a prescribed form from the head of the institution to which the applicant is attached and foreign students must in addition submit recommendations from their consuls. Students' tickets are issued for a period of six months and may be renewed subject to the government's approval. The government reserves the right to decide whether a document shall be issued for inspection, and no document of exceptional value or in a fragile condition shall be issued where certified copies exist. Search and copying charges must be paid in advance to the Treasurer, West Bengal Secretariat. No information and no copies of documents shall be given and no person shall be permitted to make a copy of any document without reference to the department concerned. A copy of any article or work based on the West Bengal records shall be deposited with the State Archives immediately after publication. Students are given facilities to work in both the buildings in which the State Archives is housed.

THE STATE OF WEST BENGAL

The large Hindu principalities in Bengal, Bihar and Orissa finally became part of the Mogul empire in 1576. The East India Company first opened trading relations with Bengal from Madras by founding a factory at Hugli, a former trading centre of the Portuguese, in 1651. This and branch factories including Patna and Dacca were administered from Fort St George (Madras) until Fort William (Calcutta), built at Sutanati in 1696, became the headquarters of the new presidency of Bengal in 1700. In return for their support, the emperor Shah Alam granted the Company the *diwani* or right to collect revenue from Bengal, Bihar and Orissa in 1765, so giving the Company the effective control of Bengal. By the Regulating Act of 1773 and later acts, Fort William was given jurisdiction over the other presidencies of Fort St George and Bombay, thus Calcutta became the seat of the supreme government of India. After the Charter Act of 1833 Bengal was divided into two presidencies, Fort William and Agra, but it was not until 1843 that the supreme Government had a secretariat of its own, distinct and separate from the secretariat of Bengal. The governor-general was relieved of the responsibilities of Bengal in 1854 and a lieu-tenant-governor of Bengal appointed. In 1874 the province was reduced to Bengal proper, Bihar and Orissa, and in 1905 a portion of Bengal together with Assam went to form a new province, Eastern Bengal and Assam. The capital of India was changed from Calcutta to Delhi in 1911 and a new presidency of Bengal, reuniting all Bengali-speaking districts, was estab-lished under a governor in council; it was constituted an autonomous province in 1937. When India was partitioned in 1947, the Chittagong and Dacca divisions and portions of the Presidency and Rajshahi divisions of Bengal, together with the Sylhet district of Assam, were apportioned to the Dominion of Pakistan to become East Pakistan. In January 1950 the territory of Cooch-Behar, and in October 1954 the former French posses-sion of Chandernagore, were merged with West Bengal. The capital is Calcutta.

ARCHIVES ADMINISTRATION IN WEST BENGAL

A General Record Office under the charge of the Presidency Committee, and after 1829 of the Territorial Department, received from district record offices lists and abstracts of useful papers and documents and copies of the most important ones. When in 1843 the supreme Government of India secretariat was separated from the Bengal secretariat the records were divided, and the office retained only the Revenue and Judicial records of the East India Company's Bengal administration prior to 1834. A committee for the destruction of useless records was set up in 1861 and in 1905 schemes to centralize the Company papers from district offices were introduced. Known successively as the Secretariat Record Room and Secretariat Record Office, it was reorganized in 1909 and a permanent post of keeper of records created the next year. Control passed to the Political Department, the Home Department and finally, in 1951, the Education Department. From 1960 reorganization and enlargement of the office began. The resulting State Archives is in two sections, a Current Section located in the Writer's Buildings, Dalhousie Square, Calcutta 1, which houses state government records from 1902 onwards, and a Historical Section at 6 Bhowani Dutta Lane, Calcutta 7, where records from the earliest period up to 1901 are housed. A research room for scholars and a library are attached to the Historical Section.

NATURE AND EXTENT OF HOLDINGS

The importance of the Bengal records is due to their relevance to many subjects and areas beyond West Bengal. Although most series created by the East India Company's Bengal administration up to November 1834 passed to the National Archives of India, the Judicial, Revenue, and other English records relate to the central government of India 1772–1854, and to areas now included in the Punjab, Delhi, Uttar Pradesh, Bihar, Orissa, East Pakistan, Sikkim, Bhutan, Assam, Tripura, Manipur and Burma. The East India Company papers are only fragmentary prior to 1770, the missing records supposedly destroyed during the cyclone and flood of 1737 and the sack of Calcutta in 1756. Their reconstruction is under consideration, and already gaps in the later collections have been filled from copies of records in the India Office Library, London. There are, in addition, Persian and Bengali records dating from 1624, Dutch records relating to Chinsura 1702–1827 and 77 volumes of surviving Danish records of Serampore. These Dutch and Danish records are on quasi-permanent loan from the central government but the correspondence between Serampore and Fort William is held in the National Archives of India. Following the partition of Bengal in 1947, copies of many documents were handed over to the Government of East Pakistan but the originals retained in Calcutta. Records concerning Chandernagore were given to the French Government. Recovery of the Purulia records from Bihar is under negotiation. Pre-Mutiny records consist of some 10,292 bundles of original consultations and 11,839 volumes of proceedings, and post-Mutiny records some 14,856 bundles of original consultations and 11,530 volumes of proceedings. Each bundle consists of about 100 documents which make a total of 2,514,800 documents. Shelving totals 22,113 running feet.

AIDS TO REFERENCE

Published handbooks include *A handbook of the records in the custody of the government of Bengal from the earliest period to 1858* (Alipore, 1946) and *Abstract catalogue of the records preserved in the Civil Secretariat from 1859* (Alipore, 1936). Published press lists and indexes of the pre-Mutiny records are listed on pp. 337-9. There are also consolidated indexes of the records of all departments from 1859 to 1928 which are mostly printed, and select indexes to the general letters of the different departments from 1771 to 1858.

HOLDINGS

Historical section, West Bengal State Archives, 6 Bhowani Dutta Lane, Calcutta 7

PRE-1858 RECORDS

ENGLISH RECORDS

1	Select Committee	1756-62
2	Comptrolling Committee of Revenue	1771-2
3	Committee of Circuit	1772-3
4	The President and Council of Revenue of the Board of Revenue consisting of the whole Council	1772-4
5	Revenue Department, governor-general in Council	1775-1815
6	Revenue—*Sayer*	1790-1805
7	Revenue—Wards	1790-1805
8	Revenue—Grain	1794-1803
9	Revenue—*Kahlsa*	1776-80
10	Revenue Proceedings (Extracts)	1772-6
11	Tea Committee (Government of India)	1839-40
12	Territorial Revenue	1815-34
13	Miscellaneous Revenue Department	1828-41 and 1853-8
14	Revenue (Judicial)	1790-3
15	Judicial (Civil)	1793-1815
16	Judicial (Criminal)	1793-1815
17	Judicial, Civil—Lower Provinces	1816-34
18	Judicial, Criminal—Lower Provinces	1816-34
19	Judicial, Civil and Criminal—Western Provinces	1816-34
20	Letters to the Court of Directors	1771-1858
21	Letters from the Court of Directors	1765-1854

22	The Resident at the Durbar of Murshidabad	1769–70
23	Controlling Council of Revenue at Murshidabad	July 1770–Sept. 1772
24	The Resident at the Durbar of Murshidabad	1772–4
25	Chief and Council at Patna and Controlling Council of Revenue at Patna	1765–72
26	Controlling Council of Revenue at Patna (Chief and Council)	Dec. 1773
27	The Calcutta Committee of Revenue	1773–81
28	Provincial Council of Revenue at Dacca	1773–9
29	Chittagong records	1771–8–85
30	Provincial Council of Revenue at Murshidabad	1773–80
31	Provincial Council of Revenue at Dinajpur	1774–80
32	Provincial Council of Revenue at Patna (Chief and Council at Patna)	1774–80
33	Provincial Council of Revenue at Burdwan	1774–9
34	Committee of Revenue	1781–6
35	Board of Revenue at Fort William	1786–1882
36	Board of Revenue—Lower Provinces	1822–8
37	Board of Revenue—*Sadar*	1829–50
38	Board of Revenue—Lower Provinces	1851–8
39	Board of Revenue—*Sayer*	1790–1806
40	Board of Revenue—Judicial	1790–1806
41	Board of Revenue—Wards	1790–1847
42	Board of Revenue—Police	1794–7
43	Board of Revenue—Grain	1795–1803
44	Board of Revenue—Invalid Proceedings	1803–29
45	Board of Revenue—Post Office	1820–9
46	Board of Revenue—Proceedings on deputation	1813–59
47	Board of Revenue—Customs	1788–93 1809–19 1851–8
48	Board of Revenue—Salt	1788–93 1851–8
49	Board of Revenue—Opium	1788–93 1851–8
50	Comptrolling Committee of Commerce	1771–3
51	Board of Revenue	1773–85
52	Board of Trade—Commerce	1774–1835
53	Board of Trade—Customs	1793–1809
54	Board of Trade—Salt	1793–1819

55	Board of Trade—Opium	1793–1819
56	Board of Trade—Hemp	1801–15
57	Board of Trade—Indigo	1811–12
58	Board of Customs, Salt and Opium—Customs	1819–50
59	Board of C.S.O.—Salt	1819–50
60	Board of C.S.O.—Opium	1819–50
61	Board of Commissioners—Ceded Provinces	1801–3
62	Board of Revenue—Ceded and Conquered Provinces	1803–7
63	Board of Revenue—Ceded and Conquered Provinces	1807–10
64	Commissioner in Bihar and Benares	1816–17
65	Board of Commissioners in Bihar and Benares	1818–22
66	Board of Revenue—Central Provinces	1822–9
67	Superintendent of the Khalsa	1772–4
68	Superintendent of the Khalsa records	1775–81
69	Preparer of Reports for the Revenue Department	1781–93
70	Commissioner of Law Suits	1777–9
71	Committee of Grain	1783–5
72	Grain Office	1795–1803
73	Presidency Committee of Records	1820–9
74	Special commissioners under regulation II of 1899 and III of 1828	1829–53
75	Presidency Commissioner Sunderban records	1829–58
76	Comptroller of Salt and Collector of the Salt Districts	1781–1893
77	Superintendent of the Salt Chowkis, Calcutta	1831–58
78	Reporter of External Commerce	1802–19
79	Calcutta Exchange Price—Current	1820–58
80	General Committee of Public Instruction (correspondence and proceedings)	1823–42
	a Miscellaneous volumes	1811–42
	b Accounts book relating to schools and colleges	1823–42
81	Revenue Department	
	a Proceedings and reports	1774–1858
	b Accounts and registers relating to Land and Land Revenue	1758–1842
82	Judicial Department	1795–1856
83	Office List of records	1790–1888
84	Miscellaneous records relating to Commerce, Customs, Salt and Opium	1778–1858
85	Miscellaneous records—Board of Revenue	
	a Office records	1767–1858
	b Register etc. relating to Land and Land Revenue	1772–1858

86 Accounts records
    a Correspondence   1834–58
    b Land Revenue and miscellaneous   1784–1858
    c Settlement   1840–58
    d *Abkari* and Stamp   1825–50

VERNACULAR RECORDS

87 *a* Persian records   1624–1828
    b Bengali records
    c Mixed Persian and Bengali records   1764–1827
    d English, Bengali and Persian registers relating to
          Bazezamin Daftar
    e Records relating to Fredericksnagar   1804–56
    f Dutch *pattahs*—relating to Chinsura   1702–1827
88 Big bundles of various Departments
89 *Nizamat* accounts books for Murshidabad Collectorate   1836–86

POST-1859 RECORDS [*for their repository see especially note on
Archives administration in West Bengal, above*]

1 Appointment Department   From 1866
2 Political Department
    a Political Branch   From 1859
    b Records Branch   From 1909
3 Police Department   From 1859
4 Jails Department   From 1859
5 Judicial Department   From 1859
6 Local Self-government Department
    a Local Self-government (afterwards Local   From 1866
          Boards) branch
    b Medical branch   From 1859
    c Public Health branch   From 1921
    d Municipal branch   From 1873
    e Municipal miscellaneous branch   1883–9
7 Education Department
    a Education branch   From 1859
    b Registration branch   From 1873
    c Miscellaneous branch   From 1921
8 Finance Department
    a Finance branch   From 1895
    b Income Tax branch   From 1863
    c Opium branch   From 1872

	d	Salt branch	From 1872
	e	Stamp branch	From 1872
	f	Stationery branch	1872–91
	g	Book depot branch	1911–34
	h	Miscellaneous branch	From 1880
	i	Customs branch	1872–1924
	j	Separate Revenue branch	1891–1924
	k	Public Works Cess branch	1874–85
9		Commerce Department	From 1914
10		Marine Department	
	a	Marine branch	From 1859
	b	Port Trust branch	1870–92
11		Agriculture and Industries Department	
	a	Industries branch	From 1921
	b	Agriculture branch	From 1873
	c	Civil Veterinary branch	From 1921
	d	Fisheries branch	1919–23
	e	Co-operative branch	From 1921
	f	Forest branch	From 1864
	g	Botanical Garden branch	From 1919
	h	Zoological Garden branch	From 1924
	i	Miscellaneous branch	From 1921
12		Revenue Department	
	a	Land Revenue branch	From 1859
	b	Jurisdiction and Boundaries branch	From 1873
	c	Excise branch	From 1872
	d	Land Acquisition branch	From 1906
	e	Emigration branch	From 1860
	f	Chincona branch	From 1921
	g	Miscellaneous branch	From 1873
	h	Excluded Area branch	From 1926
	i	Road Cess branch	1873–1910
	j	Statistics branch	1868–91
	k	Scarcity and Relief branch	1873–7
	l	Famine branch	1877–91
13		General Department	
	a	Miscellaneous branch	1859–1920
	b	Ecclesiastical branch	1859–1920
	c	Ferry branch	1879–91
	d	Sanitation branch	1868–1920
14		Legislative Departments	From 1862

15 Miscellaneous records
    a Election papers   From 1921
    b Passport papers   From 1920
    c Lists of records transferred to the Government of Bihar and Orissa
    d Lists of records transferred to the Government of the United Provinces of Agra and Oudh
    e Establishment registers   From 1859
    f Calcutta Gazette   1872, 1882, 1887 and from 1898
    g Confidential reports on newspapers   From 1873
    h Covenants of ICS officers   From 1861
       Agreements of IPS officers   From 1924
    i Convention for the maintenance of the Grand Trunk Road
16 Records of the Government of Eastern Bengal and   1905–12
Assam

under Appointment Department, Appointment (Miscellaneous), Revenue (Agriculture), Revenue (Forest Department), Public Works Department, General (Military), General Archaeology, Political Department, Police Department, Jails Department, Revenue Department, Finance (Separate Revenue), Immigration, Sanitation Department, Judicial Department, Finance Department, General Department (Municipal), General Department (Local Boards), Education Department, Education (Miscellaneous), Medical Department, Deposit Cases, General Department, General (Miscellaneous), Municipal (Miscellaneous).

ADDITIONAL PUBLICATIONS

West Bengal State Archives (formerly Secretariat Record Office), Calcutta

1 W. K. Firminger, ed. 'Bengal historical records'
Select Committee at Fort William in Bengal: *Proceedings 1758*
Resident at the Durbar at Murshidabad: *Letter copy books 1769*
Controlling Council of Revenue at Murshidabad: *Proceedings*, vol. I, *27 September–28 November 1770*; vol. II, *3–31 December 1770*; vol. III, *3 January–14 February 1771*; vol. IV, *18 February–28 March 1771*; vol. V, *April–15 July 1771*; vols. VI–VIII, *18 July–30 December 1771*; vol. VII*a*, *2 September–21 October 1771*; vol. IX, *4–28 January 1772*;

vol. x, *2 March–4 May 1772*; vol. xi, *7 May–25 June 1772*; vol. xii, *2 July–8 September 1772 and Copy book of letters issued by the Resident at the Durbar of Murshidabad, 28 September 1772–2 March 1774*
Supervisor of Rajshahi at Nator: *Letter copy book (letters issued), 30 December 1769–15 September 1772*
Committee of Circuit at Krishnagar and Kasimbazar: *Proceedings*, vols. i–iii, *10 June–17 September 1772*
Committee of Circuit at Dacca: *Proceedings*, vol. iv, 3 October–28 November 1772
Committee of Circuit at Rangpur, Dinajpur, Purnea and Rajmahal: *Proceedings*, vols. v–viii, 16 December 1772–18 February 1773

ii W. K. Firminger, ed. 'Bengal District records'
Midnapur, vol. i, 1763–67; vol. ii, 1768–70; vol. iii, 1771–4 (receipts); vol. iv, 1770–4 (issues)
Rangpur, vol. i, 1770–9 (1770, 1777–1779 supplement); vol. ii, 1779–82 (receipts); vol. iii, 1783–5 (receipts); vol. iv, 1779–85 (issues); vol. v, 1786–7 (receipts); vol. vi, 1786–7 (issues)
Dinajpur, vol. i, 1787–9; vol. ii, 1786–8 (issues)
Chittagong, vol. i, 1760–73

iii Press lists, series 1: Supreme Revenue authorities
Vol. i, Controlling Committee of Revenue at Fort William: *Proceedings, April 1771–October 1772*
Vol. ii, Committee of Circuit: *Proceedings, 10 June 1772–18 February 1773*
Vol. iii, Revenue Board of the Whole Council at Fort William: *Proceedings, 13 October 1772–30 December 1774*
Vols. iv–xi, Governor-General of Bengal in Council at Fort William: *Proceedings, 6 January–29 December 1775, 2 January–31 December 1776, 10 January–30 December 1777, 2 January–29 December 1778, 5 January 1779–20 February 1781, 6 March–18 December 1781, 3 January–24 December 1782, 21 January–19 December 1783*
Supplementary volume: *General letters to and from the Court of Directors, 1771–1775*

iv Press lists, series 2: Intermediate Revenue authorities
Vol. i, *Patna letter copy books 1765–1766, and Proceedings of the Controlling Council of Revenue at Patna etc., 1 January 1771–23 December 1773*
Vol. ii, *Letter copy books of the Resident at the Durbar at Murshidabad for 1769–1770 and 1772–1774, and Proceedings of the Controlling Council of Revenue at Murshidabad, 27 September 1770–8 September 1772 etc.*
Vol. iii, Calcutta Committee of Revenue: *Proceedings*, pt 1, *6 December 1773–28 December 1775*; pt 2, *2 January 1776–29 December 1777*; pt 3,

5 January–30 December 1778; pt 4, *2 January–30 December 1779*; pt 5, *3 January–31 August 1780 and 4 January 1781*

v Press lists, series 3: Commercial authorities

Vol. I, Controlling Committee of Commerce: *Proceedings, 28 March 1771–20 November 1773*

Vol. II, Board of Trade: *Proceedings, 24 November 1774–17 December 1776*

vi Select indexes

Select index to general letters from the Court of Directors, Judicial Department, 1795–1854

Select index to general letters to and from the Court of Directors in the:

    I, *Revenue, Territorial Revenue, Territorial Financial and Miscellaneous Revenue Departments of the Government of Bengal, 1771–1858*

    II, *Separate Revenue, Commercial, Commercial Financial and Territorial Financial Departments . . . 1765–1854*

    III, *to the Court for 1793–1858 and from the Court for 1827–1829 in the Judicial Department . . .*

    IV, *Public or General, Ecclesiastical, Public Works (Railway), Public Works (Revenue), Legislative and Financial Departments . . . 1834–56*

vii Miscellaneous publications

Catalogue of the English records 1758–1858 and vernacular records 1624–1858, preserved in the Historical Record Room, Government of Bengal

A bibliography of Bengal records 1632–1858

Jamini Mohan Ghosh: *Sannyasi and Fakir raiders in Bengal Annual reports*

PAKISTAN

INTRODUCTION

THE ISLAMIC REPUBLIC OF PAKISTAN

Pakistan was constituted a dominion on 14 August 1947 under the provisions of the Indian Independence Act. It comprised Eastern Bengal and almost all the Sylhet district of Assam in the east, and Baluchistan, North-West Frontier, West Punjab and Sind in the west, all former territories of British India, to which were added the princely states of Bahawalpur and Khairpur and the Baluchistan states. Of the merged territories, British Baluchistan had been constituted in November 1887 from the districts of Pishin, Shorarud, Duki, Sibi and Shahrig, assigned to the British in 1879, and thereafter until 1903 increased by further territory including the princely states of Kalat, Las-Bela, Kharan and Makran. North-West Frontier Province had been established from the frontier districts of Hazara, Peshawar and Mardan, Kohat, Bannu and Dera Ismail Khan upon their separation from the Punjab in 1901, and was constituted an autonomous province in 1937. Sind, annexed by the British in 1843, had been transferred from the Bombay presidency in April 1936 and constituted an autonomous province in 1937. Punjab (Pakistan) comprises the Lahore, Rawalpindi and Multan divisions of the former Punjab province. The princely states and provinces in West Pakistan integrated in November 1954 and the country was made a federation of two units, West Pakistan and East Pakistan. In March 1956 Pakistan was proclaimed an Islamic Republic.

ARCHIVES ADMINISTRATION IN PAKISTAN

At its meeting on 29 October 1947 the Supreme Partition Council decided that the original archives of the former undivided Government of India should remain with India. Other archives were to be divided on a fifty-fifty basis. In practice one finds the West Pakistan archives at Lahore more comprehensive than those of Punjab (India) at Chandigarh, but the West Bengal archives at Calcutta more comprehensive than those of East Pakistan at Dacca. In both cases however the office with the fewer originals has supplemented its holdings to some extent with copies or microfilms of the missing series. The Pakistan Historical Records and Archives Commission was constituted in 1948 and planned to set up a central records repository and a directorate of archives. However at present the administration of archives in East and West Pakistan remains separate.

EAST PAKISTAN

East Pakistan Secretariat Record Room, Eden Buildings, Ramna, Dacca
Officer in charge: Keeper of Records, Government of East Pakistan
Authority: Deputy Secretary, Services and General Administration (Common Services) Department, Dacca

RULES OF ACCESS

Records are available for bona fide historical research after reference to the department concerned. Applications for a student's ticket to consult the records should be made on a prescribed form to the keeper of records, accompanied by a recommendation on another prescribed form. Aliens are further required to supply a recommendation from their diplomatic representatives in Pakistan. Tickets are valid for six months only and may be renewed. Persons wishing to obtain information from or copies of the records should apply in writing to the keeper of records, stating their occupation and the object for which the information or copies are required. Copying charges of two annas per 100 words and search fees of two rupees a day or 60 rupees a month must be paid to the Treasury in advance.

ARCHIVES ADMINISTRATION IN EAST PAKISTAN

The East Pakistan Secretariat Record Room acquires those historically important archives from the District Record Offices of Chittagong, Noakhali, Comilla, Sylhet, Rajshahi, Chittagong Hill Tracts, Dacca, Mymensingh, Faridpur, Bakerganj, Dinajpur, Rangpur, Pabna, Bogra, Khulna, Kushtia and Jessore which may be spared by the district authorities without detriment to local interest. Otherwise the central office has no control over the District Record Offices which are administered by district officers.

NATURE AND EXTENT OF HOLDINGS

Until 1947 East Pakistan was part of the presidency of Bengal. The presidency had no central archives repository, but the secretariat records of the East India Company and the Crown were centralized in the Secretariat Record Office, Calcutta. Although the Provincial Separation Council decided that the records should be divided on a fifty-fifty basis, after Partition only existing copies of the pre-Mutiny records were transferred to

Dacca, the originals being retained in Calcutta apart from a few 'B' proceedings relating to East Pakistan districts. However, from 1859 most 'A' and 'B' proceedings relating to East Pakistan districts are held in Dacca, as of course are the East Pakistan Government records from 1947. In addition the revenue records of the districts from 1761 to 1891 and certain other pre-1900 historical documents have been collected from the district offices for preservation in Dacca.

AIDS TO REFERENCE

Annual indexes of all papers from 1858 to 1943 and the consolidated indexes of the records of several departments from 1859 to 1905 are available. Indexes of the district records are being prepared. Published press lists of the archives of the several authorities prior to 1858 are also available but the archives of those authorities are still in the custody of West Bengal.

PUBLICATIONS

No publications programme has been undertaken at present. Certain records relating to the districts of Chittagong, Rangpur, Dinajpur and Sylhet were printed *in extenso* before Partition and one copy of each of these publications is held in the Secretariat Record Room.

HOLDINGS

East Pakistan Secretariat Record Room, Dacca

District records in manuscript	1760–1891	4,220 v
Political Department		
Printed 'A' papers	1864–1900	12 bdls
Proceedings volumes	1869–1900	44 v
Police Department		
Printed 'A' papers	1860–1900	26 bdls
Proceedings volume	1899	1 v
Jail Department		
Printed 'A' and 'B' papers	1859–1900	13 bdls
Proceedings volumes	1899–1900	6 v
Appointment Department		
Printed 'A' papers	1866–1900	16 bdls
Proceedings volumes	1868–1900	46 v
Judicial Department		
Printed 'A' papers	1864–1900	49 bdls
Proceedings volumes	1859–1900	554 v

Education Department		
Printed 'A' and 'B' papers	1859–1900	46 bdls
Proceedings volumes	1873–1900	59 v
Ecclesiastical Department		
Printed 'A' papers	1862–1900	3 bdls
Finance Department		
Printed 'A' papers	1874–1900	32 bdls
Proceedings volumes	1874–1900	281 v
Law, Revenue Department		
Printed 'A' papers	1859–1900	49 bdls
Proceedings volumes	1859–1900	427 v
Medical, Public Health and Municipal Department		
Printed 'A' papers	1864–1900	70 bdls
Proceedings volumes	1880–1900	250 v
Registration Department		
Printed 'A' papers	1873–1900	3 bdls
Proceedings volumes	1895–8	4 v
Famine and Scarcity Department		
Printed 'A' papers	1873–91	16 bdls
Emigration Department		
Printed 'A' papers	1860–1900	16 bdls
Industries and Science Department		
Printed 'A' papers	1872–5	1 bdl
Port Trust and Marine Department		
Printed 'A' papers	1859–1900	88 bdls
Agriculture and Forest Department		
Printed 'A' papers	1864–1900	28 bdls
Excise Department		
Printed 'A' papers	1872–1900	7 bdls
Jurisdiction Department		
Printed 'A' papers	1873–1900	3 bdls

WEST PAKISTAN

ARCHIVES ADMINISTRATION IN WEST PAKISTAN

Until the West Pakistan Record Office is rehoused in 1970, government archives remain in the custody of several authorities. The following are the principal repositories and collections.

West Pakistan Government Record Office, described below, is heir to the Punjab Record Office and the major archival repository.

Central Record Office, N.W. Frontier Province, described below, holds the records of that province.

Sind government records are held at Hyderabad (Sind), post-1935 records having been transferred there from the office of the West Pakistan Government Press, Karachi. See *Selections from the Pre-Mutiny records of the Commissioners of Sind* (n.d.), *Alphabetical Catalogue of the contents of the Pre-Mutiny records of the Commissioner in Sind* (Karachi, 1931) and *Handbook of the government records lying in the office of the Commissioner of Sind and in district offices* (Karachi, 1933).

Police records remain under the authority of the home secretary and the inspector-general of police, W.P. Secretariat, and access is generally restricted. Each of the four branches of the C.I.D., general, criminal, special and political, had its own record and index system, described in a *Manual of the C.I.D.* (Lahore, 1915) held in the W.P. secretarial library. The special branch collection is most relevant to political studies, with information from district officers on political and semi-political movements, history sheets on individuals and movements, and a complete file of annual reports by the press sub-branch on vernacular papers, with selected translations, *c.* 1885–1922.

Education records up to 1882 are held in the W.P. Government Record Office but after that date remain in the custody of the secretary, Department of Education.

Financial commissioner records are housed in the archives of the Board of Revenue. These records, numbering some 250,000 files and volumes, complement the Revenue Department proceedings in the W.P. Government Record Office and are usually more thorough. Indexes consulted by the staff are not available to scholars, who should ask for files by subject.

High Court records after 1890 remain with the Pakistan High Court.

'Confidential' and 'secret' files, so labelled and separated by all departments from about 1880, remain generally with the section heads of the various departments and are inaccessible to scholars.

District records are gradually being moved to the two main repositories, but in many districts they still remain with the deputy commissioner.

West Pakistan Government Record Office, Anarkali's Tomb, Lahore
Officer in charge: Keeper of the Records

RULES OF ACCESS

Applications to consult the records, accompanied by the relevant credentials, should be addressed to the keeper, who secures approval from the department concerned.

HISTORY OF THE OFFICE

In 1891 the Tomb of Anarkali was acquired by the government to house the records of the Punjab secretariat and of the offices of the financial commissioner and the inspector general of police. Not until 1923 was this constituted into a proper record office under a keeper. At Partition the records of the Punjab Record Office were divided between West Pakistan and Punjab (India) [q.v.] according to primary interest, but the bulk of the English series remained at Lahore. The office will have more spacious accommodation in the new secretariat buildings planned for 1970, where it is hoped to bring together as many record collections as possible.

Any scholar gaining access to the archives automatically receives permission to use the W.P. secretariat library, which contains office manuals and rare books on the Punjab. There is a printed index. Some of the printed aids to reference mentioned in this entry are probably only available in Lahore.

AIDS TO REFERENCE

Press lists of old records in the Punjab Civil Secretariat (Lahore, 1915–42) cover the period 1799–1868 and are very thorough. The contents of the volumes are listed below. See also *List of books containing old records and memorandum showing particulars of records in the Punjab Civil Secretariat* (Lahore, 1932) and *Collections of indices and lists of important papers retained after weeding* which contains lists for the Military Department, nineteenth-century police records, confidential records 1848–*c*. 1880, Marine Department, important printed and MS files, files relating to Delhi as transferred from the North-West Provinces, and Punjab confidential printed selections. Annual and consolidated indexes have serious gaps, especially before 1880. Further reference aids are described in the holdings list with the collections to which they pertain. See also N. G. Barrier, *The Punjab in British Printed Documents* (Columbia, Missouri, 1969).

HOLDINGS
W.P. Government Record Office, Lahore

1799–1852. PERIOD OF SIKH RULE, ANNEXATION, AND BOARD OF ADMINISTRATION

1. Vernacular records of the Patiala, Nabha, Jind and Bahawalpur agencies, containing all the existing records on the political relations of these states with the British, also some material on social conditions and the relations between these states. Indexing incomplete. Approx. 100 bundles wrapped in cloth.

2. Persian records, including Ludhiana Agency papers 1809–40, Lahore Durbar Agency papers 1842–9, and papers of the first and second Sikh wars. No index, but a series of selections from these records is being prepared for publication. Approx. 100 bundles.

3. Miscellaneous papers pertaining to the agencies of Delhi, Umbala, Ludhiana, North-West Frontier and Lahore, kept in book form, issues and receipts in separate volumes. Roughly indexed in *List of books containing old records* and many papers printed in the *Press lists* series.

4. Board of Administration records, 1849–52. Records from the Military, Political, General, Judicial, Education and Revenue Departments, kept in weekly bundles. There is an index to only a small portion of these records, contained in the *Press lists* series.

1853–1947. IMPORTANT MISCELLANEOUS SERIES

1. Confidential files 1848–*c.* 1880, including extensive records on the Kuka outbreaks, the Wahabis and British political relations with chiefs and neighbouring states. The series is indexed in *Collections of Indices*.

2. Mutiny papers. See *Index to the Punjab Mutiny papers*.

3. Historical engravings, portraits, documents and artifacts relating to British rule. See *Catalogue of pictures, documents, and other objects of interest in the Punjab Government Record Office* (Lahore, 1935).

4. Judicial records relating to the Punjab Chief Court, 1865–90. Papers, circulars and letters in monthly bundles. Not indexed. Records after 1890 remain in the custody of the Pakistan High Court.

5. Delhi Agency records, comprising correspondence 1820–57. Indexed in *Collections of indices*.

6. Punjab chief commissioner records, 1853–8. These are fourfold and in weekly bundles. Indexed in *Press lists* series (q.v.).

1849–*c.* 1905. LIEUTENANT-GOVERNORSHIP AND DEPARTMENT PROCEEDINGS

From 1858 until 1868 records were fourfold and kept in weekly bundles. They are indexed in the *Press lists* series.

From 1869 a monthly volume of proceedings was printed and unimportant files kept in manuscript. Records were usually divided into three sets. 'A' proceedings were usually printed and the originals destroyed. 'B' proceedings were kept for 10–15 years and then weeded, some being printed (with pink covers) and the remainder kept in single files. Most 'B' proceedings must be requisitioned from a separate storeroom in the secretariat compound. 'C' proceedings were kept for several years and then destroyed.

From *c.* 1880 files dealing with internal security or communal disturbances were labelled 'confidential' or 'secret', and stored and indexed separately. Most are now in the custody of the section heads of the various departments and are not available for consultation.

Department	Period	Size and form	Remarks
Marine	1862–72	Fourfold, now flattened	
Police	1861–5	Fourfold, now flattened	
Military	1849–86	Fourfold, then longfold, now flattened; annual	Transferred to secretariat on abolition of Military Department
Political	1849–68	Fourfold, some flattened; monthly	
Foreign	1869–87	Fourfold, then longfold; monthly	Foreign Department subdivided in 1882 into Native States, General and Frontier.
	1888	Flat files	Redesignated Political Department with subheads General and Native States, on creation of the N.W.F.P.
General	1849–71	Fourfold, some flattened; monthly	
Education	1849–82	Fourfold, then longfold; monthly	

Judicial	1849–71	Fourfold, some flattened; monthly	
Home	1872–87	Fourfold, then longfold; monthly	Sub-heads General, Judicial, Jails, Police, Medical, Registration, Military,
	1888–	Flat files	Gazette and Education created in 1882
Financial	1862–87	Fourfold, then longfold; monthly	Sub-head Legislative created in 1899
	1888–	Flat files	
Municipal	1878–85	Longfold; monthly	
Committees	1886–7	Longfold; monthly	
	1888–	Flat files	
Boards	1886–87	Longfold; monthly	
Revenue	1849–87	Fourfold, some flattened	Divided into Revenue, Agriculture, Irrigation, Free Grants and General in 1882
	1888–	Flat files	
Scarcity	1896–	Flat files	
Commerce and industry	1905–	Flat files	

ADDITIONAL PUBLICATIONS
W.P. Government Record Office, Lahore

See the revised catalogue of *Pakistan Government Record Office publications* (Lahore, 1965)

PRESS LISTS OF OLD RECORDS IN THE PUNJAB CIVIL SECRETARIAT (Lahore, 1915–). 25 vols.

 I Delhi Residency and Agency, 1806–57
 II Delhi Residency and Ludhiana and Karnal Agencies correspondence, 1804–16
 III Ludhiana, Karnal and Ambala Agencies, receipts, 1809–40
 IV Miscellaneous correspondence, issues, Ludhiana Agency 1810–15, Karnal Agency 1815–22, Ambala Agency 1822–40. Diaries of Capt. G. Birch 1818–21
 V Ludhiana Agency, miscellaneous correspondence, 1816–40

VI Ludhiana Agency, correspondence with government, 1831–40
VII N.W. Frontier Agency, correspondence with government, 1840–5
VIII N.W. Frontier Agency, miscellaneous correspondence, 1840–5
IX Lahore Agency and Residency correspondence, 1846–7
X Lahore Resident and Cis- and Trans-Sutlej territories C.C., January 1848–April 1849
XI Board of Administration, Punjab, Military and Political Departments, April 1849–April 1853
XII Board of Administration, Punjab, General Department, April 1849–February 1853
XIII Chief Commissioner's Administration, Punjab, Political Department, February 1853–December 1858
XIV C.C.'s Administration, Punjab, Judicial Department, February 1853–December 1858
XV C.C.'s Administration, Punjab, General Department, February 1853–December 1858
XVI C.C.'s Administration, Punjab, Revenue Department, February 1853–December 1858
XVII Judicial Department, 1859–68
XVIII General Department, 1859–63
XIX General Department, 1864–8
XX Political Department, 1859–63
XXI Political Department, 1864–8
XXII Finance Department, 1862–8
XXIII Revenue Department, 1849–53, 1859–63
XXIV Revenue Department, 1864–8
XXV Education Department, 1849–61
Supplements: Revenue Department, 1849–68; Political Department, 1849–68; General Department, 1849–68; Judicial Department, 1849–53, 1859–68; Finance Department, 1862–8; Education Department, 1860–1; Mutiny papers, 1857–8; Miscellaneous, 1849–68

SELECTIONS FROM THE PUNJAB GOVERNMENT RECORDS (Allahabad and Lahore 1909–11). 9 vols.

I Delhi Residency and Agency records, 1807–57
II Ludhiana Agency records, 1808–15
III Political diaries of the agent to the governor-general, N.W. Frontier, and Resident at Lahore, Sir Henry Lawrence, 1847–8
IV Journals and diaries of the assistants to agent to the governor-general, N.W. Frontier, and Resident at Lahore, Capt. J. Abbott, 1846–9. Peshawar political diaries, 1847–8

v Political diaries of the Resident at Lahore and his assistant, H. B. Edwardes, 1847–9

vi Political diaries of the Resident at Lahore and his assistants, R. G. Taylor, P. S. Melvill, Kunahya Lal, P. A. Vans Agnew, J. Nicholson, L. Bowring, A. H. Cocks, 1847–9

vii Mutiny records: correspondence

viii Mutiny records: reports

ix Notebooks of Capt. G. Birch, 1818–21

HISTORICAL MONOGRAPHS

Nos. 1–21 (1926–43), published in conjunction with the Government and Punjab University on various aspects of administration in the Punjab, for example,

no. 3, H. L. O. Garrett, *Brief history of the old police battalions*

no. 12, A. N. Sapru, *Building of Jammu and Kashmir State, being the achievement of Maharaja Gulab Singh*

no. 19, M. B. H. Farroqi, *British relations with the Cis-Sutlej State 1809–23*

Central Record Office, North-West Frontier Province, Peshawar
Officer in charge: Keeper of the Records

NATURE AND EXTENT OF HOLDINGS

When the North-West Frontier Province was separated from the Punjab in 1901 the relevant records of the civil secretariat came into its custody. At the instigation of the Indian Historical Records Commission the Central Record Office was set up in 1946 to preserve such material. Since that date there have been large transfers of government archives and district records to the office, and the government is actively collecting and purchasing manuscripts bearing on the administration and history of the province. A library of approximately 8,000 books is attached to the office but has few old manuals or collections of circulars.

AIDS TO REFERENCE

No catalogue has yet been issued. The list of holdings has been compiled from S. M. Jaffar's *Guide to the Archives of the Central Record Office, N.W. Frontier Province* (Peshawar, 1948) and *Annual administration report of the Central Record Office* (1948–62).

HOLDINGS
Central Record Office, Peshawar
As at 1948:

FOREIGN RECORDS

Relating to political, frontier, general matters, relations with Afghanistan, Persia, Russia, Dir, Swat and Chitral.

1. Ahwal-i-Kabul. Kabul diaries, received by the Amir from the British Vakil, giving information on the Amir's relations with Khost, Kokand, Bokhara, Persia and Russia.

2. Khyber diaries. Prepared by the political officers and submitted to the government with the weekly remarks of the commissioner of Peshawar.

3. Bulletins of the news writers stationed at Jalalabad, Kabul, Herat, Kandahar.

4. Political diaries of the deputy commissioners.

5. Notes and narratives by travellers and informers, including an incomplete note on the cattle-killing disturbances of 1884–8.

MILITARY RECORDS

Few only ordnance and intelligence files.

1. Khyber, Jalalabad, Kabul, Tirah and Kurram Field Forces.

2. Mutiny papers.

3. Tirah and Samana printed series, 1897–8, incomplete.

FINANCE RECORDS

REVENUE, AGRICULTURE AND COMMERCE PROCEEDINGS

Pertaining to settlement, forest, census, famine, local self-government.

HOME RECORDS

Pertaining to judicial, police, jail, medical, education matters.

1. Police Department. District superintendent's confidential diaries to the commissioner.

2. Letters of Guru Ram Singh, 1878–9, intercepted by the police. In Gurmukhi.

3. Papers connected with the Kuka cult.

4. District files. Including documents relating to the rise of the Wahabis, Kabul, Kandahar, Seistan, Persia and Russia.